The Power to Choose

Fulfillment in Life Series: Volume One

A Practical Guide to a Quality Life

The Power to Choose

Strengthening your ability to achieve your personal goals and to enhance the quality of your life

Fulfillment in Life Series

A Practical Guide to Quality Life

Volume 1

Rabbi Shmuel Dov Eisenblatt
Jerusalem 5762

First published 2002

Copyright © 2002
by Shmuel Dov Eisenblatt

ISBN 1-58330-520-3

All rights reserved.
No part of this publication may be translated, reproduced, stored in a retrieval system or transmitted, in any form or by any means, electronic, mechanical, photocopying, recording, or otherwise, without permission in writing from the publishers.

FELDHEIM PUBLISHERS
POB 35002/Jerusalem, Israel

202 Airport Executive Park
Nanuet, NY 10954

www.feldheim.com

Printed in Israel

Rabbi Shlomo Zalman Auerbach, *ztz"l* *

הרב שלמה זלמן אויערבאך
פעיה"ק ירושלים תובב"א

I offer my recommendation of Rabbi Shmuel Dov HaKohen Eisenblatt, *shlit"a*, who has been involved in counseling Torah-observant families for many years. Over the course of his experience he has demonstrated his expertise, and many benefit from his advice and guidance in personal matters, including achieving a balanced personality, actualizing one's potential, and dealing with difficult situations.

Because so many people are in need of this type of advice and guidance, Rabbi Eisenblatt has piloted a new program to teach other young scholars to help the public. He will instruct young men — who already show a sensitivity in this area — to understand the workings of human emotions, and teach them how to guide people to understand themselves. This program is based entirely on the Torah and the sages of all generations.

Since these tasks are extremely important, and since I know the author well, I wish to extend my warm recommendation....

---

* This letter was written as a general recommendation for a program of study which the author developed.

Rabbi Chaim P. Scheinberg, *shlit"a*

Rabbi CHAIM P. SCHEINBERG
Rosh Hayeshiva "TORAH-ORE"
and Morah Hora'ah of Kiryat Mattersdorf

הרב חיים פינחס שיינברג
ראש ישיבת "תורה-אור"
ומורה הוראה דקרית מטרסדורף

    I have received the manuscript of *Fulfillment in Life* from Rabbi Shmuel D. Eisenblatt, *shlit"a*. Rabbi Eisenblatt is already widely recognized for his success in helping Torah-observant families for many years, both with his counseling and his books. This new book is an effort to help a person unlock his potential, achieving spiritual self-actualization in a relaxed and happy way, free from the bonds of tension. Along with the rest of his work, this book is based entirely on sources from our Sages and classical texts.

    I extend my blessing to the author that with G-d's help, his book be adopted by the Torah world, and that he continue teaching the public for many years in peace and tranquility. May he receive *nachas* from his children and many followers.

הכו"ח,

חיים פינחס שיינברג.

Rabbi Nissin Karelitz, *shlit"a*

הרב ש. י. נסים קרליץ
רמת אהרן
רח' ר' מאיר 6, בני-ברק

The series *Fulfillment in Life*, written by the distinguished Rabbi Shmuel D. HaKohen Eisenblatt, is intended to help people achieve self-fulfillment. To this end, the material in this book offers invaluable assistance.

I extend my blessing to Rabbi Eisenblatt that he successfully promote the well-being of our community. May his work be free of failure, may many benefit from the light of his teaching.

This volume is dedicated in honor of the lasting memory of

Rabbi Moshe Feinstein, *ztz"l*

This great leader was a *shalem* person, one whose wholeness and completeness was a shining light. His genius was integrated with humility, his determination and vitality blended with the epitome of patience and care. I am grateful for his many answers to my questions and frequent discussions — along with the influence of his phenomenal personality — which inspired me during my younger years. To a great degree, this volume is influenced by and an expression of the model provided by Rabbi Moshe, *ztz"l*.

I dedicate this series as a monument
to the memory of my father,

Rabbi Shlomo HaCohen Eisenblatt, *ztz"l*

He served as a mentor and as a beloved father figure and guiding force in the lives of many. He symbolized the mitzvah of love of Hashem both at face value and also according to our sages' explanation, "Hashem's name should become beloved through our righteous behavior". Even amidst the pains of his last years, he continued to draw those around him closer to Torah and worship of Hashem with a spell of sweetness and love until his pure soul rose to heaven on *Chol Ha-Moed Pesach,* the 17th of Nissan 5761, may his memory be blessed.

Contents

Preface 1
    About a Life of Quality • Learning the Skill

Author's Introduction 5
    The Approach of this Book • Living Examples

1: Appreciating the Range of Your Options 13
    Life Is a Rose Garden • A Wide Range of Options • Choosing an Approach • A Blend of Approaches • Broadening Your Choices • Brainstorming: Creative Solutions • Sifting: Preventing New Problems • Choosing: Determining the Direction

2: Shyness and Embarrassment 58
    What Narrows Our Options? • The Manager's Dilemma • A Time for All Things • The Paradox of Embarrassment • Stunted Relationships • How Do I Get Started? • Bashfulness in Marriage • Further Limitations • What Will People Say? • Liberating Ourselves

3: Don't Give Up! 75
    Buried Treasure • Defeatism • Impact of Defeatism • The Puny Bandit • Mountain or Hair? • The Other Side of the Coin • Achieving Balance • Where Do I Stand? • Making the Calculation • Relative Completion • Be Active! • A Promising Future

4: Other Self-Made Roadblocks 98
    Identifying Obstacles • An Examination of Attitudes • On the Home Front • Subtle Handicaps • Subtle Feelings of Shame • From Roadblocks to Road Signs

5: The Spiral Effect 114
    The Letter • Better Alternatives • Why? • The Spiral Effect • Being There • In Everyday Life • Anger Breeds Anger • The Power of Positive Thinking • An Unpleasant Surprise • Castles in the Air • Changing the Momentum • Choose Your World • Spiraling Upward and Onward • The Power of a Positive Atmosphere

6: Unveiling Deeper Emotional Forces 142
    Conflicting Levels • Blinding the Mind • Do I Want to Succeed? • Underlying Negativity • Pay Attention to Me! • Who Suffers from Self-Pity? • A Time for Everything • Weaning from Self-Pity • The Power to Choose

7: Bold As a Leopard............................... 167
   Basic Steps • Gateway to Success • Caught in the Middle • Resolving the Will • A Change in Shulamit • Other Options • Rewarding Yourself • Challenging Resistance • Temporarily Modifying the Goal • One Step at a Time • The Importance of Clarity

8: Light As an Eagle.............................. 193
   A Relaxed Approach • Tension • Types of Tension • Tension and Expectations • Tension and Responsibility • Deeper Causes of Tension • Exploring Deeper Causes of Tension • Days of Love, Days of Hatred • It Doesn't Pay to Push • Don't Try To Jump Up the Ladder! • The Results of Tension • Our Goal — The Harmonious Balance • With Lightness and Joy • Priming Your Environment • Light As an Eagle

9: Swift As a Deer 264
   Shaking Off Laziness • Justifying Sluggishness • Why Do Today What You Can Put Off Till Tomorrow? • Emotional Arteriosclerosis • Working Off the Excess Fat • Inflated Concerns • Honest Judgment • Overblown Excuses • Proceed with (Not Too Much!) Caution • "If I Am Not for Myself" • "Haste Makes Waste" • Worth It or Not?

10: Strong As a Lion............................. 302
   Marching Forward with Fortitude • Impinging on the Quality of Our Functioning • The Danger of Feeling Unfortunate • Beware of Bravado! • Building Our Inner Strength • Strong As a Lion • Ready, Set, Go!

Epilogue: The Power To Choose..................... 337
   Chapter 1: Expanding the Power of Free Choice • Chapters 2-6: The Obstacles • Chapters 7-10: On to the Solutions!

Appendix A: Comparative Success 341
   Sha'arei HaAvodah of Rabbeinu Yona, ztz"l • Letter of Encouragement from the author of the Pachad Yitzchak, ztz"l

Appendix B: Tension in Real Life Scenes 346
   Stress Due to Impatience and Lack of Self-Encouragement • Stress Due to Lack of Clarity About the Future • Stress Due to Feeling a Lack of Self-Worth • Stress Brought on When Attempting to Prepare for the Future • Accumulated Stress • Stress Brought on When Preparing for Exams • Stress That Is Part of Developing Potential • Stress Brought on by Attempting to Achieve Social Status • Stress Felt by a Hard-Working Mother • Stress That Comes from Trying To Improve the Atmosphere at Home • Stress That Is Part of Dealing with Adolescent Children

Glossary 419
Index... 427

Preface

About a Life of Quality

I thank Hashem for His constant benevolence and for enabling me to see the completion of the first two volumes of this series, Fulfillment in Life.

The subtitle, "A Practical Guide to a Quality Life," was not meant to imply that the challenge of achieving a quality life is a simple one. Since it is a complex process, a good first step would be to clarify what we mean by a "quality life." Should we be striving to attain those external earmarks of good living which are in fashion at the time, and raise our "standard of living"? Any of us could probably name a handful of people who "have it all" but hardly enjoy their lives.

It seems logical, then, that we address the more profound and subtle issues that touch all of us — the interior landscape of our lives. In that sense, we would like to suggest that the following issues are most important to our inner well-being: our familial and social relationships, our disposition, our *avodas Hashem*, and the actualization of our creative, emotional, and spiritual potential. To help us to evaluate our success in these areas, we can ask ourselves the following questions. To what extent do we:

- Enjoy all that our lives have to offer, especially in the previously listed areas?
- Invest time and effort to improve the quality of the areas which are important to us?
- Feel real meaning in our actions?

- ♦ Feel fulfilled both for the energy we have invested in improving our lives and the accomplishments we have made?
- ♦ Succeed in dealing with difficulties, and appreciate and take advantage of challenges?

As a first step toward achieving success in these areas, we need to acquire the tools that help us implement inner change and master problem-solving skills. Without these prerequisites, our aspirations remain on the ground; problems stay unsolved and changes are not made.

The present volume focuses on acquiring the tools and skills needed to succeed at our personal projects. These skills may be prerequisites, but at the same time they provide a forum in which we actualize our creative, emotional, and spiritual potential (as we mentioned above). This ability to implement inner change contributes to the quality of our emotional lives. It not only enables us to achieve our goals and to feel the satisfaction that comes with achievement; it also helps us to express our personalities. That self-expression then further enhances the quality of our lives.

Mastery of problem-solving techniques makes a contribution to the quality of our emotional lives. Efficiently solving problems eliminates the frustration connected to the problem; it leads to a distinct sensation of forward movement that feels good. And most significantly, these skills further develop our creative side, to help formulate the solutions for life's challenges, leaving us feeling less helpless and more goal-oriented. Now what could feel more fulfilling than that?

Learning the Skill

Whenever we set out to learn a practical skill, the challenges we face are usually not too daunting. After all, how many lessons and how much practice can possibly be involved? Besides, there are many people who have already mastered that skill and who would be willing to provide help and advice should any problem arise.

When it comes to the most crucial skill of all, however, the situation is markedly different. When the project being tackled is life itself, the "student" somehow encounters more than the usual obstacles.

First of all, there are attitudes that can get in the way. People generally subscribe to one of three basic opinions when it comes to improving the quality of their lives:

1. Some people are already satisfied with their lives and don't see how much room there is for improvement. Obviously, no one makes a major investment of energy when they don't anticipate enjoying substantial returns!
2. There are those who have attempted many times to make improvements and have given up. They assume that attaining a quality life is beyond them. "It's a lost cause," they sigh. "It's not realistic to be so hopeful. If I haven't changed my life yet, I never will."
3. Finally, there are those who are still trying to improve their lives. Some of these people would be happy to accept help, but haven't found the right mentor. Others are certain that they already know how to go about improving their lives; they feel no need to seek out new ideas or approaches. Although each may continue to invest a great deal of time and effort in their search for self-improvement, a closer look reveals that many of these people never even come close to achieving their goal. They are not even aware that part of their approach may be incorrect; they certainly can't pinpoint what needs to be changed in their approach to improvement.

There are other issues at work, too. For one thing, the job seems endless; there is no limit to how much a person can improve the quality of his life. What complicates things further is that most people lack a clear vision of what a quality life is, and certainly do not know how to attain it. The much sought-after ideal life is extremely subjective — people are so diverse. Everyone has his own unique personality and mentality, everyone has a completely unique set of circumstances that defines his existence.[1]

Thus, the individual who attempts to develop a vision of the way of life that is ideal for him (considering his personality and situation) undertakes a highly complex task. At the same time, few people seem to live quality lives that demonstrate a mastery of the wisdom of living — and of this small number, even fewer can readily be approached for advice.

These challenges are significant, for they prevent us from capitalizing on our most precious resource: life itself. The result is that the most important art of all — wise living — appears to be the hardest to master. Clearly, then, it is crucial that we analyze this broad and profound subject in ever-increasing depth, so that we gain the necessary insight.

NOTES TO PREFACE

1. *Berachos* 58a.

Author's Introduction

The Approach of this Book

When a book of this kind appears, questions are sure to follow: What new ideas could this one possibly have to offer? After all, there is an abundance of material in print designed to serve as practical guides to life and self-improvement. For that matter, the entire Torah is the final word on the nature of the optimal way of life; what more can any mere mortal possibly add?

Indeed, the Torah is a comprehensive guide to life's many facets: daily activities, civil litigation, interpersonal relationships, personal attitudes, as well as the activities we usually relate to as "spiritual" — like praying and fasting. The Torah and the *mitzvos* come to teach us the direction that our lives should ideally take. The Torah itself is "[Our] life and the length of [our] days...,"[1] and it testifies that we "Shall live by them [the *mitzvos*]."[2]

Most of us, however, find it difficult to understand just how personal fulfillment fits into the picture, and the extent to which it can be achieved through Torah study and *mitzvah* observance alone.

Part of the challenge may be that no single mode of living is ideal. There are many positive ways of life supported by the Torah — whether or not each is ideal has to do with who is asking the question. The members of the tribe of Zevulun lived their ideal lives as merchants whereas their counterparts, the members of the tribe of Yissachar, lived their ideal lives as full-time scholars.[3] The members of the tribe of Dan lived model Torah lives guarding the borders while the Kohanim and Levi'im had their lives filled with sacred service in the Beis HaMikdash and Torah education.[4] We see that each tribe had its own way of life, each one sanctioned by the Torah.

The halachic aspects of the Torah are certainly absolutes. But when I turn to the Torah to provide guidance for my path to personal fulfillment, I am searching for its vision of the ideal life for *me* — and that vision is not directly transferable, without alteration, to my friend, my spouse, or my child.

To complicate this job even more, every era has its own challenges. Our history abounds with a wide variety of (even apparently conflicting) approaches to understanding our lives and goals.[5] These are not just man-made spiritual or philosophical systems; they are reflections of the practical guidance that the leaders of every generation have culled from the Torah to dispense to the searching souls of their times.[6] The Torah is the flowing river from which all these streams stem, and the wide variety of approaches are testimony to the Infinite Wisdom that fashioned it.

In recent generations, people are thirsting for an understanding of their lives in what could be defined as emotional terms: how people work, what sparks their interest and why; they want to know what motivates them in a deep emotional sense. Our tradition has a wealth of resources, including the great *mussar* and chassidic texts, which contain treasures of ideas and directives, strongly entwined with discussions of emotions and character traits. In order to implement these ideas, however, a person needs to have a prerequisite level of emotional readiness, which includes prolonged states of spiritual inspiration along with adequate levels of self-control and self-mastery. These qualities were more common in previous generations, and are less so in this present era. As a result, the topics of ultimate interest and priority today have apparently shifted, becoming more geared to being able to:

◆ deal with external influences;

- achieve an in-depth understanding of self-improvement projects;
- increase motivation; and
- deepen our spiritual experience.

The purpose of this book, then, is multifaceted. On one level, it is intended to present a plan for quality living based on time-honored themes and generations-proven approaches as they apply to the situations and needs of our era. It is an attempt to deal with the problems of people living in our times, to help us achieve a more wholesome personality, and to strengthen our motivation.

On another level, the goal is to teach today's searching soul the art of sifting through various ideas in order to adapt those that are appropriate for his own personality. This series offers the reader tools for discerning which approaches apply to him personally and which approaches will work best for him. This way, he can derive the benefit of a wholesome Torah lifestyle, tailored to his own personality.

An added contribution of this series is an attempt to comprehensively translate the infinite wisdom of the Torah and our Sages into modern terms, and time-honored themes into contemporary concepts that the reader may find more easy to grasp and relate to. This series is an effort to adapt these approaches to the specific problems of our era. To this end, the reader will find quotes from many of our sacred sources, used as a basis for the means to craft a personal plan for healthy living.

I pray that I have not erred in these tasks, and that this series will help to address the needs I mentioned.

Living Examples

Our Sages have taught that the art of living can never be learned from books alone.[7] *Toras Chayim* — the Torah of life — is only internalized when we draw our instruction from a living, breathing *Talmid Chacham*. Such a person is already well into drawing his vision of life from the Torah and succeeding in honing his life skills. We can develop a vision of our ideal way of life based on his personal example. The key to the riddle of how to attain a quality life is in the hands of those who are actually living it.

Fortunate is the person who attains closeness to the leaders of the generation — to the giants of the spirit — those scholars and genuine *Tzaddikim*, true masters of the art of living![8] This does not mean simply living in the neighborhood of a scholar, or periodically seeing his glowing countenance, or even consulting with him from time to time (though all of these surely convey some benefit, to a greater or lesser degree). This means that a person can only acquire the wisdom of living by actually *attending* to a *Talmid Chacham:* assisting and being of service to him; spending time in his presence; and seeing his behavior even in mundane, personal matters to learn the Torah way of life from him.

Of course, every scholar has his own, unique personality and his own, particular style of life.[9] Yet, there is a common denominator — they are all living testimony to the fact that every human being possesses unsuspected potential waiting to be realized — and that there is a level of quality to life that is many times greater than that which most of us settle for. When a person becomes receptive to the possibility of achieving this level, he "opens up a tiny opening, the size of the eye of a needle," that expands greatly for him, to the size of "a grand entrance to a huge hall."[10]

Women should be alert to their particular opportunities to forge connections of their own. There are many *Tzidkaniyos,* great women of the spirit, to be found who can also expand a woman's awareness of the lofty quality of life to which she can aspire. For example, for all appearances, two women may have similar daily schedules. Both of them may care for their children, manage their households, be involved in a profession, and help others in their community. Yet these activities can be performed on an infinite number of planes. Their quality depends on the specific content, attitude, and depth of meaning that each woman injects into these daily activities. The alert woman will discern which of her contemporaries lead higher quality lives, and will take advantage of the opportunities to study their ways.

Clearly, we need living models of the Torah path — but logistically, things are not so simple. Most of us are preoccupied with the mundane concerns of our lives and find it difficult to devote time to attend to *Talmidei Chachamim*. We may just manage to meet these giants, glimpse a sampling of their behavior, or perhaps only see them in passing. These minimal opportunities are not to be taken lightly; every impression is valuable. But such glimpses are hardly enough to teach us to excel at the art of living.

You might think that the problem of accessibility could be solved by publishing biographies of great people, available to everyone to learn from at any time. Such works already line the bookshelves in many homes, and while they may inspire us to improve ourselves, few readers undergo an essential character and attitude overhaul. Perhaps this is because even the most well chosen words on paper cannot capture the essence of any person or experience.[11] Rav Chayim Shmuelevitz, *ztz"l*, once expressed a similar thought in a comment on the beginning of *Parashas* Vayeira. Avraham Avinu brought the angels bread and butter. Said Rav Chayim, "We might also serve guests bread and butter. But each person, according to his level, must go on to imagine to himself the saintly generosity and enthusiasm with which Avraham tended to his guests, at the height of his pain and in the middle of a scorching-hot day." The Torah and *chessed*, the fasting and prayers of the *Tzaddik* can be described, but the essence of a living personality or an exalted experience — the pure attitude, the gracious nature and rich being — aren't translated through the written word. Reading about a *Tzaddik* is not enough; one has to learn from a living Torah scroll!

Another shortcoming of biographies of *Tzaddikim* is that hardly any of them discuss the struggles of these giants and the painful process of their growth. This leaves the reader without guidance for achieving the quality life that the book describes; he still lacks a picture of all the stages and steps that will lead him to his objective.[12]

So we really have two needs here: to get a clear picture of what a quality life is and to learn how to achieve it. The most obvious solution, developing close contact with Torah giants who can guide us, is fraught with obstacles. For this reason, I have attempted to write a different sort of book to help people attain these skills in a practical way. Presented here, with Hashem's help, is a general approach that will help people like myself broaden their horizons, solve life's problems, and grow into a deeper and truer way of living; an approach that includes in it some hints of the quality life which the reader is trying to achieve. This volume develops certain crucial concepts, demonstrating how they apply to us (chapters 1-6), and then guides us through a four-point strategy (chapters 7-10). To accomplish this, I have drawn on a store of impressions that I was fortunate enough to absorb from Torah giants on many occasions. I have attempted to chart a course from those great people and to fuse their spirit into an overall outlook on life. Even a person who is fortunate enough to enjoy closeness to true *Talmidei Chachamim* will gain from these words, and be better able to integrate the ways of his mentors into his daily life.

I stress here "an overall outlook on life." This is not an anthology of personality studies of our *Gedolim*. Rather, this work is an attempt to create an atmosphere, a spirit — a sense of the path of life.

For this same reason, I have not elaborated here on many important individual topics. My primary goal in writing this series has been to help the reader find the key to unlock his own hidden potential and greatly enhance the quality of his life. I have tried to find an approach through which every intelligent person can, with Hashem's help, identify and make full use of his hidden strengths to break new ground in the areas of his choice.

Many people helped bring this book to fruition — too many to thank personally — but I am deeply grateful to them nonetheless.

NOTES TO AUTHOR'S INTRODUCTION

1. Devarim 30:20.
2. Vayikra 18:5; see also Devarim 5:30.
3. *Midrash Tanchuma, Parashas* Vayechi, 11; Bereishis 49:15 with Rashi in conjunction with I Divrei HaYamim 12:33. Also see the conclusion of the *Mesillas Yesharim.*
4. See Devarim 33:20, 22 and Rashi there; also see Devarim 33:10 and *Yoma* 26.
5. See *Shabbos,* 30b-31a; also see *Eruvin* 13b.
6. See Ritvah on *Eruvin* 13b.
7. *Berachos* 7b.
8. If a person has the opportunity to learn a way of life from two different *Talmidei Chachamim* or *Tzaddikim,* it may be preferable to concentrate on learning from the lesser of the two (see *Eruvin* 47b), especially if he is more accessible. Of course, he should try to learn from the greater scholar as well, who may still be considered his *Rav* for ruling on halachic matters (*Avodah Zarah* 19a; *Avos D'Rabbi Nosson* 3:6, 8:2). A person who has merited to attend to one great mentor may be encouraged to "take a peek" at other scholars as well, broadening his horizons still further. As we learn in *Avos D'Rabbi Nosson* 3:6, "One is required to attend to three great scholars" because he cannot know which one will make a great, lasting impression on him.
9. *Avos* 2:8.
10. *Shir HaShirim Rabbah* 1.
11. *Shiurei Da'as,* "*Chomer V'Tzurah.*"
12. *Cheshbon HaNefesh,* section I:19.

1
Appreciating the Range of Your Options

Life Is a Rose Garden

Every one of us hopes that his journey through life will be a smooth one. We would like to stride calmly and confidently down the paths of experience, untroubled by obstacles or frustrations, and be assured of success. Of course, in reality, life is full of obstacles. Our goals are like graceful roses growing among thorns in rocky soil. Anyone who attempts to walk between them must chart his course carefully to avoid being pricked by the brambles or stumbling over the stones. So, too, in life we must watch our steps and consider our moves. Only then will the journey be pleasant and culminate in success.

Most of us probably feel that we handle many of life's challenges and difficulties efficiently and successfully, but in some cases we seem to be stuck — at a loss as to how to improve the situation. In most cases, we probably tell ourselves we ought to moderate our expectations: Life isn't perfect. Sometimes we ourselves will make a mistake; sometimes the situation around us will not be so comfortable. Can we expect better than that?

If we take this mentality to its logical conclusion, then what we are basically saying is "Let's settle for the way things are. There isn't any sense in doing much more. We've tried, this is the best we can do, and these are the results. We'll just have to live with it."

But is this true? Are we to abandon our dream of life being a "rose garden"? If not, how then should we navigate our path in life? How will we arrive at our desired destination safely and happily?

In almost every difficulty that arises in life, we have a wide range of responses from which to choose. Visualize a vast field, crisscrossed by many trails. Unfortunately, it is hard to see just where most of the trails leads us. Paths that at first seem direct may prove themselves to be digressions. Rather than help us on our way, the road which we chose as a response may intensify or complicate our problems. Some routes may be so fraught with obstacles that as long as we remain on them, we make no progress.

Conversely, many alternatives are initially not clearly visible; we may not even notice them without a thorough surveying of the terrain. But if we trace courses carefully, we may find that these paths are the very ones that lead to our destination. After careful consideration, we often discover among our options a new approach that can extricate us from a baffling problem and help us on to new and better circumstances. The process of examining our options and making effective choices improves our lives — and elevates us spiritually.[1]

So on the one hand, we shouldn't expect a problem-free life, a magical realization of all our whims and dreams. On the other hand, we may and should take steps to improve our situation. Accordingly, if we find that one particular route is leading nowhere, why waste time and energy trying the same track again and again? It would be far more productive to examine alternate paths, avoiding those littered with obstacles. Once we make the right choices, we can greatly enhance our situation and enjoy the wonderful changes.[2]

In the next few pages we will discuss five basic types of responses to difficulties. The way we apply these responses will depend on the situation, allowing for many variations within each type of response. The sections that follow will provide insights about each of these basic types of responses. This can help us see how each type of response would work in general, as well as help us to discover alternatives to our usual ways of reacting in specific situations — ways which may not have occurred to us before.

In the second half of the chapter, we will discuss the process of choosing the best approach in any given situation.

A Wide Range of Options

When confronted with a challenging situation, we may choose to respond in any of five fundamental ways:

- Disregard
- Escape
- Submission
- Emotionalization and/or Internalization
- Initiating Change to Improve the Situation

Each of these basic types of responses may be helpful in some circumstances while harmful in others. We need to draw on our own common sense and life experience to determine the most suitable strategy for dealing with any given situation. The following guidelines, with examples from the Torah and our everyday life, can help us brainstorm and discover appropriate alternate responses for dealing with any difficult situation.

DISREGARD

Disregard means choosing to ignore a difficult or unpleasant situation. It is a desirable reaction in a number of cases, at times helping us to deal with:

- *Flaws:* Unless it is within our power to correct a flaw in ourselves or others, it is usually best to disregard it.[3] (This does not apply when consideration of the fault is necessary to determine a course of action — such as when choosing a business partner.)
- *Minor Issues:* If the issue is trivial, ignoring it may be the wisest choice.
- *Unreasonable Effort:* With some problems, the correction requires more effort and emotional energy than is justified. In such cases, disregarding the issue, or part of it, may also be a suitable response — as long as the problem will not develop into anything serious.
- *Inappropriate Timing:* Sometimes it is best to remain silent about a problem — at least in the interim, saving any comment for a later, more suitable moment. The Mishnah cautions: "Do not appease your friend at the moment of his anger."[4] If we attempt it, he is likely to become even more incensed.
- *Dispute:* In times of dispute, passivity is often the best option. During Korach's opposition, Aharon HaKohen did not respond to the claims made against him for several reasons: because of humility; because he felt that personal interests might prevent him from being objective; and because his response was unnecessary.[5]
- *Certain Scenarios in Child Raising:* When a child misbehaves to attract attention, it is often best to disregard his behavior (provided that it will not harm anyone or cause damage). Later, the problem can be tackled more effectively —

particularly if we then give the child positive attention for any good behavior he displays.

In contrast, disregard is not a wise choice when it will exacerbate the situation. If our constructive action has a reasonable chance of being effective, or when our inaction may result in harm to a person, ignoring the situation is unjustified.

ESCAPE

Escape means taking physical or emotional initiative to avoid being exposed to a problem. It can be an effective means of dealing with:

- *Danger:* The most obvious form that escape may take is, literally, fleeing from danger. Ya'akov Avinu followed the advice of his mother, Rivka Imeinu, and fled when his brother Esav plotted to kill him. Moshe Rabbeinu fled from the threat of death by Paroh's decree.[6]
- *Difficulties:* If the circumstance is bad enough that a person should take steps to avoid it (and there is no potential for improvement), then escape is a viable option.
- *Unreasonable Effort:* Escape is also helpful when the problem does not justify the time and effort that would be necessary to bring about an improvement (when simply disregarding the situation is not enough).
- *Illegal Action:* If offensive or unlawful action is the only way to bring about change, it is usually forbidden to take such action, and escape may be the best solution.
- *Temptation:* Escape is an effective way to keep ourselves far from the temptation to sin. Our Sages advise the *nazir*, who has vowed to abstain from all produce of the vine, to avoid even walking near a vineyard.[7] When Potiphar's wife attempted to seduce Yosef, he promptly fled.[8] In fact, daily,

in our morning prayers, we ask Hashem to keep us distant from (i.e., help us escape from) temptation.

- *Accidental Sin:* We are taught to avoid bad company and to desert a group of people who are speaking ill of others, in order to guard ourselves from stumbling into sin.[9]

- *Dispute:* When there is danger of becoming entangled in a dispute, escape may be the safest course of action. Avraham Avinu took that route when he advised Lot to set up his own camp: "Let there not be a dispute between me and you... please separate yourself from me."[10] Likewise, we are cautioned by our Sages and also by more recent commentaries to keep our distance from any scene of conflict: "Do not make any attempt to see it."[11]

- *Negative Thoughts or Emotions:* There is also cognitive and emotional escape; it is the first option to consider when suffering from negative thoughts or feelings, such as worry. Shlomo HaMelech advised: "If there is worry in a person's heart, *yashchenah*...."[12] Among the statements of the *Amoraim*, there are two different interpretations of the word *yashchenah*.[13] Rav Ami explains that the person should subdue the concern and try to put it out of his mind; Rav Asi maintains that he should, instead, unburden himself and share his concern with a confidant. The Rif reveals how both interpretations are intended by the verse: Initially, the person should shun lengthy analysis of the issue and try to expel the worry from his mind. If he fails, he should lighten his emotional load by relating the anxiety to a friend.

It is often easier to shift our thoughts to a more positive direction than to fight negative feelings head-on. The same verse from Mishlei continues, "and a good thing shall bring him joy." Rashi teaches that the anxiety-ridden person should study Torah, which is sure to bring him joy and displace the negative feeling.[14] (One convenient form of escape is to go to a *shiur* or listen to a tape, which may help a person forget about the issue. The short diversion may give a person the opportunity to look at the issue with fresh eyes later.)

Escape is not a valid choice when we can take active measures to improve the situation.

SUBMISSION

Submission means accepting a difficulty as fact and working with it rather than trying to bring about a change — a carefully directed form of "If you can't beat them, join them." It may be the most practical response when the situation is difficult or even impossible to rectify.

Let's look at some examples from the Torah to help us understand how to use submission, and what distinguishes it from the other responses. When Lavan substituted Leah for Rachel at the wedding and then demanded that Ya'akov Avinu work another seven years for his intended bride, Ya'akov Avinu acquiesced.[15] En route to Eretz Yisrael, the Jewish people met the Edomites, who denied them passage through their land and threatened them with war. The Jews submitted to the Edomites' refusal and simply took the more roundabout route.[16]

Submission can be helpful when dealing with:

◆ *Dispute:* In a dispute, submission means agreeing with or, at the very least, giving credence to the other's argument for the sake of fostering peace — provided there is no strong reason to refuse to hear the other side (as when he is trying to manipulate you and lead you astray). Often, the most effective way to attain our objective during a conflict is through some degree of submission.

> Meir asks his wife, Tzipporah, "Why don't you ever do what I ask of you?" She retorts quickly, "Because you just don't ask nicely."

Meir is offended and snaps back, "What do you mean, I never ask nicely? Just last week I asked you very nicely, and you didn't dream of doing as I asked! And do you remember, three weeks ago, when I asked you to.... Of course, you didn't do that either, even though I asked you very calmly. You're just looking for excuses."

Meir's response puts Tzipporah on the defensive; she slams the ball back into his court with equal rancor and the discussion deteriorates into a shouting match.

If Meir had shown some submission and answered early in the argument, "Okay. Do you know what? From now on I'll try to ask nicely. And if I ever forget and ask rudely, please remind me and I'll ask again nicely," Tzipporah would have been encouraged to live up to her claim. By submitting, rather than trying to argue with her, Meir may have actually succeeded where, previously, he had only met failure — by holding his ground.

- *Being Genial:* Humility and brotherly love are enhanced when we do what others want — provided there is no reason to refuse.[17]

- *Life's Difficulties:* A person is not permitted to rebel against the afflictions that Hashem sends. He must strive to accept them lovingly, bearing in mind that "everything the Merciful One does, He does for the good."[18] This obligation does not stand in the way of making constructive efforts to rectify the situation and alleviate his suffering, when possible,[19] but if these efforts don't bring about results in a reasonable time, then a person should try to submit and accept his lot.

- *Achieving Our Goals:* We can submit even while taking initiative. This means not pushing toward our goals too quickly or with too much determination, and may even mean not pushing at all. As it says in Mishlei, "Whoever is hasty, it is only to his detriment."[20] Our Sages offer a similar insight: "Whoever presses the moment, the moment presses him; whoever gives in to the moment, the moment supports him."[21]

Beware: there are some times that submission is inappropriate. The Rama cautions that when submission means accepting a spiritually unsatisfactory situation — you must not give in! "A person should not be ashamed before people who mock him for his service of Hashem."[22] Shaul lost his kingship for yielding to the demands of the masses to spare Amalek's livestock.[23]

Our history abounds with models of courage — individuals who, in the face of great danger, refused to submit to decrees and demands to violate our Torah. Consider the battles of the Maccabees against the Greeks and the perseverance of such *Tannaim* as Rabbi Akiva and Rabbi Chanina ben Teradyon, who continued teaching Torah despite Hadrian's decrees.

Submission is also undesirable when it leads us to undertake an obligation that is beyond our genuine physical, emotional, or financial limits.

EMOTIONALIZATION AND/OR INTERNALIZATION

Emotionalization means responding with strong feelings or deliberately arousing certain emotions within ourselves. Internalization means keeping our feelings to ourselves or directing them inward. One or both of these responses can be helpful especially when one needs to:

- *Face Challenges:* Conjuring up feelings of confidence and vitality can prepare us to respond effectively to a challenge.
- *Achieve Inner Balance:* We may deliberately arouse in ourselves virtuous emotions to achieve inner balance. For example, if someone close to us has caused us a problem, we might intentionally dwell on our loving and compassionate feelings for him, to counterbalance a sudden surge of anger.

Many times we emotionalize in a way that hardly affects the situation. At other times, our emotions can be helpful. Here are some examples of emotions which play a constructive role:

- *Sense of Accomplishment:* When we take correct action, we should experience the deep joy of fulfillment. This private and pleasant feeling confirms that we value doing good, and motivates us to continue doing so. While private joy is proper and beneficial, boasting for external acclaim is not.

- *Regret:* When a person realizes that he has committed a sin, he is meant to go through the process of regret, confession, and undertaking not to do the sin again,[24] which all involve emotionalizing and internalizing the appropriate feelings. Throughout the generations, righteous people have always been open to feeling regretful and deeply saddened when they sinned.[25] Our Sages call Adam HaRishon very pious because "when he saw that death was decreed upon the world because of him, he sat and fasted for 130 years, and separated himself from his wife for 130 years, and wore bands of figs on his flesh for 130 years."[26]

  Regret also helps us to correct mistakes that are not necessarily sins. A person who has done something wrong should not ignore the error, as long as he can take action to improve or correct it. Mistakes of this type include accidentally losing, forgetting, or breaking things. Although we wouldn't call these types of incidents sin, they still need to be corrected. In situations like these, internalizing feelings of regret can motivate us to make amends.

- *Appreciating Kindness:* Internalization is desirable when acknowledging Hashem's Kindness or another's favor. A person should attempt to be aware of the good he has received, and to inculcate a feeling of indebtedness within himself. Many parts of the Torah serve to develop a feeling of gratitude — Shabbos and festivals, praises to Hashem, honor of parents, closeness with friends, and so on.

In order to encourage closeness and endearment between friends, you should tell your friend if you did him a favor, unless he will discover, on his own, that you did this favor for him. That way you can promote feelings of warmth between you, which might otherwise have remained hidden.[27]

On the other hand, there are times when emotionalization and internalization can be detrimental. When we accomplish something, we may get carried away with the feeling of pride. More pride than is necessary to maintain a positive self-image and encourage ourselves to continue doing good is destructive.[28]

We also should not emotionalize another person's shortcomings. If someone refuses a favor, we may not hold his denial against him, since the Torah prohibits bearing a grudge.[29] While it might be appropriate to consider how we can work on improving the relationship — by trying to initiate change — we must disregard the lack of kindness.

If someone hurts us, it is forbidden to internalize our negative feelings toward them. The classic example of internalizing animosity is Esav's resolution to kill Ya'akov Avinu after he discovered that Ya'akov had appropriated the blessing that Esav had expected for himself.[30] The Torah warns us not to harbor hatred in our hearts. We should, instead, rebuke a fellow Jew for his misdeed, and clear the air.[31]

It would seem that the only alternative to internalizing negative emotions toward someone is to suppress them, but there is another option. Rather than swallow our feelings. we are commanded to engage him in constructive discussion. It is considered *middas chassidus* (exceptionally righteous behavior) to sincerely forgive *(disregard)* the wrong that a friend did to us, even before he asks for our forgiveness.[32] If someone causes us monetary damage, we may ask for an explanation, or for compensation; but we should not feel hostile.

If our child misbehaves, anger or other emotionalizing will often be counterproductive. Instead, we should usually take action by correcting the child gently, but firmly.

When we discover a need for repentance in ourselves, we should not wallow in unproductive feelings like guilt or depression, but use these feelings only to the extent that they encourage change.[33] Our task is to regret the wrongdoing and get on with our repairs.

In general, we should not lose control over negative emotions like jealousy, anger, apathy, or sadness — our focus should be on generating a positive atmosphere and a more constructive reaction.

INITIATING CHANGE

Initiating change means taking action to improve our situation. It is desirable when there is:

- ◆ *Room to Improve the Situation:* When we have the strength and ability to take constructive action, and there is a reasonable chance of success, it is best to try to take the initiative. This is true whether the situation is difficult or pleasant, as long as it can be improved.

- ◆ *Room to Improve Our Personality:* Any effort toward self-improvement is also a form of initiating change. The Talmud says, "If a person suffers, he should review his deeds."[34] Similarly, "Repentance, prayer, and charity nullify the harsh decree."[35]

Let's look at some examples. Ya'akov Avinu dealt actively with Lavan's scheming. He approached his father-in-law directly concerning the problem of fair payment for his work tending the flocks. By using various strategies, such as setting up branches with peeled bark by the water troughs, Ya'akov ensured that his own flocks would not dwindle.[36]

Yosef dealt actively with the threat of famine in Egypt by suggesting and implementing a national program for stockpiling grain.[37]

Many prophets and sages spent a good part of their time traveling through the country, trying to help people improve their lives.[38]

Attempting to initiate change is not appropriate when it will cause undesirable consequences. We should not undertake challenges that are beyond our capabilities. If we become very tense when we deal actively with a problem, the result may be that we mishandle it or offend others and cause them to respond in ways that lead to even more trouble. We need to either learn to take action without becoming tense[39] or abandon the plan of action in instances where we stand to lose more than we can gain *(escape* or *disregard)*. Similarly, it is not advisable to take someone to a *din Torah* for petty matters, but only when the issue really justifies the trouble and aggravation involved.

We also should not try to initiate change when it will have undesirable consequences for someone else, such as the infringement of his rights, or causing him undue pain.

Anger is often an attempt to initiate change by influencing another person. However, expressing an emotion in an uncontrolled manner rarely benefits anybody.

THINK ABOUT IT

HOW DOES THIS EXPLAIN:

♦ the difference between the functions of *escape* and *disregard?*

♦ the proper use of *emotions? submission?*

What can be the advantages of using the response called *initiating change?*

Choosing an Approach

Until now, we have discussed five types of responses to a situation — *disregard, escape, submission, emotionalizations/ internalization,* and *initiating change* — and explored the times we might, and times we shouldn't, use them. As these five types of responses are very general, each can be employed in many different ways and in different measures — some which will be positive and constructive, and others which will be negative and possibly even harmful.

Let's take a specific scenario and see the different ways in which a person can relate to the situation.

> Chayim and his wife recently bought a house of their own for the first time. In honor of the occasion, Chayim's long-time friend, Dovid, an accomplished artist, painted a breathtaking winter landscape. When the picture was finally ready, Dovid wrapped it carefully and hurried over to Chayim's house, elated at the thought of the pleasure that it would bring his friend.
> Chayim unwrapped the painting and stared at it in silence for a moment. When he finally spoke, his words were laced with sarcasm.
> "So," he said, "this is the present you kept talking about. It figures that you'd paint a frigid winter landscape. In fact, it chills me to the bone."
> Dovid was appalled. For a moment, he stood in shocked silence, unsure of how to respond.

Most of us would agree that Chayim's statement was extremely inappropriate and that he needs to do some serious soul searching. But, for now, let's focus on Dovid's possible responses.

Possibility #1: If Dovid has (or has acquired) a unique level of patience and restraint, and easily controls his feelings, he may choose to *disregard* Chayim's rudeness. He might recall their many years of friendship and the many favors they have done for each other. He may assume that Chayim had either been in a particularly bad mood to start with, or that the picture had disturbed him in some way that he, Dovid, did not understand.

Dovid can also remind himself that he had hoped to strengthen the bond between them, and therefore he will not allow an ugly response to undermine his effort or harm their long-standing relationship. He may then manage to calmly pronounce, "Well, then, what kind of a present *would* you enjoy?" *(submission* and *initiating change)*

Possibility #2: If Dovid is struggling with the character trait of over-sensitivity, he would feel deeply hurt when hearing these words; he might leave without saying a word and go home to brood over the incident *(internalization)*. He could become so perplexed at what went wrong that he might not know how to relate to Chayim in the future. Instead of continuing their friendship, he might cultivate a cool detachment when dealing with Chayim *(escape)*. But in an incident like this, both internalization and prolonged escape are likely to bring suffering to everyone involved.

Possibility #3: Should Dovid be quick-tempered, he may shout, "Is that what you have to say about the present after I worked so hard for so many hours?!" *(emotionalization)* While he might intend to teach Chayim how wrong his behavior is, this negative way of trying to *initiate change* will probably backfire.

Possibility #4: If Dovid is practical and composed, he could consider both Chayim's acute disappointment at receiving a gift that was not to his liking, and his own intense hurt at the unexpected rebuff. He may leave quietly, without saying anything, in order to avoid making matters worse *(escape)*. He might wait a few days until both he and Chayim have had a chance to calm down, and then call Chayim and say, "I'm sorry that you were so disappointed. But your words did hurt. What do you suggest we do?" *(initiating change)*

Although Chayim's rejection of the gift was quite extreme, problems like this do frequently occur. Sometimes we do a favor for a friend, expecting a good word in return. But instead of accolades, we get criticism. In such a situation, we gain nothing by getting drawn into the newly poisoned atmosphere. Instead, we can try to understand the critic's point of view, and, if circumstances allow, gently point out the error of his fault-finding. In this way, we can foster an atmosphere of good will, which, after all, was our original goal.

Taking a quick look at the story from a different angle, we can now relate to Chayim's outburst, which we probably found so objectionable. We can use this perspective to inspire ourselves to be extra careful to feel and show enough appreciation when someone does *us* a favor. Even if the favor disappointed us, we should appreciate and acknowledge the good intentions with which it was done. If we do need to make our objections known, we should do so only in a tactful, considerate way — perhaps waiting for a few hours or days so it doesn't seem like we're rejecting the favor, and the person who did it for us.

Let us now examine some more day-to-day examples.

> Miriam's upstairs neighbor, Elisheva, sometimes hangs dripping laundry right over Miriam's laundry.

Miriam has several available options:

- ◆ *Disregard:* If the dripping is not excessive, if it does not happen too often, or if it is not too difficult for Miriam to wait for her laundry to dry a second time, then ignoring the disturbance might be the most appropriate response.
- ◆ *Submission:* If Elisheva points out that she has no other time or place to hang her laundry, but that Miriam could easily hang her laundry at a different time or in a different place, Miriam should strongly consider making a new arrangement, if it is not too inconvenient.

- *Escape:* Miriam could find ways to avoid the situation. For instance, if it is feasible, she could take note of when Elisheva usually hangs out laundry and schedule her own washing for different times.
- *Emotionalization/Internalization:* Neither exploding in anger nor swallowing her bad feelings would be helpful. However, Miriam could counterbalance her frustrations with positive memories of times when Elisheva was courteous and helpful to put her in a better frame of mind. This will also help her to deal with the situation more effectively.
- *Initiating Change:* Miriam could discuss the problem with Elisheva in a calm, straightforward manner. She could ask her to hang up her laundry somewhere else, or to wring it out better so that it will not drip so much. She might suggest that the two of them work out a schedule so they do not have laundry hanging simultaneously. In addition, Miriam could try to improve their overall relationship, which would make it easier to discuss this issue and any others that arise.

Perhaps Miriam already tried to discuss the problem with Elisheva *(initiating change)* but, unfortunately, it led to an argument. In that case, Miriam may want to avoid meeting up with her neighbor for a while, until Elisheva has had a chance to calm down (*temporary escape*). During that time, Miriam could try to figure out a new way to approach the subject (again, *initiating change*). She might, for instance, enlist the help of another neighbor to speak to Elisheva. Or she might reconsider and decide that the most practical solution is *submission*, taking Elisheva's suggestion that she hang up her own laundry somewhere else after all. If nothing else works, she might suggest that they go to a rabbi or a *din Torah* about the matter.

Sometimes one type of response works for a while, but a change in the situation makes it necessary to look for new solutions. In this scenario, perhaps Miriam originally decided to disregard the unpleasantness. But, as time went on and both women had more children (and more laundry), ignoring it was no longer practical. At this point, Miriam would need to reassess her options in light of the altered circumstances.

> **Note**: The idea of a "Peace Fund" is brought by the Chofetz Chayim,[40] in which each person regularly puts aside some money that he can draw upon when a small expenditure would help to solve a problem. Sometimes it may be worthwhile to spend a little bit of money — or even more than a little bit — to avoid a dispute between Jews and maintain peace and harmony. Hashem will surely repay a person for whatever loss a person suffers in his attempts to promote peace. (Here, "Peace Fund" money could be used to relocate the washlines, buy a portable washline, or even invest in a dryer.)

Let's look at another situation.

> Gershon is bothered by the fact that his wife, Chana, does not keep the house tidy.

He has several options:

- *Disregard:* Gershon could choose to ignore the messy state of the house. After all, Chana does do many good things for him.
- *Escape:* Gershon might decide to stay away from the house as much as possible to avoid being irritated by the mess and castigating Chana for it. It is likely, however, that frequently using this approach will, in the long run, cause him to internalize his ill feelings, hurt her feelings, and cause harm to their marriage and to the emotional health of their children.
- *Submission:* Gershon could decide to accept Chana's attitude about the house. He might also straighten out the house himself.

- *Emotionalization/Internalization:* Gershon might explode in anger or suppress his negative feelings, but neither of these would be constructive responses. He could also empathize with his wife's situation. This might create a catalyst to encourage his wife to understand *him.*
- *Initiating Change:* Gershon could discuss the matter with Chana, all the while keeping both of their interests in mind. He could try to help her understand how much he is bothered by the mess, *while* he himself is trying to understand why she keeps house this way. If she says that she dislikes straightening up the house or finds it too difficult, perhaps the two of them can come up with ideas to make it easier for her. Gershon should also remember to show his appreciation for whatever cleaning up Chana actually does.

A Blend of Approaches

We have just discussed how each of the five basic types of responses to challenges *(disregard, escape,* etc.) can be accomplished in a variety of ways. Now let's go a step further and add that in many cases, it is best to respond with a *combination* of more than one type of response, as we see in the actions of Ya'akov Avinu when he was about to face Esav. He prepared himself with conciliatory gifts and prayer, and readied himself for battle (all forms of *initiating change),* but he also divided his family into separate camps so that if one group had to fight, the other could *escape.*[41]

In every case, we must weigh our options — remembering to take our own and other people's emotions into account — and then choose or fuse together the most effective and practical response.

Even when a person is escaping from negative emotions, he must make plans to improve his situation and his attitude to prevent these feelings from recurring. For example:

> Baruch was insulted by Avrummi.

Baruch should try to dispel his anger as much as possible *(escape)*. At the same time, he should try to figure out how to avoid such incidents in the future, and how to improve his overall relationship with Avrummi *(initiating change)*.

Sometimes a single course of action can, in fact, be a combination of two approaches. For example, seeking a compromise is a positive solution that combines *submission* with *initiating change*.[42]

Similarly, we must strike a delicate balance between accepting life's trials *(submission)* and *initiating change* to improve our condition. If while trying to improve our situation we are careful not to push too quickly or with too much determination (a modified form of *submission*), our efforts are most likely to be effective.

In our service of Hashem, as well, we must find the middle road between losing heart when we encounter difficulties and pushing ourselves too hard. We must progress energetically, but patiently.[43]

In the previous story of Gershon and Chana, Gershon could resolve to put off looking for ways to make changes in his house *(disregard)* until he develops his appreciation for the positive aspects of their relationship. Then, perhaps, he will be able to move on to a different strategy for dealing with the problem. For instance, he may realize that there is something preventing Chana from doing the job properly, such as: she doesn't have enough time, she never learned housekeeping and organizational skills, or she's tired. It may be that some help from the outside, in the form of hired help or guidance, could help improve the situation *(initiating change)*.

Broadening Your Choices

As we encounter a specific situation, we may intuitively choose a way to apply one of these types of responses, and that choice may

Appreciating the Range of Your Options 33

or may not work. We may even feel that we've exhausted the type of response we have chosen, and reacted in every way within that type that is practical — but it hasn't brought satisfactory results. We may be stuck, in need of a way to discover alternative approaches within the type (or types) of response we have chosen, or even within other types of responses we may not have considered before. Once we have new alternatives at our disposal, we can choose the most preferable approach, one which is practical to apply and likely to be effective. It is probably most efficient to increase our alternatives in a three-step process:

1. Brainstorm: Use your creativity to drum up as many alternative approaches as possible, including those which seem remote or uncomfortable. Seeing how many options you can come up with within each of the five basic types of responses *(disregard, escape, submission, emotionalization/internalization, and initiating change.)* (You can refer to exercises at the end of the chapter for a convenient chart.) At this stage, every option is a possibility.

2. Sift: Weed out the approaches that will clearly not work in your present situation, or that are risky, as they can be harmful or negative. For example, if you are considering using a form of *escape,* you need to be alert to detect whether it might lead to a worse situation, or would be likely to cause an intense reaction from another person. Or, alternatively, if you choose *submission,* you need to draw lines — to what extent is it appropriate and practical to submit to the other person's demands? *Disregard* can be effective when it is subtle; it can be risky when employed in a way that may make other people upset, possibly aggravating the situation. When using *emotionalization/internalization,* we express or internalize positive or negative emotions to different degrees — which may affect us in different ways. It becomes clear that we need to sift out those approaches which could hurt us and others. In this stage, every option is challenged. Only safe and effective alternatives will qualify to be listed as viable options.

3. Choose: Lastly, we can review our remaining list of approaches (within any of the five basic responses we have decided is appropriate for this situation). We should objectively try to figure out the influence each option will have on the problem and on our lives, and choose the approach that we hope will be the best for our situation.

This 3-step process of brainstorming, sifting, and choosing requires a bit more time and thought than the more intuitive method, but it will hopefully save us from the danger of making the situation worse — from becoming more negative and even harmful. In the long run, it will also save us the time that we would probably have invested in an incorrect approach, and the repercussions we would have needed to correct.

Let's look at a simple example of how this 3-step process could be applied:

> Mr. Braun was known as the "green thumb" of the apartment building. He had potted plants in all corners of his home, as well as climbing vines on his walls. But his pride was the small flower patch in the yard outside his ground-floor window, which he tended most carefully.
> One day, he came home to find a number of his prize petunias trampled mercilessly. He grimly saved whatever he could. The next day, he happened to get off of work early and came home when the boys in the building were still out playing in the yard. He stood at the window drinking a cup of coffee and observed the boys' game. Before long, a ball came hurtling in his direction, landing right in the middle of the flowers. Before he had a chance to react, he saw Shimmy, the son of the new upstairs neighbor, stomping his way through the flower patch to reach the ball, giving no thought at all to the destruction he was wreaking. He quickly stepped out and gave Shimmy a talking to. Shimmy mumbled an apology and went back to the game.

That Friday, when Mr. Braun approached the building on his way home from work, he saw another game in progress. From across the street, he could see what appeared to be an "instant replay" of the previous incident: A ball flew straight into his flower patch, and a boy went charging over to retrieve it. Yes, it was Shimmy again.

Mr. Braun stopped in his tracks, feeling the anger rising in him. He felt like letting loose, but he caught himself and decided to logically consider his options. First, he *brainstormed* to see what his alternatives were. He came up with several options. He could go out and yell at the boy again *(emotionalization)*. He could ignore it completely *(disregard)*. He could go to the neighbor and demand that he give his child an appropriate punishment *(initiating change)*. He could move to a different house *(escape)*. He could bring up the problem at the next tenants' meeting *(initiating change)*. He could have all the neighbors sign a petition forbidding the boys from playing ball in the yard *(initiating change)*. He could fence off the garden to reduce the likelihood of such incidents recurring *(initiating change)*. He could give up on the outdoor garden, and replant the flowers in window boxes, realizing that "boys will be boys" *(submission)*.

Next, Mr. Braun examined each of the possibilities he had come up with to *sift* out the ones that were impractical or risky. Yelling at the boy was obviously not accomplishing very much; there wasn't much point in trying that again. Ignoring what happened was not a practical option, since he was too upset by it. He briefly considered the idea of approaching the boy's father, but decided that it was not worth the risk of causing a rift between him and the new neighbors. It was ridiculous to consider moving away from a perfectly good home because of this problem, so that idea was easily dropped. He admitted that it was not fair to prohibit ball playing in the yard on account of his flowers, so that alternative was dropped. He was left with the options of bringing up the problem at the tenants' meeting, fencing in the garden, or moving his flowers to a window box.

After considering the items on his list, Mr. Braun *chose* to first put up a fence and see if that would resolve the problem. If the flowers were trampled again, even with the fence, he would try one of the other options.

Despite his strong emotions, Mr. Braun decided that instead of acting impulsively, he would take the time to find a response which

would not only keep the peace, but also produce a solution which he would benefit from and be happy with. The *brainstorming* stage allowed his mind to flow freely; notice how acknowledging even his more reactive and possibly confrontational responses gave him the emotional freedom to come up with other options which would be good for everyone.

After brainstorming, Mr. Braun *sifted* through his options with honesty and integrity, trying to switch the focus from his own needs and feelings to what was most likely to work. He resisted taking action that might accomplish nothing but provoking negative feelings between neighbors.

Finally, Mr. Braun *chose* to start with some of the few options still available to him. Nevertheless, he kept his "sifted" list handy, since in life, we never know for sure what will work and what won't.

Let's take a closer look at each stage of this process.

Brainstorming: Creative Solutions

Obviously, a crucial aspect of success in discovering efficient solutions lies in stage 1 — in the ability to brainstorm and come up with new ideas of different types. Having a large pool of ideas helps with the other stages as well; it is easier to let go of the alternatives that seem a bit risky or less efficient when there are several options available.

Every situation we encounter in life can actually be dealt with in an endless number of ways. Yet it seems that many of us find ourselves reacting the same way again and again in certain situations, regardless of our degree of success. Is there a reason behind this tendency?

There are various factors that may prevent us from discovering creative solutions and employing options we may not have used before. One is that many of us may have only partially developed our creative, constructive side. Some may not be used to the concept of letting their imagination run free, taking in the wide gamut of options, as is necessary in the *brainstorming* process. Others are not accustomed to seeking out innovative solutions; they simply do not know where to start and how to go about it.

Another obstacle to creative solutions is the habit many develop of handling certain types of problems in a set way. People get stuck in a particular style of reaction and they automatically, almost instinctively, apply that same style of reaction to all similar types of situations.

The first of these factors, a lack of experience in creative problem solving, often has its roots, as well as its prevention, in early childhood.

Young children have little control over their lives. In his early years, a child's problem-solving skills basically consist of crying for help. As he gets older and develops more understanding, competence, and independence, he becomes more equipped to take charge of his life and deal creatively and independently with his problems. This ability, however, is unlikely to develop automatically. Like any other life skill, the art of problem solving must be learned. If it is not, that child, now grown, is likely to handle problems in a way that is not constructive, and perhaps even make them worse.

There is much that parents can do to create an atmosphere which will help their children develop creative problem-solving skills. Parents should be careful not to lean to either of two extremes: some parents over-identify with their children and become so empathetic that they cannot see situations objectively and provide their children with guidance on how to relate to their dilemmas. At the other extreme are parents who are too demanding of their children, expecting them to already know how to solve their own problems. Ideally, parents should be empathetic, and with patience and understanding provide guidance to help their children solve their problems creatively.

This will create an atmosphere that will allow the children to develop a desire for problem-solving skills, while helping them to actually integrate the skills successfully.

Furthermore, parents themselves should focus on learning and practicing these skills within the family. When children see problem solving in practice and have living models to emulate, acting with creative, constructive approaches will become natural to them. They will find it easy to come up with all types of ideas, weigh them objectively, and choose an effective solution. Perhaps the day will come when, along with the wealth of material taught in schools, students will receive much clearer instruction about how to use innovative thought to solve day-to-day problems.

The second factor that may prevent us from discovering creative solutions to problems develops over the course of years. Those who do not appreciate just how many options they have may find themselves constantly choosing from just two or three options. Eventually they will develop a habit of using those particular reactions. They may even become attached to those responses, regardless of their effectiveness. Ironically, this is especially true when a situation is important to us. We often get tense in such situations, which impairs our creative abilities.

To discourage this pattern, we need to encourage constructive flexibility within ourselves. In situations where success doesn't seem to come, even if we feel we have already considered all the possibilities, it is important to review our options. We should try to think of new options, reconsider the ones we already have, and ask ourselves: "Is there a better way to handle this?"

Bear in mind, too, that any one approach may include many possible options. For example, there may be several constructive ways to escape from a problematic situation. There may be many kinds of actions that initiate a desired change, and even more than one way to submit to and live with a situation that we cannot alter.

We should be open to a whole variety of ideas and be ready to implement them.

An example of applying this kind of flexibility is illustrated in the story of N., a convert to Judaism:

> After a difficult childhood, N. felt compelled to run away from home. She wandered around the world, searching for some meaning in her life, until she stumbled upon a community of Jews. The experience left an indelible impression on her, and some time later, she made the bold decision to become a Jew.
>
> When her family learned of her conversion, they were outraged and cut off all connection with her. N. found herself alone in the world.
>
> She found that the transition to an entirely new way of life was far more difficult than she had expected. N. had hoped that her fellow Jews would have the time and patience to offer her emotional support and provide her with a sense of security — to be the family that she never really had. But it didn't quite work out that way. The local women were not her type. They had no common personal history, and she found it hard to relate to them. Every time she encountered some difficulty in communicating, or a lack of understanding, she became more afraid that she would always remain estranged and alone. As her anxieties grew, she became more difficult to approach — perhaps, too, these women did not sufficiently understand the challenges faced by converts.
>
> The communication gap widened, and N.'s tense efforts to improve relations with her neighbors met with dismal failure (unsuccessful *initiative*). For years, N. agonized over her bitter lot (*emotionalization*).
>
> Finally, she reached the conclusion that there was no point in tensely waiting for society to change its attitude toward her. She realized that she would have to learn to adapt herself to society (*submission*). N. also decided that the chances of correcting matters in her neighborhood were very slim, since the women there were so different from her. So she began looking around for a different place to live, one that would be more suited to her personality. Eventually, she found her niche (*escape* and *initiating change*).
>
> With great effort, N. adopted a cheerful, positive attitude with which to rebuild her life (*initiating change*). The women in her new

neighborhood found N. to be quite likeable and were happy to befriend and help her.

N.'s earlier failure stemmed from insisting on dealing with her situation in only one, specific way. Success came when she adopted a flexible approach and ventured in a new direction.

Major difficulties like N.'s are not the only situations in which a variety of options may need to be explored. In a more common application, when attempting to improve our children's behavior and character, patient flexibility is vital. We cannot expect our efforts to show results immediately, and must recognize when it is time to try a different course.

If, for example, a parent has been unsuccessful with one particular method for influencing his child, there is no point in sticking obstinately to that approach. Instead of becoming angry with the child for not improving, he should seek alternative methods.

> Mr. Millstein was at his wits' end with his son, Yonasan, who had recently begun exhibiting poor study habits and rude behavior.
> Mr. Millstein's first reaction was *emotionalization*: he resented his son's behavior and berated him constantly.
> As time went on, Mr. Millstein saw that Yonasan's behavior was only deteriorating, so he decided to take constructive action to *initiate change*. He began with a series of earnest discussions with his son. In these talks, Yonasan expressed willingness to change, but, afterward, he would revert to his unacceptable behavior.
> After a month of having these talks once or twice a week, Mr. Millstein concluded that, although he had chosen a seemingly logical and constructive approach, it wasn't working. It was time to reconsider his options. He then decided to *initiate change* in a different way. He told Yonasan that at a certain time every evening, they would sit and review his schoolwork together. At first, Yonasan grumbled and acted bored, but as the weeks went by, he began to expect and then look forward to these sessions and even prepare himself for them. As time went on, the relationship between father and son began to deepen. By the time two months had passed,

there was a noticeable improvement in Yonasan's study habits and behavior.

We have seen that it is important not to get stuck in a problem-solving approach that isn't working. Conversely, lack of immediate results shouldn't lead to discouragement or desperate jumping from tactic to tactic. When working toward a goal, devote yourself consistently to the method you have chosen and *give it a reasonable chance to work*. If, however, you see that your approach still isn't working after time, reconsider the available possibilities and try to discover new ones.

We call this approach "constructive flexibility" to differentiate it from "floppy flexibility" — which stems from a lack of the backbone necessary to maintain an approach, and to differentiate it from "impatient flexibility" — which stems from not being ready to give an approach a reasonable chance to work. On the other hand, one does have to keep his distance from stubbornness or simple naivete — sticking blindly to an approach in the hope that even if it did not work in the reasonable period allotted, it may work some time.

Someone who has not assimilated effective problem-solving techniques can always acquire these skills later. But first, he must be prepared to break away from his set, unchanging patterns — only then can he learn more constructive approaches. He must become aware that, thank G-d, as an adult he has the competence, wisdom, and life experience that can help him determine the best way to improve his skills, personal qualities, and situation. He can develop the creativity needed to come up with more viable options. He also has the strength to break away from habitual responses and the control over himself that he needs to carry out his decisions. In the course of this series, we will discuss a number of ways in which we can free ourselves of old habits even more effectively, and learn to take appropriate action.

Sifting: Preventing New Problems

During the sifting stage, we weed out options which are risky or clearly ineffective — this stage is essential for reacting in a constructive, healthy way. The process of sifting can be rather complex if we're not alert. The most complicated areas when it comes to sifting out the wrong types of reactions are probably *initiating change* and *emotionalization*. With the other three responses, it is often easier to identify the steps that will bring us closer, not further, from our desired goal. But when we emotionalize, we sometimes get so caught up in our emotions that we cannot direct them constructively. Initiating change can also have an elusive effect; steps that at first seem constructive can actually be destructive.

One of the most common ways to express emotions or initiate change is by communicating. So let's direct our discussion to communication, which will help us to learn the importance of sifting through different ways of applying emotionalization and initiating change in order to succeed. In addition, our conclusions from this discussion may help us understand how to sift through various ways of emotionalizing and initiating change, as well as the other responses.

When we emotionalize, we often feel the need to convey our emotions and share our feelings with the person who provoked us. Usually we hope to get an appropriate response in which the listener conveys care and sympathy. Unfortunately, the listener does not always respond as we had hoped. This problem is especially common between family members. Let us examine the following examples, and see how brainstorming for ideas for how to communicate, and then sifting out the risky or impractical options, could greatly improve the success of our communication of emotion:

Mr. Goldstein was rather upset about the weekend he and his wife had spent at her parents' house. Both his father-in-law and mother-in-law had refuted a number of the opinions he voiced, and he was hurt by their attitude.

The next evening, he found himself wandering around the house with a gloomy face, silently hoping that his wife would notice his dejection and sympathize with him about what had happened.

After a day or two of such behavior, his wife had still not said a word on the subject or even asked why he was feeling down, and he noticed that he was starting to feel angry. That anger erupted the next time his wife did not promptly answer a question he asked. In the heated debate that followed, Mr. Goldstein accused his wife of being cold as ice. After revealing to her how hurt he was from her parents' words, he claimed that she did not know how to love or care; she didn't even notice how gloomy he had been all that time. That comment did not help the situation much; instead of softness and sympathy, he received a heaping serving of reminders of the many times he hadn't shown *her* love or care. Both left the argument discouraged.

Mr. Goldstein wanted to communicate the pain he felt from what he considered to be his in-laws' lack of respect for his opinions. As he understood it, putting on a gloomy countenance should have been sufficient to arouse his wife's concern and bring up the subject of his hurt feelings. When this method did not achieve the expected results, instead of trying to come up with other ideas, he simply allowed his frustration to build up until he expressed his feelings in a clearly nonconstructive manner.

If Mr. Goldstein had stopped to brainstorm for different options, he might have come up with a number of alternative ways to communicate his emotions: Simplest of all, he could sit down with his wife right away and calmly speak out his feelings about what happened, asking her to show sympathy. Or, in a slightly different version, he could say that he needs her advice, since he has a problem working through his feelings. A third option: he could wait for an opportunity when his wife demonstrated her respect for his views, and at that point, thank her for her vote of confidence, while adding that he had been hurt when her parents had demonstrated their lack of consideration of his opinions. Or, he could write his wife a note explaining what was bothering him.

Once he finished brainstorming for new solutions, Mr. Goldstein would have to sift through the ideas he had, to decide which would be most constructive. Although talking things out was most direct — and what he believed to be the most natural way of conveying his emotions — quite often their discussions would turn into arguments and end unproductively, so that option was rather risky. On the other hand, if he would take responsibility for his feelings, as if they were his problem, and approach his wife asking for her advice, that probably would not be hazardous. His wife might even appreciate the fact that he was approaching her for help.

While demonstrating respect for his wife's views would probably sit well with her, he knew that, at this point, he was not really in the mood to show such respect just now, especially since his wife didn't always show respect for his opinions. He was concerned that his request wouldn't come out sounding natural, and his wife would notice and be sensitive to the lack of sincerity.

Mr. Goldstein realized that the note could be the best idea, but he knew he would have to be sure it said something nice there too; otherwise, it also would be risky. At the end he was left with two valid options: asking his wife for advice (being careful to speak with sincerity), or using a nice letter to ask her to sympathize with him.

Let's take a look at another not uncommon scenario of faulty communication, but this time we will see how sifting out negative options can alter the results:

> Mrs. Spiegel had a hard time taking care of the baby and her seven-year old twins who were home from school with the flu. At noontime, when her husband called from work to ask how things were doing, she said everything was all right and that she really hoped to manage. But from mid-afternoon, when the twins got into an argument about the game they were playing while she was

nursing the baby, she felt it was too much to handle. She really wanted to share with her husband the difficulties of the day, but she felt that reciting a long list of all she had gone through would be rather boring. So instead, when her husband came home, she found herself in a generally irritable mood — complaining about the rainy weather and cranky, undisciplined children, and grumbling about the amount of laundry and garbage which piled up endlessly in their house.

Mr. Spiegel had experienced his share of aggravation at work, and was hoping to come back to a nice quiet home. He was rather disappointed by the atmosphere that greeted him. He told his wife, "This isn't the first time you've been in such a *kvetchy* mood lately. I wonder if crankiness is hereditary from your side of the family."

Mrs. Spiegel felt like bursting into tears. Why didn't he understand what a miserable day she had gone through? Then, in a sudden spark of inspiration, she realized that her indirect communication simply hadn't worked: her husband was still unaware that she had such a difficult day, especially after she had assured him just a few hours earlier that everything was under control. She considered her options: She could break down and cry, in the hope that she would arouse his sympathy. She could try explaining how she felt now, or she could postpone the discussion to a more appropriate time. She could answer him in kind, and let out her frustrations in a nasty outburst. Or, she could use some self-effacing humor to defuse the tension and express what was bothering her, while admitting that it was her responsibility to some extent. She quickly sifted out the first two options. She wasn't sure her husband would understand just why she was crying, and that would hurt even more. She was a bit concerned about directly explaining, although the postponing idea seemed like a good one. She surely didn't want to increase the tension with more hurtful words. Left with the postponing and self-effacing humor options, she decided to try the latter:

"You know what — you're right! I *am* cranky. And whenever the kids are cranky, I send them in for a nap. So you know what — do me a favor and take over for just fifteen minutes while I lie down a bit and come back to myself." Mr. Spiegel readily agreed, glad to put a stop to the escalating tension. A short while later, as they both sat at the dinner table, each one calmly shared with the other the difficulties and small victories of their day.

Mrs. Spiegel was able to brainstorm and sift "on the spot," quickly running through the pros and cons of each response. Her success was largely due to her recognition that the best options would be worthwhile for both parties, and her staunch belief that there must be a way for her to communicate her feelings so that her husband would understand. This concept of being "worthwhile" guided her sifting process much better than overwrought emotions would have, and it allowed her to reach a successful solution, instead of remaining stuck in emotional venting.

In *initiating change,* communication is used to discuss an issue openly with a person who can potentially correct, or help us to correct, a problem. Unfortunately, many people think they are being open and direct, but their discussions fail because they are not wielding this powerful tool correctly. The purpose of communication, when discussing a problem, is to encourage improvement and mutual growth. To paraphrase the remarks of one astute individual, "Effective communication will take into consideration the person, the time, and the situation. Our success in finding and using that right way to communicate will be measured by the quality of the results." Improper communication can make matters worse rather than better; that is what makes it one of the most dangerous threats to a marriage.[44] Since our emotions can confuse us at times, it is crucial to thoroughly sift through our verbal options and master the art of conducting a fruitful discussion. Here are some suggestions:

- ♦ Keep the focus on fostering good will and creating an atmosphere that encourages improvement.
- ♦ Watch your tone — it should be friendly and pleasant. Choose words that exhibit patience and understanding. Remember, "the words of the wise, spoken gently, are accepted."[45]
- ♦ Don't insult the other person or dredge up past failures or conflicts.

- Be a good listener — pay attention and don't interrupt. Sincerely desire to hear and understand the other person's ideas. It's usually worthwhile to try to repeat back to the other person, in your own words, what you understand he is saying. By showing that you're listening closely and trying to understand what's been said, you create trust and strengthen the bond between you.

- Don't listen with the sole intention of refuting what the other person says. Chances are that he is saying something that you need to hear, absorb, and take into account when you answer. Show respect for what he has to say, even if you disagree. As Shlomo HaMelech teaches, "Whoever answers before he hears will be viewed as a fool and will be shamed by it."[46]

The other person will respond in kind to your expression of anger or good will, argumentative edge or amicability. Be aware that your feelings will manifest themselves involuntarily in your speech, gestures, and facial expressions. Negative feelings poison the atmosphere, add fuel to the fire, and cause the other person to take a defensive or aggressive stance. A positive approach sweetens the atmosphere and puts you closer to success right from the start. Again Shlomo HaMelech explains, "Just as in water, face reflects face, so does the heart of man to man."[47]

Now let's see what can happen as a result of a little incident in which a person preferred to respond spontaneously rather than to weigh and sift through his options.

> Chaya and Rochel were both neighbors and classmates in junior high. They went everywhere together — to school, to the library, to the grocery store. The problem was that Chaya was extremely punctual, while Rochel was more easygoing and was frequently late. One day, after waiting for Rochel at the corner for almost twenty minutes, Chaya was fed up. "It's time to put a stop to this," she

decided. "I'm going to tell her just what I think about her intolerable lateness so she'll change her habit from now on!"

When Rochel finally arrived a few minutes later, Chaya exploded at her, "Enough is enough! That was the fifth time this week that you made me wait for you. I'm sure we missed the bus, and now we'll get to the performance late. You're impossible. When are you going to learn to come on time?"

Rochel was taken aback by the unexpected outburst. She began to explain, "It's not my fault. Just as I was about to leave, my baby sister woke up and I had to help..."

"Oh yes, there's always some excuse. So how is it that I'm always on time? Don't I have a baby sister, too?"

It didn't take too many days for Chaya to notice that Rochel was rather cool to her. Apparently, their relationship had suffered an immense blow.

Chaya believed she was only addressing a small problem in their relationship. However, not only did their conversation offer Rochel little motivation to become more prompt in her meetings with Chaya, the damage was far deeper. Chaya used to feel that her friend Rochel understood her well. This harsh incident undermined her earlier feelings and eroded her trust. Chaya violated almost all the "rules of constructive communication": Her tone was aggressive and her angry words did not foster good will. She dredged up Rochel's past offenses and insulted her. She interrupted Rochel's attempts to justify her lateness, and clearly was not interested in listening to her side of the story. It will now take time and decided effort on Chaya's part to rebuild what was knocked down in those few moments, if she can.

Had Chaya used her waiting time more constructively, she might have brainstormed for more options that would express her feelings without hurting Rochel or endangering the relationship. Had she then sifted out the inferior options, she might have realized that a condescending outburst was not only unlikely to achieve the desired results, but might also irreversibly damage their relationship. What sometimes happens, and could have happened to

Chaya, is that the sifting stage could have brought Chaya to realize that none of the options she envisioned would be good for their relationship, forcing her to return to the brainstorming stage. The sifting stage often has this effect: helping us realize that we need to brainstorm a bit more in order to come up with better options.

After thorough brainstorming and sifting stages, Chaya might have ultimately chosen to greet Rochel cordially, saying "I'm happy you're here," and listening patiently to Rochel's apologetic explanation. Then Rochel might have even admitted that keeping people waiting is inconsiderate, and that she should find ways to avoid such incidents. At that point, they could have calmly discussed ways of initiating change — perhaps by Chaya giving Rochel a quick ring before leaving the house, to remind her to drop everything and go. While doing so, Chaya would have to be careful not to be controlling or to tread on her friend's sensitivities. These types of options allow for positive communication, and when the communication is positive, the atmosphere promotes real change and may even enhance a relationship.

As powerful as the tool of communication can be, the results depend on how it is used, for better or for worse. We have to make sure to sift out any approaches which could endanger our desired goals, not to mention our relationship. This rule applies equally to all of the five basic approaches to difficult situations. It is not just the type of approach that affects the results. The *way* we apply that approach is just as crucial to our success.

The best proof that there's a need to reevaluate an approach is failure. If you've tried an approach a reasonable number of times, enough times that it "should" work, and it hasn't, it is time to do some reevaluation.

Let's look at one of our previous examples to review the ideas of brainstorming and sifting we have discussed thus far. We can return to the story of Gershon, who is frustrated about the constant untidiness in the house and would like to *initiate change*. He first tries the approach of direct discussion in the hope of bringing about this change. Perhaps Gershon explains to Chana how much the disorder upsets him. After discussing it a number of times, to no avail, he is tempted to *emotionalize* and lose his temper. "I explained it to her patiently over and over again," he thinks, "and she still refuses to listen!" Each time he tries to explain it to her, he comes away angrier and more hurt because she is apparently ignoring his needs and his clear request.

Gershon needs to realize that his repeated failure to inspire Chana to change her behavior indicates that he has not chosen the most effective methods in this particular case. Now he must reevaluate his options and consider what made his approaches unsuccessful.

At this point, it is time to brainstorm, culling together all possible ideas to deal with the situation. There may be other ways of *initiating change* — such as some we mentioned earlier, like pitching in to help, or arranging for hired help. Maybe he should attempt a less direct way of motivating his wife to keep the house clean — perhaps by using warm encouragement along with investing in a general improvement in their relationship, so that Chana will want to please him by seeing to it that the house is kept as he likes it: orderly.

Perhaps direct discussion is still an option, and it is only the manner of speaking that needs adjusting. It may be that Gershon's words to Chana were tinged with a critical tone — however unintentional — making them hard for her to hear and accept. She may feel that she does put a lot of energy into the house and that her husband does not appreciate her efforts enough. In that case, if he prefaces his request with clear appreciation for what she does already, that might be sufficient to initiate change. He can also try presenting the discussion as a request for her input: "Chana, I know you don't like when I talk about the tidiness of the house, but it is still bothering me. It would really make me feel better if you could tell me what I can do to help." He can only use this approach if he is ready to be very open to hearing what she has to say. Even if he thinks her suggestion is illogical or inaccurate, he will have to genuinely try to adopt it, in the hope that if carries out his side, it will encourage improvement on her side. Or, he may conclude that initiating change simply is not practical, and he will have to settle for one of the other four options.

Once the list of options is complete, Gershon needs to sift out the ones that cannot or should not be implemented. For example, if finances are extremely tight, then hired help may not be practical. He may also feel that since previous discussions were so tense, a new try at direct discussion is too risky.

Finally, Gershon must choose the option that seems most likely to succeed at that juncture. Analyzing why the previous approaches failed can be very helpful in facilitating the sifting and choosing process, since it gives clear guideposts as to what best to avoid, and what option might work better.

THINK ABOUT IT

HOW DOES THIS EXPLAIN:

◆ the different ways each type of response can be applied?
◆ how to choose between the different modes?

What lesson can be derived from the discussion about communication?

Choosing: Determining the Direction

Choosing is different from sifting because at this last stage, you are working only with viable options. Your task is simply to decide which option looks most appropriate at this time and in this situation. When possible, it is usually best to decide at a time when your perspective is most objective. Here are some pointers that can help you examine your options when faced with a problem, and help you to make a wise decision:

- Weigh the various possibilities at a time when you feel alert and refreshed. For some people, the ideal time is bright and early in the morning. For you, it may be at night, after the day's work is off your mind, you've had a bit of a rest, and the house is quiet. In either case, when your mind is fresh and undistracted, problems seem smaller and more manageable.
- Before tackling the subject, release tension in a way that works for you, perhaps by taking a long walk, engaging in some other form of physical activity, or reading about an unrelated topic.
- Analyze your past successes in dealing with other situations. Identify the elements that contributed to the desired outcome.
- Discuss your options with another person — a friend, a family member, or mentor. Some people may find that the process of preparing the question is helpful enough, without even having to pose it to another. Yet others may do best with a pen and paper, writing down each option, along with its pros and cons.
- Consider the ramifications of each option carefully, thinking as far ahead as you're able to. How is each person involved likely to be affected? How will he then react? As our Sages say, "Who is wise? He who can foresee what will happen."[48]

Keep in mind that you want your choices to be *effective* and *agreeable* to all parties involved. Try to implement those options that will not only relieve your own difficulty, but also take into consideration the other person's beliefs and feelings and encourage him to join you in looking for a solution which would be best for all.

Throughout your efforts, keep the perspective that a wide range of options is open to you. Careful consideration, spiced with patience, flexibility, and life experience can take you a long way toward finding a constructive response — one that will yield rich results.

> **THINK ABOUT IT**
>
> **HOW DOES THIS EXPLAIN:**
>
> ◆ why a person may not develop effective problem-solving skills?
>
> ◆ why we should sometimes use different approaches to problem solving simultaneously?
>
> As adults, how can we bring out the full potential of our problem-solving capabilities?

FINDING YOURSELF IN WHAT YOU'VE LEARNED

1. How do you generally approach challenges? List ten goals or challenges that you have to face. Examine them one by one.

2. Of the five possible responses (disregard, escape, submission, emotionalization/internalization, initiating change), which do you tend to choose? Weigh the pros and cons of your usual reactions.

3. If a new option has greater advantages, what has been preventing you from using it until now? Did it not occur to you? Is it too unfamiliar? Is there some other reason, perhaps?

4. Mentally review a time that you've worked toward a goal and not succeeded. Examine it for signs of insufficient flexibility in your method.

5. The chart on the following page lists some common situations that call for responses. Fill in all the constructive possibilities that you can imagine.

6. Look over your responses. Do you feel uncomfortable about using any of them? If so, why? If a particular response wouldn't always be appropriate, would there be similar situations where it would be helpful?

Difficult Situation \ Constructive Option	Disregard	Escape	Submission	Emotionalization /Internalization	Initiating Change (Since there are many forms, use this space to describe 3 that you could use)		
					A	B	C
1) A neighbor's child hit your child.							
2) Someone unfairly stepped ahead of you in line.							
3) You are unsatisfied with the service you received from some tradesman, professional, or clerk.							
4) List three other situations you feel are important or common. a) b) c)							

55

NOTES TO CHAPTER ONE

1. See *Sotah* 5b, "He who weighs his words..."
2. Rambam, *Moreh Nevuchim* 3:12.
3. Zechariah 7:10; Ibn Ezra on Zechariah 8:16; *Iggeres HaKodesh* of the Vilna Gaon, end of chapter 22.
4. *Avos* 4:23.
5. See Ramban and Rabbeinu Bachaya on Bamidbar 16:4.
6. Bereishis 27:41-45; Shemos 2:15.
7. *Avodah Zarah* 17a.
8. Bereishis 39:12.
9. *Avos* 1:7; Rambam, *Hilchos De'os* 6:1; *Chofetz Chayim, klal* 6.
10. Bereishis 13:89.
11. *Avos D'Rabbi Nosson* 29; *Shemos Rabbah* 31. See also Rabbi Shmuel D. Eisenblatt, *Chayim Shel Shalom, Chayim Shel Berachah* (Jerusalem: 5749), book 1, *klal* 13:15; book 2, *klal* 13.
12. Mishlei 12:25.
13. *Yoma* 75a.
14. See *Likutei Amarim: Tanya*, chapters 26-28.
15. Bereishis 29:28.
16. Bamidbar 20:21.
17. "'A person should always be genial to the people around him.' — to do for each person as that person likes" (*Kesubos* 17a, and Rashi there); "I never refused to do what another person instructed me to do" (*Shabbos* 118b).
18. *Berachos* 60b. See also volume 2 of this series, appendix B, condensed from the work *Chavivim Yesurim*.
19. "And he shall cause him to be healed" (Shemos 21:19). "From here we learn that the physician is permitted to heal his patients" (*Bava Kama* 85a). Rashi and Tosafos explain that we should not say that since Hashem made the patient sick, any effort to cure him contravenes the Divine decree. Rather, the Torah itself establishes that we are permitted to do whatever can be done to heal the patient.
20. Mishlei 31:5.
21. *Eruvin* 13b; *Berachos* 64a.
22. Rama, *Orach Chayim* 1:1.
23. I Shmuel 15:9, 15:15, 15:24.

24. See Rambam, *Hilchos Teshuvah* 2:2.
25. See *Mesillas Yesharim*, chapter 22.
26. *Eruvin* 18b.
27. "We have seen great, pious people who were punished for giving themselves too much credit, despite all their piety" (*Mesillas Yesharim*, chapter 2).
28. Vayikra 19:18.
29. Bereishis 27:41.
30. Vayikra 19:17.
31. Rambam, *Hilchos De'os* 6:9.
32. See *Beitzah* 6a, and Rashi there.
33. See *Likutei Amarim: Tanya*, chapter 27.
34. *Berachos* 5a.
35. *Rosh HaShanah* 16b.
36. Bereishis 30:37-39.
37. Bereishis 41:34-36.
38. See I Shmuel 7:16; *Berachos* 11b; and *Tanna D'Bei Eliyahu Rabbah*, end of chapter 8.
39. See chapter 8 of this volume.
40. See the Chofetz Chayim's *Shemiras HaLashon, Chasimah*, chapter 6, where the Chofetz Chayim suggests that a person set aside "4-5 rubles a year," or the price of a *lulav*, along with small change now and then, as a fund for keeping the peace.
41. Bereishis 32:8-21.
42. In fact, it is a *mitzvah* to make a compromise with an opponent. See *Shulchan Aruch, Choshen Mishpat* 12.
43. See chapter 8 of this volume.
44. See Rabbi Shmuel D. Eisenblatt, *Fulfillment in Marriage*, 2 volumes, (Jerusalem: Feldheim, 5748), volume 1, part 2, chapters 2-4.
45. Koheles 9:17.
46. Mishlei 18:13. Also see *Bava Basra* 98b: "I weighed everything on the scale and found nothing lighter than bran. But lighter than bran is... a guest who brings a guest of his own. And lighter than such a guest is one who responds before he hears."
47. Mishlei 27:19.
48. *Tamid* 32a.

~·2·~
Shyness and Embarrassment

What Narrows Our Options?

Even after recognizing our broad range of options, and determining what ought to be done, it may prove difficult to implement the constructive solutions that we have planned. A course of action may seem logical, yet we cannot bring ourselves to take the necessary steps. In these next five chapters we will examine the handicaps that block our potential to discover and implement the solutions that help us attain our goals. We will then look at ways to free ourselves from these handicaps. Our goal is to reach the point where it is almost simple for us to arrive at and execute correct decisions.

Let's begin by taking a look at the limitations associated with shyness and embarrassment.

The Manager's Dilemma

J.P. was a successful, ambitious manager employed by a well-established firm. He enjoyed his work immensely — until he was promoted to a more prestigious position. The new assignment was not to his liking. The location was inconvenient; the work, boring; the people, unfriendly. J.P. would gladly have returned to his old position, but he felt that to make such a request was out of the question; it would be too humiliating. And so, he remained in his prestigious new position, bored and unhappy.

Notice, it is not difficult people or circumstances that prevent J.P. from leaving his miserable situation and returning to his former, more beloved job. What holds J.P. back from taking the initiative to improve his situation is something within him: his sense of shame.

Like J.P., we, too, sometimes find ourselves unable to take action to initiate change, not because we are blocked by our circumstances, but because some limiting force exists inside us. The result is that we can suffer from the effects of our inner limitations as much as from the original problem.

A Time for All Things

When discussing the need to overcome shyness and embarrassment (our first example of a self-made limitation), a question immediately arises: In the Torah world-view, shyness and a sense of shame are considered positive qualities that play an important role in the service of Hashem. Why, then, are we belittling these valuable traits? To further complicate matters, it seems that even in the Talmud there are differing ideas about shyness and its opposite, boldness.

> *Rabbi Yehuda ben Teima said: Be bold as a leopard... to fulfill the Will of your Father in Heaven.... The boldfaced person is headed for Gehennom; the shamefaced person, for the Garden of Eden.*[1]

These two statements seem to contradict each other. How can the same *Tanna* advise us to be bold as a leopard, and then, in the next breath, tell us that the boldfaced person is plunging toward *Gehennom*? The answer is that the absolute, unqualified form of any character trait should be avoided. As Shlomo HaMelech said, "Everything has a season, and there is a time for every endeavor under Heaven."[2] This includes the emotional realm, as well. Every attribute should find expression in its proper time and place.

A sense of shame does have a constructive role; it can prevent us from acting in ways that are evil, harmful, bizarre, or foolishly impulsive. Our sense of shame keeps us from being overly stubborn and prods us to be considerate of the views and needs of others. As the Mishnah teaches, a proper sense of shame can powerfully direct a person onto the path toward the Garden of Eden. At the same time, excessive or misplaced embarrassment can make us feel overly self-conscious, and prevent us from taking positive action. A person must therefore selectively employ bold tactics to do the Will of his Father in Heaven.

On the other hand, in order for boldness to be beneficial, it must be used in moderation. A person must not become what the Mishnah calls a "boldfaced person," that is, someone who is habitually and conspicuously brazen. Not only is it a bad personality trait in itself, but with it, a person can't develop those positive qualities, described in the last paragraph, which are associated with shamefacedness. Audacity, like all emotional attributes, should be a tool in our hands to maneuver or even avoid using, as the situation demands.

Before beginning a painting, the skilled artist prepares a palette in the range of colors that he expects to use. Then he selects just the right color, sometimes mixing or even diluting his paint to get exactly the shade that expresses his intention. Our emotions, too, offer us a wide range of ways in which to express ourselves in the world. We must skillfully use our palette so that we choose the most beneficial response in every situation.

Each of us is born with a fundamental personality that has various tendencies, including the inclination toward either bashfulness or audacity. But we must take charge of those tendencies, and not allow them to hinder us from acting in ways that we deem most appropriate.

The decision whether to employ a trait in a given situation should always be an honest, objective one. We must develop in ourselves the inner strength needed to make responsible decisions unburdened by people's opinions — so that we may act with determined self-assurance. We cannot allow ourselves to be dominated by either insensitive brazenness or by timid submissiveness. Our goal should be to become truly free — capable of meeting the demands of the moment with the best emotional response, unencumbered by restrictive inclinations to either extreme.[3]

To locate your golden mean, try examining where you stand in the *middah* of sensitivity to those around you. Ask yourself:

1. How heavily am I influenced by other people's opinions?
2. To what extent are my decisions dictated by the views of others?
3. Does fear of criticism make it difficult for me to weigh the sides of an issue and develop an unbiased opinion?
4. On the other hand, do I make decisions and form opinions without seriously considering the views and needs of others?

By carefully evaluating your responses, you can see whether you are inclined toward oversensitivity and timidity, or toward lack of consideration and audacity. Once you are aware of this, you can know where to invest your efforts in order to achieve a harmonious balance between the two extremes.

THINK ABOUT IT

HOW DOES THIS EXPLAIN THE DIFFERENCE BETWEEN:

◆ constructive embarrassment and that which is not constructive?

◆ the proper and improper use of boldness?

What is the best gauge for applying these two *middos* in harmony?

The Paradox of Embarrassment

The effects of embarrassment are paradoxical — in some cases, it causes excessive bashfulness and timidity; in others, it leads to outbursts of anger and aggression.

> Jack and Ken are driving down a narrow street in opposite directions. As their cars pass, they sideswipe each other. The two drivers jump out to inspect the damage and find that both cars are barely scratched.
>
> There is clearly no need for either Jack or Ken to file an insurance claim or demand compensation from the other. But instead of forgiving each other and going their separate ways, each blames the other for driving carelessly.
>
> Tempers flare. Jack declares his readiness to call the police. "Call them!" shouts Ken. "I'm not afraid of the law!"
>
> The two waste much time shouting as their cars continue to block the road. In the end, someone else calls the police, and both of them are fined — all because it was beneath their dignity to give in, apologize, and drive on.

In any kind of dispute, some people tend to respond as did Jack and Ken. Although the best solution may be to forgive and forget or to reach a compromise, both sides insist on having their "day in court," with all the bother and ill feelings involved, because they consider it shameful to appear submissive. To them, any concession is a sign of weakness.

It is important to remember that escape from a problem is sometimes the most positive solution (see chapter 1 of this volume). Sometimes we reject the option of escape, even though it is appropriate, because we are ashamed that "they" will think we are unable to face the problem head-on. But we need to weigh the alternatives objectively. If escape appears to be the best choice, let's not discard it because of considerations which are not constructive.

> Refael is miserable in his present school. After doing everything within his power to succeed there, he has come to the conclusion that the setting is simply not right for him. He knows that what he

really needs to do is transfer to a different school, one more appropriate for him, where he will be able to grow to his full potential. But he is ashamed to take that step. He fears that his friends will consider him a quitter and look down upon him for not succeeding at their school. So he spends a lot of his time hoping that things will somehow improve by themselves.

If only Refael saw clearly what he is doing to himself — trading his emotional and spiritual growth for relief from the temporary discomfort of embarrassment — he would probably be able to overcome his shame and initiate change by transferring to a more appropriate school.[4]

> **THINK ABOUT IT**
>
> **HOW DOES FEELING BOLD OR EMBARRASSED AFFECT:**
> ◆ our reactions to difficult situations?
> ◆ our ability to make choices?
>
> How might a clearer understanding of our feelings of boldness and shyness help us to control them?

Stunted Relationships

Bashfulness can affect relationships by hampering their development. When it prevents us from forming social or business associations with potentially harmful influences, it is desirable. But bashfulness can also stunt the blossoming of positive relationships: between student and teacher, between neighbors or friends, even between husband and wife. The relationship hits an impasse because those involved are too shy to draw as close to each other as they would like.

> Leah and Shulamit are neighbors. Both women are lonely and would like to get to know each other better, but each is waiting for the other to break the ice. Leah, who has five little children, longs for adult companionship, but she hesitates to make the first move toward a neighbor who is unfamiliar. Shulamit, who has no children, imagines that Leah is probably contentedly busy with her family and with other mothers like herself.
>
> What's more, each of them questions how the other one will relate to her. "Shulamit is busy with her job and her community activities," muses Leah. "She probably thinks that women like me who are home with children all day long are boring."
>
> At the same time, Shulamit is thinking, "Leah is involved with her family all the time. She probably isn't interested in the things that I do during my day. Maybe she'll give me a hard time because I don't have any children."
>
> Each of them tells herself, "Why doesn't *she* approach *me?* If she wanted to strike up a friendship, she would find a way. Evidently, she isn't interested."

Both Shulamit and Leah are bashful about speaking to each other openly. They are too shy to discover whether they really have common interests and whether the other is interested in becoming closer. And so, each of them remains lonely. Let's look at another example.

> Nosson wants to become closer to his teacher, Reb Peretz. He would like to be able to talk with his teacher and benefit from his wise insight. He would love to see how Reb Peretz interacts with his family; he is sure he could learn a lot from it. But Nosson is embarrassed to indicate his interest in such a relationship.

It is likely that Reb Peretz would, indeed, appreciate a closer relationship with his student. Perhaps the reason he does not initiate it himself is that he's concerned that Nosson may not be interested and that a move on his part might embarrass his student or put him under pressure.

This situation was described by our Sages:

> *The shy person cannot learn and the stern person cannot teach.*[5]

> *If you see a student whose studies are as hard as iron for him, it is because his teacher does not treat him with warmth.*[6]

A student cannot achieve a more personal relationship with his teacher unless he clearly indicates his interest. At the same time, a teacher must maintain a warm and approachable manner with his students and make it clear that he is open and interested in them.

In the course of our daily lives we may have many other potential relationships that never get a chance to flourish, simply because of shyness and embarrassment. For example:

> Ben, who has recently started attending a new school, feels lonely, but is too shy to approach other students and make new friends.

> Mr. Horowitz, an elderly widower with no family nearby, has been living in Bayfield for ten years. He has many acquaintances and casual friends from his day-to-day activities, but no one with whom he feels close. He would love to have a few really good friends, but he is embarrassed about taking the initiative to try to strengthen any of his relationships because he is afraid of seeming pushy or being a "fifth wheel" among people who have spouses and children.

Both Ben and Mr. Horowitz remain lonely because they allow shyness to prevent them from taking action to improve their situations.

> Victor needs help fixing something in his house. He's certain that his neighbor, Yitzchak, knows how to do it and could help him, but he is embarrassed to ask him for a favor.

Actually, Yitzchak would be more than happy to do the favor. And because of his reluctance to ask, Victor may run into unnecessary problems — and not only with the repair job, either. Deep down inside, he may even start to have hard feelings toward Yitzchak for not having offered to be of service whenever help was needed.

> When Alice went through a long illness, Sharon was very helpful to her, bringing Alice's children to kindergarten and back, and even taking care of them in the afternoon on those days when Alice had

to go for medical treatments. Now that she has finally recovered, Alice gives Sharon a gift to show how much she appreciates all of Sharon's kindness. But Sharon, embarrassed, refuses to accept the gift because she is ashamed of looking as though she gave her help expecting some sort of compensation.

What Sharon overlooks is that, by refusing the gift, she is denying Alice the good feeling of giving it to her and expressing her appreciation. Worse still, she may be hurting Alice's feelings and harming their friendship.

How Do I Get Started?

Most shy people, even if they know and admit to themselves that they do want to foster closer friendships, simply don't know where to start. When they try, they sometimes misjudge other people and make awkward overtures, or give only the subtlest of hints ("Didn't I nod good morning to him?" "Didn't I pick up and return the object that he dropped on the street the other day?") and think that they've done their part and that the ball is now in the other person's court. They don't grasp that it would take a *very* perceptive person to recognize that some of these actions and gestures are intended as moves toward friendship, rather than simply being casual encounters or routine politeness. The reality is that some people who could potentially be very good friends aren't necessarily able to read such subtle cues.

On the other hand, a shy person may become so firm in his resolve to initiate relationships that he gets a bit too forthright in his efforts. In a moment of great boldness, he may come right out and inform someone, "I want to become closer to you." This may work, occasionally; he may be surprised and delighted to discover that the other person has had the same thought but was equally shy. But many people are embarrassed or intimidated by such directness, or feel as though they are being asked to sign some sort of contract with the other person. Lasting, real friendships often develop slowly but surely.

As we move on, hopefully, the reader will absorb enough cognitive tools and perspectives to help himself strike a healthy balance between shyness and boldness. This, in turn, will make it easier and more natural to approach another person in a properly balanced way. For the time being, a simple yet successful way to show your desire for friendship is to approach people gradually. You might start with greetings and smiles, and then go on to friendly comments and questions — but don't get too personal! Topics of common interest are a good focus and, when appropriate, you may even want to give occasional small, sincere compliments. From there you can go on to broader remarks that invite discussion. Words that express your concern and awareness of the other person's situation ("Are you managing all right in this cold weather?") are usually appreciated.

Involvement in real-life situations with other people is an excellent springboard for friendships. Try offering your own able assistance to someone you believe might need it. Don't forget that when you need help, you don't have to be afraid of graciously accepting it, or, if necessary, even asking for help from someone who is likely to be able to give it to you. The other person may be quite happy to help and may relish feeling needed and being kind. (If it turns out that he can't help, he can always apologize and say no, and he won't think any less of you if you asked politely and don't hold it against him.) If you are involved in some organization or community work, try volunteering to collaborate on a project with others, instead of always working alone.

When you have a conversation with someone, don't forget to listen — really listen — to what he says and direct the conversation to him as well as to yourself. Even if you disagree with his opinions, show respect for them.

Once you know someone casually and would like to deepen the relationship, don't be afraid of accepting or giving invitations. Don't be embarrassed if, for example, your house isn't as fancy as his; that isn't what determines the quality of the relationship. The more you feel self-conscious, the more conspicuous you'll be. The more you relax and focus on your friends, the more authentic that friendship can be.

Now that you have some simple ideas for deepening your friendships, you shouldn't need to drum up too much courage to make a start. If you haven't been able to bring yourself to launch the project, don't be hard on yourself — keep a positive self-image. Appreciate yourself: "I am a good person and many other fine people will probably like me. As time goes on and my personality becomes more balanced and my skills improve, I'll learn to succeed more at this. Meanwhile, I'll do my best to enjoy those relationships that I already do have."

Bashfulness in Marriage

Some of us may be surprised to realize how often the handicap of shyness finds its way into a marriage. We might not expect that a husband and wife would allow such feelings to come between them. After all, the hope of sharing a good life together is crucial to both spouses. What's more, if they communicate well, they will see that their basic expectations of each other are really in alignment. What each of them hopes for is attention, appreciation, and mutual understanding. Both partners could more easily achieve these aspirations by sharing their thoughts, needs, and hopes with one another.

> Shimon Brown would like more encouragement and appreciation from his wife, Tehila. But Shimon is embarrassed to tell Tehila how important her words of encouragement are to him. The need for such attention seems to him silly, childish, and not worth mention-

ing; he is somewhat ashamed that he even cares about it. Little does Shimon realize that, at the same time, Tehila is longing for a little more attention from him.

The need for attention and encouragement is not something silly or childish. It is a very real human need that remains with us our entire lives. There is no more reason to be ashamed of it than there is to be ashamed of the need to eat. Those who claim that attention is not important to them are fooling themselves and are preventing themselves from taking steps to achieve richer, more meaningful relationships. Suppressing a need does not make it vanish!

What is the result of Shimon and Tehila's shyness, which keeps them from expressing their needs for attention in an honest and amicable way?

> Shimon still wants these "unimportant" things that he is ashamed to ask for directly, and eventually this need does show itself. Rather than explain his feelings to Tehila openly and pleasantly, inspiring a generous response by asking her directly for more attention and encouragement, he lashes out about something else entirely. "Why didn't you take my suit to the cleaners? How come you didn't do what I asked? Don't you care about what I need?"

Instead of asking for what he really wants and discussing ways of developing mutual consideration, Shimon makes demands of his wife in the hope of reassuring himself that she really does care about him. And when he doesn't get what he wants, he demands all the more.

> Tehila, of course, cannot read Shimon's mind, and can't understand why he is in such a hostile mood. At the same time, she, herself, has been trying to get some attention from Shimon by asking him to do trivial odds and ends for her. She is embarrassed to explain to him how much good a little quality time would do her. And Shimon can't understand why Tehila is pestering him with petty requests.

The result is that the Browns are suffering from disappointment with occasional outbursts of resentment when they could have tenderness, understanding, and mutual fulfillment.

Husbands and wives need to be honest and ask themselves and each other, "What does my spouse lack? What do I lack? How can we satisfy each other's needs?"

If your spouse says, "I lack nothing," ask, "Are you really happy? If not, then why not? Don't be ashamed to tell me!" You may need to reassure one another that you will not let the discussion turn into an argument. It is therefore important for both of you to be able to listen to each other's answers without feeling hurt or taking personal offense. In fact, encourage each other to overcome your shyness and open up!

Further Limitations

We have seen many kinds of damage, social and practical, that are caused by shyness. The *Orchos Tzaddikim*[7] mentions even more ways in which unnecessary bashfulness can cause difficulty and loss:

- ♦ A person who is timid about asking a scholar to explain things that are unfamiliar or unclear may remain ignorant.
- ♦ A person who is ashamed to seek the counsel of wise people in material, emotional, or spiritual matters may carry a problem with him for his entire life.
- ♦ A person may refrain from undertaking a worthwhile or enjoyable project out of concern for someone else's opinion.[8]
- ♦ A person may not dare to disagree with contemptible people at a time when it is important to stand up for what he knows is true and good.

What Will People Say?

Mrs. Douglas bought an uncomfortable new sofa because of its elegant appearance. She is convinced that her motives are purely aesthetic and denies to herself that she has a particular interest in impressing visitors.

Mrs. Douglas's choice came at the expense of her own family's ease. She has sacrificed their comfort and her own because of her excessive concern with what people will think of her.

Mrs. Englard is overly meticulous about the cleanliness of her home. If she spots a bit of dust in a corner or under a bed, she drops whatever she is doing and hurries to clean it up immediately. She is proud of her excellent housekeeping, which she is sure she does for her family's benefit.

Mrs. Englard certainly has a right to feel proud of her efficiency and orderliness. But when her fastidiousness conflicts with the needs and comfort of her family, she is doing anything but benefiting them; she is making life less pleasant for those who are dearest to her. (Nor is she being too kind to herself! Consider all the times she has insisted on making the house gleam even though she was exhausted.) Her preoccupation with perfect housekeeping handicaps and restricts her. Perhaps her meticulousness actually comes from a sense of shame: How embarrassed she would be if a neighbor or a visiting relative were to see her home in less than perfect condition!

THINK ABOUT IT

HOW CAN EMBARRASSMENT:

◆ create tension?
◆ dictate tension?

What types of questions would help determine if embarrassment has pushed a person too far?

Liberating Ourselves

If we honestly acknowledge our need for rewarding relationships and show others that we want to come closer to them, then we can enjoy many rich friendships.

If, as the Mishnah tells us, the shy one cannot learn, then whoever *does* muster the courage to question his teacher until the material is clear (and requests guidance when he needs it) *will* succeed in his studies and enjoy the spiritual pleasure of understanding and growing in Torah.

A husband and wife who are prepared to communicate and be genuinely open with each other in a pleasant, constructive way will find that the results are well worth the effort. They will be rewarded with all the blessings that married life has to offer.

In relationships between neighbors, acquaintances, and friends, between teacher and students, and between husband and wife, there is so much potential benefit to be harvested. Why allow a misplaced sense of shame to lessen the quality of your relationships or stand in the way of fulfilling the *mitzvah* of loving your fellow man? Why not take advantage of opportunities to resolve problems and disagreements? For our own emotional and spiritual growth, as well as for others, overcoming inappropriate bashfulness and freeing ourselves from oversensitivity to other people's opinions are essential for realizing our potential and creating an environment in which we can flourish. We can enrich our lives so much — if only we will be bold as a leopard to do the Will of our Father in Heaven!

FINDING YOURSELF IN WHAT YOU'VE LEARNED

1. Make a list of activities or projects that you avoid because of shyness or embarrassment. Are each of these hesitations justified?

2. Make a list of the situations where you normally assert yourself. Is each instance free of contentiousness or insufficient consideration of others?

3. Compare your shy list with your bold list — which is longer?

4. Try to remember when you met your current closest friend. How long did it take you to become acquainted? How did you show each other interest in a way that was comfortable?

5. Which relationships in your life need strengthening, but because of your unwillingness to make the first move, are weak? Come up with three appropriate ways to approach the other person.

6. Sit down and visualize the face of someone close to you. Tell yourself, "I need him/her." Try it again with several different people. How can you make them aware of this without overwhelming them?

7. Ask yourself, if it's applicable, "Am I ashamed to have open discussions with my children's teachers?" If so, what can you do about it?

8. Which people do you believe would like to improve their relationship with you, but hesitate because of feelings of bashfulness? How might you reach out to them?

NOTES TO CHAPTER TWO

1. *Avos* 5:24-25.
2. *Koheles* 3:1.
3. See Rabbi Shmuel D. Eisenblatt, *Fulfillment in Marriage*, 2 volumes (Jerusalem: Feldheim, 5748), volume 2, part 1, chapter 5.

4. See chapters 7-10 of this volume and all of volume 3.
5. *Avos* 2:5.
6. *Ta'anis* 8a.
7. See *Orchos Tzaddikim,* chapter 4.
8. See Tur and Beis Yosef at the beginning of *Shulchan Aruch, Ohr HaChayim* 1.

❧ 3 ❧
Don't Give Up!

Buried Treasure

We each possess reservoirs of emotional and spiritual potential. The physical heart pumps vast quantities of blood daily, distributing life-giving oxygen and nutrients to every organ of the body. Its spiritual and emotional counterpart, what we'll call the "inner heart," is entrusted with tasks that are no less vital.[1] The Midrash ascribes no less than fifty-five emotional powers to the inner heart.[2] Shlomo HaMelech compared the vastness of its potential to the sea. Just as "all the rivers flow to the sea, yet the sea is not filled...," so does the inner heart carry the entirety of a person's wisdom and Torah knowledge within itself — also without ever being filled. Consider the *Tannaim* and the *Amoraim* — they studied the Talmud from memory alone and held the equivalent of entire volumes in their mental libraries!

The question arises — if these resources are ours, why don't we draw upon them? Why do most of us use only a tiny fraction of our vast emotional, spiritual, and intellectual potential?

Defeatism

We are about to explore one of the most common ways in which we limit ourselves: by our modest estimation of our abilities. We're all aware of the role defeatism plays in preventing problem solving. When a person believes that he lacks the potential to deal with a difficult situation — he thoroughly paralyzes his potential and creates a feeling of sluggishness in himself. That sluggishness makes it difficult for him to take constructive action. In fact, one of the main reasons why people fail to overcome their problems is that their efforts are made only half-heartedly, without conviction to the real possibility of success. Since they lack awareness of their own powers, every obstacle seems insurmountable. By resigning themselves to eventual defeat, their innate abilities to take constructive action are paralyzed; hopelessness — along with underestimating their own abilities — causes the very failure that they fear![3]

Detecting a leaning toward defeatism, recognizing its pervasive effect, and overcoming this tendency play a crucial role in our work. Undervaluing our potential doesn't only get in the way of successful problem resolution. It also impedes the discovery and development of our latent potential. When we have a vivid awareness of the true extent of our capabilities, we can maintain an optimistic attitude, and constantly discover and develop our talents. Without an appreciation of the treasures that are buried within, how is it possible to muster the resolve and emotional energy necessary to succeed? Or to even make the attempt?

> On several occasions, Fred found that he didn't recall his friends' phone numbers. This has made him certain that he has no memory for numbers. Now he does not try to remember even phone numbers that he uses almost daily.

Actually, there is nothing defective about Fred's memory — the problem is that he has convinced himself that remembering numbers is beyond him, and that making the attempt is not worthwhile. Fred has, himself, closed the door on his memory, and that act prevents him from taking advantage of his potential.

The Torah teaches that we are held accountable for the effects of a defeatist attitude. As Shlomo HaMelech warns, by being "lax on a day of adversity, your strength is diminished.... And if you say, 'But we did not know [how to deal with the problem]...,' He that keeps your soul knows, and He will repay each man according to his deeds."[4] Rabbeinu Yona explains: If you have the power to rescue yourself by your resourcefulness, but act as if you are unable to do so, then your strength will be cut short — measure for measure.

This loss of strength is not a punishment; it is a consequence that is as inevitable as it is self-inflicted. Shlomo HaMelech and Rabbeinu Yona are informing us about one of the ways that Hashem operates the universe: by convincing ourselves that we lack the knowledge or ability to accomplish a task, the spark of potential that was hidden deep within, but is still burning, is temporarily smothered. In other words, every difficult task, or *nisayon*, will strengthen us if we persevere. By admitting defeat before we really try, we not only deny our present capability, but we also do not gain the strength that could be actualized in the *nisayon*. So the first step is to know that we do possess such potential. Once we appreciate what we truly have, we will find ourselves accomplishing more and more, and realizing our goals more easily.

THINK ABOUT IT

HOW DOES THIS EXPLAIN:

◆ how a person can get in touch with untapped potential?
◆ what the different forms of defeatism are?

Is there any difference between problem solving and actualizing potential?

Impact of Defeatism

Determination, and its polar opposite, defeatism, are so powerful that choosing one or the other can sometimes mean the difference between dying and living.

Survivors of the concentration camps and Siberian labor camps speak of those who arrived at the camp at least as strong and healthy as they had been, who were subjected to the very same conditions as they, but who quickly weakened and died from the hunger, cold, and rampant disease. How is it that the stronger ones succumbed while the seemingly weaker ones survived? We will leave the dynamics of Divine Providence out of the discussion for the moment. In many cases, the survivors testify that what kept them alive was their belief that their lives had a purpose — together with a determination as strong as iron to survive.

We, ourselves, may know people who defied their doctor's prognosis and have lived years beyond what was expected of them. Some, perhaps, recovered completely and went on to live long, fulfilling lives. If we look into the details of such cases, time after time we find that the patients have in common the belief that their life has meaning, the determination to survive, and the conviction that they can conquer their disease. Medical research has clearly shown that a defeatist attitude invites illness and that, conversely, a positive outlook actually enhances the autoimmune response.

Despair can mean life or death. Certainly, in more ordinary circumstances, it has the power to make it difficult for us to carry out our responsibilities. Despair may persuade us to limit our attempts; it may drain us physically and emotionally and even inhibit our desire to act. A wise man once remarked, "If you think you can succeed, you're right. And if you think you can't, you're also right."

Resignation not only affects the despairing person, it even influences the way others relate to him. The Torah tells us that the spies sent by Moshe Rabbeinu to the Land of Israel returned with a disturbing report: "We were in our eyes like grasshoppers, and so we were in their eyes."[5] As the commentators tell us, the spies' view of themselves as insignificant made the Canaanites see them in the same dismal light.[6] It stands to reason, then, that if a person who lives his life in an upright way finds that others belittle him, he should examine himself; perhaps he undervalues his own accomplishments and efforts? With an enhanced appreciation of the value of his own deeds, he may find that others respect him more, too.

The Puny Bandit

Life presents us with a myriad of opportunities;[7] and yet, we may not notice them or may even be unmotivated to take advantage of them. Perhaps we fail to realize that lack of self-confidence prevents us from making positive changes and moving forward. By underrating our potential, we resign ourselves to failure when we could be flourishing. What lies at the root of such self-defeating behavior?

While it may seem rather simplistic to some, these internal processes should be seen as ploys of the *yetzer hara*. This wellspring of self-defeating counsel dwelling in our inner heart has a keen interest in making us fail in our life's journey. It sometimes accomplishes this by exaggerating the difficulty of a task, while simultaneously persuading us to underestimate our potential. We feel defeated even before we begin!

The Midrash[8] offers the following parable: A puny bandit sat at a crossroads, threatening each passer-by. "Give me your money, or else!" he said, and all the travelers fearfully obeyed. At last, one clever fellow came by; he realized that the bandit was all bark and no bite. The traveler toppled the thug and continued safely on his way.

The *yetzer hara* uses a similar tactic. Its strength lies in the threat, the bark, the magnified view of the difficulty. When confronted with firm opposition, the *yetzer hara* retreats. If a person doesn't take a strong stand, the *yetzer hara*'s messages of imminent failure gain this "puny bandit" victories time and time again.

> An experienced student believes that he cannot review three pages of Talmud — even simple ones — in an hour.

The student is selling himself short. With an awareness of his real capabilities, he could use his time more efficiently, amass more knowledge, and develop his learning skills further.

> A young mother is convinced that looking after her two little children and keeping house is just too much for her to handle.

Objectively, this woman's situation is not too difficult. But by telling herself, "I can't do it; it's too hard for me," this woman forces limits and low spirits on herself.

We should always remember that in the case of a reasonable goal, the Torah assures us that "It is very close to you; in your speech and your heart to do it!"[9] The Talmud reiterates: "Hashem does not make unreasonable demands on His creations."[10] If we overstate the difficulty of a spiritual challenge, we don't fool Hashem, but we can deceive ourselves. On the other hand, a lighter approach to life prevents obstacles and brings us closer to realization of our potential.

THINK ABOUT IT

HOW DOES THIS EXPLAIN:

♦ the way the *yetzer hara* uses defeatism to its advantage?
♦ why we are sometimes convinced of things which are not accurate?

How can a person can overcome the *yetzer hara*'s defeatist trap?

Mountain or Hair?

The way we tend to determine if the challenges in front of us are easy or difficult may lead us to big surprises in the future.

> In the future, Hashem will bring out the yetzer hara and kill it in the presence of both the righteous and the wicked. To the righteous, it [the yetzer] will appear like a high mountain; to the wicked, it will appear like a strand of hair.[11]

What is the meaning of this strange difference in perception? The *mussar* giant, Rabbi Yisrael Salanter, explains:

> By encouraging their desires, the wicked made it more and more difficult for themselves to overcome their inclination for evil, even in trivial things. They presume that at the final judgment, they will be judged as failing at a difficult task and will, therefore, be shown more leniency than those who failed at a simpler challenge. However, they will be shown no leniency when judged for those original, simple tasks, since it was they who chose to intensify and strengthen their desires until their battle against the yetzer hara became such a difficult one. Therefore, the yetzer hara appears to them in its original form, as [thin as] a strand of hair — the opposite of what they had imagined.
>
> On the other hand, the righteous, who toiled in the service of Hashem until even difficult tasks became a pleasure for them, presume that their reward will be minimal, since it was so simple for them to fulfill their duties. But this will not be the case. Since difficult tasks became easy only because of their choice, they will be judged as succeeding at difficult tasks, and the reward will be commensurately great. Therefore, the yetzer hara will appear to the righteous on their day of judgment as a mountain; they will be rewarded as if the task had been as difficult for them as it originally was.[12]

In his explanation, Rabbi Salanter focuses on those who make obedience to Hashem easier by experiencing the pleasure of serving Him, and those who make it harder by feeding their desires. But the message of the Talmud also applies to the way we relate to our daily tasks, since they, too, are forms of serving Hashem. While "venting" about a challenge can sometimes be therapeutic, we have to be careful not to overdo it. Some people convince themselves that their day's "assignment" from Hashem is far more difficult than it actually is, repeatedly telling themselves, "It's so hard!" or "How am I ever going to do it?" Such a person talks himself into difficulty and failure. In the future, he will be embarrassed to learn that, objectively, he was capable of doing the task, and that it could even have been easy. On the other hand, we can imagine the reward of someone who is faced with a truly difficult challenge, but brings himself to see it as a relatively simple matter and accomplishes it successfully.

A practical, easy-going attitude makes life's challenges appear less formidable and paves the way for ever-increasing success. The student slowly accustoms himself to reviewing a bit more material in an hour of study. The young mother gradually works toward relating to her work with a lighter, more pleasant attitude, and discovers that she does, indeed, have the ability to accomplish most of the items on her agenda — and feel good about it, too!

So, if you find yourself bogged down by defeatism, try taking a more objective look at your present situation and past accomplishments. You are certain to find that you have been successful at many different times, in many different roles, and in a variety of circumstances. This reveals that the inept image you have painted of yourself is simply inaccurate.

Especially in the spiritual realm, it is possible for a person to attain heights beyond his modest estimation. One may think that fulfilling a particular *mitzvah*, avoiding a certain prohibition, or controlling his own thoughts surpasses his ability. But these assumptions are just another form of despair. The Torah itself testifies:

> Its [the yetzer hara's] desire is toward you [to cause you to stumble], but you can be victorious over it.[13]

The *yetzer* can be overcome. And the more confidence you have in your ability to overcome it, the closer you are to winning!

The Other Side of the Coin

The tendency to underestimate our abilities is certainly damaging, but overestimation can also be detrimental. If a person overestimates his capabilities or ignores his limitations and faults, he may undertake tasks that are beyond him. Not only is this a waste of time and effort — he may even harm himself or others.

The most obvious illustration of this is the overestimation of knowledge or skills. We can probably predict the outcome if someone ignorant of first-aid techniques tries to care for the injured; or someone attempts to fix a broken machine without having the slightest understanding of how it works; or a scholar dispenses halachic decisions without sufficient knowledge. Although even a qualified person may sometimes fail, an unqualified person still has no license to make attempts at projects that clearly invite failure.

A person may also overestimate his physical stamina:

> Reuven, suffused with enthusiasm to devote himself to Torah study, has decided to cut down his sleep by two hours a night — all at once — so he can spend the time studying.
>
> Rivka, whose four little children always keep her busy and tired, has, nonetheless, volunteered to make *sheva berachos* for two pairs of newlyweds in one week.
>
> Mrs. Spiegel, whose own health is far from ideal, has offered to let her sister-in-law stay in her house for a month while she recuperates after surgery, even though this means that she will have to lift her sister-in-law in and out of a wheelchair and perform other strenuous tasks.

Although all these people have the best intentions, they are unaware (or perhaps unwilling to admit) that they are undertaking tasks beyond their limits. Their acceptance of overly burdensome commitments may be due to concern that a refusal would jeopardize their image (or self-image). But how much more unpleasant would it be to have to abandon their projects in the middle, or want to drop them, but find themselves stuck? Even if they manage to accomplish what they set out to do, the effort may take its toll on their physical and emotional health and on the nerves of everyone around them. And perhaps they will come away from the experience with such bitter feelings that, in the future, they will no longer be willing to make even a more modest effort.

A person may also overestimate his abilities in the realm of self-improvement, either because he has a distorted self-image or because his desire for personal transformation is so intense. He may then make resolutions that are, for him, entirely unrealistic. For example, he declares that, from this point onward, he will *always* be cheerful and friendly to *everyone*, even to the most obnoxious people; or that he will *never* be jealous of anyone.

Such a person's exaggerated expectations of himself lead to failure and send him straight into the arms of despair. Since he feels that he has already invested all he has by showing love and friendship to others or by purifying his speech, the inevitable fall will cause him to give up altogether.

This shows us how important it is to avoid tackling overly ambitious projects. Instead, the way to self-improvement is by dividing large goals into more manageable, intermediate sub-goals. We advance, then, with smaller, more sure steps. Once we succeed with an intermediate goal, we can continue on to the next leg of the journey.

THINK ABOUT IT

HOW DOES THIS EXPLAIN:

◆ why the *yetzer hara* doesn't like when we remember our achievements?

◆ why the *yetzer hara* sometimes tries to encourage us to take on large projects?

What is meant by "honest self-assessment"?

Don't Give Up!

Achieving Balance

Our Sages strongly caution against both extremes of under- and overestimation and lay the full burden of responsibility on the unqualified person for any damage he incurs. The qualified person, on the contrary, enjoys a certain degree of immunity according to the halachah. For example, in certain cases, a *shochet* who inadvertently renders an animal *treife*, and a money changer who misjudges the value of a coin, are not required to pay for the loss they bring to the respective owners if they can prove that they are experts in their fields. But if they cannot prove their expertise, they must pay for the losses they cause.[14]

At the same time, our Sages do encourage us to always develop our talents further.

> Whoever does not add [virtues to those he already possesses][15] will be cut off.... If I do not do for myself [fulfill my responsibilities], who will do for me?[16]
>
> Rabbi Tarfon says: The day is short, the labor is great, the workers are lazy, the reward is vast, and the Master urges on![17]
>
> Be bold as a leopard — to strengthen yourself in mitzvos beyond your ability.[18]

When a person suffers from inappropriate self-doubt, he often avoids doing what he should because he judges himself incapable, or assumes that there must be other, more suitable candidates. It is important to remember that the Torah repeatedly warns against any kind of apathy or inaction. If you find a lost object, don't ignore it. If you see another Jew's animal struggling under its burden, stop to help.[19] And most crucially, "Do not stand by your brother's blood! ...Love your fellow man as yourself."[20]

Simply developing strength is not enough. Devora, the prophetess, berates the silent observer; Shlomo HaMelech calls him destructive. Devora berated the people of Meroz, who lived near the battlefield and could have come to the army's assistance against the enemy, but did not.[21] Shlomo HaMelech warns us that "he who is slack in his work is a brother to the destructive one."[22]

Of course, people who avoid taking action usually can offer abundant rationalizations. But, clearly, the Torah finds many of these reasons inadequate and takes a harsh view of those who, though capable, do not do their part.

Where Do I Stand?

All this leads us to a dilemma. On the one hand, we must not overestimate our abilities and commit ourselves to projects for which we're unqualified. On the other hand, we must not underestimate ourselves and remain passive when fulfilling a task that is within our grasp.

When we face a challenge or a prospective project, how can we know where we really stand? If we assume that it's manageable, how can we be sure that we are not simply overrating ourselves? Or, if we are apprehensive, how can we know whether our modest self-assessment is correct, or is an underestimation due to laziness or apathy? How can we figure out whether we are evaluating our talents accurately or fooling ourselves?

Actually, both overestimation and underestimation have certain indicative symptoms that are recognizable when we make an honest self-evaluation. The following questions can help clarify where we stand.

1. If you feel reluctant to take action in the face of uncertain success, ask yourself:
    a) Are you reluctant to approach the task at all, even though you know that at least part of it can be accomplished and is worth attempting?
    This is a danger signal: it's likely that your hesitation comes from apathy, laziness, stubbornness, or defeatism.

b) Do you feel weighed down by sadness or a feeling of heaviness that makes it emotionally difficult for you to take action?

This is a sure sign of defeatism.

c) Are you so concerned about the harm you might cause that you are afraid to get involved even in the "safe" parts of the project?

Two things might be at the root of this concern: apathy about the importance of the project, and a sophisticated form of laziness.

2. If you feel capable and confident in the face of a challenge, there are three signs of hastiness or of overestimating yourself:

a) Are you impatient or so eager to achieve your goal that you are unwilling to take your goal one step at a time?

If so, you need to remind yourself that the sub-goal system works best.

b) Do you feel that slow progress doesn't befit a person of your stature?

If you answered yes, you need to focus on your goal, and reaffirm that slow, steady progress is the proven way to get there.

c) Do you dismiss all concerns about harm that you might cause if you do prove unsuccessful?

If so, watch out for hastiness! Carefully plan the ramifications of your actions — you are responsible for the effect you have on others.

3. To determine if you are estimating your abilities accurately, see if you:

a) are eager to do what's required to succeed — but still careful to prevent doing harm to others;

b) are prepared to consider sub-goals and to progress slowly when necessary;

c) are eager to take whatever action is within your capacity, with whatever measure of success it can bring — even if complete success appears unattainable.

A "yes" answer to any of the parts of question 3 above shows a healthy attitude. Your concern that you may not be able to complete the job is a sign of practicality, since it doesn't prevent you from doing what you can. When you assume that you can meet the challenge, your estimation is probably accurate and practical.

Keep your answers to these questions in mind when approaching your next challenge, and try to use them when gauging your response.

Making the Calculation

Finding the practical approach becomes one of life's important skills.

> Kalman and Levi both want to work on their *davening*. Their goal is to pronounce every word with feeling and concentration, with full awareness that they stand before the King of kings. Kalman is an apprehensive type. When he considers his goal, he feels intimidated; it seems far beyond his reach. He is tempted to abandon the project altogether.

If Kalman gives up on his desired goal, he will be giving in to defeatism. A more realistic approach would be for Kalman to accept upon himself, for the time being, a modified goal: to concentrate while saying a small number of *berachos* and to gradually increase the number. Although he has temporarily shelved his ultimate objective, Kalman is being practical, not defeatist. He does the best he can and advances optimistically.

Levi, on the other hand, is very ambitious. He is ready to leap forward to his goal. He reluctantly acknowledges that he can't achieve perfect concentration in *all* of his prayers immediately, but he feels that he *ought* to be able to get there in just a few steps. The idea of having to divide his project into many, small sub-goals doesn't appeal to him, and he refuses to consider the possibility that his ambitious plan may fail.

Since he is unwilling to pace himself and is convinced that quick advancement is the only option, Levi is probably acting hastily and overestimating himself. He needs to reconsider his method and the size of his sub-goals. If he'll focus on doing the Will of his Creator, Levi will be more inclined to seek out the most effective way to achieve his goal. As a first stage, he will only try to concentrate on certain *berachos*, as was suggested for Kalman. He will do what he can and advance cheerfully at his own pace. Let's look at another example.

Linda and Miriam both want to cultivate patience and avoid angering easily. While Linda tends to be very cautious, Miriam is ever enthusiastic — always ready to "take the plunge." Linda finds it easy to recognize that saying "I will never lose my temper again" is unrealistic and overly ambitious. In fact, even a less extreme goal looks so intimidating to her that she considers giving up completely. But she recovers her determination and recognizes that she can handle the challenge without feeling overwhelmed if she organizes a gradual plan to become more patient.

Miriam's first impulse is to jump beyond her level and take on the impossible goal of not losing her temper at all. But she stops herself and thinks about whether this would be realistic. She, too, concludes that it would make the most sense to work toward her goal step by step, not expecting immediate, dynamic change.

For both Linda and Miriam, the balanced approach is to undertake a reasonable sub-goal: to be on guard against anger for a specific amount of time each day, starting with those periods that are not highly pressured. Gradually, they should increase the length of that time and include the more hectic hours of the day. They should also remain aware of their goal at other times and stay on the lookout for practical hints that will help them to develop patience.

If a person untrained in first-aid techniques comes upon a seriously injured person, a balanced approach would be to avoid overconfidence and not try to treat him alone. Nevertheless, he must not evade acting responsibly — qualified help has to be summoned immediately. While he waits for them to arrive, he needs the self-confidence and determination to administer any assistance that cannot wait and which clearly can be provided by someone lacking special training. And if he lives in a place where accidents occur frequently, he may make it his business to enroll in a first-aid course.

In the balanced approach, a scholar who is not yet fit to rule on halachic questions will not rush to issue decisions, but will, instead, make an effort to verify the halachah from a more competent source. His awareness that his knowledge is insufficient may inspire him to apply himself and master the halachos.

So when can we rely on our assessment? When the generally cautious person is prepared to extend himself and act when the situation demands it, he can assume that his more frequent decisions to stop trying are motivated by honest self-assessment, and not by a sense of defeatism or apathy. And when an ambitious, confident person responds to the needs of the moment and is ready to proceed slowly or even refrain from acting, he can assume that his usual decisions to "jump in" stem from a realistic awareness of his capabilities, not from an overestimation of them.

Relative Completion

Partial completion may be a new concept for many of us, or a new life mode for others. Many may feel that if they can't do the job completely, better not to do it. They see an incomplete job as proof of incompetence and believe they won't be appreciated by Hashem or man. This can be the case if a project can and should be completed. However, as we learn from *Pirkei Avos* and the commentaries there, it is definitely not the case if action is necessary but a person is powerless to completely change the situation.[23]

> "Rabbi Tarfon says: You are not required to complete the task, but you are not free to withdraw from it..." — *to give up entirely.*[24] You should not say, "Since I cannot finish it, what is the point of putting in any effort at all?[25] — "And your Employer can be relied upon to recompense you for your labor."[26]

The tasks that are set before us in this world are far greater than we can ever accomplish. But as we learn from Shlomo HaMelech, "In the morning, sow your seeds, and in the evening, do not lay down your hand,"[27] and "All that you find within your power to do — do!"[28]

When a person resolves to do something and does his utmost, even in those areas in which he is incapable of completing the job, he is considered to have completed the job relative to his ability — or at least to have fulfilled his responsibility in that area. Furthermore, he will be surprised to discover how much Hashem supports his efforts and how successful he can be. He expands the limits of his possible accomplishments in this world, and can look forward to the vast reward that awaits him in the World to Come.

THINK ABOUT IT

HOW DOES THIS EXPLAIN:

◆ why responsibility should be relative?

How can a person achieve harmony between his enthusiasm and his concerns?

Be Active!

When we have doubts about whether we can carry out a particular project, taking gradual action of a limited scope is the best strategy. But there will still be some cases in which, despite our willingness to act, we are concerned that our efforts will turn out to be a waste of time. Usually, when we are in doubt, if the goal is an important one and there is a reasonable chance that we can possibly succeed, to make the attempt and risk failure is better than not trying at all. Then, even if the effort does prove unsuccessful, it doesn't mean that it was a waste of time — after all, we were working toward something good in the world!

Our Sages expounded on the verse in Mishlei[29] that "Many has he struck down" refers to the scholar who issues halachic decisions before he is fit to do so, and "...mighty in number are those he has slain" refers to the scholar who is fit to issue halachic decisions but refrains from doing so.[30]

Rav Moshe Feinstein, *ztz"l*, pointed out that since "Mighty in number" is a stronger expression than "many," we can deduce that avoiding the responsibility of issuing decisions when one is qualified to do so is actually worse than issuing decisions when one is not competent.[31]

We see, then, that the possibility that we may err by overestimating our abilities does not justify abandoning the challenge and opting for inaction. In many cases, it is even preferable to exaggerate our abilities somewhat rather than to be overly reserved in our estimate.

Many opportunities for personality improvement arise in daily life, but if we lack confidence, we may avoid seizing them. The means to take advantage of our opportunities may lie within us, but if we magnify our own limitations, we may not be able to discover them. For this reason, it is important to learn to appreciate our potential. Similarly, if we really are not sufficiently competent but the task cannot be postponed, and there is no candidate more suitable, we should not shirk our responsibility.

A Promising Future

As our Sages say, "All beginnings are difficult."[32] Sometimes we invest a great deal of time and effort in a project but, at the start, don't make much progress. If we are impatient and insist on instant results, disappointment and resignation follow all too often.

To counterbalance this frustration, we can encourage ourselves by visualizing our desired outcome as we work slowly but surely toward our goal. This Midrash reveals that in time, our diligence and patience will bear fruit that was well worth the wait. The Midrash shows us that we find examples of this throughout the Tanach:

> *Your beginning shall be constrained, and your end shall be exceedingly prosperous.*[33]
>
> *Whoever suffers at the beginning will merit a tranquil end. No one suffered at the beginning as much as Avraham. He was thrown into the furnace, exiled from his father's house, and pursued by sixteen kings. He withstood ten tests and buried his wife, Sarah. But, in the end, he attained tranquility, as it says, "And Avraham became old, and advanced in years, and Hashem blessed Avraham in every way."*[34]
>
> *Yitzchak, too, suffered in his youth. The Philistines envied him, as it says, "And Avimelech said, 'Go away from us.'"*[35] *But in the end they sought after him.*
>
> *Ya'akov — how much he suffered!... While he was still in his mother's womb, Esav tried to kill him.... When he received the blessings, Esav hated him even more and awaited their father's death so he could kill him. Ya'akov ran away to Lavan in Charan and Lavan deceived him about his daughters. And later, Lavan tried to kill him.... He left Lavan, only to meet up with Esav. Then came his troubles with Dina, Rachel, and then Yosef. But in the end, he attained tranquility, as it says, "Yosef supported his father and his*

brothers."[36] Hence: "Your beginning shall be constrained, and your end shall be exceedingly prosperous."[37]

So be strong, and don't give up! The prophet reassures us, "My redemption is close in coming and My justice will soon be revealed."[38] Our Sages also encourage us:

> Rabbi Yochanan said: All forty days that Moshe spent on the mountain, he learned the Torah and forgot it until, in the end, it was granted to him as a gift. Why was that? To encourage those who forget what they learn to review their studies.[39]

So, if our learning isn't going smoothly, we should not say to ourselves, "Why should I work for nothing?"[40] We can take heart from the example of Moshe Rabbeinu and patiently review the material yet again.

The same is true of other worthy goals — no effort goes unrewarded. Sometimes the initial investment is considerable, and it doesn't turn a fast profit, but we are assured that, eventually, some measure of success commensurate with our efforts will materialize. As Dovid HaMelech promises:

> Those who sow in tears shall reap in joy. He who goes weeping, carrying his bag of seeds, shall return joyfully, carrying his sheaves.[41]

Don't give up! Our job is to sow good seeds. Even though we may struggle under the load, eventually, with patience and perseverance, we will return joyfully with our harvest. The prophet promises, "Say unto the righteous that it is good, for they shall eat the fruits of their labors."[42]

Why should you deny your buried treasure — it's within you to do so much more!

APPLYING WHAT YOU'VE LEARNED

1. Pinpoint the areas in which you believe you are emotionally weak. For each of them, is your evaluation accurate and justified, or is it a low estimation which actually limits your emotional strength?
2. In what types of situations do you tend to underestimate your ability to change things for the better? Choose one of these areas and work on overcoming this tendency.
3. Choose an area that is important to you, but on which you've already given up hopes of success. In light of this chapter, review the challenge — is it really as hopeless as you'd thought? Take the problem and break it into more manageable bits. Resolve to work on the issue piecemeal.
4. Think of situations from the past where the beginning was difficult but you later found great satisfaction in the success you achieved.
5. Pinpoint those areas that you believe are your emotional strong points. For each of them, is your evaluation accurate and justified, or does your high estimation sometimes cause you to push yourself too far?
6. Analyze your answers to questions 1 and 5 — do you see any patterns? In what realms do you tend to under- or overestimate yourself?

NOTES TO CHAPTER THREE

1. See *Reishis Chochmah Sha'ar HaYirah*, chapters 7 and 8 concerning counterpart organs.
2. *Koheles Rabbah* 1:16; see also Rabbi Chayim Shmuelevitz, *Sichos Mussar* 1:5 (Jerusalem: 5740).
3. See *Chosen Yehoshua* 1:8 where he expands on this concept.

4. Mishlei 24:10, 12; see also *Bava Metzia* 33a, "He who pretends [to be unable to help others] will at the end reach that [being unable]."
5. Bamidbar 13:33.
6. See also *Gur Aryeh* and *HaEmek Davar* on Bamidbar 13:33.
7. See *Mesillas Yesharim*, chapter 1.
8. *Bereishis Rabbah* 22:6.
9. Devarim 30:14.
10. *Avodah Zarah* 3a.
11. *Sukkah* 52a.
12. Rabbi Yisrael Salanter, *Ohr Yisrael*, Eighth Letter.
13. Bereishis 4:7.
14. This immunity applies only if the professional is providing his services free of charge. If he is being paid for his services, he becomes responsible for any loss he causes. The nonprofessional, however, is responsible even when he is not paid for his services. See *Shulchan Aruch, Yoreh De'ah* 337:1, unqualified doctor; *Choshen Mishpat* 25:3, unqualified rabbi. See also *Choshen Mishpat* 306:6.
15. Ya'avetz on *Avos* 13-14.
16. *Avos* 1:13-14.
17. Ibid. 2:20.
18. *Pesachim* 112a; Rashi, Rashbam there.
19. Devarim 22:3-4.
20. Vayikra 19:16, 18. The Ramban there notes that the commandment to love one's fellow man means acting in a loving way: benefiting him in whatever way possible, as one would do for oneself.
21. Shoftim 5:23.
22. Mishlei 18:9.
23. See Devarim 4:41 and Rashi on "Then Moshe set aside..."
24. Rashi on *Avos* 2:16.
25. See Rabbeinu Yonah there.
26. *Avos* 2:16.
27. Koheles 11:6.
28. Koheles 9:10.
29. Mishlei 7:26.
30. *Sotah* 22a.

31. Heard personally from the Rav by the author. In contrast, the Talmud in *Eruvin* (100b) explains that the rule of [When in doubt], "being passive is better" (only) applies to situations in which there is a risk of violating a prohibition. In our situation, if there is a definite possibility that by taking action he will cause damage, he should probably be passive.
32. *Mechilta*, Yisro.
33. Iyov 8:7.
34. Bereishis 24:1.
35. Ibid. 26:16.
36. Ibid. 47:12.
37. *Tanchuma Eikev* 3.
38. Yeshayahu 56:1.
39. *Yerushalmi Horios* 3:5.
40. Pnei Moshe on *Yerushalmi Horios* 3:5.
41. Tehillim 126:5-6.
42. Yeshayahu 3:10.

4
Other Self-Made Roadblocks

Identifying Obstacles

Shyness and defeatism are only two of the emotional characteristics that limit our success in life. Many other negative attitudes and nonconstructive thought processes also act like roadblocks that we erect in our own path. To progress in life, we must clear away these obstacles.

In this chapter our goal is not to comprehensively analyze each specific negative characteristic. Instead, we hope to appreciate that, for the most part, our difficulties with actualizing our full potential may be due to restricting factors that exist within us. Nevertheless, just identifying the obstacles and understanding how they hold us back can be enough to neutralize them. In other cases, identification serves as a necessary first step of a more active process — something that will be discussed further on in this and later volumes of this book.

Some negative emotional states hurt us by preempting constructive action. This is the primary function of *depression*, which saps our vital energy, so that it's difficult for us to improve the situation. Other emotional states, like *tension*, don't block the beginning, but, instead, cause us to botch things and distance ourselves from our goal. In actuality, most negative emotional

Other Self–Made Roadblocks 99

states affect us in both ways — they thwart our initial improvement and damage any steps we do take.

Fear and *pessimism* may prevent us from exploring new solutions to old problems or trying out new programs for self-improvement. The student may shy away from looking into a better learning setting, or a worker may fail to investigate a better job opportunity or push for a promotion. A child who is teased by his classmates may be timid about finding a solution — even though he has little to lose by it.

These states not only discourage first forward steps — they may even sabotage an effort that is already under way. Because pessimism and fear can paralyze our ability to think clearly and act proficiently, they may even cause us to set ourselves up for failure. In that way, a bleak outlook becomes a self-fulfilling prophecy.

Just imagine taking a strong wooden plank, 20 feet long by 8 inches wide, and laying it on the sidewalk. Could you walk the length of it without falling off? Not much of a problem, right?

Now picture setting up the plank at a height of 30 feet and securing it well. You would probably be afraid to walk along the board and, if you tried it, you would be likely to fall. Why? In a state of fear, you feel unsteady; it becomes hard to keep your balance. The fear of falling makes you fall!

We see this phenomenon clearly in job interviews. Some people become so anxious about impressing their prospective employer that they act in a stiff, unnatural way, avoiding eye contact and answering every question in monosyllables. Others crank up their bravado and gush on and on about their accomplishments. In both cases, the result is a poor impression, one that doesn't accurately reflect the job applicant's personality or capabilities — because he was afraid of not making a good impression!

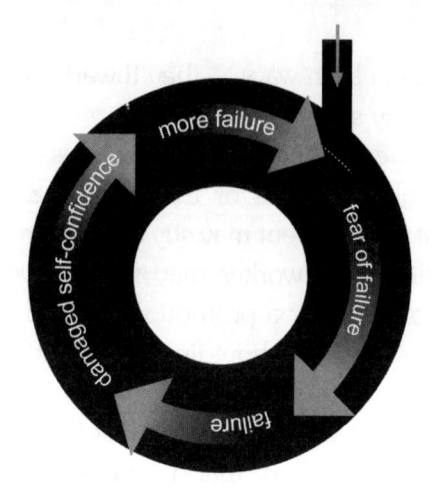

THE CYCLE OF APPREHENSION

(Cycle diagram: more failure → fear of failure → failure → damaged self-confidence → more failure)

Fear is the catalyst of a destructive cycle: the greater the fear of failure, the more likely it is that failure comes. And this failure erodes the self-confidence so that in the future, every reminder of the incident intensifies the anxiety.

How can we break that cycle? One solution is to relax and focus on the value of the goal. This serves as a distraction and releases a person's focus from his fears or the "trial" of the moment. By reorienting his focus on the value of his goal, a person will also naturally think more about the positive aspects of his situation, and feel less emotional about the negative ones. For example, a job applicant can think of the fulfillment he will feel providing for his family or about the type of work he would like to be doing. A person who is about to speak can focus on the impact that he hopes his words will have (to bring joy to a newlywed couple at a *sheva berachos*; or to persuade people of a worthwhile idea). A parent focuses on whether his response to a situation will contribute to his child's *chinuch,* rather than on the opinions of outsiders. This works because in these types of situations, feelings of anxiousness often come from issues which are not central at the time, like a lack of self-confidence or a fear of failure. If a person would concentrate on the positive sides of the issue at hand, he might just be distracted from those peripheral issues that may confuse him.

We should see these challenges as opportunities to develop our *emunah*. We can remind ourselves, "Whatever the outcome, Hashem knows and I know that I made my effort. Those people whose opinions are important to me know it and will appreciate it, also. The outcome is already in Hashem's Hands. Even if my efforts don't succeed this time — I'm trying to do something worthwhile and that effort, in itself, is valuable."

Cynicism, sarcasm, and a *dismissive attitude* prevent enjoyment of life because with them, all the good and beauty of the world is minimized or explained away. The cynic doesn't recognize the value of ideas or people that can bring him benefit and is deaf to words of guidance.[1] He either distorts serious words or lets them roll off him without penetrating, like raindrops off an umbrella. The sarcastic individual doesn't really communicate — a sparring partner is intensely tempted to deliver sharp retorts, and he is not interested in relating to constructive explanations. How can we turn around these negative attitudes? One approach is to try an exercise, asking yourself: If there were something positive in this situation, what would it be? For a further discussion about seeing the positive in all situations and people, see volume 2, chapters 2, 3, 5, and 6.

Anger and *hypersensitivity* prevent a person from developing relationships with people, even if doing so would be to his advantage. The hypersensitive person finds many people intimidating and avoids them, or he may project the image of being "complicated" — so people don't want to get involved with him. Sometimes he may be convinced that no relationship is ever "bruise-free," and so decides to avoid situations of intimacy, which he finds threatening.

Anger can make other people intimidated; the angry person also tends to choose coarse solutions to interpersonal problems that make others shy away from him. A thorough discussion of anger — and how to overcome it — can be found in volume 2, chapter 2.

Tension and *sensitivity to pressure* can trigger impulsive responses to situations and block the mental clarity needed to find efficient solutions. The measures taken under pressure are more likely to aggravate problems than to solve them. When tense, it's easier to become entangled in interpersonal conflicts with neighbors, co-workers, clients, one's boss, spouse, or children. It can also lead to a kind of self-sabotage. A tense technician may find himself acting butter-fingered as he attempts to make a repair, even one with which he has experience. A housewife who feels pressured may have difficulty organizing her normally manageable, daily responsibilities. See chapter 8 of this volume for ways to work through project-related tension. Volume 2, chapter 2 discusses situation-related tension.

The *compulsive winner* must always be in the right. He would rather have his way than learn the secret of the other guy's advantage or find practical solutions that are fair all around. Students who are compulsive winners don't seek the truth; they prefer to feel that they know everything already. Principals and managers brush aside sound advice about running their institutions because they feel that it compromises their authority as "the boss." Spouses argue continually and find it difficult to improve their relationship because each feels a need to have the last word. The compulsive winner might get past this roadblock if he redefined "winning" in healthy terms like winning a better solution, winning a compromise, or winning a better relationship with his counterpart.

The *sadness* and *depression* that can come in the course of a problem often compound that problem. They slow a person down, and block him from taking action to make the situation more encouraging. They both are related to the despair discussed in the previous chapter, and will be dealt with more thoroughly in volume 2, chapter 1.

An Examination of Attitudes

Let's examine some rather typical situations and notice that while they affect different people differently, the common denominator remains: negative tendencies act as roadblocks standing in the way of our goals.

> Twenty people are seated in a room, about to take a test. The tension is palpable. Although nearly all the examinees feel pressured to some extent, they all react to it in different ways. Dan finds it difficult to concentrate. Ed panics and makes many careless mistakes. Fred wants so badly to escape from the room, that he rushes to complete the exam and hands in his paper without checking his answers. He would rather accept the possibility of a lower grade and have it over and done with, than remain in the pressured state of feeling that he must do his best.
>
> For some of the examinees, additional feelings come into play. Allen despairs of getting a good grade right from the start. Ben feels hostile toward the examiner for preparing such a difficult test. Carl is sure that his friends will get higher grades than him and he starts to feel jealous of them even before the test has begun.

Again we see the paradoxical outcome: the *fear* of doing poorly causes these examinees to actually perform below their ability. And, of course, without the pressure and the anxiety it fosters, they would have a better chance at a high score.

Interpersonal relations, too, elicit a wide variety of attitudes from people, many of which act as roadblocks to finding productive modes of action.

> A new neighbor, Zelda, has moved into an apartment building. Almost immediately, Zelda begins complaining about nearly everything that the other tenants do.

Let's observe their reactions.

> Harriet becomes angry at Zelda, but avoids confronting her directly. Inwardly, Harriet feels hostile toward her. Irene can't control her outrage and yells back at Zelda or answers her sarcastically. Joyce feels intimidated by Zelda. She gives in to her every demand,

whether reasonable or not, and goes out of her way to avoid giving her cause for complaint. Karen resents Zelda's behavior, but avoids dealing with her directly. Instead, she lectures her husband, accusing him of being someone who takes matters too much to heart. Leah simply ignores Zelda completely. Let Zelda scream to her heart's content; Leah goes on doing as she wishes.

Judging the reactions of these neighbors, we find manifestations of emotions such as anger, defeatism, and cynicism, all of which create roadblocks. If these neighbors would identify their emotional roadblocks, it would be easier, either individually or as a group, to discover many better alternatives to neutralize Zelda's negativity. It would make it easier — perhaps even pleasant — to live with her. They might, for instance, write her a frank letter, being careful to explain the problem gently; or ask her, in person or in writing, to come to a rabbi or some other respected third party for arbitration. They could try inviting her over socially and including her with the other neighbors in events such as *kiddushim*. They might even consider sending her flowers before a *Yom Tov* to indicate their friendly intentions. They could try to find out whether Zelda needs some particular kind of help that they can offer, or whether she has some talent or expertise to contribute that will make her feel more a part of the group.

In a case like this, when a neighbor's behavior exceeds the accepted norm, it may be appropriate to inquire, with sensibility, (being careful not to hurt anyone's feelings or meddle in her affairs), if Zelda isn't dealing with some serious problem that causes her to unburden her stress on those around her; perhaps, G-d forbid, there is a sick family member under her care, and she is under tremendous strain. Whatever route you finally choose, if the cause of the problem is not so clear, trying an approach which includes understanding, friendship, warmth, and encouragement may help the situation, and the rate of complaints might decrease considerably.

📝 **Note**: All the neighbors should also try to overcome negative responses when relating to each other as they coordinate to solve the problem. Even if these neighbors don't find a perfect solution, whatever they do accomplish is preferable to allowing the negative roadblocks to take over. At the very least, they will have the satisfaction of knowing that they had the self-control to act constructively.

Our emotions should never block our ability to make wise decisions! When we're angry, we can't be gentle. If we panic, our level-headedness is gone. Depression undercuts our drive to function properly, and fearfulness makes us hide from our problems. If we are arrogant, we resist negotiating and compromising, even when standing our ground means losing more than we gain.

A negative disposition is also contagious: the next person may well reflect it right back at us. Our goal, then, is to identify the negative emotions that get in our way. We can then be free to operate according to reason.

THINK ABOUT IT

HOW DOES THIS EXPLAIN:

◆ how different attitudes become roadblocks?
◆ which roadblocks can be resolved merely by identifying them?

Which roadblocks do you consider to be the most challenging?

On the Home Front

At home, too, our emotions and attitudes can obstruct lucid thought and effective communication. But if we "try on" a different attitude, it can clear the way for us.

> Michael, who is self-employed, needs to get some important papers to his accountant by the end of the week. But this is his busy season; he is swamped with work and can't free up time to bring over the papers. He knows that his wife, Navah, passes the accountant's office on her way to and from work and could stop off there on her way home. He also knows that Navah doesn't like going there; it means a long wait for a second bus, and the accountant's secretary is sometimes rude.
>
> Because Michael knows that Navah would really rather not go, he feels anxious about asking her. In addition, he's feeling pressured because of his workload. Michael could use a little help and a little sympathy; he wants very much to feel that his wife is on his side. He's really not in the mood to hear "no" right now.
>
> All the pent-up pressure and anxiety have their effect: Michael ends up asking Navah for the favor in a demanding, accusatory tone. For her part, Navah would have agreed to do the errand for Michael if she had been asked in a reasonable manner. Even though she doesn't like going to the accountant's office, she knows that Michael could use her help right now. But when confronted with demands, she becomes defensive and insists that she absolutely *will not* go there!
>
> The result is that Michael's anxiety causes the very thing he wants least to happen.

If Michael had recognized and worked through the roadblocks of his difficult feelings, he might have thought of a way to elicit Navah's help while also encouraging both of them to be cooperative and pleasant. So much can be accomplished with the help of a smile, gentle words, and good will. For instance, if Michael had said, simply and without accusations, "I know this is unpleasant for you to do, but your help is so important to me right now," Navah would, most likely, have set aside her own comfort to help her husband.

The favor that Michael was asking of Navah was an urgently needed one. Sometimes, though, one spouse asks the other to do something that itself is insignificant, almost as a way of testing the other spouse. The favor isn't what matters — it's the love that is revealed when the favor is done. Here too, if there is too much anxiety about the reaction it will bring, the request might be phrased in a way that only makes it harder for the other partner to reveal that love. A husband and wife are usually willing to do so much for each other, if only each feels sure of the other's appreciation!

Subtle Handicaps

Negative traits often exist in subtle, hard-to-detect forms; this may make it all the more difficult to detect their presence and recognize the effect that they have on our lives. Even when we discover these traits in ourselves, their apparent triviality undermines our motivation to deal with them aggressively.

Consider fear. We tend to assume that we are afraid only when confronted by a serious threat. When a person must appear in court or undergo major surgery, he knows that what he feels is fear. Even when approaching a major exam, a person can easily discern how fear disturbs his tranquility and mental clarity.

But we are often unaware of fear's more subtle manifestations, and do not realize how limiting such fear can be. We may be skittish about trying even simple new ideas or projects because we may not succeed. We may be preoccupied by other people's opinions of our lifestyle. Such anxieties can restrict our behavior. They may dictate anything from where we shop to how we educate our children. For example:

- ◆ Stage fright can cause an actor to give a poor performance or a public speaker to become tongue-tied.

- ♦ An anxious student may hesitate to ask a question in class for fear of looking foolish.
- ♦ A citizen may avoid taking an active role in community affairs, even though he feels dedicated to a certain cause, for fear that his skills are not up to the demands of the project or that someone will take a cynical attitude toward his attempts to contribute.
- ♦ A mother might be apprehensive about using a new technique in child raising or a new recipe, lest she fail.

Always try to examine if there are subtle anxieties and fears blocking your way to achieving your goals. By identifying them, you make it so much easier for yourself to clear away those roadblocks and forge ahead!

Subtle Feelings of Shame

Just as subtle fears affect us profoundly, so can subtle feelings of shame. One of the most far-reaching ramifications of such hidden shame is that it prevents us from accurately pinpointing those areas in which we can improve our situation.

> Throughout the day Josh wondered, "What happened to everyone today? My neighbor seems to be angry with me; the grocer didn't smile at me this morning; the family is quieter than usual; and my friends are avoiding me. What's the matter with everybody today?"

It doesn't occur to Josh that "the matter" might be with *him*. He tries to understand why the world seems strange, and looks for the answer in everyone and everything: his office, the weather, the financial state of the country. It's all part of an unconscious effort to avoid acknowledging his own hand in the situation.

Chances are that if you asked him, Josh would agree that he sometimes does have days when he walks around in a bad mood.

But, although he may admit to this in theory, he probably feels a trifle embarrassed about it. This small trace of shame is powerful enough to keep Josh from recognizing his "bad days" when they do come around. Because his shame keeps him from identifying the real source of his uneasiness, any attempts to improve his situation are liable to be misdirected.

> Rav Chayim Shmuelevitz, ztz"l, the late Rosh Yeshivah of Mir, was once asked for advice by a certain student of a different yeshivah. The student had despaired of succeeding in his studies at the yeshivah he was attending at the time. He explained his difficulties to Rav Chayim and listed the factors that he considered to be responsible for his failure. He asked the Rosh Yeshivah's advice on whether or not to switch to another yeshivah. Rav Chayim gave the student a penetrating look and then recounted a parable from a midrash:
>
> There was once a bird whose tail emitted a foul odor. The bird tried to escape from the smell by flying away. The problem was, of course, that the bird's tail was attached to him, so wherever the bird flew, his tail followed. But the bird did not understand that he, himself, was the source of the odor. And so he spent most of his life running away from his own tail.
>
> "So you see," concluded Rav Chayim, "switching yeshivos will not solve your problems. Your problems will follow right behind you."[2]

Certainly, the student wanted to improve his situation. But the subtle shame of admitting to himself that he had a part in causing his own problems blurred his vision. For this reason, he could see no way to correct his situation except by making unnecessary changes in his environment. Were it not for Rav Chayim's astute comment, the student would have wasted a great deal of time and energy trying to alter his situation in any number of ways. Worse than that, he would have missed out on the real option to initiate change — by working on changing himself.

> Levi Bluth is having trouble in school: his grades have taken a nosedive and he is misbehaving. Mr. and Mrs. Bluth are prepared to

sacrifice a great deal for their son. They have pleaded with him, yelled at him, and worried over him. The one thing they won't do is speak openly with Levi's teacher about his problems — they fear they will have to admit to a flaw in themselves.

Sometimes two friends who are quarreling will try to restore their relationship, or a couple will attempt to improve the atmosphere in their home, but find that they don't make any headway. Each of them is ashamed to openly admit his part in the problem and his responsibility for improving matters. They each feel more comfortable pinning the blame on the other or on some outside circumstance, even though if both were to accept more responsibility and try to work on their share, it would certainly improve both of their lives.

THINK ABOUT IT

HOW DOES THIS EXPLAIN:

◆ how a person can detect subtle roadblocks?

◆ how such a discovery enhances the quality of our relationships?

What other benefits are achieved by identifying subtle roadblocks?

From Roadblocks to Road Signs

Throughout this chapter, we have been working together to sharpen our ability to detect roadblocks. In many cases, once an obstacle is seen clearly, it becomes simple to get around it. In other cases, as we identify the roadblocks, we change them to road signs — they become goals to achieve along the way. As we remove the roadblock, we allow our potential to flow and develop.

Having listed and discussed many types of roadblocks, we will spend the next two chapters deepening our understanding of how they (and others) work. Clarity will increase our confidence, making us more able to do away with obstacles and pave the way for change — with confidence.

FINDING YOURSELF IN WHAT YOU'VE LEARNED

1. Fill in the chart on the following page with descriptions of how these tendencies affect different areas of your life.

2. In what situations have you succeeded in overcoming the above tendencies and handicaps? How did you accomplish it?

3. In which of the areas listed above do you intend to overcome these tendencies first?

4. Are your life's goals being limited by the roadblocks of negative traits? To find out, ask yourself:

    a) Am I involved in clearly defined self-improvement projects? If yes, move on to question b).

    If not, why not? What are the three most likely reasons? Write them down, put the paper away for a day or two, and afterward, read them over and examine those possibilities.

    b) What do I consider to be a reasonable rate of progress in a project like this for a person like me? Would other people agree? Am I moving at that rate?
    If yes, move on to question c).

    If not, why not? Think of the three most likely reasons and write them down. Examine them again after a day or two.

Situation	Tendency	Apprehension	Cynicism	Anger	Tension	Need to Win	Sadness	Worry
Family								
School/Work								
Social Environment								
Relationship with Hashem								

c) Am I generally satisfied with my progress?
d) Am I satisfied with my long-term program for self-improvement? Are my goals sufficient but not excessive for a person with my potential?

Most people will answer "no" to some of these questions. Examining the "no's" will help you discover the areas in which your potential is being inhibited, and in what ways.

If you are one of the few who answer "yes" to all four questions, either you are doing a great job, or you have missed an important point and need to reexamine your answers carefully.

In the course of any self-improvement project, it is recommended that you periodically ask yourself questions b) through d). Do it as often as necessary to keep yourself on track.

NOTES TO CHAPTER FOUR

1. *Mesillas Yesharim*, chapter 5.
2. Told to the author by Rav Chayim's son.

❦ 5 ❧
The Spiral Effect

The Letter

Let's open our discussion of the Spiral Effect with the story of a young man named David Baum.

> David Baum, a sensitive young man, was studying at a yeshivah away from home when a married friend suggested that he meet his wife's cousin, Sarah. After describing her exceptional qualities, the friend added, "There are two cases of illness in the family, but they aren't hereditary."
>
> David, an only child, would have liked to discuss the idea with his parents, and he knew that they would expect him to. But he was sure that his father, possessive and particular as he was, would never even consider such a possible *shidduch*. Father and son had never felt all that comfortable speaking openly with each other, and it seemed to David that discussing a *shidduch* with some drawbacks wasn't the time to start trying. David, however, did want to meet Sarah. He decided that, in order to avoid a needless confrontation, he would meet her once and see what he thought before consulting his parents.
>
> David met Sarah and was very impressed with her. However, he learned of two more disturbing details: one of her brothers was in trouble with the law, and her family was virtually penniless.
>
> David pondered his situation. On one hand, he was interested in continuing the *shidduch*. On the other hand, it was now clearer than ever that his father would oppose the idea. He would be furious that

David had initiated a *shidduch* without consulting his parents. So David decided that he would see Sarah a few more times and then decide whether he was interested enough in her to tell his parents about her.

After meeting a number of times, David and Sarah felt certain that the match was "made in Heaven." The only question was how to break the news to David's parents. David considered his options and decided that it would be best to break the news in a letter. He wrote:

Dear Dad and Mom,

My friend Daniel suggested introducing me to his wife's cousin, Sarah. He spoke highly of her and thought we would be good for each other. I met Sarah several times and was very impressed with her. We are seriously considering marriage.

However, there are a few side issues to deal with. There are two cases of illness in the family, and one of her brothers seems to have been involved in theft. One more thing: they are a poor family and cannot afford the cost of a wedding or of setting up a household.

I was afraid we might get drawn into an argument or that you might not give your approval to our marriage. That is why I chose to inform you in a letter.

Sarah and I would like to become engaged already. I hope you understand my feelings.

Love,
David

Meanwhile, David's parents had been wondering why David, who usually called home two or three times a week, had begun calling only once a week. When he did call, he sounded anxious to keep the conversation short.

Mr. and Mrs. Baum had gone through a great deal during their lives. Ever since the death of their older son, their devotion had been focused on their only surviving child. They thought of David constantly and spared neither money nor effort when it came to their son's well-being. Now they found it strange that David seemed to be holding back about something. And then they received David's letter.

Why had David written instead of calling as usual? Fearing that something terrible had happened, Mr. Baum anxiously tore open the envelope and read the letter out loud. By the time he finished, he felt that his whole world had come crashing down.

"How can he do this to us?" Mr. Baum fumed to his wife. "We've always done all we possibly could for him. It will be hard enough for me to let him go — and that's if the girl he finds is ideal! And now he's on the verge of getting engaged — without telling us first! It sounds as if he's determined to marry her, whether we approve or not. And who is she? Some pathetic girl from an awful family! What got into him? Why didn't he discuss it with me? I would have explained to him that it's not the right thing to do — that a fine, intelligent boy like him could do a lot better for himself!"

Mr. Baum threw the letter onto the table and paced back and forth, repeating to himself, "What got into him? How could he do such a thing?"

Mrs. Baum picked up the letter and read it silently. Too shocked to speak or even to cry, she could only sit and shake her head.

A few moments passed in tense silence. Mr. Baum took the letter, read it again to himself, and remarked, "Her family doesn't have money for a wedding. I guess they expect us to foot the bill. So that's all we're here for: our checkbook. No discussion, no consultation, just a note informing us that they don't have money! This is more than I can take. I'm going to tell that boy just what he's done to us."

He grabbed the phone and dialed the yeshivah's dormitory number. While he waited for a younger *bochur* to go pull his son out of the *beis medrash*, he paced, muttering, "What's going on here? Why hasn't he called? I don't understand that boy!"

By the time David came to the phone and said, "Hello?" Mr. Baum had already launched into a loud tirade. "I just don't know what happened to you. What have your mother and I done to deserve such treatment? Tell us! Don't you know how we've cared for you since you were a baby — how many sleepless nights we worried over you? Don't you remember when you were in the hospital for six weeks and Mother sat by your bed all day, while I stayed through the nights? Tell us, where did we go wrong? Didn't we do enough for you? Why are you behaving this way?"

His father's words came fast and furious. David stood, stunned, at the other end of the line. He shook himself out of his stupor and quickly interjected, "But Dad, Sarah's a great girl — you'd really like her. All the other things are just side issues..."

Mr. Baum cut his son short. "Speaking of *her*, how can you get engaged to a girl your parents haven't even met? What's the tremendous hurry? You're young. Why should you rush into a marriage like this? You could have your pick of *shidduchim!* And what do you need with this pathetic girl — just look at the family! You think the apple falls far from the tree?"

At that, David bristled. "Are you saying that just because her family has some problems, she's no good?"

"Some problems?" said Mr. Baum, "Theft, illness, and poverty are not what I'd call minor details! Your mother and I insist that you call this *shidduch* off immediately!"

"I'm sure that Sarah is the right one, Dad. I'm not breaking it off!"

For a moment, there was dead silence.

"If this is what you decided, there isn't too much I can do, but don't expect my support. If you can't even accept simple logic, you're on your own!"

David shook his head. "I'm not calling it off!"

Mr. Baum intoned, "Then I haven't got anything more to say. Just don't expect one red cent out of me." He hung up. David was left holding the phone, wondering how he could possibly make a wedding on his own.

After hanging up, Mr. Baum turned to his wife and said, "I can't believe he had the *chutzpah* to slap me in the face that way. As far as I'm concerned, he's on his own with this. I don't want to hear another word about it. Just thinking about his ingratitude gets me so angry!" He stalked out of the room and slammed the door.

The engagement and marriage took place without Mr. Baum's presence. Mrs. Baum came to the wedding, but stood at a distance from the crowd and left right after the *chuppah,* unable to restrain her sobs. Both the parents and the newlyweds are depressed, and the young couple is drowning in debt. Each side blames the other for the bitter situation.

Who is right, the father or the son?

Better Alternatives

Actually, both father and son committed grave errors which cost them dearly. From David's point of view, it was hard to judge at precisely what point he should have discussed the matter with his parents, and in what way. Let's assume for now that a letter was appropriate for such an important subject. But it should have sounded something like this:

> Dear Dad and Mom,
>
> My good friend Daniel Roth suggested that I meet his wife's cousin. She seems to be an excellent choice for me. I would like to discuss the matter with you very much. But, to tell you the truth, I'm afraid to because there are some drawbacks – not in the girl herself, but in her circumstances. I would like to tell you all the details, but I'm afraid of getting into an argument – I love you and I wouldn't want either of us to accidentally hurt the other. Can we talk this out in a calm, relaxed way? I really want to hear your ideas about how to go about this.
>
> Your loving son,
> David

Notice that this letter does not bombard David's parents with a list of all the shortcomings of the match before giving them a chance to hear about the girl's merits. It also emphasizes his concern for their feelings. A letter of this kind wouldn't have incited Mr. Baum to be so confrontational. It might even have led him to be more open-minded about the *shidduch*, if only to prove to his son that free discussion was possible.

David made another mistake — he decided from the outset that there was nothing to be gained from hearing his parents' opinion.

He should have been prepared, instead, to weigh their words seriously and objectively. If, after hearing them out, he were to find himself in doubt about what to do, or if the discussion had been unproductive, he could then seek advice from his Rebbe or another advisor.

Mr. Baum erred, as well. Had he thought things over calmly, he might have been able to express himself in a way that would have encouraged David to relate seriously to his opinion. Rather than making a phone call in the heat of anger, he might have instead sent David a letter which could have read something like this:

> Dear Son,
> Your mother and I were very hurt by the tone of your letter. It's not like you. We just don't know how to respond to such behavior. I think you ought to come home and discuss the whole thing with us face to face — both this shidduch and your approach.
> Your loving father.
> P.S. I'll try to hear what you have to say, too.

If Mr. Baum had written such a letter, and if David had come to discuss the situation with his parents, then several issues might have been resolved. Mr. and Mrs. Baum could have attempted to understand David's rationale, and David could have seen exactly why his parents were so hurt and what he should have done differently. All of them could have looked for ways to correct whatever was faulty in their relationship.

David made another critical mistake after their explosive phone conversation. Instead of accepting the break in their relationship, he should have done everything possible to become reconciled with his father. It is true that, according to halachah, he can marry whomever he wants. Although he doesn't need the consent of his parents, he is still not exempt from the obligation to respect them. Even if a child sees his parents transgressing a Torah commandment, he is obligated to act with the greatest of sensitivity to avoid causing his parents any more pain than is absolutely necessary. In this case, even if David was correct in deciding to marry Sarah over his parents' objections, he should have apologized sincerely for the distress that he caused and asked his parents how he could restore good relations with them. If he had any problems with the way his father handled the situation, he should have brought them up in a respectful manner.

The discussion in chapter 2 ("Shyness and Embarrassment") might offer clues to the cause of the terrible mishandling of this situation. Perhaps Mr. Baum's underlying sense of shame about his need to be involved in his son's life led him to choose an aggressive approach. David, for his part, was embarrassed to admit that his relationship with his parents could be destroyed by his obstinacy and independence when handling such a big issue. This may be part of what led him to adopt a closed, defensive attitude with them. In this way, hidden shame contributed to the tragic rift in their relationship.

Why?

Incidents as dramatic as what happened to the Baums do not happen often. But in the course of everyday life, arguments do occur in which both parties end up making choices that bring unnecessary pain to everyone involved.

Why do people do this to themselves? Why don't people choose better, less painful alternatives? Why don't they make more of an effort to seek positive solutions instead of those that result in disappointment or misery? What prevents them from making wise decisions and hampers their ability to achieve a happy outcome? Rather often the answer is the Spiral Effect.

The Spiral Effect

A major principle that explains some mysteries of human behavior is that every action creates a magnetic force that pulls him to perform other, similar actions.[1] As our Sages phrased it:

> One good deed pulls along another; one evil act pulls along another.[2]

This principle holds true not only for actions, but for thoughts and feelings as well. Every thought engenders a similar thought, and every emotion gives rise to a similar emotion.[3] While a person who is in a good mood finds it easy to continue on the same positive track, a person who is in a bad frame of mind feels irresistibly drawn to more negativity. He doesn't only continue along the same level path. His actions and decisions while in that state often give rise to similar situations that reinforce and intensify his mindset and bring about even more problematic situations. The result is that the magnetic pull of his actions creates a spiral that drags him ever deeper into the circle of his mindset and intensifies his emotions.

For this reason, one irritation tends to be followed by another. The solutions that we devise tend to reflect our emotional state at the time the decision was made.

Being There

The Ba'al Shem Tov reveals a principle that is crucial in understanding this phenomenon: "Where a person's thought are, that's where he is."[4]

When a person is angry, he *exists* in that world. He sees everything through the lens of anger. In that state, he is unlikely to find constructive solutions for his problems — neither for the problem that originally provoked his anger, nor for any other. He simply can't envision a solution whose outcome might be conciliation, serenity, and good will — the antithesis of where he is. The Ba'al Shem Tov's statement is illustrated by the following story which happened over 200 years ago.

> A young couple got married. After a few weeks of marriage, they ran into a serious problem, and the husband left home without giving a hint about where he was headed. All efforts to track him down were unsuccessful. The woman had no choice but to return to the home of her parents, were she lived as an *agunah*.
>
> Ten years passed. Then, one day, a man knocked at the door and introduced himself as the long-lost husband, now returning home for good. He claimed that he had wanted to return long ago, but that various hindrances had prevented him from coming. Now he begged the woman's forgiveness.
>
> The *agunah's* parents were ecstatic, but the *agunah* did not believe that this was indeed her husband. While he did resemble her husband in many ways, and he did know all sorts of details about her husband's past and about her family, she remained unconvinced. Her heart told her otherwise, and she refused to let the man approach her.
>
> Was the man really her long-lost husband, or a vulgar imposter? The woman's father went to the Vilna Gaon and explained their dilemma. The Gaon gave the following advice: On Shabbos eve, the father should take the man to *shul*. There, the father should ask the man to lead him to the father's customary seat. At that point, all would become clear. The Gaon explained that were the fellow an imposter, he could somehow have found out all the information that he knew about the *agunah* and her family. He would have pumped the real missing husband for all the details necessary to carry out his lowly scheme, but it would never have occurred to his depraved mind to ask about a holy place. He would never have thought to ask for details relating to the *shul*.
>
> Following the Gaon's advice, the father took the man to *shul* with him the very next Shabbos eve. When they entered, the father said, "Please show me to my usual seat." The man stood there, helpless. When he realized that he had been caught, the imposter confessed that a year earlier, he had fallen in with a group of wandering beggars, one of whom was the real husband. After he found out that the husband had deserted his wife years before, he began to hatch his deplorable scheme. Slowly but surely he drew many details out

of the husband, until he thought that he knew enough to be able to impersonate him and deceive his wife and her family.

The imposter concluded by announcing that the real husband had, indeed, decided to return home and would be arriving within a few weeks. And so it was.

The Vilna Gaon's logic paralleled the Ba'al Shem Tov's principle: a person is where his thoughts are. The Gaon understood that such a scoundrel, whose mind was bent on deceiving innocent people, was not capable of thinking about holy matters at the same time.

In Everyday Life

The words of these two great *tzaddikim* apply to us in our daily lives, as well. A person who is occupied with pleasant, constructive thoughts will find it difficult to dwell on the negative. Conversely, when a person is in a state of anger and irritation, he is totally immersed in that world, and it can be difficult for him to contemplate practical solutions that will ease the atmosphere. He may think that he is working to correct the situation. But, unless he first extricates himself from his original, negative mindset, he will only gravitate toward choices that reinforce those ill feelings that already exist.

In the same way, someone who is busy worrying about himself exists in a world of self-centeredness. In such a state he is unlikely to consider the effects his automatic reactions have on others, and just how they'll be influenced by his conscious decisions. His only thought is — what's in it for me? Again, this initiates a Spiral Effect: the person becomes less and less able to focus on the needs of others, and so he creates situations that cause increasing trouble in his relationships.

The Spiral Effect was also at work in the case of David Baum and his father (see page 114). The son's thoughts about his father — that he was too particular and was likely to deny him permission to give Sarah a chance — made him tense. In this state of tension, in which he visualized the difficulties awaiting him and what he could expect to happen, it was hard for him to plan ways to defuse the situation. Perhaps David also felt frustrated and angry about not being able to find a suitable way to discuss the matter with his father. The solution that came to him was based on his mindset at the time. True, he made an effort to control his feelings and even succeeded in using more delicate language than his emotions might have dictated. But he still was miles away from realizing his goal of finding the best possible solution for everyone.

The same thing happened to Mr. Baum. He read his son's letter and immediately sank into a state of pain and anger. He was shaken by his perception of his son's attitude, and by the thought of the proposed match — which seemed so terribly unsuitable. It was difficult for Mr. Baum to formulate a plan that would respect everyone's feelings, restore their strained relationship, and protect his son from the harm he feared. Sure enough, the "solution" at which he arrived — while caught in the whirlwind of his pain and anger — did nothing to improve matters. On the contrary, it escalated the conflict.

THINK ABOUT IT

HOW CAN THE SPIRAL EFFECT:

♦ be driven by a person's mood instead of his overall feelings of love and care?

♦ lead even loving gestures down a path of misunderstanding?

Which other areas of life can be affected by downward spirals?

Anger Breeds Anger

The limiting effect of this spiraling, magnetic force is often observed when a worker is fired. Insult is added to injury; in addition to his concerns about finding new work and surviving until then, he has to deal with the emotional burden of an assault to his dignity. He may be angry with his employer, who he feels was ungrateful for all his hard work and devotion over the years. He may also judge himself harshly and believe he is a failure.

While the predicament of losing a job is a difficult one, it is possible for a person to liberate himself from these crushing emotions. He should open his mind to the possibility that being fired might have some beneficial aspects, and start searching for them in the experience. What he really needs to do is to internalize the teaching of our Sages, "Everything that the Merciful One does, He does for our good."[5] He can see the loss of his job as a challenge to overcome — as a Heaven-sent opportunity to begin a new chapter in his life by finding different, and perhaps even better, employment. This perspective can go a long way toward improving his state of mind.

If he doesn't adopt this attitude, the magnetic, spiraling force may take effect. If the worker subconsciously chooses to retain the negative attitude (that justifies his continued anger against his former employer), and dwells on his initial feelings of resentment, any bad feelings will only snowball. He is likely to commit himself to future actions that further reinforce his anger. He may even sabotage his own job search by finding any number of reasons to disqualify the offers that come his way. And even if he does try his hand at a new job, he may lack motivation and eventually fail in his new endeavor. All this can happen without the person being aware that he has developed an inner program for failure.

The Power of Positive Thinking

When you find yourself stuck in a downward spiral, take a break for a minute. In order to get out of that spiral, you can bring yourself to a neutral state perhaps by reading a book or listening to relaxing music; or even better, you can put yourself in an upbeat mood by reminding yourself of something positive, like a pleasant memory. Stepping out of a negative mood, at least long enough to reassess the situation and determine how to improve it, is a fast but effective way to escape from the Spiral Effect.

This process can be further simplified by using a combination of self-awareness and consciousness of the power of our mindset. We can learn to recognize our negative state of mind and understand how it influences us to choose ineffective or even destructive solutions. At the same time, we can learn to pay attention to the way that a positive frame of mind and an optimistic mood contribute to finding workable, effective solutions. We need to focus on how such a mindset can also generate an equally powerful, spiraling magnetic force, drawing us irresistibly toward more positivity.

Once these concepts are clear and deeply ingrained in us, it takes minimal effort to escape a negative state of mind for just a moment — knowing that the power of practical, positive thinking will then make it possible for us to escape our predicament entirely. A quick jump into a positive mindset facilitates more constructive thinking and action — drawing us into an upward-tending spiral. Truthfully, we should get used to turning a suspicious eye onto all the choices we make while in a negative state of mind. Preferably, we should put more trust in choices we make when our disposition is more positive.

If the worker discussed above had such an awareness and adopted such an optimistic attitude, he would be inviting success. He would be more alert to promising opportunities, and would take advantage of them in an effective way. At the same time, his domestic and social life would clearly be enhanced.

If the Baums, father and son, had freed themselves from the obstruction of a doom and gloom mindset, they might have been able to see the positive — after all, they were discussing a prospective spouse, which should be reason for happiness. By dwelling on the positive, they could have discussed their different viewpoints in a lighter, freer way. This could have brought father and son closer, and perhaps they would have discovered a way to resolve their differences of opinion.

An Unpleasant Surprise

Sometimes, we begin a new enterprise feeling buoyant, when suddenly, we are hit with something unexpected that jolts us out of our positive state. It takes deliberate effort to neutralize our disappointment and the other negative emotions that it generates. But the effort is worthwhile, since without it, the repercussions can be devastating.

> One Wednesday evening, Tova went out to a *shiur*. Before she left, she told her husband, Meir, that she planned to start cooking for Shabbos when she returned. After Meir tucked the last of the children into bed, he decided to surprise Tova by doing some of the cooking for her. She would certainly be glad to have a little less work to do. He was a competent cook and sometimes prepared weekday meals for the family, although it had been a while since he had cooked for Shabbos.
>
> What should he make? A noodle kugel seemed like a good idea. Meir set to work, humming, feeling good about helping Tova and anticipating her pleased look when she would see his creation. An hour later, when Tova came home, Meir opened the oven with a flourish and presented the kugel, now turning a lovely golden brown. He waited for her appreciative remarks.
>
> Instead, Tova took one look and sank into a chair. "Oh, no, Meir!" she sighed, "What did you do? I was going to make a potato

kugel this week, because Uncle Nachum is coming, and that's what he likes. And I was going to use those noodles for tomorrow's lunch. And I need that baking pan for the cake. I always make the cake first, and then the kugel, so that the kugel can stay in the pan when it's done. Why did you have to mess up my plans?"

Meir felt so disappointed and hurt that at first he couldn't answer. When he did speak, he launched into an angry list of all the things he had done recently that he felt she didn't appreciate enough.

Tova responded with some angry remarks of her own, and they ended up arguing for a long time that night. In the course of the evening, the kugel had to be rescued from burning, Tova had no time or energy left to do any other cooking, and Meir's plan to help his wife and strengthen the good feelings between them had turned into a dismal failure.

What happened here? Why didn't Tova show appreciation for Meir's nice gesture? From the opposite perspective, why did Meir help to aggravate the situation further, in sharp contrast with his original, caring intentions?

Tova became quite frustrated when she discovered that Meir, by attempting to help, had actually complicated her work. Meir had put in work, and she couldn't see how she could benefit from it! At that moment, relating to the situation in an appropriate and tactful way was just too hard for her.

Meir, in the meantime, had anticipated a warm response to his help. When Tova expressed her criticisms, surprise and disappointment deflated Meir's positive mood. In that state, he could not transcend his hurt feelings to imagine a solution that would restore a positive atmosphere. The initial disappointment led to a spiral of deeper disappointment, complaints, and arguments.

How could they have handled the situation better? They should have paused before reacting. Meir should have reminded himself of his original goal: to make life a bit easier for his wife and enhance their relationship. He should not have lost control or given up, but rather regrouped and gotten back on the track to his original goal. He might have defused her anger by reemphasizing his original intention — that he wanted to help her — and was still glad that he made an effort to help her, his beloved wife — even though his work hadn't come to much. Tova should have thought about Meir's motivations and appreciated those intentions. Thinking about his devotion and desire to help could have put her into a positive mood, in which she could have explained his mistake to him gently and tactfully. Both of them would then have been able to collaborate and figure out how to get the Shabbos preparations back on schedule — in a spirit of caring companionship.

Practically speaking, Tova might have smiled at Meir and expressed her genuine pleasure and gratitude for his consideration and desire to help her. Her appreciation would have created a far more pleasant frame of mind, in which she could have tried to find a way to remedy the situation without spoiling the home atmosphere. It may have been possible, after all, to save Meir's kugel for Shabbos, either buying a kugel for Uncle Nachum, or buying a disposable baking pan to make a potato kugel, so that Tova wouldn't have to clean the pan. While it would require spending some money, a small expenditure would be justified in this case — in order to keep peace and good feelings in their home.

For his part, Meir could have made it up to Tova by going to the grocery store early the next morning to buy another package of noodles for the children's lunch. In these ways, both Tova and Meir could have raised themselves above the situation, relating to it from a more true and constructive angle.

Once it becomes clear that both husband and wife are trying to find mutually beneficial solutions, a better atmosphere can be created. A peaceful and accepting atmosphere in the home can then transform a "mess" into a problem that is much smaller than the way it originally appeared.

Here's an illustration of tactful redirection:

> Mrs. Rosenfeld was shopping in a large department store when she saw a rack of girls' spring dresses on sale. Just the thing for her

granddaughters! After several years, she still wasn't so attentive to the particulars of her daughter and son-in-law's religious way of life, but she did know that the girls didn't wear pants and that they had to have sleeves. And here were such cute dresses, and for such a good price! Of course she knew all the children's sizes and was happy to be able to save her daughter some money, not to mention the trouble of a trip downtown.

Unfortunately, Mrs. Rosenfeld didn't understand that these dresses weren't right for her granddaughters. They had sleeves, but the sleeves and hems were too short, the necks were too open, and the prints were too loud for her daughter's standards of modesty.

When Mrs. Rosenfeld brought the dresses over, her daughter, Lisa, looked at them and groped for the right words. "Mom," she began, "I know that you wanted to help me and that you enjoy buying things for the kids. I'm sorry to have to say it, but the girls just can't wear dresses like these." Mrs. Rosenfeld was momentarily taken aback and disappointed. Here she had thought that she was getting exactly the right thing! But she caught herself from slipping into hurt feelings. She thought for a moment and then said, "Well, it's certainly a pity. I thought they were such cute dresses. You know I only wanted to do something nice for you and the children. I suppose I can return the dresses to the store. But why don't you tell me clearly what is all right, so that this doesn't happen again."

Years later, Lisa's eight-year-old daughter, Shoshana, came home crying. She had gone to see a sick friend and had brought her a doll as a gift.

"A doll?" the friend had exclaimed, "I'm not a baby anymore!" Shoshana was very hurt, but she held back her tears until she got home. Then she poured out her disappointment on her mother's shoulder. Lisa wiped away Shoshana's tears and sympathized with her. Remembering how her mother had once handled a similar situation, she said to Shoshana, "Do you know that Savta once made a mistake like that?" and told her the story. She ended by saying, "Sometimes we want to give someone something nice, but we don't realize what's right for them. Why don't you call your friend and tell her, 'I'm sorry I didn't know how you felt about dolls. I wanted so much to give you something that you would enjoy.'?"

The exact words don't matter; the main thing is to neutralize negative thoughts and emotions — and the earlier the better! Then you can work to maintain a positive atmosphere — one that helps you reach your original goal.

> **THINK ABOUT IT**
>
> **IN WHAT WAYS IS THE SPIRAL EFFECT:**
> ◆ avoidable? interruptible?
> ◆ workable? reversible?
>
> How can the Spiral Effect be used positively?

Castles in the Air

If it is not stopped in time, the Spiral Effect can easily make a simple bad mood explode, causing a great deal of unnecessary damage. The following well-worn joke is an extreme example of this phenomenon.

> Reuven came home from work at eleven o'clock one winter night. Snow had fallen all day long, and the ride home had been hard and slow, with traffic jams all over town. When he finally got home, Reuven looked at the white blanket of snow covering his sidewalk. The local law required that he clear away the snow in front of his house by morning.
>
> Reuven decided to shovel the snow right then, since he would have to leave for work early the next morning. But, suddenly, he remembered that his snow shovel was broken. Perhaps his friend, Moshe, who lived on the next block, would be able to lend him one.
>
> As Reuven plodded wearily toward Moshe's house, it occurred to him that Moshe might not open the door for him because it was so late. He might be trudging through the snow for nothing!

"I'll appeal to his sympathy," Reuven told himself. "I'll say, 'Please be a good friend and help me out. I have to shovel the snow now. I'm awfully sorry to have to disturb you at such a late hour.'" He continued to anticipate the conversation. "But what if Moshe answers, 'You can buy yourself a new shovel in the morning. It won't be so terrible if you get to work late one day'?"

The closer Reuven got to Moshe's house, the more agitated he became. "Well, then I'll remind him of how I lent him my lawn mower last summer. I'll tell him, 'That was a valuable piece of machinery I trusted you with. Where's some common decency? How can you be so ungrateful for all the things I do for you?'

"But Moshe might just answer, 'You're talking about decency? A decent person doesn't disturb his neighbors at eleven o'clock at night!'"

As Reuven continued to anticipate all kinds of degrading and humiliating responses that he was likely to hear, the imaginary argument grew more and more heated. By the time Reuven arrived at Moshe's house, he was fuming. He kicked at the door in rage.

Moshe, a pleasant, soft-hearted fellow, jumped out of bed in alarm and asked through the locked door, "Who is it? What do you want?"

Reuven shrieked, "You selfish, no-good, fair-weather friend! I don't need you or your snow shovel! I'll manage on my own!" With that, he turned and stomped off for home, steaming with fury.

In the story, Reuven's exhaustion put him into a negative mood, and that mood triggered apprehensions, which in turn fostered resentment, so that his negative state of mind grew and swelled. In the end, Reuven's attitude and imagination built a towering edifice of negativity based on — absolutely nothing.

A much more modest version of Reuven's story often takes place in our own lives. A minor incident puts us into a bad mood, so we construct a pessimistic scenario in our minds and dread the worst. If we have to discuss something with someone, we agonize in advance over the anticipated answer. Through fantasy, we create an atmosphere of antagonism with little or no basis in reality. Perhaps we almost wait for the other person to recite the lines of our imaginary script. Usually, it makes little difference what he actually says, we may interpret his intention as negative or "hear" the words we assumed we would hear — and then respond in kind. Instead of improving the situation, we accelerate its deterioration.

While we would all like to avoid getting caught in this trap, many of us do, at times, build such castles in the air. This is most likely to occur when we already feel down, angry, or resentful. At those times, we get preoccupied with analysis of the other person's "real" motivation for acting as he did. "He did it deliberately, and then he pretends it was all in innocence. But I can see straight through him. He clearly intended to hurt me!"

Even when no one else is involved, we may build castles in the air when analyzing our own situation. We replay the film of an unpleasant incident until we find more and more to get depressed about. The negative feelings we arouse in ourselves make it impossible for us to deal with our problems objectively or productively. In the end, this exaggeration of the negative harms us greatly.

The detrimental effects of castels in the air aren't limited to negative cycles. Sometimes our imagination may be enticed to exaggerated our *positive* thoughts and assemble a picture that is out of proportion with reality. We may then act to our own disadvantage based on those unrealistic positive thoughts. For example, a person convinced that his new business will succeed may not adequately research the market or take the time to manage his new business appropriately. Similarly, a person might spend more money than his current income permits based on exaggerated expectations that he will make a great deal of money in the near future.

Once we are conscious of the castle-building phenomenon, we are well on our way to uprooting this destructive and absurd tendency. If we can retain a level-headed approach, we can substitute a constructive attitude that will enable us to deal successfully with life's challenges. One of the primary goals of this book is to learn how to successfully carry out the commandment to "choose life."[6] The first and most crucial step is to remove ourselves from the excited emotions of the unrealistic mindset we're in, which will allow us to turn our attention to constructive action. We need only to avoid letting ourselves get carried away by the disposition we're in, perhaps by taking a small "coffee break." Once we're in a more composed frame of mind, we can refocus on setting up a realistic goal and moving forward to attain it.

Changing the Momentum

Sometimes a person feels as if he just doesn't have it in him to smile; he doesn't have the energy to stay calm; he can't muster up the strength to be patient and understanding toward his friends or children. Yet if someone speaks to him in the wrong tone of voice or refuses to do as he asks, he somehow conjures up the energy to respond with angry screaming. At home, he may get involved in protracted arguments, often stretching late into the night.

Where did this person, who was too weak to drum up a bit of patience, find the energy to scream and argue? Where did he get the strength for a vehement reaction? If he was too tired to be understanding, how did he manage to stay up so late arguing, which certainly demands more energy?

When a person is tired and is already in a bad mood, little energy is needed to continue gliding on the same downward spiral for another few moments, and then another few, until they turn into hours. Like a car in neutral that, once rolling downhill, will keep going of its own momentum, the downward spiral produces a great deal of the energy required to maintain and intensify a bad mood. This is why it is vital to stop that downhill slide before the momentum escalates out of control. But to stop that car, turn it around and get it going in a new direction — that demands a new infusion of pure effort. The thoughtful person realizes that the extra effort is still far less than the price he will pay if he allows things to continue to roll downhill.

A person who is tired, but in a positive mood, has even less strength for fighting; he finds it so much easier to smile, or perhaps to engage in a calm, productive discussion. Any argument is a major emotional effort for him, and he is not interested in wasting his energy that way.

> **THINK ABOUT IT**
>
> **HOW DOES MOMENTUM:**
> ◆ propel us forward with little additional effort?
> ◆ save us from difficulties when we're feeling good?
>
> How can a person learn to recognize and correct the current trend of his energy?

Choose Your World

As our Sages say:

> *Who is wise? He who foresees the future.*[7]

A wise person acts with foresight. If you feel yourself beginning to be pulled into a negative spiral, especially if the reason is that you are tired, catch yourself quickly. Think about how much time and effort you are likely to waste in a negative state of mind, and how much your energy will be sapped by arguments. If you can summon up so much energy for negative action, then you aren't as exhausted as you think. It's only the force of habit that misleads you into thinking that you can't smile or act with patience and consideration right now. But once you've caught yourself, you can detour around that old habit and redirect yourself. Once you become aware that the reflex doesn't have to confine you — that you really do have the energy for something more constructive — you'll be able to invest your energy in an emotional venture that will turn a bigger profit. It may take some energy to climb over the fence into the garden of positivity, but it saves much more energy in the long run.

Spiraling Upward and Onward

A positive spiral not only helps us fight negative emotions, it can have its own beneficial impact on our lives. Imagine waking up in a good mood, then hearing good news about your financial situation and getting a call from an old and dear friend — all within the same hour. All that positive energy can not only support a person's good mood, but feed it, allowing him to interpret everything around him in a positive light. As he discovers more reasons to be happy, upbeat emotions build, and he gathers the energy to flavor his entire day with optimism. He may even interpret otherwise difficult circumstances as a challenge to his abilities and a chance to grow and truly shine. This is how a positive emotional spiral works — each moment is happier than the last, each moment gives us the energy and ability to interpret, and use, the next moment judiciously and contentedly, and so our positive moments add up. We'll discuss this idea at length in volume 2 of this series, chapter 3, *Transforming the Negative*.

This information can be helpful in two ways: it can help us to create an upward spiral, and it can help us harness that spiral to make constructive changes in our lives.

Until we develop the skill, building a positive spiral may take considerable effort. We might just have to lay in wait, on the lookout for any opportunity — any flicker of positive emotion — to get the upward spiral going. Small inspiring moments can take us by surprise at any time: the overwhelming feeling of gratitude for a friend's care, seeing a small act of kindness on the bus, or perhaps a slight, enjoyable change in the routine. When that moment comes, we can be ready for it and let our whole mind feel it for a brief moment. It's at that moment that we're free to start the upward momentum going. We can continue to try to see more and more of the wonder around us, both in nature and people. We can then harness that energy to work for us, bringing us ever upward and onward, investing ourselves with the momentum to grow.

Once a strong positive spiral has developed, we can use it to work for us. When we notice that our mood is not only good, but helping us to interpret life's events in a positive way, we can look back on other events that may have left us frustrated in the past. Our upbeat mood might give us a fresh perspective, while our positive momentum might help us push through any blockages we may have encountered and make changes that help us improve situations we thought were hopeless.

The Power of a Positive Atmosphere

Appreciating the importance of positivity and creating a positive atmosphere should not mean ignoring the negative. Many negative situations, both great and small, arise throughout life. As human beings, we are emotionally affected by these situations to some extent, and a person is not meant to "make believe" that he isn't affected. At the same time, many such situations definitely call for a constructive response.

The problem arises when we let down our guard and allow ourselves to get "worked up" by difficulty. This is more likely when we are affected by fatigue, hunger, or even concern. If we do allow ourselves to get drawn in, we lose our entire equilibrium — that's how the downward Spiral Effect takes hold. We find ourselves becoming more intensely drawn into a negative disposition, and from that mindset, we are prone to view situations in an even more negative light. By seeing things so negatively, we become irritated further, and it becomes even easier to translate details in a negative way, or to exaggerate the intensity of the difficulty. These factors cause us to suffer far more than is warranted by the situation.

This spiral not only intensifies the distress; it makes it difficult to take constructive action to remedy the situation, and sabotages any positive action that we do take. As constructive as we'd like to be, steps to improve a situation taken in a negative atmosphere have poor chances of accomplishing anything positive — and there's a reasonable chance that it will aggravate the situation even further. You, the reader, may remember a number of times when you thought you were doing something to correct a problem and it boomeranged right back. Check if you weren't acting from a negative disposition.

In contrast, if we pull ourselves out of a negative mindset and put ourselves into a positive one, our chances of success increase. In this positive mindset, we finds ourselves using positively charged tools. A well-placed, kind word is more likely to encourage positive growth than a generous helping of criticism. A pleasant face does more to lighten a tense atmosphere than well-thought-out reasoning. A cheerful smile can go further toward melting icy resentment than fights and stubborn arguments. All of these gestures create an environment in which other positive efforts can succeed. When the fuel of negative energy is removed, the fires of anger, hostility, and tension die all by themselves.

So when we encounter difficulties, it's important to maintain our guard. Being on guard does not mean that a person should deny that he is being affected by a situation. It is important to recognize our hurt or anger, but we should maintain control by counterbalancing our reaction. This will put us in a position in which we can make sure we will respond constructively. Similarly, if you have been trying to deal with a problematic relationship, and all the negative energy you've poured into it hasn't gotten you very far, then the time has come for a change of attitude. From now on, invest your energy into genuinely sweetening the atmosphere so that you and the people around you will feel naturally drawn toward actions and reactions that repair your relationship. What you need to do is to jump out of the negative spiral that you're in now, release yourself from its downward drag, and build up a new spiral of good will — one that generates peace and friendship. What better use is there for your precious energy?

Of course, the truly wise person is looking one step farther down the road of the future and seeks not only cures, but prevention. He doesn't wait for tense situations to crop up, but starts right in from the beginning with a cheerful expression and pleasant words. Everyone delights in his presence, and his aura of upbeat geniality can be infectious. This is a way to create peace among people, for which the Mishnah tells us that a person eats the fruits of his efforts in this world, while the principal of his reward awaits him in the World to Come.[8]

FINDING YOURSELF IN WHAT YOU'VE LEARNED

1. List, on a separate page, a few of those times that you built castles in the air. For example: you expected a negative response from someone, or a negative outcome to a situation. How did your expectations affect the way you handled the situation?
    a) Put your list aside for a day or two and then come back to it. Has your perspective changed since the time of those incidents? Or have your negative feelings gotten stronger?
    b) What might you learn from this?

2. Be aware of how your mood influences your actions and the way you relate to matters unconnected to the cause of your mood.

   a) Focus on situations when you were drawn into unpleasantness because you were already in a bad frame of mind.

   b) Now pay attention to those times when you were in a good mood, and because of it, you succeeded in relating to a challenging situation positively. It's beneficial to write it all down so that you can review it later. That way, you may see that many responses aren't necessarily made objectively.

3. Were there ever times when you managed to shake off a bad mood temporarily, and happily found that you really had succeeded in transforming your state of mind and bringing about an improvement in your situation? Jot down a short description of those times to demonstrate to yourself how you did it, and to reinforce a feeling of accomplishment.

NOTES TO CHAPTER FIVE

1. See *Kiddushin* 40a: "If a person has violated a commandment one time, and another, it becomes permissible in his eyes."

   See also the Apter Rav in *Ohev Yisrael*, where he suggests a metaphysical explanation for this phenomenon: "When a person does a deed with worthy intentions, he creates a holy angel. That angelic force rises to Heaven and speaks in defense of the person who, in essence, gave the angel its existence and life-force.... This angel (aramaic, '*IR*') arouses (is '*ml'oRer*') the person to further service of Hashem."

2. *Avos* 4:2.

3. See our Sages' statement: "Whoever does one *mitzvah* in this world, it precedes him and goes before him in the World to Come; whoever commits one transgression in this world, it winds itself around him and goes before him on the Day of Judgment" (*Sotah* 3b).

   See also *Avodah Zarah* 5a, and Maharsha there; Rabbeinu Bachaya on Devarim 29:18, regarding the statement "Thoughts of sin are more severe than the sin itself"; the Gra's commentary on Mishlei 1:23; and

Rav Tzadok HaKohen, *Tzidkas HaTzaddik*, essay 241.

The explanation in note 1 apparently clarifies what our Sages (*Mechilta*) said on the verse "If [you] listen, you shall listen" (Shemos 15:26): "If a person listens to one *mitzvah*, he is led to listen to many *mitzvos*, as it is written, 'If [you] listen, you shall listen' (Devarim 28:1). If a person forgets one *mitzvah*, he is caused to forget many *mitzvos*, as is written, 'If [you] forget, you shall forget'" (Devarim 8:19).

Our Sages also say, "'If [you] listen, you shall listen' — and if not, you shall not listen. Another explanation: if you listen to the old, you shall listen to the new. If you turn your heart aside, you shall not listen again" (*Sukkah* 46b). The difference between these two explanations is that in the first, we're referring to the same *mitzvah:* doing the *mitzvah* paves the way to keeping that same *mitzvah* in the future. The second explanation seems to add that such listening also brings a person to keep other *mitzvos*.

See also *Yalkut Shimoni* (*Ha'azinu*) on the verse "The Rock is perfect in His Actions" (Devarim 32:4), where it explains the verse "A person's foolishness shall distort his way" (Mishlei 19:2) according to what is written in *Tanna D'Bei Eliyahu Zuta* 3.

See also Rashi on Hoshea 14:2, "Because you have stumbled in your sin..."; Rabbi Eliyahu Dessler, *Michtav Me'Eliyahu*, 5 volumes (Jerusalem: Sifrati, 5757), volume I, p. 234; *Bereishis Rabbah* 71:4, that the deeds of a person have an influence and a continuation even in future generations; *Degel Machaneh Efrayim* on *Parashas* Behar, and Rav Levi Yitzchak mi'Berditchev, *Kedushas Levi* on *Parashas* Naso, on the verse "Hashem is your Shadow" (Tehillim 121:5).

4. See *Keser Shem Tov* 56, 275; Rav Efrayim mi'Sudylkov, *Degel Machaneh Efrayim*, *Parshas* Bereishis, and *Parashas* Shemos.

    See also *Sotah* 21a, "A *mitzvah*, at the time one is involved in it, protects and saves...," and Rashi there.

    See also Rabbeinu Tam, *Sefer HaYashar*, end of section 5; Ramban, *Da'as HaKedushah*, end of chapter 5: "You already know that a person is not considered as knowing something until the idea has become one with the thinker. Understand this well." *Likutei Amarim: Tanya*, chapter 5, elaborates on this concept.

5. *Berachos* 60b.
6. See *Degel Machaneh Efrayim, Parashas* Shemos.
7. *Tamid* 32a.
8. *Pe'ah* 1:1.

~*~ 6 ~*~
Unveiling Deeper Emotional Forces

Conflicting Levels

Since the beginning of this book, we have examined the profound effect that our *middos* (character traits) have on the quality of our lives. We have honed our understanding of the ways that negative emotional responses can further complicate issues: a negative attitude not only makes life more uncomfortable, it can have secondary effects that inhibit optimal functioning. As we have discussed, despair can make it difficult to manage, and anger can make it hard to make friends. A negative attitude can tie a person down, imprison him in his predicament, and even pave the way to failure.

In this chapter, we will delve into the psychological mechanism responsible for even deeper forms of self-sabotage. We will see that a person may work toward some goal, and yet, without his being aware of it, have certain internal forces that oppose his goal and prevent him from attaining it. He may even make repeated efforts to advance in some direction and be utterly baffled by his lack of progress. As far as he understands, he has no reason to stand in the way of his own advancement. We will call this phenomenon *conflicting layers of will*. Consciously, within the thoughts that a person can access easily, the person wants to reach his objective. On a deeper, subconscious level, where thoughts operate beyond a person's awareness, there is opposition.

Sometimes we have conflicts of will that are all on the conscious level. For example, I want to buy a new couch. Now, that is a genuine desire. But if the new couch is expensive — there is a part of me that doesn't want to buy it. I am in touch with both my desire for the new couch and my desire to save myself the money. I will have to make a decision that either chooses one side (to buy or not buy the couch) or that balances and harmonizes these two conflicting wills. This kind of realignment can take several different forms — I may settle for a less pricey model, or delay the purchase of my first choice until my financial situation is better.

When the two sides of an issue, or the two desires, are both operating on the conscious level, reaching a solution or a compromise is relatively easy. When the conflict is between the conscious and the subconscious levels, however, finding a solution becomes much more complicated.

The nature of the subconscious is that it's obscure, unclear. Part of the drawing power of subconscious desires is the very fact that we're unaware of them. Since we often aren't aware that within us exists a conflicting will which is holding us back, that will retains an exaggerated amount of power over us. It can therefore be a challenge to identify, understand, negate, or transcend that will. It can even be difficult to ascertain when there is an inner will trying to *improve* our behavior — in which case we would like to strengthen its efforts. However, we will not explore this last, positive influence of the subconscious in this chapter; it will be dealt with in volume 3 of this series. Our discussion in this chapter will deal with dual wills specifically in situations where the subconscious will interferes with our success.

To illustrate this phenomenon of dual wills, let's examine the case of Mr. Levy.

Despite his full schedule, Mr. Levy has, for many years, designated two hours a week as family time — one to learn with his children and the other hour for discussions or playtime. These sessions have always been quality time: the learning enthusiastic, the conversations warm and filled with mutual understanding.

But lately, the two hours have become boring for everyone. Mr. Levy has tried several different tactics to rekindle his children's interest, but none of them have succeeded. He cannot understand why.

Talking it over with a friend gave Mr. Levy a deeper perspective on the problem. He had already realized how much his children would benefit by receiving more of his attention. But he found only two hours a week for them, and even that with difficulty. He knew that he really should spend more time than that with them.

Mr. Levy was locked in a psychological bind. It had been difficult for him to find more time for his children, yet he felt guilty about his lack of time. He had been deeply disappointed in himself for not being more dedicated.

Eventually, Mr. Levy's subconscious found a way out of his guilt pangs: if the two hours that he *did* devote to his children would prove unsuccessful, then it clearly would not be worthwhile to make an effort to free up more time for them. And so, without being aware of it, Mr. Levy created an atmosphere of boredom and subtly introduced disturbances, so that the time he spent with his children would become unpleasant for everyone.

These sessions did, in fact, become unsuccessful — so much so that they alleviated Mr. Levy's guilt feelings. He "gained" from failure: he no longer felt that he was shirking his fatherly duty by not giving his children more of his time, since even more hours of tedium would certainly not do them any good.

Had Mr. Levy been conscious of this while he was doing it, he would have felt even guiltier — ruining the little time he did set aside for his children. For this reason, the inner force that opposed his overt will had operated subconsciously, so that even he could not detect it.

The brief, open discussion with his friend helped Mr. Levy adopt a healthier attitude. He no longer suffers from tension and misplaced guilt feelings. If, during a given week, he is able to make more time for his children, he does; if he can't, he doesn't. He acknowledges that he would like to give them more of his time, but that is not always practicable; we cannot always do all the things that we would like. In the interim, he invests his best efforts in order to make those two hours real quality time — interesting and valuable for both his children and himself.

Notice that, on the conscious level, Mr. Levy wanted to and really tried to succeed with his children. He was not aware that, below the surface, a battle was raging between his dual wills: his desire to succeed with his children and his fear that success would make him feel obligated to spend much more time with them than he already did.

In the previous example, we've seen how subconscious feelings and attitudes can interfere with a person's conscious efforts. We've also learned that an unbalanced view of responsibility and capability can restrict a person and make success difficult. Once Mr. Levy became aware of the conflicting forces within, he found ways to reconcile them and develop solutions that would further both his conscious and subconscious objectives.

Not all difficulties in family relationships stem from subconscious conflicts. The example of Mr. Levy's problem merely serves to demonstrate how deep-seated, internal feelings may bring failure even when we are trying hard to succeed. Let's look at another scenario.

> Danny is the kind of person who always hates to ask for advice. Now he is thinking about buying a used car for the first time. After hearing about his plans, Danny's friend Shmuel, a professional mechanic, takes him aside and offers him some advice about what to look for and what to avoid.
>
> Danny knows that Shmuel's advice is valuable — and he didn't even have to "stoop" to ask for it. But if the advice leads him to a good buy, he'll feel obligated to become more willing to ask people for help in the future. And he cannot bear the thought of doing that.

So, what happens now? Without Danny being aware of what is really happening, all kinds of reasons crop up that make it difficult for him to follow Shmuel's advice. He claims that he doesn't like any of the kinds of cars that Shmuel recommended. Or he tries out the advice, but, "unfortunately," it doesn't help because his subconscious throws a wrench into the works. Perhaps he will end up buying a car that he should have known to avoid. All this is actually a defense mechanism designed to spare Danny the unpleasantness — to him, the humiliation — of having to seek advice in the future.

Understanding dual wills gives us deeper insight with which to understand the examples we explored in chapter 5. In the sad story of the Baums, both father and son believed that they were seeking a practical solution to their conflict. Each of them wanted to find a tactful way to impose his viewpoint without alienating the other. They were unaware that, because of their pain, they were subconsciously searching for reasons to be angry with each other. A resentful mindset caused them both to adopt poor approaches which caused them to fail in their attempts to respond constructively.

We looked at a worker who was angry and resentful about being fired from his job. Without realizing it, he behaved counter-productively and failed to find new employment — which justified his protracted resentment. In chapter 5, we discussed his difficulties in terms of the Spiral Effect: his resentment snowballed into failure. In this chapter, we can understand his difficulty as a conflict of wills. One part of him — the part he is aware of — wants to find a new job and actively searches for one. But, at the same time, another side of him — the part that wants to hold onto his anger — secretly sabotages his efforts.

Many times we, ourselves, don't recognize that we are acting in ways that lead to failure — even in projects that are important to us. Perhaps we don't realize it because any benefit we derive from failing, along with the ways we cause ourselves to fail, are less than obvious. We may remain oblivious to the fact that deep within us exists a "fifth column" that works against the very thing we are trying to achieve.

Blinding the Mind

The phenomena of blind spots and hidden thought processes are not new concepts. The Torah warns us that "Bribery blinds the eyes of the wise and distorts the words of the righteous."[1] Our Sages explain[2] that this statement refers even to the wise and righteous judge who accepts a gift from one party to a dispute, but fully intends to judge the case exactly as proscribed by Torah law. This judge does not want, and would never consent, to distort justice. But once he accepts the gift, little by little, his subconscious begins to unearth seemingly "incontrovertible proofs" that favor the party who gave him the gift. On the conscious level, the judge strives to arrive at a just verdict, and he is confident that his logic is seamless. He is unaware that the brilliant reasoning he has developed is critically flawed at its foundation, causing an apparently solid structure to lean drastically in one direction. As we learn from the Talmud:

> "Bribery blinds the eyes of the wise" — *even if he is a great scholar, once he has accepted a bribe, he does not leave this world without a blinded heart* — "...and distorts the words of the righteous" — *even if he is completely righteous, once he has accepted a bribe, he does not leave this world without confusion of mind.*[3]

The damaging effects of the bribe are not confined to the particular instance when it was accepted. Once a judge has accepted a bribe, bribery begins to permeate his thinking. As a result, his judicial vision will be distorted in the future, making him vulnerable to bias in other situations, even if he never accepts another bribe — as long as he hasn't fundamentally repented.

It is true that the Torah's prohibition against bribery refers specifically to court cases. While other distortions of a person's judgment are not direct violations of this prohibition, the principle behind it also holds true in personal situations.[4] Subtle biases and ulterior motives may affect any aspect of a person's life. Like a judge analyzing a case, our conscious mind can be swayed by internal forces. The previous quote from the Talmud teaches us just how far-reaching the ramifications of these feelings and motives can be. We also learn the importance of self-evaluation in verifying that such inclinations and biases are not commandeering our thoughts and actions.

The more care we take to recognize these mental influences, the more clarity of thought we will be given.[5] The efforts we invest to eliminate prejudices are never wasted. Mental lucidity, deepened cognitive powers, and an enhanced ability to pursue truth are the dividends we can enjoy.

Do I Want to Succeed?

Most of us would answer "yes" to the question. Some may tack on another question, "But how?"

If the influence of our inner conflicts was limited to trivial issues only, life would be complicated enough. Unfortunately, it isn't — *our general preparedness for success can be fundamentally affected.* If we didn't have secondary considerations hiding inside us, we wouldn't get stuck on that second question, "But, how?" We would simply say "yes" to the first and move forward from there. If you feel that undercurrents in your will might be dragging you down, keep an eye out for the following mental indicators:

- ♦ *Lack of Interest in Change:* Are you so attached to your present situation that you don't want to let go? This may stem from unhealthy self-love.[6]

- *Responsibility Aversion:* Is the lazy part of you anxious that initial, small changes will yield so much success that you will feel obliged to make other, larger changes too?[7]
- *Fear of Change:* Is the unknown frightening enough to you that you would rather be stuck with a familiar problem than try out an unfamiliar solution? This may be due to a lack of trust — in the situation or yourself — that it is within your ability to achieve new and unfamiliar levels of accomplishment.[8]
- *Self-Flagellation:* Do you feel a deep-seated need to punish yourself with failure? Are you begrudging yourself social or personal successes? ("I do not deserve to make this progress, since I am still...") This may be due to a repentant attitude that isn't constructive.[9]
- *Self-Pity Habit:* Do you sometimes feel nurtured by a brand of self-pity that would be threatened by success? We will discuss this deep issue presently.

Some of these issues, in extreme manifestations, can be considered pathological. Yet, we should be aware that in subtle ways, any and all of them can infiltrate our personalities and interfere with the attainment of our life goals.

Underlying Negativity

We have probably all been in contact with a chronically negative person, whether in passing or in a closer, more involved way. He can be called a "grumbler," the constant complainer who exposes those around him to his malcontented view of the world. There are two types of grumblers. The *universal grumbler* perceives the world around him as negative. He believes we live in a horrible world, and that we all (perhaps excluding himself) have a hand in ruining it. The other type of grumbler, the *self-involved grumbler*, operates in a more personal vein. He sees himself as a victim of egoistic and aggressive people who have, for no good reason, chosen him as a target for their critical impulses. Common to both grumblers is their ability to interpret life situations negatively. It is not so pleasant to be around either of them. As the verse explains, "His words are like hammer blows, and they penetrate to the innermost parts of the stomach."[10]

This inclination toward negativity seems puzzling. Why in the world would someone choose to be preoccupied with seeing things as bad? What do they stand to gain with their constant complaining?

The answer is found in the commentaries on the verse quoted above. The message is clear and sharp: "The grumbler exercises his fertile imagination to invent complaints about everything and nothing, like people who feign being abused so that others will pity them."[11]

The grumbler finds it hard to forge relationships based on the positive. He focuses on the negative and tries to convey it to others, hoping to arouse their pity. If the grumbler would only stop complaining, he would discover more and more of the blessing around each of us, including himself, and that even difficult things are really for the best.

THINK ABOUT IT

HOW DOES THIS EXPLAIN:

♦ what drives a person to complain constantly?
♦ what the chronic complainer is lacking?

How does constant griping make success difficult?

Pay Attention to Me!

Most of us are very different from the grumbler. We do enjoy things to a reasonable extent, and we share our positive feelings with others. Some people are even embarrassed to complain, and scorn the idea of other people treating them as pitiful, as a *nebuch*. Yet most of us may suffer from a more subtle and private version of negativity. We only have a weak appreciation for everything good in our life: Hashem's Kindness, the good we receive from other people, and for that matter — our own accomplishments and the genuine good within us, as we shall soon discuss.

Here again the question arises: What holds us back from this more wholesome and powerful cheerfulness and brightness? Can there be some inner part of us that has a vested interest in restricting our positive disposition? If yes, why *would* a rather healthy person want to write the role of victim for himself? Even if his life isn't always a pleasure, why should he choose to focus on the negative, and underplay the good that he has?

The answer in this case is not an attempt to elicit pity from others, but rather *self-pity*. A person dwells on his problems and difficulties, and comes to the conclusion that his life is filled with suffering and he is deprived. Let us understand the dynamics of this tendency.

Self-pity often has deep roots in childhood. Of course, parents want the best for their children, and make many sacrifices for them. They may, however, be insufficiently aware that their attention is one of the most important things they can give their children. Actually, attention is a general category, and there are a number of different forms of attention that should be offered to a child since they are vital to his development. Attention, when it is wholesome, is well balanced and given at appropriate times — rather generously when practical. It alternates between the following, at times being:

- *Spontaneous:* expressing the parent's good feelings toward the child and flowing naturally, on the spur of the moment
- *Responsive:* relating to the child when he asks directly, or constructively displays a need for attention
- *Caring:* guiding or assisting with a project or problem
- *Encouraging:* showing appreciation, praising, or rewarding proper behavior or success
- *Disciplining:* giving firm, constructive guidance, sometimes accompanied by a punishment, that serves to correct or improve the child's behavior
- *Sympathetic:* sharing feelings and being supportive when a child is going through a physical or emotional difficulty, like when he fails or is hurt

Unfortunately, there are parents who don't have the time or patience to give their children adequate attention for more positive reasons. If the child helps his parent or a sibling, the parent feels he has fulfilled his "obligation" with a few short, hurried words like "Thank you, sweetie." But when the child gets hurt or fails at some endeavor, he becomes the object of more genuine and more intense sympathy that takes the form of hugs and kisses, gentle words, or a treat. When parents behave this way, they are actually teaching their child that the surest way to secure the rare commodity of their attention is by arousing their pity.

Like every adult, every child craves attention. In a healthy situation, a child knows that his parents will usually pay attention to him if he does something good or if he asks for attention clearly and pleasantly. When a child does not get enough of the natural, positive attention that he really deserves and needs, he will seek other means to procure it — even negative ones. After all, he has learned well that arousing the pity of his parents is the most reliable way to get their attention. If his tactic works, this negative attention-seeking is likely to become a habit.

Let's watch the process at work. While playing, a child falls down and gets a light bruise. We would expect him to cry a little, wipe his tears, and return to his play. But, instead, he continues to cry pathetically, out of proportion to the severity of his injury. Why? Sometimes a child's cries can be exaggerated because he's sick, tired, or hungry. But if such excessive crying happens often, it is likely that he's spotted a good opportunity to get the attention he lacks. This is the first stage in the formation of the self-pity addiction.

The child slowly habituates to attention-seeking behavior in unpleasant situations. He then progresses to the second stage. Since he knows that the surest way to get attention is through pity, he begins to "stumble" into situations that arouse it. He may provoke a sibling into hitting him, taking care that his parents only see the blow, but not the provocation. He instigates those situations that arouse pity so that his emotional needs are satisfied, since he simply has no other sure-fire method of getting his parents' attention.

The solution in such cases is *not* to immediately withhold expressions of warmth in pitiful situations, since that may induce the child to seek other, more negative ways of getting attention. The correct approach is to respond with more generous, spontaneous warmth when the child behaves well or asks for attention in a straightforward, healthy manner. Make sure this warmth is at least as intense as the warmth that you project in a "crisis." Once you've gotten past that stage, you can begin to slowly decrease the amount of attention that you give when he cries over minor or imaginary troubles. Keep in mind, though, that crying does call for attention when there is a significant problem.

When he was little, this child learned to get attention by arousing pity. But as he gets older, and especially as he approaches adolescence, he begins to realize that this tactic is no longer effective. Once he is too old to be cute, his woes don't arouse people's sympathies the way they used to. Moreover, he, himself, may recognize that it is humiliating to play the role of *nebuch* in public.

The more mature, constructive, and creative the developing adolescent is, the more clearly he sees the advantage of engaging in positive and respectable attention-providing behaviors. He may choose to apply his energies to some laudable activity, or work on being pleasant and friendly so that people will enjoy his company. In that way, he could truly take advantage of the altered situation (his own maturity and the lack of overdone sympathy) to devise a healthy solution.

If, however, he became accustomed to pity-seeking in early childhood, he will probably be affected, to some degree, by inertia. He cannot expect much positive encouragement from those around him, either, since there seems to be, in society at large, a general lack of appreciation for the simple good in people. It is likely, then, that the new source of attention he finds to ease his cravings will be a recycled form of pity-seeking. (Worse still, he may discover that being a troublemaker or a delinquent will get him attention in the form of disapproval.) He will conclude that, since the world around him does not provide him with enough attention, he will provide it himself.

The kind of attention that he now gives himself is the same kind that is familiar to him from his childhood. When things don't go his way, he exploits the opportunity to silently bemoan his oppression. It's as though he strokes himself emotionally, and consoles himself for his terrible suffering. In this way, he becomes used to enjoying a new form of a familiar type of attention: self-pity.

Of course, warmth generated by failure is a poor substitute for the healthy glow that is kindled by success or love. And feeling sorry for oneself is a poor substitute for genuine caring offered by another. But he takes what he can get; he doesn't see anything more satisfying on the horizon. Over time, without realizing it, he may even seek out or go so far as to invent increasing difficulties so that he will have more excuses to pity himself, or more justification for the compassion he showers upon himself.

Sometimes the self-pity habit develops in childhood, without the prior stage of seeking pity from parents. This is especially likely if the child is the target of excessive criticism or tragic circumstances. In such a case, the child is likely to absorb the criticism or believe he is at fault for causing the mishap. He may then develop a self-image of victim. Then, when he searches for sources of warmth, he is likely to opt for those which are most compatible with his assumed identity: self-sympathy for his troubles, or in other words, self-pity.

In time, the tendency to pity himself and to maintain the self-image of *nebuch* becomes a basic part of the person's psyche — so much so that, when spouses argue, the real, unspoken argument is often about which of them is more unfortunate. Then, even when an opportunity to get some positive attention arises, he is likely to sabotage it for fear that, if he succeeds, the self-pity that is his emotional nourishment will no longer be justified. Since while he is caught in this syndrome, success and positive attention will leave him at a loss, he feels as though it actually pays for him to fail!

Passing up the genuine good feelings of success and of being sincerely appreciated in favor of the dubious pleasure of "victim status" may seem to be an irrational choice. Yet it does have its own, strange logic. Since it's impossible to be both a success and a victim simultaneously, the degree of success that a person chooses will dictate the extent to which he must abandon his status as a victim. The more of a winner he becomes, the less he can coddle himself. But does he trust himself to be able to maintain his role as a success? Does he trust the world to provide him with at least a minimal amount of recognition and appreciation? This wariness puts the brakes on his drive to pull free from the *nebuch* role and enjoy the fruits of success — self-fulfillment.

So, before he can adequately internalize positive attention, he must become aware of this opposition buried deep within. He needs to withdraw from his need for self-pity with a gradual, step-by-step process, and simultaneously learn to elicit positive attention. In that way, he won't feel threatened by an abrupt cutoff from his main source of attention as he becomes more familiar and confident with his new, healthier sources. This weaning process will soon be discussed.

> **THINK ABOUT IT**
>
> **HOW DOES THIS EXPLAIN:**
>
> ◆ how an understanding of a person's past can help break the self-pity cycle?
>
> ◆ the underlying effects of positive versus negative attention?
>
> How does self-pity act as a roadblock to prevent people from reaching their true potential?

Who Suffers from Self-Pity?

The self-pity habit is not confined to a small number of troubled individuals. Nearly all of us pander to it to some extent. The very common tendency to de-emphasize the good in our lives, and not focus on how much we have to be happy about, is actually a form of self-pity. The self-pitying part of us wants to feel deprived, so if we start noticing, appreciating, and enjoying all that is good in our situation, we would neutralize any reason to feel deprived.

This self-pity hurts us more than we realize. The obvious result of self-pity is that we cannot attain the happiness that would be ours if we learned to enjoy all the good things in our midst. With self-pity a person usually sees his life as trying or somewhat trying, while reluctantly agreeing that it does contain positive elements. In contrast, the person without self-pity will usually see his life as flourishing, while admitting that it does contain difficulties. And this thin line determines whether or not we're suffering from self-pity.

The negative effects of this mindset go far beyond affecting our level of happiness. Self-pity lowers our readiness for success and reduces the quality of our interpersonal or social situations. Unfortunately, the greatest damage is usually felt precisely in our closest relationships. If we were to notice and fully enjoy all the positive qualities of the people closest to us — parents, siblings, friends, spouse, children — and how much we gain from those relationships, what an intensely encouraging effect it would have on everyone! It would bring out everyone's best. Were we to enjoy those relationships, we would have even more reason to notice and express positive feelings.

But someone who is unused to thoroughly enjoying large doses of positive attention may not be ready to consider himself so fortunate. After all, if things are so perfect, he will feel compelled to express his appreciation to Hashem and to those around him. He would be overflowing with joy and good will. He wouldn't have any excuse for anger or resentment, and certainly not for self-pity!

As a result, we are not quite ready to be so perfectly content. We try to justify this flaw in our personalities by searching, more than we realize or are ready to admit, for all sorts of defects in our environment, exaggerating existing difficulties and inventing others. We may convince ourselves that we were deprived as children; our spouse does less for us than we do for him; our neighbors and friends are not friendly enough; our Rosh Yeshivah or boss is too imposing; our mother-in-law interferes too much; and our children are not giving us enough *nachas*. Even if these things are partially true, we can get caught up in it. In this way, we find reasons to continue in our less than happy state. Our lives become interspersed with a few persistent touches of tension, anger, sadness, and, of course, self-pity, and we distance ourselves from appreciation, enjoyment, and success.

Self-pity is one of the most substantial subconscious factors that may undermine success. It is probably responsible for an alarming proportion of the serious failures in our lives. For that reason, it is important to detect when self-pity is affecting us, and to check for its symptoms any time we are not enjoying a reasonable degree of success.

> Molly feels that her husband does not appreciate her enough. The logical solution would be for her to find ways to encourage him to appreciate her more. Molly knows that succeeding at this would bring her happiness. Wouldn't any woman be thrilled to be considered the fulfillment of her husband's dreams?

Unfortunately, Molly is not ready for such happiness because she is already habituated to the negative attention she gives herself when indulging in occasional bouts of self-pity. Subconsciously, she fears that if her relationship with her husband is too good, she will have much less reason to pity herself, and then she will feel that she is lacking that form of attention. If she has to appreciate all the good that she has, she will no longer have the excuse to occasionally gripe. She will have to be in good spirits because of her wonderful situation. She will also owe appreciation to her husband for all that he gives her — and she is not ready to assume all these unfamiliar habits.

Molly would certainly admit that genuine appreciation from her husband would be worth many times as much self-pity. But she is too unfamiliar with this form of warmth. She is afraid to relinquish the old, reliable source of comfort, however second-rate it is.

> Without realizing it, Molly seeks ways to guarantee herself a reason for self-pity. On a conscious level, she seems to be striving to attain her husband's good will. But, subconsciously, she is sabotaging her own success. Instead of acting in a pleasant manner that would win

her husband's appreciation and affection, she shouts at him for not appreciating what she does for him.

Deep inside, Molly is aware that her husband will not value her more if she attacks him with complaints and criticism. She also knows that he will either defend himself ("How can you say that I don't appreciate you? Why don't you notice all the times when I show you my appreciation?") or counterattack ("How much appreciation do you ever show me?"). We would have expected Molly to be sensible enough to anticipate her husband's reaction. At least, once she has seen how he reacts, we would think that she would revise her strategy and act logically. But, since she is unaware of the subconscious battle within her, she will only end up feeling even more hostile: "I came to my husband with a reasonable request: that he appreciate what I do for him. Instead, he has the nerve to stack up even more complaints against me." In this way, she has gotten herself another excuse for self-pity.

Although unaware, Molly is moving away from her articulated goal, not toward it. If she were aware of her inner struggle and was truly determined to help herself, then, instead of aggravating the situation, she could plan an escape from her self-pity habit. And *that* would bring satisfaction and joy to the both of them.

A Time for Everything

Along with every other character trait, self-pity has its positive application. Attention is vital for human beings and its absence can cause problems of many kinds, with varying degrees of intensity. They range from a simple lack of self-confidence to deep existential anxiety. Even though self-pity is a poor substitute for healthy attention, if a person cannot get that, self-pity is better than nothing at all. A person may not thrive on it, but he can survive.

Nonetheless, self-pity is usually destructive in the long run. Once a person is accustomed to it, he craves this familiar, easily procured form of attention. It becomes harder and harder for him to notice or take advantage of opportunities to get the positive attention that encourages growth and emotional health.

If a person continues to live on self-pity, unaware of this danger, then what started out as a survival tactic will turn into a destructive force. But if he is conscious of his tendency to pity himself and keeps it under control, then he can gradually wean himself from his habit and learn to get attention in healthy and positive ways. Thus the thinking person will acknowledge his feelings, and take advantage of the benefits that self-pity can provide. At the same time, he will be careful to avoid the extensive pitfalls that he risks when indulging in self-pity.

Self-pity, then, is an excellent example of the power of deep-seated emotions and hidden feelings. On one hand, they serve a vital purpose. On the other hand, there is a constant risk of damage as long as we don't recognize them.

Weaning from Self-Pity

By patiently working through the following seven-step process, a person can make the transition from dependence on self-pity to healthy receptivity, and finally to positive attention.

1. Identify

Recognize if you have any subtle symptoms of self-pity. Learn to identify the thought process which leads to it. Notice when the "poor me" syndrome is in effect. See how it makes you personalize your difficulties and dismiss the good in your life. Be sensitive to even subtle manifestations of this dynamic.

Awareness of this pattern is a major step toward curing yourself of it. Once you realize that objectively, your perspective is skewed —

that your troubles aren't quite so monumental, that life is sweeter than you thought — your self-pity is dealt a major blow. You have recognized that it is not based on fact; you have let your self-pity infiltrate and color your reality.

2. Visualize the Goal

Spend time visualizing yourself as you would like to be — free to live with the mentality of success and suffused with appreciation of all the people around you, and of yourself and your goals. In your imagination, "try on" the emotional robustness that accompanies feeling positive and fulfilled.

3. Temporarily Justify Your Self-Pity

Accept the fact that you can't change yourself all at once. In the meantime, appreciate that your self-pity is fulfilling a constructive purpose: it substitutes for the attention that you lack.

Seeing your self-pity as something constructive helps put it under your control — you manipulate it, it doesn't manipulate you. Remember, you are using it for a positive purpose until you can develop healthier sources of attention. Keeping this clear will help you stay in a constructive state of mind and prevent you from despairing about the elements of self-pity that you haven't conquered yet. Of course, don't overdo the justifying! You might come to feel comfortable with self-pity.

4. Encourage Yourself

When you do express appreciation for the good in your life, send yourself encouraging, affirming messages. Pay attention to those times when you lighten up about your challenges so that you can see how you really are progressing. Gradually work toward focusing more and more on all the good that you are, do, and receive in life. Learn to deepen your appreciation for all of it.[12]

5. Be Bold

Realize that you can let go of self-pity and not feel abandoned. Appreciate that you have the strength to nurture yourself by valuing your accomplishments[13] and by absorbing positive energy from your relationships with others.

6. Avoid Roadblocks

Any of a variety of nonconstructive attitudes may be hampering your ability to appreciate yourself, what you do, and what you receive in life, and may even make you justify negative ways of thinking. See chapter 10 of this volume, and chapters 1 and 6 of volume 2 for further discussion.

7. Sharpen Your Technique

Learn to use the techniques for determined and wholesome progression described in the next four chapters, and the technique for developing proper perspectives described in volume 3 of this series.[14]

8. Reap Your Rewards

Think positively, act positively, and watch how it affects your disposition and the way that others relate to you!

Freedom from self-pity finds its apex when we shift our focus and recognize that Hashem cares for us and watches over us with special, individual concern. Noticing and appreciating the many times that Hashem has arranged events for our benefit bathes us in a feeling of being loved and nurtured that is both comforting and elevating. Knowing that Hashem hears our prayers and is intimately aware of all our thoughts, feelings, and troubles makes us certain that we are receiving attention in the most beneficial, dependable way there is.

> **THINK ABOUT IT**
>
> **HOW DOES THIS EXPLAIN:**
>
> ♦ what a person stands to lose by giving up self-pity?
> ♦ what a person stands to gain by learning to thrive on positive attention?
>
> Why would it take many steps to wean a person from self-pity?

The Power to Choose

Self-pity is one of the most dynamic of the deeper forces, affecting most of us in at least a subtle way to form a barrier between us and the achievement of a quality life. In addition, each of us may have his own subjective issues that are getting in the way of his progress and the fulfillment of his potential.

In reality, greater feelings of contentment and well-being are often within our reach; perhaps only a few steps away. The power to take hold of the good that life has to offer is in our hands; all we have to do is face our problems with the right attitude. This may simply require a slightly altered approach, or a minor correction of an old habit. Still, some force holds us back and makes it seem difficult to make those needed changes. This force may very well be some form of apprehensiveness — we may fear that success is something unfamiliar, with which we need to learn to feel more comfortable.

Hashem's organization of the world and human nature rests on the reality of true freedom to choose. But this freedom — this power over the many forces at work within us — is not always apparent. Only through constant self-awareness can we learn to recognize and control the subconscious tendencies that affect our actions and decisions, so that we can truly become the masters of this power of choice that Hashem has given us. Then we can choose wisely, act sanely, and go great distances toward the most fulfilling goals in life.

The inner conflicts and tendencies of which we are unaware interfere with our logic and our power of free choice. But if we understand ourselves and work to remove our limitations, then we can think clearly and freely choose the straight and proper path in life. We can, in the Rambam's words, "stand before Hashem and... walk upright as [we were] originally created by the Al-mighty,"[15] and limitless horizons will open up for us.

Until this point, we have examined the factors that interfere with our ability to make wise, beneficial choices. In the coming chapters we will discuss how to overcome or avoid these obstacles entirely so that we can actualize our goals.

FINDING YOURSELF IN WHAT YOU'VE LEARNED

1. Draw up a list of goals that you set for yourself in the past, but were unable to achieve. Ask yourself what subconscious, secondary will may have prevented your success.
2. Fill in the following chart to help pinpoint secondary, obstructive elements of your will:

Tendencies \ Questions	Can you identify in yourself a tendency toward...?	In what areas of your life has this tendency affected you?	How does this tendency influence the way you relate to those closest to you?
Fear of Change			
Lack of Interest in Change			
Responsibility Aversion			
Self-Flagellation			
Self-Pity Habit			

NOTES TO CHAPTER SIX

1. Shemos 23:8, Devarim 16:19.
2. Rashi and Sifri on Shemos 23:8, Devarim 16:19.
3. *Kesubos* 105b.
4. *Sanhedrin* 18b, "Neither the king "nor the *Kohen Gadol* are permitted to intercalate the year. The king, because of his mercenaries (Rashi: whom he pays at a yearly rate; it is to his benefit to have thirteen-month years, every year); the *Kohen Gadol*, because of the chill (Rashi: since he has to immerse five times on Yom HaKippurim, it is to his benefit to always have Tishrei fall earlier in the year)." See also *Kovetz Ma'amarim*, Rabbi Elchonon Wasserman, essay 1.
5. For "the measure of reward always exceeds the measure of punishment" (*Sotah* 11a). If allowing biases to influence us causes the blinding of the mind, then distancing ourselves from bias will surely be rewarded with an even greater measure of clarity of mind.
6. See volume 5 of this series, chapter 10.
7. See chapter 9 of this volume.
8. See chapters 7-10 of this volume.
9. See volume 2 of this series, chapter 1.
10. Mishlei 18:8; 26:22.
11. Ralbag, Mishlei 18:8 on "The words of the complainer."
12. See volume 2 of this series, chapters 57.
13. See chapter 10 of this volume.
14. Also see volume 2 of this series, chapter 6, and volume 3, chapter 1.
15. Rambam, *Hilchos Shmittah V'Yovel* 13:13.

7
Bold As a Leopard

Basic Steps

We have seen that even when a person chooses the best available option to overcome a challenging situation (chapter 1), any of several limitations may still keep him from carrying out his resolution and reaching his goals (chapters 2-4). A magnetic force exists, too, that reinforces a negative state once a person is in it (chapter 5). He may also be hindered by the existence of multiple and contradictory layers in his will: even if he has a strongly articulated desire to succeed, he may have deep, hidden pockets of resistance that cause him to covertly undermine his own efforts (chapter 6).

What can we do so that our capabilities will not be confined by these handicaps? How can we keep the gateway to our success wide open?

Gateway to Success

> *Rabbi Yehuda ben Teima says: Be bold as a leopard, light as an eagle, swift as a deer, and strong as a lion to do the Will of your Father in Heaven.*[1]

From this mishnah we can derive a four-point plan that will lead to success in almost any area and can totally change the quality of our life.

1. *Be bold as a leopard:* Strengthen your resolve to succeed. Forge yourself a will of iron to reach your goal and eliminate or avoid any factor that stands in your way — with the boldness of the leopard.
2. *Be light as an eagle:* Avoid the lead-like seriousness that can come from determination. Instead, approach your goal free from worry or tension and progress with the lightness of the eagle that soars to great heights.
3. *Be swift as a deer:* Break out of any feelings of malaise and lifelessness. Call forth your energy and let it spread through you as you bound toward your goal with the vitality and swiftness of the deer.
4. *Be strong as a lion:* Arm yourself with emotional power. Advance toward your goal with a feeling of self-confidence and competence. Be secure in the knowledge that you have lots of untapped potential. Emulate the mighty lion with power of purpose and confidence in your ability to succeed.

In this final group of chapters (7-10), we will explain each technique individually, starting with the first step: becoming as bold as a leopard.

Caught in the Middle

We have already learned a bit about the nature of the will and the role it plays in determining our path in life. We saw in the last chapter that different layers exist within the will: we may want something on one level and, on a different level, we may wish to avoid it.

As we ponder deeper, we notice that inner conflict can cause us great pain and stress, and can effectively block our advancement. If we are not conscious of the opposing forces within our will, we are likely to become disappointed and frustrated by our slow progress. We may wonder why, despite our plans and efforts, we feel as though we are trying to break through a brick wall.

When a person has a strong, healthy, and consistent desire that permeates all levels of his personality, he becomes bold as a leopard. He can go far and achieve lofty and longed-for goals. "Where there's a will, there's a way" — "a" will, *one* will, whose layers are unified. Or, as our Sages phrased it, "A person is helped along *the* path [the specific path] on which he desires to go."[2] With this unity, we feel at peace with ourselves and can realize our goals without experiencing internal friction or conflicts. With it, we can make major changes in ourselves with relatively little effort. Without it, even large investments of effort don't yield much.

> It bothers Mike that he loses his temper easily, and he would like to overcome this tendency. Over and over again he has declared, "From now on, I won't lose my temper!" But, in fact, he seldom overcomes the temptation. He has tried a number of techniques to improve his patience. Even so, the degree of success he does achieve never lasts.

Why does Mike find it so hard to control his anger?

The answer lies within Mike himself. If he were to have a deep, honest conversation with his inner self, and ask if he really wants to rid himself completely of anger, he might be surprised to discover that — even though his knee-jerk response is "yes" — it isn't firm, or unequivocal. If he listens carefully, Mike may hear a distant voice piping up from deep within: "But if I don't raise my voice, my friend won't understand how wrong he is. I won't be able to convince my wife that she really hurt me, and my children won't see that I mean business. It's true that I lose my temper too often and that it causes me problems, but how can I give up my anger altogether?"

Along with his strong desire to rid himself of the handicap of anger, Mike still keeps the option of expressing it in reserve. He fears that if he drops it entirely, he will lose its "benefits." Obviously, it is difficult to free a prisoner when he, himself, is grasping his chains tightly!

> Freeda feels that her *davening* lacks life and she would like to pray with more concentration and feeling. Time after time, however, she finds herself thinking about arrangements that she has to make, or daydreaming about things that have nothing to do with her *tefillah*.

The first thing that Freeda ought to do is ask herself, "Do I honestly want to *daven* with complete *kavanah* — always? Am I really ready to stop thinking about all the important things that I have on my mind or drifting off into some pleasant memory or fantasy in the middle of my prayers?"

Freeda certainly wants to *daven* properly. Embarrassing as it is to admit, however, she is not really willing to concede her entire prayer time. If she did concentrate consistently, she would not be able to focus on anything extraneous during that time. (A student resolving to learn diligently and without interruption or a person resolving to fulfill his obligations joyfully and for the sake of Heaven may also make a similar subconscious calculation.)

A part of Freeda really does want to pray with concentration, but she simply lacks the wholehearted, unreserved desire to do so. This underlying conflict of will prevents her from succeeding at her goal of *davening* properly.

Resolving the Will

When we have undertaken a project, failure to complete it in a reasonable amount of time is a signal that we need to do some introspection. If we weren't harboring any reservations at all, our goal could be achieved quite easily. We need to learn the art of discovering our innermost desire. By being in touch with our desires, we can devise a way to consolidate our diverse motives into a single, harmonious force that's eager to achieve our established goals. All buried pockets of resistance must be dealt with properly.

But, *how* do we make ourselves "bold as a leopard"? How do we fortify our will and sharpen our determination to overcome all obstacles? What follows is a multi-step method for resolving such conflicting fragments of our will, which we will call "Resolving the Will."

1. Identify the Conflicting Will — What It Wants

Whenever you see that a self-improvement project is not progressing at a reasonable pace, you should suspect that the opposition is coming from a inner, resisting will. Your first order of business is to try to determine what it is, exactly, that you do not want to change. You should ask yourself: Do I have some emotional force or way of thinking that is resisting my goal? Why don't I want to do what I am setting out to do? Why might I prefer not to change myself in this way? Cross-examine yourself until you discover exactly what these resisting forces are.

It may be easier to ask the question in a less direct, more hypothetical format: "If I were not so interested in making this change, what would be my vested interest in maintaining the status quo?"[3]

To some extent, any attempt at self-improvement engenders fear of change. This apprehensiveness about improving ourselves is sometimes a simple wariness of the unknown — we are concerned that making this improvement will create an unfamiliar situation. While it doesn't have to take long to become familiar with and begin to enjoy the new, improved situation, adjustments always have to be made, and feeling some discomfort can be expected in the beginning.

2. Understand the Conflicting Will — Why It Wants

As simple as the conflicting will's objection may be, it is important to get to the bottom of it so that it can be dealt with correctly and efficiently.

> Mordechai has a problem getting up on time. It's been a few weeks since he made a firm resolution to get up promptly at 6:30. The first few days were successful, but since then, he's been locked in a daily struggle to stay with it.
>
> It was obvious that some part of him objected to the new regime — his lazy side. It required some introspection, however, to uncover the deeper reason why he wanted that little extra snooze. After a few days of thinking it over, he realized that he felt he wasn't pampered enough; the extra twenty minutes in bed were his way of pampering himself.

Introspection is a valuable tool for understanding the conflicting will. Returning to Mike's situation again (page 169), Mike asked himself why he wanted to feel authoritative — was it only for constructive purposes, or did he have ulterior motives? He realized that he wanted to command respect as well as impress his needs upon others.

Freeda (page 170) also benefited from introspection: she thoroughly analyzed why she needed her mind to wander during *tefillas Amidah*. She came to the conclusion that it felt good to have some private time just to mull over her needs and experiences.

It's important to pursue the issue of *why* we want what we want as far as it takes us — so that our underlying motivation becomes crystal clear.

3. Challenge Its Logic

Analyze whether the conflicting will is really being satisfied by its obstructionist tactics. "Lawyer it out" with your opposing will — continue asking yourself questions until you pinpoint the faulty logic. You may be able to demonstrate to your conflicting will that even with the obstacles it lays down, its desires aren't being met. That alone may be enough to dampen its enthusiasm for resistance.

> Mordechai realizes that although the extra twenty minutes of rest do make him feel more pampered in the morning, the rest of the day he kicks himself for not being more responsible and prompt. He asks himself, "Do those twenty minutes really make me feel more pampered if the rest of the day I feel lousy about it?"
>
> Mike, too, sees that his outbursts (which are meant to bolster his authority and ensure that his needs are met) are counterproductive. Every incident demands an escalated response, and no overall improvements have been made at all. True, his family members may listen to him momentarily, but every time he wants something, he starts over at square one.
>
> Freeda comes to the conclusion that although she needs some private time, *Shemoneh Esrei* is really not the best place for it. While she prays, even though she may daydream, she always pulls herself together to try to concentrate on her *tefillah*. Freeda has decided that those intermittent moments stolen from her *davening* just aren't adding up to the quality time she would like for herself.

4. Organize Alternatives

The conflicting wills within Mordechai, Mike, and Freeda may have some legitimate justifications. Their problems stem from the clumsy way that their subconscious is trying to resolve those issues. They each have the option of organizing alternate means which are more effective and constructive, and will provide what their conflicting wills want.

In Mordechai's case, since what his conflicting will wants is pampering, he will have to find another way to pamper himself that doesn't block him from achieving his goal — rising early to start his day. He may need to set aside some time during his day to indulge in a favorite activity that he normally doesn't make time for. Even better, he may learn to focus on the fulfillment he feels from his achievements during the day so that his need for pampering will be satisfied. Not only would his conflicting will be getting its "due" by being flooded with good feelings all day long; Mordechai would have all the more reason to get up early in the morning, and be enthusiastic about a new, fulfilling day.

Mike needs to work on improving communication with his wife and friends so that he will feel less of a need to express displeasure or urgency through anger. For instance, at a quiet time he can sit down with his wife and discuss his goal of remaining calm along with any reservations he has about it. The two of them can make an agreement that each will respond to the other's requests only when they are articulated pleasantly. If an angry demand is voiced, the response can be, "I would be happy to do as you ask. But, as we agreed, I can only do it on the condition that you ask again in a pleasant way." By using this method, Mike will begin to realize that his wife is paying attention to and respecting his requests, even though — or, in this case, because — they are voiced without anger. When he is feeling angry, Mike can inform his wife of his anger and explain why he feels that way, without having to prove it by demonstrating just how angry he is.

Mike may choose to work on his child-raising and discipline techniques so that he won't feel the need to assert his authority by flying into a rage when one of his children misbehaves. If he will work on strategies to inspire his family's respect of his authority, the part of his will that insists on showing anger can work together with his conscious desire to control his anger. Since the "objector" is provided with an alternate means of getting what it wants (respect), it doesn't mind giving up the destructive behavior (shouting).

Freeda discovered that her busy schedule doesn't allow her the time she needs for herself, so she may choose to take a fifteen or twenty minute walk around the park several times a week. On the days that she doesn't take her walk, she may want to write in her new diary — which is a safe place for her thoughts and feelings. If

Freeda begins this new system, a degree of success is sure to follow; her *tefillah* still may not be perfect, but it should definitely improve.

A Change in Shulamit

Let's follow Shulamit as she works through the stages of her self-improvement process.

> Shulamit had a sharp tongue and excelled at ridiculing others. She was aware that she was hurting people and even recognized that her unrestrained barbs occasionally landed her in trouble. At several different periods, Shulamit had tried to break the habit — with some success. Yet, she still found that she would revert to her old pattern; all too often, an irresistibly sharp quip would slip out.
>
> She tried to uncover her conflicting will (#1 *Identify*) and came to a conclusion — she realized that she felt an inner sort of vacuum; she was unfulfilled. She used her knack for making people laugh to mask her feelings and give her temporary fulfillment (even if it was at the expense of her victims). She just didn't feel as though she could pinpoint anything deeper. After some persistent introspection (#2 *Understand*), she unveiled that she was sensitive to criticism. She was employing the strategy of "the best defense is a good offense" so that critical eyes would be focused on others. At the same time, her image would be intimidating enough to scare away potential derogators. Shulamit also realized that she felt a need for appreciation — and that her caustic wit served her by inspiring laughs, as well.
>
> She then entered into a conversation with her conflicting will (#3 *Challenge*): "Is this the kind of appreciation I'm seeking? How do I know that those people who laugh at my jokes don't turn around and degrade me for being callous when they're out of earshot? Just because people are afraid to voice their criticism... does that mean I'm appreciated?" These questions put Shulamit in a quandary.
>
> Later that week, Shulamit attended a lecture on the topic of "Who is truly honorable? The one who honors others."[4] After the lecture, she felt very inspired and began to see how her conflicting will could be satisfied differently. Shulamit has since resolved to focus more on showing respect to other people so that she can

become a more honorable woman, and be less concerned about criticism (*#4 Organize Alternatives*) — and she has found that her tongue is starting to give her less and less trouble.

> **THINK ABOUT IT**
>
> **HOW DOES THIS EXPLAIN:**
>
> ♦ the warning signs of a conflicting will?
> ♦ the importance of identifying the conflicting will?
>
> How do each of the steps described above help a person to become bold as a leopard?

Other Options

The method described above is a thorough way to resolve the conflict between the inner wills. It has a disadvantage, though: it requires that a person satisfy the demands of the conflicting will, which isn't always easy. Satisfying the conflicting will often involves correcting a fundamentally problematic situation, like improving communication in a family, or putting an end to abuse. Such a change is definitely beneficial, but it is difficult and will take time to materialize. In the meantime, while working on long-term solutions, some short-term solutions can also be helpful.

Another drawback of the previous method is that it involves finding the logic and justification for the resistance — and it may be risky to look for anything that would justify the resisting will's position. This may lead to vindicating the problematic behavior so much that it weakens a person's resolve to overcome it. Therefore, care is necessary to make sure that as a person tries to understand his conflicting will, he shouldn't begin to validate it.

The following methods represent more direct solutions, offering different ways to confront the problematic part of the will. Experiment with them to see which works best in different situations. These alternatives have one point in common with the previous method: a person must determine what, exactly, is interfering with his desire for change (#1 Identify, see page 171.) Once we have pinpointed the source of our hesitation, we can try the more direct methods listed below to neutralize that desire. These methods include:

◆ *Neutralizing Resistance*
◆ *Rewarding Your Efforts*
◆ *Challenging Resistance*
◆ *Temporarily Modifying the Goal*

NEUTRALIZING RESISTANCE

Our Sages advise us to neutralize negative feelings by venting them. As it says in Mishlei, "[If there is] worry in the heart of a person, *yashchenah*"[5] Our Sages explain the word "*yashchenah*" to mean that a person should speak out his worry to others.[6] The *Anaf Yosef* adds, "When a person articulates the worry in his heart, he feels relieved. This is not the case when the worry remains in the heart — it festers there and causes him more distress. Accordingly, we may see that someone who is angry with his friend may want to punish him, take vengeance with blows and wounds and the like. Should the angry one approach his friend and rail at him, saying, "I'll do this to you, and that...!" *that itself* cools off his anger. His fury settles because he vented it."[7]

Rebbe Kalonymos Kalmish Shapira, the martyred Rebbe of the Warsaw ghetto, bases his statements on the words of the Alshich and expands on this approach.

You may be unable to free yourself from some suppressed anger at your friend. Chances are that, since you hate him, you view him negatively, finding faults and sins in him that make it all the more difficult to reconcile with him. Only after you've cleared the anger out of your heart will you be able to truly see whether his faults are any greater than your own. I just said, however, that you'd like to jettison your hatred, but you can't. So, write him a letter — don't send it — hide it away. In it, tell him off to your heart's content. Over the next few days, read it aloud, imagining that you're standing right in front of him, cursing him with those curses. After some time, it's certain that the anger in your heart will disappear; and if you're a sensitive, spiritual person, you'll hurry to make amends.

Don't be amazed at this piece of advice, and don't chalk it up to one of two things: "Either it's untrue, or it's some sort of magic. Is it possible that just by writing a letter and cursing him [in that letter] that I'll want to reconcile with him and even appease him?" This is neither a lie nor magic — it merely conforms with a law of human nature. When a person vents his anger, it subsides a bit (as we find in Sifsei Tzaddikim, Parashas Vayigash, in the name of the Alshich, z"l, on the verse "And Hashem regretted..."). Only when the foe answers back while he's venting does his anger multiply.

You, however, should write an appropriately stinging letter, and read it yourself, and tell him off. You will find that your anger cools off just by cursing him. When you read it again the second day, after your anger has already gotten smaller, you'll be reading insults you had written while under the spell of a much bigger fury. Your conscience will start to prick at you and say, "I wrote this?" At that point, you won't be able to read the letter in quite the same way you did before. Even so, since you accepted upon yourself to read it, and you still are somewhat angry, you'll force yourself to read it again. By the third day, when your anger is even weaker after the second day's reading, you won't be able to read it again at all. You'll already regret what your heart exposed — that you were capable of such an outpouring of vitriol. By then you'll be looking for strategies to appease him. A good-hearted person will rush to make amends, and someone stubborn will need to read the letter again and again. With Hashem's help, however, everyone winds up reconciling through this technique.

If you write such a letter, do it only at rare intervals, and be extremely careful not to lose it or show it to even your closest friends. *If the subject of the letter should find out that you wrote such things about him, it would only infuriate him.*[8]

Just like anger, almost any negative emotion can be defused with a similar technique. It can, therefore, be used to neutralize the feelings that are impeding progress. A person needs to isolate whatever point is holding him back, and to express that point many times. In that way, he can cause the feeling to weaken and abate.

For example, if a person would like to be liberated from anger generally, he should pinpoint the issue that makes it difficult to free himself from his anger, construct an appropriate sentence that expresses the sentiment, and repeat it many times. If he felt that he needed the anger to protect his interests, he might say, "I don't want to completely free myself from anger since... the members of my family won't accept my authority if I speak calmly." Adressing his resistance verbally, whether aloud or in written form, should help him to break his habit of anger. Once he has addressed his resistance to letting go of the anger, he may actually find himself feeling free of that resistance. This method can liberate a person from his anger even if he has not yet figured out what caused his anger in the first place — by describing his feelings in a general way, "I am very angry at _____, and I don't care what it's about...," he should repeat this many times.

Rewarding Yourself

Some people benefit from giving themselves positive reinforcement[9] to override their reluctance. Try to find a reward system that works for you, either by yourself or with someone else who can keep tabs on your progress.

Mike and his wife can agree that each of them will give the other[10] a warm compliment or even a token gift after each day that the other does not lose his or her temper. This reward can help

Mike to feel that giving up the "benefits" of anger is worthwhile after all.[11]

Freeda can treat herself to some small prize — a moderate amount of some favorite food,[12] some small object, or some time spent on an activity that she enjoys — each time she notices an improvement in her praying. She might also encourage herself by taking a moment at the end of her prayers to sit quietly and reflect on the improvement in the quality of her *davening*.

The best prize of all, of course, is the sweetness of success. Mike can notice how much more he enjoys his family and the atmosphere in his home when he is calm and patient. Freeda can envision her joy when she succeeds in *davening* without interruption, and bask in the good feeling that envelops her every time she enjoys a moment, even a brief one, of focused, devoted *tefillah*.[13]

It is very important not to discourage ourselves by dismissing the progress we have made and by feeling that what we have done is never good enough. As we strive toward continued improvement, we must remember to enjoy the success we have already achieved. If we don't appreciate our accomplishments enough, we deprive ourselves of our most important source of encouragement and motivation, and actually lessen our chances of more complete success.

Challenging Resistance

The following three alternatives do not modify or neutralize obstacles to self-improvement. Rather they are simple techniques to help win a direct confrontation with your own inner resistance to change.[14]

USING "NEVERTHELESS..."

Acknowledging an obstacle is a very powerful tool for challenging its resistance and overcoming it.[15] Let's look at this technique in terms of the scenarios we have already discussed. Mordechai might say to himself, "Yes, I deserve to be pampered — *nevertheless*, I am determined that my desire to get up early will override my desire for pampering."

Mike can affirm, "It is true that I want to maintain my anger so that I can wield my authority — *nevertheless*, I see how damaging it is for everyone. I plan to be free of it even though I'll have to forgo its 'benefits'."

Freeda might admit, "I really do need some time to organize my thoughts about different matters — *nevertheless*, focusing on *davening* is important enough to justify giving up that undisturbed, quiet time."

Here's how it works. When an obstacle is concealed, it is difficult to relate to it, and even harder to understand the way it affects us. Since a concealed obstacle is so elusive, it can influence a person without him knowing it — against his will. Once a person identifies an obstacle and then indicates (particularly orally) that the obstacle is undesirable, he is seeing it clearly. When it is exposed, the obstacle takes on realistic proportions, and so it becomes conquerable. Once he realizes he can conquer the obstacle, he limits its potential influence.[16]

WAIT IT OUT

You might find it easier to use the Kotzker Rebbe's advice: "When the *yetzer* tries to take over, push it off for five minutes." When a person feels inner resistance to his project, one way to overcome that resistance is to wait a little while and then try begin your project again. If we put off giving in to the resistance, it can be less threatening than engaging in an all-out challenge at the heat of the moment — and may defuse the challenging situation altogether.

DO IT RIGHT

Freeda should also comply with the ruling of the *Shulchan Aruch*,[17] "If a foreign thought occurs to a person while praying, he should remain silent until the thought dissipates." She can tell herself, "I refuse to submit to the *yetzer*. Its goal is to get me to *daven* unconsciously while planning my day. If I really need the time for myself — I'll take it. But I don't have to pray *while* I plan. I'll stop *davening* for a moment and plan to my heart's content. When I finish, I can resume with a mindful *tefillah*."

If she is set on *davening* properly while offering herself this compromise, the element of her will that wants to think about other things will receive its due. Even though it seems like she is giving in, eventually, the number of times she has to interrupt her prayers and wait until the thought passes will begin to annoy her so much that she will feel completely ready to *daven* in a way that befits the act of offering praise and supplications before the Master of the Universe.

Temporarily Modifying the Goal

Strengthen your determination and avoid inner resistance by adjusting the size of your immediate goal. Limit your efforts to slow and steady progress. Your subconscious is less likely to put up serious resistance to a small step, so divide your overall goal into bite-sized ones.

Mike can tell himself, "I would really like to be completely free of my anger habit, but that is too big a goal. For the time being, I will try to step out of it for just half an hour a day. The best time for me to choose is the half-hour from 8:00 to 8:30 every evening. That way, I'll have nearly the whole day to take care of my anger 'needs.' I'll set aside just this one half-hour for calmness and patience."

To disarm his inner opposition even more, Mike can adopt even this limited resolution on a trial basis: "If I see that I lose out on anything too important because of this half-hour of calm, I won't continue the project. I also won't add any more calm time unless I see that I haven't suffered because of it."

After a while, Mike's half-hour a day of controlling his temper will become a habit. He will begin to feel that this calm time is no great sacrifice and that, in fact, he has gained by it: he feels more serene inside and his relationships have improved.

Once he recognizes this accomplishment, Mike will feel ready to add another half-hour of calm time to his day, still leaving himself more than enough time for any "necessary" outbursts of anger. To satisfy his inner opposition, he will continue to check that he has not suffered any significant loss from the added half-hour. In this way, he can continue adding a half-hour every month, until he learns to manage virtually without anger.

If Freeda concentrates on saying just one paragraph of the *tefillah* intently, she will have enough time during the rest of her prayers for all her other thoughts and arrangements, ill-timed though they may be. Even if her mind wants to wander off to the ends of the earth, she will still have enough time for a complete round trip. Meanwhile, she reserves only one specific paragraph during which she will breathe life into her *tefillah*.

In the course of time, Freeda will experience the pleasure of praying with devotion. She will discover that those crucial deliberations can be accomplished quite well in that much less time. Every month she can add one more paragraph of quality *tefillah* with which she does not allow her active imagination to tamper, and dedicate it to the sole purpose of communion with her Creator.

Mordechai may find that if he initially limits his early rising to once or twice a week, and gradually increases it, the project may progress more successfully.

Similarly, the student who is struggling to concentrate on his studies can resolve to engage in diligent, focused learning for just half an hour of his learning time. Plenty of time will still remain for half-hearted learning and daydreaming.

> **THINK ABOUT IT**
>
> **HOW DOES THIS EXPLAIN:**
>
> ♦ when it would be preferable to use the "resolving the will" technique?
>
> ♦ the advantages of these last options instead of, or in addition to, "resolving the will"?
>
> When might a person use a combination of approaches?

One Step at a Time

It may be hard for a person who aspires to genuine spiritual growth to force himself to concede and agree not to try to improve his *middos, davening,* or attention to his learning the rest of the time. His response to our suggestion is likely to be, "What kind of *yiras Shamayim* is this? Everyone knows that we are obligated to avoid anger all day and that we must concentrate on all of our *davening!* How can anyone say that this little bit is enough of an effort?" The answer has already been offered by our Sages:

> *If you reach for too much, you have not taken hold at all; but if you reach for a little, then you've caught hold!*[18]

It won't take long to notice how much easier it is to overcome your inner opposition by the method of reaching for just a little at a time. Although our way may seem long, in the end it is the short and sure road, while the other path — attempting to change ourselves completely in one giant leap — has been tried often without success.

The idea of starting off with small, attainable goals finds strong support in our classic sources. The Vilna Gaon, in his commentary on Mishlei,[19] explains that failures in the service of Hashem most often result from a desire to jump to a lofty level all at once.

> Our Sages said, "One who comes to purify himself merits Heavenly assistance.[20] Yet sometimes a person begins learning Torah or observing mitzvos, finds it too hard, and abandons his efforts. He does not feel that he has received any assistance, and he rages against Hashem for not helping him. His failure, though, really results from his own foolishness, as it is written, "The foolishness of man distorts his path, and his heart rages against Hashem.[21] Every person must go according to his own level. If he does, he will advance safely and surely and will also merit Heavenly assistance. When he tries to leap ahead, however, he will not merit Hashem's help. This is the "foolishness of man": by acting without presence of mind he, himself, distorts his path, yet he directs his rage against Hashem for not coming to his aid.

Similarly, a person is simply not ready immediately, at the onset of his Torah learning and *mitzvah* observance, to act out of purely spiritual motivations. Rav Chayim of Volozhin, in his commentary on *Avos*,[22] compares the process of the ascent from worldly motivations to heavenly ones to a king commanding his servant to go up into the attic. "There is no reason in the world for the king to become angry with the servant for going up the rungs of the ladder and not jumping in one great leap from the ground floor to the attic, because it is impossible to ascend without advancing up the ladder one rung at a time."

Most importantly, the Vilna Gaon advises further[23] that a person should not directly work against his nature. The Talmud gives a parable[24] which also illustrates this idea. It involves a camel, which is an animal with small ears. In the parable, the camel actually starts off with large ears, but is not satisfied. He goes to look for horns, a quality not aligned with his nature, and instead of getting them, even the ears that he has are cut off. Similarly, a person must always weigh the goal he has set for himself, to determine if it is appropriate for him.

Rav Yisrael Salanter considered the gradual approach to be a special skill and called it "The art of wise living — knowing how to anticipate the future... to minimize the goal and lighten the trial, until the motivation generated by fear of Heaven can overwhelm the specific desire." Rav Salanter would emphasize that if we do not yet possess enough fear of Heaven to overcome a great challenge, we should try to minimize the challenge until our fear of Heaven is strong enough to overcome it. The art of serving Hashem is to know our abilities and to ensure that we will be victorious in our spiritual battles by setting ourselves attainable goals. Then, after winning the fight a number of times, our power will have grown and we will be equipped to face challenges at the next level of difficulty.

Some people find it hard to proceed with baby steps because they never learned to appreciate the value of small changes. Slow progress does not satisfy their desire to see how much they are advancing, and they may not yet have experienced the sweetness that can be found in steady growth, accomplished one small step at a time.[25]

Truthfully, starting small is the time-tested technique of the *yetzer hara*. It usually does not tempt us right from the start with major felonies, but rather attempts to trip us up with misdemeanors. The author of the *Chovos HaLevavos* warns us "not to underestimate the evil inclination's small successes. These small victories whet his appetite to do further battle; however, if you stand up to him, he will not be able to prevail against you.... Therefore, do not be intimidated by his words or by the might of his soldiers."[26] This is one of the talents of the evil inclination and one of the keys to its success; it recognizes the potential of the slightest foothold as a stepping stone to greater things. We can learn this trick of the *yetzer hara* in order to overcome its influence and lead ourselves, with even greater success, in a positive direction. The key is to really appreciate the significance of each and every bit of progress. Our small but determined steps will then prove to be great, firm strides toward our goals.

> **THINK ABOUT IT**
>
> **HOW DOES THIS EXPLAIN:**
> ◆ how solving a problem piecemeal doesn't mean you're not a *yirei Shamayim*?
> ◆ the advantage of breaking a big problem into smaller stages?
>
> How could taking small steps actually make a person as daring and bold as a leopard?

The Importance of Clarity

We've learned the importance of clarifying goals and having an accurate grasp of our obstacles. The Ramchal emphasizes this approach in his *Mesillas Yesharim* and it is one of the main devices that permeate the book. In the introduction to the book, the Ramchal laments that the basic tenets of life are considered obvious — that people don't realize that what they took for obvious actually needs to be examined, worked out, and absorbed. He opens the book with the words "The foundation of piety and the root of pure Divine service is that it should become clear and confirmed in a person's mind what his obligation in the world is, and on what he will focus and make his objective."

The Ramchal expands on this point in the second chapter and introduces us to the challenges that beset the person who searches for clarity:

> This is truly one of the plots of the yetzer and its cleverness — to constantly burden the hearts of people with his labor so that they aren't even left with enough mental space to contemplate their situation. It is certain, though, that if they only paid the slightest bit of attention to their ways, they would immediately begin to regret their deeds. Their remorse would continue to intensify until they would abandon their sins altogether. This was one of the plots of the wicked Paroh who said, "Increase the workload on the people...."[27] He intended to deny them any space, so that they wouldn't have the time to think or devise some strategy against him.
>
> This is exactly the yetzer hara's tactic against a person.... This is just what the prophet cried out, "Pay attention to your ways...."[28] Our Sages also said, "Anyone who maps out his path in this world merits to see Hashem's salvation."[29] If a person keeps track of himself, Hashem helps him, and he will be saved from the yetzer hara.

The Ramchal teaches us that success in self-improvement projects is contingent on setting aside and using the time necessary for constructive self-evaluation. Self-evaluation is vital because it allows us to determine clear paths and objectives. If we don't invest the time, the *yetzer* gets the better of us.

In chapter 3 of *Mesillas Yesharim*, the Ramchal again encourages the reader to firmly establish both his goals and the best path to attain them. After discussing potential pitfalls, he concludes, "Through this [contemplation], it is certain that it will be easy to purify himself from all evil and rectify his ways."

The Ramchal closes chapter 9 with a similar sentiment, "After a person has already opened his eyes to see his deeds and to be careful with them... it will be easy for him to avoid evil, to long for and be zealous for the good; this is obvious."

One who attends carefully to the structure of *Mesillas Yesharim* will notice that the book is built around developing clarity about goals at every stage of progress. Likewise, the Ramchal emphasizes the need to recognize and be in contact with the obstacles that lurk at every stage so that they can be eliminated. He advises that the "bliss of clarity"[30] makes it possible to approach our goals. The Ramchal encourages us to develop our ability to reflect and evaluate our true selves (*hisbonenus*) and use it as a starting point to develop our relationship with Hashem.[31] However, self-reflection is never meant to be an exercise in self-flagellation — on the contrary, our clarity and awareness should provide a means to detour around obstacles and naturally pave a smooth road toward true self-improvement.

A strong, consolidated will is essential for progress, and clarity is one of the important components. The goal should be well defined, its purpose clear, the approach well mapped. At the same time, one must be in touch with any opposition in the will, understand just what that opposition wants, and either neutralize it or organize constructive alternatives.

All these steps pave the way for us to be able to move toward our goals in a bold, determined fashion. While it may require an investment of effort at the outset, it saves so much time by preventing us from getting bogged down along the way.

Think of the last time you saw a leopard pacing his cage. Now picture the leopard stalking its prey. What mesmerizes us the most is the very quality of its movement — every step is absolutely deliberate. It may be a slow and steady flow or an intense rush, but he never projects a hint of apprehensiveness or hesitation; the leopard is a solid mass of directed motion completely focused on his objective. Once our wills are fully consolidated, we too can approach our goals in the daring, forceful, and determined way that our Sages exhorted — and be bold as brazen leopards to fulfill the Will of our Father in Heaven!

APPLYING WHAT YOU'VE LEARNED

1. Refer back to chapter 4, question 1, along with the chart there. Choose up to three of the tendencies that you listed there which have hindered you in important areas and jot them down in the blank spaces provided in the boxes marked "Obstacles". Use the following chart to explore different ways that you might use to resolve those conflicts.

Obstacles / Techniques	Obstacle #1*	Obstacle #2*	Obstacle #3*
1. Organize Alternatives			
2. Neutralize by Venting "I find it hard to... because..."			
3. Reward			
4. Challenge Resistance a) "Nevertheless..."			
b) Wait It Out			
c) Do It Right			
5. Temporarily Modify the Goal			

* Write one of your obstacles in this box — see question 1 for suggestions.

NOTES TO CHAPTER SEVEN

1. *Avos* 5:24.
2. *Makos* 10b (emphasis mine).
3. We will discuss tuning in to inner reasoning in greater detail in volume 3 of this series.
4. *Avos* 4:1.
5. *Mishlei* 12:25.
6. *Yoma* 75.
7. *Ein Ya'akov, Yoma* 75.
8. Rabbi Kalonymous Kalmish Shapira, *Chovas HaTalmidim*, chapter 9.
9. "A person must consantly occupy himself with Torah and do *mitzvos*, even if not for their own sake; since through ulterior motivation a person can come to learn Torah and do *mitzvos* for their own sake" (*Pesachim* 50b) Beware: not all people relate well to reward systems — they may find that the rewards "cheapen" the project, or that the rewards themselves can become objects of desires that will themselves need work later on.
10. *Taz, Yoreh De'ah* 361:2.
11. *Mishlei* 31:28.
12. *Shabbos* 118b-119a — Abaye would make a feast when a student finished a tractate; *Shulchan Aruch, Yoreh De'ah* 246:26 — One should prepare a feast and invite others.
13. See volume 2 of this series, chapter 10; and volume 3, chapter 5.
14. More sophisticated methods of challenging preconceptions will be presented in volume 3 of this series.
15. *Berachos* 5, "A person should engage his *yetzer tov* in a constant battle with his *yetzer hara*." See also *Sanhedrin* 111, Rashi on the words "And the one who overpowers his *yetzer*..."
16. This is similar to what we find in *Pesachim* 11: Although a person is no permitted to handle food that is forbidden, since he may forget and place i in his mouth — if he is taking it to be burned, we are not concerned about him handling the food, since the activity is only geared toward destroying it See Rashi on the words "He himself..."
17. *Orach Chayim* 98:1.
18. *Rosh HaShanah* 4b.
19. Vilna Gaon on *Mishlei* 19:3.
20. *Yoma* 38b, and commentary there.
21. *Mishlei* 19:3.
22. Rabbi Chayim Volozhin on *Avos* 3:1.

23. *Even Shleimah* 1:7.
24. *Sanhedrin* 106a.
25. To better appreciate the significance of small acts, see Rabbi Shmuel D. Eisenblatt, *Fulfillment in Marriage*, 2 volumes (Jerusalem: Feldheim, 5748), throughout volume 1, and volume 2, part 1, chapter 5.
26. *Chovos HaLevavos, Sha'ar Yichud HaMa'aseh*, chapter 4.
27. *Shemos* 5:7.
28. *Chagai* 1.
29. *Mo'ed Katan* 5a.
30. Introduction to Ramchal's *Derech Hashem*.
31. Ramchal, *Derech Etz Chayim*.

✥ 8 ✥
Light As an Eagle

A Relaxed Approach

As we become "bold as leopards" and learn to face our goals with growing determination and a stronger will, we must take care not to be drawn to extremes. We shouldn't be so riveted to success that we begin to feel pressured and tense.

Earlier, in chapters 6 and 7, we discussed the need to appreciate the importance of our goal and to consolidate all the levels of our will while working toward that goal. But once we have achieved such a clear focus, we may stumble into a new trap. This trap is set by the *yetzer hara*, who may change tactics and "righteously" urge us on, trying to convince us that our task is so vital that success is absolutely imperative. In this way, our *yetzer hara* throws us into a state of anxiety.

In the *Ma'ariv* prayer, we ask of Hashem, "Remove the *Satan* from before us and behind us." At times, the *Satan* (a.k.a. the *yetzer hara*[1]) stands before us, blocking our way. At other times, he stands behind us and pushes us to move hastily, or with too much tension.[2]

Our objective in this chapter is to learn how to liberate ourselves from tension and pressure so that we can approach our goals with the lightness and ease of a soaring eagle.

Tension

What's so terrible about tension? Why do we have to be so careful to avoid it?

We often witness the damaging effects that the tense person's agitation has on the people around him. They may be bombarded with criticism that is not constructive, anger, or suspicion. We may not realize, however, the extent to which stress blocks the tense person, himself, from achieving the very objective that concerns him.

The Talmud discusses a common disorder: constipation.

Various medical solutions are offered, followed by the opinion of the majority: "He should remove his attention."[3]

The Talmud then challenges this advice: "If he removes his attention, won't it be even more difficult for him to relieve himself?" Our Sages reply that he should turn his attention away from *everything else* and concentrate only on his need to relieve himself. This explanation seems rather forced — we would expect that "removing his attention" means distracting himself from his problem, not focusing on it. It is also unusual for the Talmud to do an apparent about-face between the first and second recommendations.

The Talmud may actually be suggesting a step-by-step solution. Stress can affect many bodily functions, particularly those of the digestive system. It is quite likely that the constipation problem was initially tension-induced. Now that this person has something else to be "stressed" about — the constipation, itself — he is likely to become even more anxious. This added stress may well intensify the physical problem even further, creating a vicious cycle. The first step, then, toward implementing the solution is for the sufferer to break the cycle by turning his attention away from the problem and adopting so relaxed an attitude, that it should be as if he couldn't care less about his constipation.

Once he is relaxed enough to be emotionally unaffected by his condition, he can move on to the next step. In his new, tranquil state, he does an about-face and gets down to work, rerouting his attention from other things so that he can focus on solving the problem. The Talmud's discussion is suddenly much more clear, and both aspects are correct. The pivotal word is *distraction*: first, from the problem and his anxiety, and later, from everything else as he refocuses his attention.

We can extrapolate a general lesson about facing life's other challenges from the advice of our Sages about this common, tension-induced ailment. Superficially, we would say that the stronger a person's will is, the greater are his chances of achieving his goal. There exists, however, a type of determination that can actually hamper success: determination that results in anxiety. The more tense we are, the less calm and flexible we will be — and calmness and flexibility are crucial for success.

So, if you find yourself taking your situation too seriously, begin to remedy matters by heading for the opposite extreme. Try to neutralize yourself emotionally about the task at hand until you feel relaxed, emotionally weightless, and unconcerned about success. Once you have this attitude, you will be able to resume your projects, addressing each of your goals with lightness and tranquility. After a little experimentation in crossing over to the other side, you will strike a harmonious balance and appreciate the importance of your goal while retaining a relaxed attitude as you work toward it.

The idea that tension sabotages the achievement of goals is clear from the words of the *Avos D'Rabbi Nosson*: "[A person should be] calm and thoughtful in his words and not over-exacting. Whoever is irritable... causes his ideas to be forgotten."[4] We might have thought that there is an advantage for a person to be overzealous about his worthwhile ideas; it indicates that he feels intensely about them. In reality, though, such an attitude makes him lose touch with his ideas. He may have learned a great deal or originated some new insight, but since his learning was done in a state of stress or irritability, the knowledge doesn't penetrate to the depths of his mind and, ultimately, is forgotten.

Our Sages teach us that one of the forty-eight prerequisites for the true integration of Torah is through happiness with one's lot. Rav Chayim of Volozhin explains that such a state is achieved by not being overly ambitious, even about learning. The one who possesses this attribute "Learns a little bit at a time until he is proficient at it. He does not pride himself on acquiring a great deal of knowledge at one time, which would cause him to forget everything."[5]

Tension is counterproductive not only in the active pursuit of positive goals, but also in our efforts to avoid the negative. Rav Yisrael Salanter advises us not to make too concentrated an effort to rid ourselves of impure thoughts since anxious preoccupation with them is likely to intensify them rather than drive them away.[6] The same can be said, Rav Yisrael explains, about distracting thoughts that interfere with our *kavanah* while praying. Excessive effort to drive these thoughts away is likely to have the exact opposite effect.

Instead, we can employ any of several tactics to calmly redirect our attention away from such thoughts:

♦ The Rambam teaches that the best way to avoid improper thoughts is to distance oneself from improper stimuli, like frivolity, drunkenness, and unbecoming songs, and to turn one's mind to thoughts of Torah. He does not advise a head-on confrontation with undesirable thoughts, since it would only generate anxiety. He recommends, instead, avoiding the problem by removing the stimulus and by diverting the mind to a more positive direction.[7]

- Every time such a thought enters your mind, remind yourself that you now have the opportunity to fulfill the *mitzvah* of not straying after your heart.[8] Even if you can't divest yourself of the thought immediately, be happy that you are *osek b'mitzvah*. Think to yourself, "Sooner or later, I will get rid of this thought," and be happy with your future success instead of tensing up about the fact that you haven't yet succeeded.

- When you do succeed in freeing yourself of the thought, rejoice that you were able to fulfill Hashem's command. The joy of doing a *mitzvah* not only puts a stop to the cycle of counterproductive tension — it also is an antidote for the depression and self-pity that breed disruptive thoughts in the first place. Anxiety concerning our ability to overcome these thoughts — and sadness if, at times, we do not succeed in ridding ourselves of them — only chip away at our ability to concentrate, and open the door to more depressing, bothersome thoughts.

- Every time such a thought intrudes, be happy that you've been sent an opportunity to simply make a conscious *effort* to pray or study with devotion and, in this way, show Hashem that you want and are trying to *daven* and learn properly. And, when you do succeed in overcoming the challenge, you have cause to be even happier! By focusing on the eternal value of not only the success, but every effort and desire to serve Hashem wholeheartedly, you will free yourself of anxiety and sadness and make it easier to achieve you goal.

Keep in mind that Hashem values each small struggle and improvement, even though it may not seem like a big achievement to you. We'll discuss this idea more throughout this series.

Types of Tension

To control tension, we first need to deepen our understanding of it. What is tension? What causes us to be tense?

Tension is a manifestation of unwillingness to accept difficulty; it is found in two general frameworks:

- ◆ *Task-Related Tension:* stress related to the process of pursuing and attaining specific goals
- ◆ *Situation-Oriented Tension:* stress brought on by some painful or uncomfortable event (the provocation can even be as minor as breaking a glass)

We will discuss the second variety of tension in volume 2, chapter 2. For the present, we will focus on the tension that arises from meeting up with obstacles while working on projects and toward goals.

While a person is making headway with some project, he can become more preoccupied with constant evaluation of his efforts and his progress than he realizes. In addition, he will most likely need to deal with all sorts of obstacles that crop up unexpectedly. Each of these elements is likely to cause tension. If we try to understand how these trouble-spots cause tension, we may discover subtly distorted perspectives regarding two major issues:

- ◆ *Expectations:* when a person has exaggerated hopes; and
- ◆ *Responsibility:* when feelings of obligation are out of balance.

Whereas expectations can involve both the final goal and the process of reaching it, a person's attitude to responsibility mainly involves the process of attaining his goal. We'll examine both areas closely.

Tension and Expectations

It is essential to find a golden mean for our expectations. While it is healthy to have hopes and aspirations, we still cannot expect that all of our dreams will materialize in exactly the way we would like. And we certainly shouldn't "count our eggs before they hatch" — and be disappointed if they don't!

There are three different objects of our expectations: ourselves, other people, and Hashem, Who directs our life.[9]

1. *Ourselves:* Although it is important to be aware of our strengths and abilities (see chapter 10 of this volume), overestimating them can cause a serious problem. If an inaccurate self-evaluation leads us to demand more from ourselves than we're capable of producing, failure to see the results we expect can make us tense.

2. *Others:* Human beings are social creatures, and often need to rely on assistance from others. When we expect help from others — whether it's their time, advice, money, or the like — with an "it's coming to me" attitude and it doesn't come, what happens? We may then pulse with tension, feel overwhelmed, and fret, "What will I do now?"

3. *Hashem, or "Life":* Hashem does love us and wants the best for us — however, we should not think this means that Hashem *must* help us in ways that conform to our understanding of "good." We should not be under the mistaken impression that we deserve to receive such help, that our lives in this world are supposed to be beds of roses, or even that our vision of what is good for us is really to our benefit. We might expect that we will always be graced with success, and that obstacles will never get in our way. When they inevitably do, and we don't progress as fantastically as we would have liked, we can become filled with tension.

In this chapter, which deals with task-related tension, we will devote ourselves mostly to the first and third types of expectations. Situation-related tension is discussed in volume 2, chapter 2. There we shall concentrate on the expectations of others, and delve further into our expectations from "life."

Now that we've named the primary realms of tension, let's identify the various ways in which we distort our expectations and sense of responsibility that make us tense.

COMMON AREAS OF OVER-EXPECTATIONS

What types of expectations does the person approaching a task have? In general, it is healthy to expect to function properly, and to get reasonable responses from others — and even from "life." Even so, without flexibility and the ability to deal with unanticipated outcomes, the person with specific expectations is consigning himself to stress and disappointment. In other words, not everything that one believes "should" happen *will* happen, and that is quite normal. Believing that everything will happen as it "should" is itself an exaggerated expectation.

It is common for people to have unreasonable expectations in the following areas:

- *Energy Investment:* We may want to achieve a certain goal but, at the same time, bristle at the demands of the task. We expect to be able to attain our objective with ease, and when we don't... we get agitated. This type of tension is an expression of our resistance to exert the required effort.

    Similarly, sometimes we may be unwilling to make peace with the fact that problems do arise along the course of all processes. This insistence that everything should always go smoothly can result in stress.

- *The Quality of the Results:* We may have exceedingly high expectations of what the end product of our endeavor will look like, or worry that the result will not measure up to the demands of others. Either way, an inability to gracefully accept the outcome, whatever it may be, can provoke a great deal of tension.

- *How Long It Takes to See Results:* We might want to see immediate results. This causes us to be frustrated by the length of time it takes to achieve the desired outcome. This is particularly the case when we underestimate the time a job will take. In those situations, tension is a manifestation of impatience.

In our times when we hear so much about products and ideas that guarantee instant results, we our especially vulnerable to such expectations in many areas (which could be especially damaging when they are not practical.)

Tension and Responsibility

The nature of a person's feelings of responsibility plays a decisive role in determining his future. The Ramchal, in the opening words of *Mesillas Yesharim* and throughout *Derech Etz Chayim*, discusses the importance of clearly understanding your responsibilities. He starts *Mesillas Yesharim* by saying, "The foundation of piety and the root of pure Divine service is that it should become clear and confirmed in a person's mind what his obligation in the world is. What will he focus on and make his objective throughout his life's work?" When a person is clear and determined about the positive direction his life should take, he has already taken the first steps of scaling the greatest heights of piety and pure *avodas Hashem*.

We will not concern ourselves with clarity of purpose. The issue at hand is the character of a person's *feelings* about his obligations. Without appreciating his responsibilities, a person drags himself through his life, tackling his daily routine mechanically. Worse, he may slip into inertia and inaction. At the other extreme, with an overblown sense of responsibility, he may feel filled with tension and stumble on the path toward his goals — leaving in his wake anger, rigidity, and small-mindedness which may cause others to trip as well. Compare that with the person whose sense of obligation is infused with joy! The door to success is open wide before him; he can reach the highest levels and inspire those around him, too.

COMMON AREAS OF AN EXAGGERATED SENSE OF RESPONSIBILITY

There are times when a person can have a practical picture of the resources he needs to invest in his project and a reasonable idea of what the outcome may be. Yet he finds projects stressful instead of challenging. This feeling of stress can be caused by taking his responsibilities much too seriously. This excessive concern takes various forms:

- *An Exaggerated Sense of Obligation:* A person can be so concerned with success that he drives himself into hyperactivity. He feels such an obligation to channel all his energies into his task, that he may drive himself to invest more physical or emotional energy than he has — so as to satisfy his sense of obligation. A housewife who feels obligated to accomplish *everything* is a good example of this. So is a dedicated and sympathetic public servant who deals with the problems of many people.

- *Anxiousness to Complete a Project:* A person may have undertaken (or been assigned) a large project which he would like to have behind him. In the case where there is a deadline, his uncertainty about finishing in time can add to his tension. Some examples of people who are vulnerable to this type of tension are people who plan events, and those who are writing term papers.

- *Hyper-Concern for Success:* A person can be so concerned about a project that his stomach gets tied in knots. He probably exaggerates the possibility of failure or the seriousness of the issue. Sometimes he doesn't give the project that much importance on an intellectual level, yet he finds that emotionally it is hard for him to relax, feeling compelled to succeed.

   When in this mode, a person may not exert himself to succeed much more than otherwise; to the contrary — this form of tension makes a person freeze up, and makes preparation even more difficult. It can ruin his appetite, cause sleepless nights, and make his overall disposition rather unpleasant. Prime candidates for this form of tension are students before a test, applicants before an interview, or speakers/actors before a public performance.

- *Hyper-Concern About Decisions:* Whenever a person has more than one option, he can become confused. Since the most productive choice is not always clear, coming to a decision can become a real challenge. It is very probable that his decision will not be the ideal option. Feeling anxious (stress) when making such types of decisions indicates a lack of willingness to take responsibility for producing anything less than "the best." This concern can often have a paralyzing effect, especially in older bachelors.

COMPENSATING FOR A LACK OF HEALTHY RESPONSIBILITY

The previous list discussed types of tension whose common thread was an exaggerated sense of responsibility. A person suffering from those forms of tension would usually want to rid himself of such feelings. There are, however, times when some people actually summon up tension from within themselves to serve a particular purpose. In this mode, a person uses the serious way in which he relates to responsibility for a distinct function. This can happen in two areas:

- *The Need to Prove "I Care":* A person may want to attribute more importance to some issue than he really feels. He may suspect, beneath the surface, that if he weren't to exhibit signs of stress — especially when his projects don't proceed according to plan — it would amount to a declaration of apathy. In such a situation, he uses the tension as a performance for his own or others' sake to convince them (or himself) that he attributes great personal importance to the issue.

- *Stress, the Motivator:* Whenever we approach a task, we need to evaluate the benefit that comes with completion of the project. When we do that, we activate our feelings of responsibility and joy about working to bring the plan to fruition. If those good feelings are absent, we may lack the motivation to fulfill our responsibilities. Accordingly, we may wind up trying to over-compensate with feelings of accountability and seriousness that force us to get the job done.

Both of these motives reflect a lack of a more natural sense of care, interest, and concern. We then invite tension to substitute for more healthy forms of concern or motivation. In essence, though, we allow ourselves to be weighed down by lead-like feelings of duty (in excess of what is needed to get us to work) and the stress is an unnecessary and unwanted addition to the situation.

Even after pointing out the various conditions that lead to stress, we need to understand what makes us susceptible to those conditions in the first place. In the case of unrealistic expectations, what makes us minimize the need to put in effort? Why are we so keen on quality results, produced quickly? In the case of an unhealthy approach to responsibility, why do we overemphasize our own control over the outcome? What follows are some underlying factors that promote the attitudes described above.

Deeper Causes of Tension

In this section, we will explore the *underlying factors* that create the previously mentioned distorted perspectives. What brings a person to be overly concerned about his responsibilities? What leads him to be overly focused on and concerned about the expected results? Why would a person resort to invoking and using feelings of tension? We'll list the factors briefly here; the next section will include an in-depth explanation of each factor.

- *Insufficient Understanding:* A person might not understand the purpose of investing effort and overcoming challenges. Similarly, he doesn't understand why immediate and gratifying results aren't always forthcoming. Since he doesn't understand the benefits of a challenge, he experiences internal resistance.
- *Insufficient Awareness:* He doesn't recognize to what extent it is necessary — universally — to put in very real effort, and how common it is to get stuck in difficulties. Similarly, he is unaware that even after making suitable attempts, the results are often not as good as what was expected. He then expresses his refusal to accept a situation that, in his opinion, "didn't have to happen."
- *Preoccupation with the Opinions of Others:* It is extremely important to him that others see him always attaining impressive results. It might be important to him that others perceive him as efficient and capable of producing good results quickly — that he be known as a serious, diligent worker. Or, he may want others to view him as a kind of magician, capable of producing spectacular results without appearing to expend much effort. It is difficult for him to make peace with the

possibility of not impressing others as he would like, and certainly that others may bear witness to his failure.

Since the opinion of others is so important to him, he may drive himself to invest more energy than he really can or ought to in the project.

♦ *Preoccupation with Self-Image:* A person may interpret the presence of obstacles, or results that are less than what he expected, to be proof of low self-worth. In his mind, if he were "okay," he wouldn't have trouble making decisions or find himself stuck while trying to actualize either a simple or significant goal. It is as though the existence of the problem itself proves that he isn't equipped to handle that job or any other — and that he isn't a good enough person to be worthy of Hashem's assistance. Obviously, no one really wants to reach those conclusions, so he expresses resistance to this unexpressed judgment with tension.

♦ *Egocentricity:* Hidden beneath these four points is subtle self-centeredness. It becomes difficult for a person to deal with conditions that don't conform to his desires or plan, and this leads to impatience and unhappiness.

If a person weren't to some degree egocentric, the fact that he didn't understand the purpose of his challenges wouldn't impel him to rebel against his situation. He wouldn't be so disturbed when the process took more time or effort than he had anticipated, and it wouldn't grate on him if others didn't seem to be impressed by his achievements. He would not be so sensitive to an issue that he would consider it an overall indictment on his value as a person.

He may be unaware of it, but he nevertheless assumes that he deserves a tranquil life free of disturbances — and even glowing success in every endeavor. When this doesn't happen, he loses his equanimity, and begins to rebel against his situation. If he is prepared to accept some setbacks, fine; if not, anxiety engulfs him.

Sometimes, the other attributes of his personality contribute to his feelings of tension. A finicky person will be overly sensitive to difficulties; if a person is tired, it can be harder for him to deal with problems. The fiery personality has a greater than average need to see immediate results. When a person's overall attitude makes obstacles more of an annoyance, he is that much closer to frustration and tension. The degree to which a person is influenced by egoism will determine how difficult it will be to transcend his natural tendencies so that he can maintain equanimity even under stressful conditions.

- *Insufficient Faith and Trust in Hashem:* Unrealistic expectations and unhealthy attitudes about responsibility usually involve insufficient faith and trust in Hashem. If a person were to believe that Hashem arranges everything for our ultimate benefit, he would do whatever he could and rely on Hashem to direct his efforts to produce the best possible results. He wouldn't take the apparent quality of the results or the presence of obstacles to heart, since he knows that they are created by the Will of Hashem.
- *Insufficient Appreciation of Good Deeds:* A person may want to value the good that he does, but finds that it doesn't come naturally. When that is the case, he may attempt to force himself to feel concerned, as if pressure will convince him or others that he really does value and care about what he is doing.

Alternatively, a person may realize that some action needs to be taken, but since he doesn't have a natural appreciation for the task, he won't have sufficient motivation to complete it. He might then use tension (even without being aware of it) as a means to jump-start himself to tackle what needs to be done.

Everyday examples of these tendencies can be found in appendix B, at the end of this volume.

Exploring Deeper Causes of Tension

Now that we have listed the underlying factors briefly, we can examine each one of the points in depth, along with its effects on unhealthy expectations and approaches to responsibility. Subheadings will indicate if the discussion refers to expectations, responsibilities, or both. With this deeper understanding, we can learn how to recognize a tense response and prevent its occurrence.

INSUFFICIENT UNDERSTANDING
Expectations

A person may have aspirations, yet feel unable to accept that he will have to work a bit for them. "Maybe there are goals to work toward," he says to himself, "but why isn't it easier or less time-consuming to attain them?" By resisting the need to invest energy in a project, the whole enterprise becomes that much more tension-provoking. Without accepting the need to overcome difficulties, a vicious cycle can set in: His resistance to the situation causes tense feelings. In this tense state, the person is prone to further exaggerate difficulties, and that exaggeration can intensify his resistance to dealing properly with those difficulties. This resistance can lead a person to feel even more tense. His momentum could continue in a rhythm which clashes with the natural flow of energy which he would otherwise direct into a the general success of the project. This friction between positive energy flow and resistance creates yet another source of tension. (See figure 1.)

POSITIVE ENERGY FLOW
AND TENSION CYCLE

Figure 2a

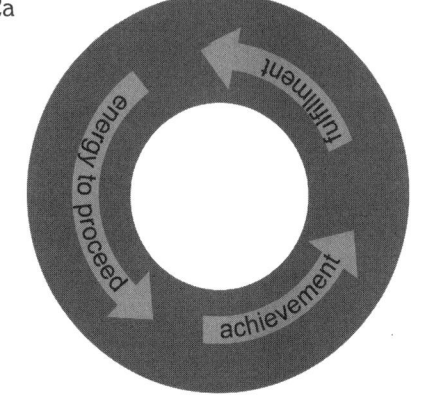

This diagram shows the natural Positive Energy Flow of a person in a healthy frame of mind. He uses his energy to achieve his goals, which leads to a sense of fulfillment. This fulfillment creates new positive energy — and that feeds his efforts further, helping him even more. Thus the positive energy flow drives itself and creates new, constructive energy.

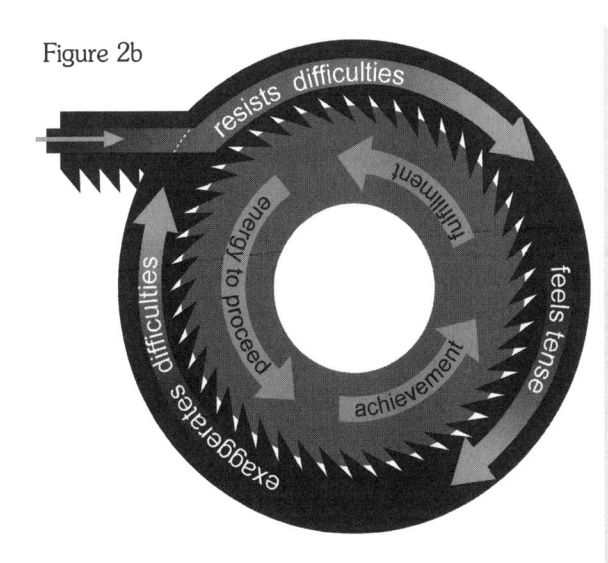

Figure 2b

This expanded diagram illustrates the Tension Cycle, represented by the outer circle. A person usually encounters difficulties in his path. If he resists those difficulties instead of accepting them and taking time to deal with them, he generates tension. In this mindset, he will resist difficulties even more. Thus the tension cycle continues to produce more and more tension. Furthermore, tension abrades the flow of positive energy (represented here by the inner circle), restricting its flow.

It is important for us to be aware that the Jewish world-view includes a vision of effort as an end in itself, not merely as a means to achieve some outcome. Our efforts have value, even if we don't achieve anything. This importance placed on effort could explain why we find few worthwhile goals in this world that do not demand an investment of energy.

Once we recognize the inherent value of our efforts, we won't resist the time and energy it takes to pursue our goals, and we won't get frustrated when we encounter obstacles. We will begin to uproot the Tension Cycle, thereby freeing our natural positive energy, and giving us the ability to overcome obstacles and achieve our goals in a tranquil frame of mind.

We were placed in this world to serve our Creator with our deeds — and to be actively involved in our own inner perfection and character development. In this way we make ourselves worthy of cleaving to our Creator in this world and basking blissfully in His Presence in the World to Come.[10]

When we consider serving Hashem with our performance of *mitzvos*, it is relatively easy to see the value of the effort itself: the more intense the effort we invest, the more we express and actualize our desire to serve Him properly. When it comes to serving Hashem by improving our inner selves, however, some people think that all that matters is the final product, and they ascribe little significance to the very effort that gets them there.

We were not put into this world to pick perfection off a tree; if that were the case, we could have entered a world devoid of challenges and free of the allure of evil. Hashem placed us in this world of challenge so that we would, through our own efforts, become partners in our own creation by developing what is best within ourselves. The only good that can really be called ours is that which we've sweated over — it is "Called by [our] name."[11] Whatever merits we have are precious to us because we worked for them and did not just happen upon them.[12]

The Chofetz Chayim addresses the question "Could He not have arranged matters so that man could earn the merit of *mitzvos* and Torah study in the upper worlds?" He concludes:

> *The reward for mitzvos is earned by the toil and challenge that a person experiences in carrying them out. If a person were to be stripped of his physical aspect and become a totally spiritual being, he would undoubtedly recognize the glory of Hashem and the awe He instills in all His creations, and it would be no challenge for him to do what is good.*[13]

Many statements of our Sages[14] point to a related principle, reiterated by many of our greatest luminaries throughout the generations: that the effort is primary, not necessarily the results.[15] The following mishnah sums it up well:

> *The reward is commensurate with the pain.*[16]

We tend to be concerned with our final accomplishments. Nevertheless, what we do and how we act along the way are factors that are no less significant. The effort is what Hashem values most and wants from us. Appreciating the value of that effort and investing it happily is the key to attaining true virtue.[17]

Many simple acts that we do routinely in the course of our day are genuine *ma'asim tovim*, good deeds, that, slowly but surely, implant within us elements of spiritual wholeness. Every positive act helps us to acquire a stronger foothold in some good quality.[18] The husband and father who works an honest job is caring for his family's needs as he makes his contribution to society. The wife and mother who lovingly takes care of her home and her family nurtures them emotionally and spiritually; she tends to the miniature sanctuary for which she is responsible. It is vital that we appreciate the value of all the effort we invest into these and other similar activities.

Furthermore, it is reasonable to believe that our achievements will endure only when proper efforts have been invested in a project.[19]

> A wealthy businessman once wanted to build a sixty-story office building. He published a bid notice offering excellent payment to the building contractor who would commit himself to complete the construction within a year. The advertisement also stipulated, however, that if the deadline was not met, a steep penalty would be imposed for every week of delay.
>
> For weeks, the businessman received no bids; no builder wanted to undertake the project and risk incurring such heavy fines. Finally, one daring, energetic contractor presented a bid. The deal was closed and the contract signed.
>
> The businessman sat in his office, feeling pleased, and began calculating the rate at which the construction would have to proceed. "It's a matter of simple arithmetic," he thought. "To build sixty stories in a year, the contractor will have to put up five stories a month, or a little more than one floor a week."
>
> At the end of two weeks, the businessman visited the building site to see at least the first two and a half stories. To his chagrin, he found only a deep pit in the ground. He returned a week later and saw that the huge pit was even deeper. Puzzled and annoyed, he called up the contractor and demanded, "Are you building me an office building or a bomb shelter?"
>
> The contractor patiently explained, "If you don't want your building to collapse, you have to begin with a deep, solid foundation. It's no trick to throw a building up quickly. The trick is to build it so it will last. If you want your office building to stand for years and years, you have to build it properly, step by step. And the first step is to dig down deep and lay a proper foundation."

The same can be said of us — if we want to "build" ourselves, develop our abilities, and improve our *middos*, we must begin by laying a strong foundation. For those changes to last, they must stand on the solid base of our willingness to weather the storms that are part of the process of initial change and later maintenance. To review, putting in effort:

- makes the achievement truly yours;
- is rewarded (especially when done willingly);
- means the best chance at lasting success!

This story from *Bava Metzia* illustrates the point:

> *Rabbi Chiya acted to ensure that Torah would not be forgotten by the people of Israel. Rabbi Chiya planted flax, wove nets, and caught deer. He fed their meat to orphans, made their skin into parchment, and wrote on them the five books of the Torah. Then he went to a town where there were no teachers. He taught each of five children a different one of the five books. Then he taught each of six children a different one of the six sections of the Mishnah. He told them, "Until I return, teach one another."*[20]

It may seem to us that Rabbi Chiya went to a lot of unnecessary trouble. Why didn't he simply teach Torah to these children, without spending so much time on all the preliminaries? The Maharsha explains that Rabbi Chiya wanted to make certain that all the preparatory steps were done for the sake of Heaven; he believed that pure motives were necessary from the very start.

The Ben Yehoyada says that Rabbi Chiya behaved this way because, when it comes to the teaching of Torah, it is crucial to invest effort in every step of the process and not settle for shortcuts. To take it further — if we appreciate that the task at hand is of great, or even eternal, significance, we will be willing to exert ourselves at every stage.

In most situations, our job is not to seek out the longest, most difficult route. When, however, the task at hand demands effort, we should appreciate its temporal as well as its eternal value. The minutiae of keeping a home, raising children, or any other noble pursuit are opportunities to reflect on the importance of the tiniest cog in the grandest design.

Work also has its own, intrinsic value.[21] Being active not only contributes greatly to our physical and emotional health — it has spiritual benefits, as well. Since we are meant to take care of our physical needs, the effort we invest in every constructive material pursuit has spiritual significance, too.[22] Beyond that, the hard work and difficulties that are part and parcel of reaching a goal are sometimes meant to be a *kaparah*, a divinely sent means of atonement.[23]

We see, then, the important role that our efforts play on the physical, emotional, and spiritual planes. We should expect that, at times, our effort will be required, and when that happens, we should embrace the opportunity — instead of feeling angry and disappointed.

THINK ABOUT IT

HOW DOES THIS EXPLAIN:

◆ why the world was designed in such a way that it takes time to achieve results?

How should my expectations be tempered by my awareness of the need to invest energy?

INSUFFICIENT AWARENESS

Expectations

Disappointment and guilt feelings may stem from the unrealistic expectation that we can get things done and not run into obstacles.[24]

We need to accept and remain aware of the fundamental fact that we are in *this* world, not in the World to Come. The next world is a garden of limitless, spiritual delight. However, duty beckons in this world of action, which is, by its nature, rife with challenges and pitfalls.

Hashem said to the woman, "I shall increase your suffering and your childbearing; with pain shall you bear children...." And to Adam He said, "Since... you ate of the tree from which I commanded you not to eat... by the sweat of your brow shall you eat bread."[25] It is pointless to rail against Hashem's decree, to try to sidestep reality and seek a life devoid of difficulty, pain, and toil — or even delayed results. It is far more helpful to accept our roles in *this world* — which is merely a corridor leading to the next world — with understanding and appreciation, and to rejoice at every opportunity to work for the good and make it our own.

PREOCCUPATION WITH THE OPINIONS OF OTHERS

"Insufficient understanding" and "insufficient awareness" both affect our expectations. When a person doesn't understand that projects aren't easy or done quickly, this can lead to a lack of understanding and unrealistic hopes. On top of that, concern with what others think can have an influence on both our expectations and feelings of responsibility, in slightly different ways.

Expectations

A person who is sensitive to the question "What will they think?" is focused on whether the work he does will be appreciated by others. Those "others" may be specific people or a community; a person's Rav, or his students, the members of his extended family, or his neighbors.

> Leah feels, sometimes justifiably, that her mother-in-law doesn't appreciate her. Whenever she is in the presence of her mother-in-law, she becomes tense, and worries over the negative impression her mother-in-law might have of what she does and how she does it.

Leah's tension is a result of her fear of making a bad impression — and the consequences (real or imagined). She is also tense because she does not know how to behave in a way that would avoid this problem altogether.

Occasionally, a person is plagued by thoughts of "What will they think?" about *everyone*.

> Ya'akov, a decidedly amateur carpenter, has committed himself to building a bookcase. As the project takes shape, his worries grow. It appears as if the final product will only be a mediocre piece of work — it will stand okay, and even hold the books, but it won't be quality craftsmanship. Ya'akov becomes anxious. What can he do to make it more impressive-looking? How will he feel if those who see it don't shower him with compliments? What if they even express their disappointment with his workmanship? All of Ya'akov's anxieties are manifested as tension that can be felt by anyone who comes upon him while he is working on the bookcase.

At times, a person is capable of dismissing his accomplishments, since they don't measure up to the success he had hoped for. He may even get overwrought beforehand, and obsess about imagined reactions to an outcome that, most likely, will never exist!

> Rachel is busy preparing for a *seudas mitzvah*. Even though most of the dishes are already finished, she is still extremely anxious about the coming reaction of her guests and the success of the affair.

Although Rachel really has no reason to worry, she is still plagued with anxieties over any, even the most minute, possibility of failure.

There are various reasons why a person may be prone to ask himself, "What will they think?" He might not know how to focus on the real value of what he is doing. If he doesn't enjoy his task all that much, and doesn't value it, but decides to stick with it anyway — he will need to find some rationale for continuing. It will be easier for him to keep at his task if others appreciate him for it. In other words, if a person doesn't derive genuine, inner fulfillment from what he does, he will be forced to seek out some superficial and external source of gratification.[26]

Sometimes, a person suffers from a low self-image, and his attempts to make others appreciate him are really a way of seeking support. Clearly, it would be preferable that he build himself up by working on finding fulfillment in what he does instead of relying on the compliments that he receives, or the impression he believes he's making.[27]

At times, arrogance plays a part in bringing a person to seek respect from those around him.

The bottom line is, though, that a person gradually frees himself of the tension that comes from that question "What will they think?" by focusing more on the essential good that he is doing, and less on the reactions of others.

THINK ABOUT IT

WHY DO PEOPLE GET TENSE ABOUT:

♦ the quality of results?
♦ the time it takes to produce them?

How does what I've read help me to modify my expectations?

Responsibility

When a person is about to embark on a new project, he needs to determine just what is included in his objective, to estimate how much time and energy needs to be invested, etc. He must assess what is involved and prioritize the other elements of his life in relation to the project. How much time or money will he divert from some other use to complete the job ahead of him? What areas of his life are sacrosanct and can't be infringed upon at all, and what concerns is he willing to shelve minimally?

> During the preparations for a cousin's *sheva berachos*, Mrs. Green announced to her family that for three days she will "...*not* be available to cook and serve hot meals or help the children with homework."

Should Mrs. Green have settled on a less elaborate affair so as not to sacrifice hot meals for her family? What about helping any or all of the children with their homework?

Here, the decision is not too crucial; to have settled for a simpler affair would not have been any great tragedy — and the children could have, most likely, made do without hot meals or assistance with their work for just a few days. What interests us here is, on what basis did Mrs. Green draw her conclusions? Did she compare how important an elegant meal would be to the *chosson* and *kallah* (and the guests) with how important hot meals and help would be for the children?

Chances are that Mrs. Green's main motivation was that she expected that a change in schedule and her anticipation of a social event would be a nice change in her routine and have a pleasant effect on her. But if she is preoccupied with the desire to impress other people, needing to make the best impression, she might commit herself to responsibilities that are really beyond her. Her flurry of preparations might not put her in the pleasant state she anticipated.

In different situations, a person's concern to make a good impression may cause him to abandon high-priority tasks in order to devote more of his resources to rescue the job at hand. The impossible desire to work "full steam ahead" on both projects will invariably cause stress. Worse still, he may become so deeply absorbed in the task (for instance, while preparing for tests, on *erev Pesach*, etc.) that he sacrifices his own, basic needs — like taking the time to eat healthfully, sleep, or take a walk for a breath of fresh air.

Everyone needs to make an honest assessment of his decisions — especially those that concern allocating his personal resources. When making these types of decisions, keep in mind that it's impossible to do everything at once, and there are always bound to be people that remain unsatisfied. For example, in the case of Mrs. Green, in order to counterbalance her desire to make a good impression, she could have taken equally into account the importance of the atmosphere of the banquet itself — would she be happy, relaxed, and conscious of each and every guest and their needs?

When we focus on the intrinsic value of what we are doing, we can avoid getting tense about impressing people, and save ourselves from accepting responsibility for that which is beyond our ability to handle.

THINK ABOUT IT

WHY DO PEOPLE TENSE UP AND:

◆ overexert themselves to succeed?

◆ get bogged down when making decisions?

How might what you've read contribute to a more wholesome sense of responsibility?

PREOCCUPATION WITH SELF-IMAGE

Every single Jew wants to be good and act appropriately.[28] Notwithstanding attempts to choose the best course of action — the straight path — a person will find it difficult to determine if all his choices and attempts have really succeeded. The healthy person is capable of carrying on a constant balancing-act: "A person should always see himself as though he is half guilty and half innocent."[29] On one hand, he should never see himself as wicked,[30] and on the other, he should never be too sure of himself.[31] When a person acts with the right intentions; when he finds fulfillment in the good that he does; and if he has a connection with a rabbi and G-d-fearing friends that are open and trustworthy and offer him direction — a healthy balance comes naturally. He appreciates his abilities, disposition, and good deeds,[32] which gives him a general feeling of self-worth. Yet he remains constantly aware of the need for introspection and internal accounting, to ascertain whether he is still moving in the right direction.[33]

In our generation, however, most people are lacking in the areas of intention and fulfillment and so find themselves in need of a substitute. People feel that it's necessary to *prove* that they are "worth something."

Expectations

One way that a person evaluates himself is by making comparisons with others. He examines himself and compares his achievements to those of other people. He may make comparisons in many different areas, including: activities, abilities, Torah learning, *yiras Shamayim*, and character development. It's natural for a person to feel at ease and pleased when he reaches the conclusion that he is better than average in some area. He reasons that if he is better than others, he must have worth. If he is, instead, sub-average in some field that is important to him, he feels disappointed in himself.

Disappointment which results from comparing can sometimes be useful, as our Sages say, "Jealousy among the learned increases wisdom."[34] When a school teacher sees that a colleague is more successful, he may learn that he, himself, is not dedicated enough, not investing enough of himself. He then exerts more energy because he doesn't want to remain with a feeling of not being "okay." Not that he expects everyone to notice — but he wants to feel better about himself.

Light As an Eagle

The tendency to want to approach or even surpass the achievements of another person can be an excellent motivating tool. However, as we see in the Mishnah, when this tendency runs amok, it can have disastrous results...

> Originally, anyone who wanted to volunteer for the Altar service would volunteer. When the number of kohanim was excessive, those who wanted to serve would run up the ramp and whoever outpaced his friend by four amos won the privilege. Once, two kohanim were racing neck and neck and one pushed the other so that he fell and broke his leg. When the court saw that the competition was dangerous, they decreed that volunteers would be selected by drawing lots.[35]

The Talmud relates a prior incident that is even more disturbing: "There were once two *kohanim* that were racing up the ramp.... When one entered the four *amos* of his friend, he took out a knife and stabbed him in the heart...."[36] (The court, however, only changed the system when they saw the problem was a recurring one instead of the isolated act of a troubled person.)

When a person is tensely absorbed in his task, even the elevated aspiration to serve in the Beis HaMikdash and surpass his friend spiritually can lead a person to the depths of depravity.

With this, we can better appreciate the words of Rabbi Yechezkel Levenstein, *ztz"l*:

> The aspiration to be like others is a force of human nature, and it is necessary for advancement in Torah — as it says, "Jealousy among scribes increases wisdom." This, however, should only be the first push for advancement. Its power should impel a person to a greater, inner recognition of the importance of the learning. Certainly, remaining at the level of "jealousy among scribes" is not the right path.[37]

This leads us into the subject of competition among students (and even among adults). Examinations are known to be a cause of stress. We practically grant grades the power to measure personality. "What did I get compared to the others?" and "How many students got a higher grade than I did?" becomes another way of asking, "Am I as good or better than the others?"

On the one hand, it's easy to see the benefit of that kind of stress. Those students that lack self-motivation for schoolwork feel compelled to learn and know the material. On the other hand, too much stress can cause psychological damage. Even worse, the student may begin to judge his entire self-worth (and the worth of others) based on grades. Too much emphasis on "making the grade" can force a student to measure up in terms of available units of memory, and not as a human being. This distorted way of judging students can, unjustifiably, undercut their self-esteem. Ultimately, it becomes difficult for the student to learn for the sheer pleasure of it, and the entire enterprise becomes a competition. It isn't even necessarily the case that the student is seeking honor when he shows off a great mark — more likely, he needs it to bolster his flagging self-respect.

Clearly the "competition game" isn't restricted to students and exams. Adults compare everything — their status, homes, and behavior — with others. Often, the real motive for the extension of courtesies and kindness doesn't stem from caring, value, or love for others. It comes, instead, from the desire to be seen as no less of a "mensch" than anyone else. Shlomo HaMelech complained about this, long ago:

> "I, myself, have seen all the effort and ability to act" — *even those good and worthy acts that are done for ulterior motives*[38] — *"for it is"* — *originates from* — *"interpersonal jealousy..."* — *that he wants to lord it over his friend and not have inferior accommodations, clothing, children, food, wisdom, or reputation*[39] — *"this, too, is vanity and breaks the spirit."*[40]

The results: action is taken without the right intention, the quality of interpersonal relations plummets, and tension builds in a competition that has few winners.

For these reasons, it is crucial that a person learns to act for the right reasons and feel fulfillment from what he does — that way, he can attain real self-worth and will no longer feel the need to rely on comparisons with others.

Another way that people tend to evaluate whether or not they're behaving properly is by focusing on the outcome of their deeds. When the results have been good, they feel encouraged that they're moving in the right direction. If, however, the results have been less than ideal, they mistakenly interpret failure as an accusation against them. In *"Sha'ar HaBitachon"* of the *Chovos HaLevavos*, this phenomena is discussed at length. The author concludes that our job is simply to make active efforts; afterward, when the task is no longer in our hands, we need to trust that Hashem will manipulate the outcome to serve the best possible purpose.

> Devora loves to babysit. Once, while she was watching the neighbor's children, she decided that since she knows the children well, she would try to teach them a new game. They couldn't grasp how to play, and Devora felt like a failure.
>
> Dovid didn't feel that, from a practical point of view, his success on a certain exam was all that important. Even so, he took failure to heart, since he felt that it would prove his inadequacy.

Like Dovid, Devora also wasn't all that concerned whether or not the neighbor's children picked up her game — what bothered her was how she interpreted that failure. She saw it as an indicator that she lacked a talent for teaching or engaging the children.

As a result of the difficulties they experience in trying to reach their goal (or if the results are poor or slow in coming), some people arrive at the mistaken conclusion that they are inadequate. If they want to avoid such a conclusion, they fight the difficulty, as though they are angry that it exists. This resistance can make a person extremely tense.

Although obstacles are a normal part of life, some people think that they shouldn't happen (at least not to *them*). When some difficulty does come up, they see it as a reflection of their imperfections. The way they see it, a person is "no good" if on a particular day things didn't go his way. He feels that failing to progress in a certain project as quickly as anticipated, the myriad challenges of child rearing, and even minor mishaps like a broken plate in the kitchen, are all personal judgments against him.

When we appreciate the inherent value of our efforts, then even if we do not achieve the results we had hoped for, we can feel free from apprehension about the outcome of our projects. Our approach should be to make our best effort to be decent human beings. We should focus on doing what is right as we do the Will of our Creator, and ask Him to bless us with success if it conforms to what He knows is truly best for us.[41]

People who suffer from either an inflated or poor self-image are especially vulnerable to this type of tension. Someone who suffers from an exaggerated sense of self-importance believes he can do everything, perfectly. Since any trace of imperfection is devastating to his ego, he will fight passionately against anything that points to his fallibility.

On the other hand, if a person already suffers from a poor self-image, any setback in life will only reinforce his conviction that he is incompetent, a born failure.[42] Whatever the circumstance, if we keep in mind that we are human beings and not angels, we will be able to set reasonable goals and avoid this source of tension.

When we approach our tasks with the right intention, with a feeling of joy and fulfillment, we save ourselves from the need to find superficial proof of our value.

THINK ABOUT IT

WHY DO WE BECOME TENSE ABOUT:

♦ the quality of results?
♦ the time it takes to produce them?

How does what's written above help us modify our expectations?

Responsibility

Likewise, a person may feel as though he's "no good" if he doesn't invest the time or energy required to produce better or faster results. This includes the student who develops an overly serious attitude to preparing for examinations. That it is possible to use a little tension to approach exams more diligently doesn't justify putting himself under stress and overdrawing on his physical or psychological reserves.

A person must be particularly careful when he is involved in a project that extends over a long period of time — such as dealing with illness, learning for *semichah*, publishing a book, or collecting funds to pay off debts or make a wedding. At times, the scope of the project and the period that it is in are unlimited, for example: dedicating oneself to continuously learn or help out in the community beyond his physical capacities, or the one who is responsible for communal affairs and is dedicated to a degree that is beyond his capability. Such people are likely to be in situations of long-term stress that can cause them to become impatient, damage their personalities, and provoke them to make unrealistic demands on others. Additionally, it can lead to "burnout" and its symptoms: resistance to the daily schedule and even exhaustion. If a person is particularly sensitive, and if there is substantial cause for disappointment, he may show the first signs of chronic fatigue, which can manifest as a physical illness (like mononucleosis) or a psychological breakdown.

Therefore, anyone who commits himself to large responsibilities like the ones just mentioned should try to identify his possible motivations, and whether he is pushing himself too hard. He should concern himself with the joy and fulfillment of his objective, and work on establishing a balanced daily schedule (as discussed at the end of the chapter).

An additional aspect of an unbalanced approach to responsibility is perfectionism, and it will be discussed at length in volume 2, chapter 4.

> **THINK ABOUT IT**
>
> **HOW DOES THIS EXPLAIN WHY WE BECOME TENSE AND:**
> ♦ overexert ourselves to succeed?
> ♦ get bogged down making decisions?
>
> How can what you've read contribute to a more wholesome sense of responsibility?

EGOCENTRICITY
Expectations and Responsibility

When a person suffers from egoism, he finds it difficult to deal with things that contradict his will or aren't in alignment with his plans. This affects both his expectations and his attitude toward responsibility in a similar way. Without being aware of it, he assumes that an *easy* life crowned with stunning successes and free from all problems is "coming to him." If this doesn't work out, he loses his equanimity and begins to complain and rebel against the situation. Any time that things don't go his way, or he has to put in effort, or the results aren't as good as he wants them to be, he makes a point of venting his bitterness and frustration.

When a person sets a goal for himself, he may want to get there immediately. If it takes time, he may become tense. Let's look at this cycle at work.

> Sam has ordered new furniture — and he wants it without delay.
>
> Shira awaits a positive answer about a suggested *shidduch* — and she wants to hear from the *shadchan* on the double!
>
> Martin has invested money in a promising venture — and he wants to see profits *now*.
>
> Elissa sends off a letter — and she wants a reply *yesterday*.
>
> Chayim takes steps to improve a relationship — and he wants to see a change then and there, not next month.

They've each set a deadline for their goal, and every passing day beyond it causes them tension.

This "no sooner said than done" attitude can make a person so impatient that he becomes tense even over trivial matters. It is hard for him to cope with the idea that his needs aren't being met instantly, that others don't just drop everything to attend to him, and that the world at large doesn't revolve around his concerns. He can become so impatient that the slightest setbacks spark an exaggerated response — and even merely unpleasant situations make him tense.

> A father asks his child a question and doesn't get an immediate answer.
>
> A mother is about to go out to a wedding and leaves a baby intercom with a neighbor. As she makes her way out the door, the baby wakes up, and she must go back to attend to him.
>
> A teenager is trying to write a long-overdue letter to a friend, and her little sister interrupts her twice with the same, inane question.

The more trapped a person is by the influence of his ego, the more easily he can be shaken by trivial disturbances, and the more exaggerated his tense response will be.

When we get impatient about our spiritual projects, we can also be drawn into harmful tension. A strongly negative response to a spiritual setback can actually be an indicator of tension and egocentricity. Whether our goals are in the emotional or spiritual realms, the possibility always exists that the project will take longer than we estimate. Growth can never be forced by taking quick leaps while under pressure. Such leaps are difficult and draining, and the person who insists on trying to progress in this way is likely to fall or get "burned-out" in the process. Progress in gradual, more reasonable steps is easier and more likely to have the lasting, positive effects that all of us hope for.

Our Sages understood that the education of children is a process that spans many years, with much work to be invested all along the way. Even so, many parents want to see their child transform into a person of talent and sterling character, functioning almost like an adult, when he is hardly out of kindergarten. This kind of impatience can cause serious emotional damage and should be avoided — especially with firstborn children.

In general, the influence of the ego can blind a person so that it becomes difficult to see any perspective other than his own. He is less likely to make the effort to transcend his unique character traits that contribute to tension; his many needs feel intense and have a profound influence on his expectations of himself and his attitude toward responsibility. Since his self is at the epicenter of his world view, every situation becomes a forum for meeting those needs — even if it involves unreasonable expectations, or taking on more than he can handle.[43]

Conversely, when a person isn't caught up with his own needs, it becomes easier to maintain a healthy perspective of the demands of the moment. Furthermore, when a person accustoms himself to remain unfazed by a challenge, his tendency to egocentricity is weakened. A positive momentum develops, and the process of patiently accepting challenges becomes that much easier.

> **THINK ABOUT IT**
>
> **WHY DO WE GET TENSE ABOUT:**
> - energy investment?
> - the quality of the results?
> - how long it takes to produce them?
>
> How might what you've read contribute to a more wholesome sense of responsibility?

INSUFFICIENT FAITH AND TRUST IN HASHEM
Expectations and Responsibility

Due to the importance of this subject, a brief treatment really doesn't suffice. Therefore, the beginning of volume 5 has been devoted to the issue, along with the subject of equanimity and patience.

There is, nonetheless, a point that should be discussed here.

Job interviews and first dates (among other things) are usually catalysts of intense, although temporary, anxiety. If a person is seriously interested in that job or in that *shidduch*, he is likely to feel nervous because it is possible that he may not get what he was hoping for. He may also fear having to deal with the unpleasantness of rejection.

In such situations, it is important to keep in mind that all that is required of us is to make *our* best effort, and not measure that effort by comparing it to what others can do. The rest is in Hashem's Hands. Tension and nervousness about the response from the opposite side will not help and are likely to only get in the way.

Furthermore, can we really know that the job or the suggested match is right for us? Can we be sure that a positive response would be to our benefit in the long run? We need to learn to trust in Hashem and rely only on Him to make sure that the matter at hand will conclude in the best way possible, whether that means that the response is "yes" or "no."

Even when our undertaking is a spiritual one, we must avoid a sense of tension about the results we get, remembering that "It is the same whether one accomplishes much or little, as long as his heart is directed Heavenward."[44]

Faith and trust in Hashem instills equanimity, so that we can be powerfully motivated to meet our challenges, yet remain joyful and relaxed all the while.

> **THINK ABOUT IT**
>
> **HOW DOES THIS EXPLAIN WHY WE MAY:**
>
> ◆ overexert ourselves to succeed?
> ◆ be overly concerned about the decisions we make?
>
> How might what's written above modify our expectations?
>
> How might it contribute to a more wholesome sense of responsibility?

INSUFFICIENT APPRECIATION OF GOOD DEEDS
Responsibility

A healthy person fulfills his responsibilities and does good deeds out of self-discipline and personal motivation. On the one hand, he recognizes the need (and perhaps the obligation) to act; in a spirit of responsibility and decisiveness, he applies himself to his mission. On the other hand, he sees the good and positive effect of the task before him, and so he sets out to bring it to fruition filled with determination and joy.

Understandably, a person is not always inspired by the same spectrum of feelings. Some tasks are more pleasurable or we see more value in them. In those cases, our inspiration and interest will be strong enough to carry us through to accomplish the task. Other tasks are less engaging but, nonetheless, need to be tackled. At those times, a person needs to activate a sense of urgency and self-discipline in order to get to work. The nature of the task is not always the factor which determines the degree of motivation. For example, some days are more high-energy than others, so what gets done during those times has an aura of joy and ease to it. Other times, a person may feel more sluggish and "wiped out" and so most of what he does during those times is lackluster and somewhat dry. During such a down period, a person must activate the self-discipline to take care of things that, during better times, he might have done more energetically and joyfully.

These two approaches towards motivation and self-discipline correspond to the attributes of love and fear. A person who acts out of self-discipline is acting out of recognition of (and fear of) the consequences of inaction; a person with inner motivation acts out of love. We fulfill *mitzvos* out of love, desire, and joy, as well as out of fear of punishment and shame-filled unwillingness to disobey the command of the elevated and exalted King — because we are in awe of His Greatness. The *mitzvah* to love Hashem and the *mitzvah* to fear Hashem are always intertwined — a person needs to hold on to both simultaneously.[45]

The Torah also exhorts us to combine the two approaches. Our Sages posit, "One verse says, 'You should love Hashem, your G-d...,'[46] [apparently, one should serve Him from love]. Another says, 'You should fear Hashem, your G-d, and serve Him...'[47] [apparently, one should serve Him from fear]. Do it, then, out of love and do it out of fear."[48]

Most of what we do has some aspect of fulfillment of a *mitzvah* to it. It is fitting, then, that we approach our tasks with enthusiasm and awareness: the enthusiasm of fulfilling the Will of Hashem, and the somber awareness of our obligation to accept the yoke of Hashem's Kingship.[49] Only then can we can act accordingly.

Although we may approach some *mitzvos* with enthusiasm, many of us unfortunately lack a wholesome appreciation for the smaller tasks. Daily chores such as sewing on buttons and dealing with paperwork are necessary in life. Yet they don't seem to be very interesting or meaningful unless we learn to recognize their significance. We also lack a deep, vibrant awareness of the value of the acts of physical, emotional, and spiritual kindness that we do every day for ourselves, our families, and other people around us. Without that awareness, we find many activities uninteresting and unsatisfying, and so find ourselves short of being stimulated to function in a healthy way.

1. One Manifestation — The Use of Stress As a Motivator

A person *does* have to function, after all, and many things must get done in life. So how can he get himself to do what he has to?

To create a drive to function, many people use tension in place of motivation. They develop an exaggerated concern for what might happen if things would not get done. They focus on the "dire consequences" that will ensue if they fail to achieve their goal, and their overplayed fear of a job left undone is the force that propels them to achieve. They cook this tension up and keep it simmering on their back burner to ensure that they will keep on working. Some will even tell you outright, "If I didn't get upset, I wouldn't get anything done." Instead of combining love with fear, they add pressure and stress onto their anxieties.

When a person lacks motivation, but still pushes himself to act, he becomes more sensitive to the discomforts of putting in necessary effort and dealing with obstacles. Also, he is more prone to feel tense about results that are slow to come since he is, anyway, in an unpleasant state of tension and pressure. Aside from all the anxiety and ulcers that it causes (to both the tense person and those who have to live with him!), this form of motivation is not an acceptable way to live our lives in the service of Hashem. The Torah provides a reason for the Jewish people's long, bitter exile: "Because you did not serve Hashem, your God, with joy and good-heartedness amidst your great bounty."[50] We should not be driven to accomplish our tasks and achieve our goals by anxiety and self-made fears. Our sense of responsibility should, instead, be inspired by an appreciation of the full value of the task and its results, and by the desire to do what is right — with joyful enthusiasm.

THINK ABOUT IT

HOW DOES THIS EXPLAIN:

◆ the drawbacks of using stress as a motivator?

How does what you've read contribute to a more wholesome sense of responsibility?

---

2. A Second Manifestation — The Need to Prove "I Care"

When a person who is in touch with himself performs actions superficially, by rote, he feels a kind of emptiness inside. This emptiness is like the sensation of thirst — it indicates his need to add mindfulness and emotion to his life and to make sure that his good deeds are of a high quality. Unfortunately, though, he may not always have a clear picture of how to go about doing these deeds in a more mindful, emotional way. Rather than working, step by step, to build up genuine pleasure and deep appreciation for the good that he does,[51] he instead chooses to act *as though* he possesses these lofty feelings. He tries to convince himself that what he does is valuable, but he doesn't understand or develop in himself a feel for *why* it really is so significant.

An *avreich* would like to learn in a more elevated way, but he doesn't know where to begin. He lacks a model of joyful learning that is inspired by inner pleasure, or perhaps the necessary psychological groundwork hasn't been laid. If he doesn't have the tools to direct himself properly, his attempt to awaken an awareness of the importance of Torah learning may instead activate negative feelings. For example, if his learning is interrupted, he may feel frustrated: "How can it be that these people don't appreciate that I'm learning and are bothering me?" It is also possible that feelings of anger will be aroused and directed at whomever dares to make light of the fact that he is trying to learn.

While it is true that a person should make an attempt to learn with a minimum of interruptions, certainly the loftiness of Torah study isn't actualized by feelings of frustration and anger. Learning at a high level should prove to be full of enthusiasm, joy, and excitement, grounded by a profound grasp of the subject and the reason for learning along with any enjoyment that could come from studying that topic. These feelings are positive; any interruptions should be handled patiently and efficiently. If anyone has a reasonable request that crops up in the middle of learning, it should be dealt with — willingly. If the request is not pressing, the two can discuss it at an appropriate moment. The person who was interrupted can then explain why the middle of learning was not a suitable time to deal with the issue. He can also provide directions for a similar situation in the future. If the children are noisy, he should decide carefully whether he should steer them to a different place or activity, ignore them, or move himself somewhere else. Certainly, though, handling the situation tactfully, without frustration or anger, does not mean that he lacks respect for his learning; on the contrary, it shows he has properly integrated his learning.

In another setting, a woman may not have had a good working model to learn how to relate to her children. It is possible that, in her childhood, she craved, and didn't receive, warmth and understanding. This lack may inspire her to pay special attention to her children, since she feels the need to offer them that which she never had. Basically, this can be an excellent response. Since she never had a good model of parental giving, however, she may, instead, project intensified feelings of worry and overprotectiveness.

It is the duty of every parent to be concerned with the technical aspects of child rearing: teaching children to be careful in dangerous places (like crossing the street), making certain they eat enough, that they dress warmly, etc. The overprotective mother, however, makes such concerns into forced issues by asking about them constantly, and radiating tension when she does. She feels that if she doesn't act this way, she isn't a good mother. Truthfully, she isn't psychologically prepared to unlock her internal treasure-trove of warmth, understanding, and patience. It's as though she remains bottled up, and consoles herself with displays of worry and excessive responsibility.

This same mechanism is noticeably at work among many young couples in the most vulnerable period of their marriages — the first few years after the wedding. Both partners approach marriage with a complete desire to forge a deep connection. Somehow, though, either because there weren't good models, proper guidance, or psychological preparation, instead of letting feelings of love, understanding, and patience flow, they settle into a pattern of overbearing concern or possessiveness. Each spouse displays worry over how the other is acting (when it differs from their experience or expectations), and every mistake takes on global proportions. Somewhere, inside, each believes he is revealing how much he cares by questioning his spouse's behavior. He is shocked to discover that his spouse, instead of being grateful for his concern and constructive comments, responds sharply! This couple has simply allowed worry and anger to fill the vacuum created in the absence of love, understanding, and patience.

In the same way, many of us lack a free-flow of positive emotions, and a void is formed. We'd like to feel that we're filling this void and are expressing care in both our actions and relationships, but we're not in the habit of expressing such rich emotions. Instead, we use tension as a distorted substitute for appreciation and care.

It should be understood, though, that our goal is to be aware of our thought processes to the best of our ability, and to fill our lives and our actions with genuine and rich, meaningful emotions. If we want to stop using worry as a substitute for motivation and avoid excessive displays of concern to prove that we are involved, we need first to be well equipped with inner joy and patience.

THINK ABOUT IT

WHY DO WE GET TENSE ABOUT:

◆ our need to prove "I care"?

How might what you've read contribute to a more wholesome sense of responsibility?

A RELAXED ATMOSPHERE, A BALANCED APPROACH

Thus far, we have identified different types of tension and tried to understand what underlies them. We have also seen how tension fosters a mental state that inhibits success. Now we will examine the nature of tension more closely, seeing how it can encourage failure in other ways, too. As it says in Mishlei:

> "If you see a hasty person, [know that] a fool has more hope [of success] than he." — *Since the fool is aware of his limitations, he rightly seeks counsel from the wise.*[52]

The hasty person is rash to speak, respond, and act. He considers *himself* wise and does not allow for retractions of his impetuous decisions.

It is important to appreciate the difference between vivacity's alacrity and the pressured haste of rashness. The vivacious, energetic person retains his composure; the tense, pressured individual finds it impossible to maintain equilibrium.

So, contrary to what many highly pressured people think, patience and a sense of equanimity are by no means synonymous with apathy and laziness. The former qualities contribute, instead, to the well-balanced attitude that enables us to get things done with minimum errors.

When a person frees himself from tension, he also creates a comfortable atmosphere that encourages the cooperation of others.

"The words of the wise, spoken gently, are heard."[53] We can assume that the subjects on which the wise do comment are important, perhaps even urgent. Still, wise people (precisely because they *are* wise) make their statements gently. They understand how to sweeten the atmosphere so that their words are most likely to be accepted. Fortunately, everyone can be wise in this way. As the Talmud tells us, "A person should say three things in his home *erev Shabbos* before sundown.... And he should say them gently, so that they will be accepted."[54] Although these words concern urgent matters — necessary things that will prevent the violation of Shabbos — the householder is warned that his words should *still* be delivered gently, since that is the only way that they will be accepted.[55]

Days of Love, Days of Hatred

Life has its own emotional ebb and flow, and so there are days that are more conducive to growth and others when growth is more difficult. A cycle of attraction and aversion underlies all matters, both worldly and spiritual. Learning to recognize and take advantage of those times helps growth come more naturally, with minimal stress. Once a person is aware of this subtle mechanism, he can persist in working at almost any challenge. Rabbeinu Tam explores this cycle in depth:

> *Any action that produces pleasure will introduce an initial state of attraction into a person's heart. After a while, this state of attraction fades, and a state of aversion takes its placed.... They continue to interchange in this way....*
>
> *If a person derives great pleasure from his work, however, and has a well-balanced mind, then the state of attraction will last for many days and the state of aversion only a short time.*
>
> *The inverse holds true, too. If a person lacks a balanced disposition, if the work isn't pleasurable, or if the satisfaction it brings is tempered with complications, then the state of aversion will be protracted, and attraction will last just a short while.*
>
> *The introduction of new, positive factors tip the balance of a person's attitude toward attraction, and new, negative factors toward aversion. Without any new variables entering the equation, the situation remains in stasis, until personality factors or the faculty of reason determines the direction of his attitude.*
>
> *A person who wants to work on himself must realize that at the start of his efforts, these states of attraction and aversion compete with each other. At times, one will prevail; at times, the other. He should not be concerned if, at an early stage, he feels repelled by his task, for this is the normal pattern of desire: it stands suspended — only later does it grow again in strength. If the person is aware of this tendency in advance, then when the attraction subsides and the aversion intensifies, he will not be discouraged. He will know that, with time, this phase will pass. If, however, a person isn't attuned to the pleasures of serving his Creator, then the stage of aversion extends, while the days of attraction will dwindle....*[56]

A balanced person eases himself into his work so that his spirit doesn't rebel against the task. If he feels the desire to perform a *mitzvah*, he does it promptly — but if he experiences aversion, he focuses on holding his own until the negative feeling subsides. Some people foolishly set aside their project when a wave of aversion hits them, only to find that later, when they are inspired to pick it up again, they've lost their grip on it, and have to start again from scratch. Rabbeinu Tam continues:

> A wise man, then, when he feels hostility and aversion to his work, should not drop the matter entirely or tell himself, "I will put it aside for now, and get back to it later." If he does that, it will slip from his hand. If, however, he holds onto it, even minimally, it will not be lost....
> I say that a person who wishes to work on himself should start with simple tasks. And if he cannot do them, he should do them partially and add to them as he goes along. If he sees that he is beginning to feel repelled by them, then he should ease off and do them only in part. But he should never drop them entirely....[57]

It is only natural that a person will not be in the same mood all the time; emotions are not consistent. Sometimes we feel more motivated and energetic; at other times, less so. Since emotion is such a central element of a person's character, Rabbeinu Tam advises us to move forward at those times when we feel motivated, but, at times when we feel down, simply to hang on to our level, trying not to fall back but not attempting to press ahead.

Rav Chayim of Volozhin directs us onto a parallel path in his commentary on *Avos*:

> A human being constantly experiences ups and downs. During a down-phase, though, it seems to him as though all of his Torah study and service of Hashem is half-hearted and unsuccessful. At such times, he'd like to rest and sleep it off until he regains his usual alacrity. This is a common experience for those who are familiar with the way of Torah. There is a fallacy to this mentality, [since] the person who holds on, even in a weak way, finds it simple to get back to his original level afterward. The one who avoids learning at all then has a much harder time getting his energy back, since he has distanced himself from the Torah.[58]

Here, too, we see how common the approach built around an understanding of spiritual ups and downs is, and how important it is just to hold our own during the down-phase of the cycle. We are rewarded for holding our ground during a rough period, since we must work hard to counteract a natural tendency.

We can compare this to a person at the seashore who wades into the water until it reaches up to his neck. Suddenly, the water becomes rougher, and he finds it hard to walk or even keep his balance. How can he get back to shore safely?

If this person keeps his wits about him, he will take advantage of the waves rushing toward the shore and will coast with them. When they recede, he won't strain against them, and risk losing his footing. Instead, he will stand still and plant his feet as firmly as possible in the ocean floor to resist the pull of the undertow. All his energy is concentrated on standing firmly, so that the tide doesn't drag him even further out. Only afterward, when the waves again push toward the shore, does he advance with them.[59] Shlomo HaMelech advises,

> *On a day that goes well, do good deeds, but on a day of adversity, reflect.*[60]

This principle applies not only to our internal ebb and flow, but also to times when we encounter external obstacles. Forcing progress can be a waste of energy when external factors stand in the way. Instead of putting more pressure on ourselves, we should try to pinpoint the problematic factor, get rid of it, or avoid it. Sometimes, though, the solution is simply to bide our time until the next "right moment" comes along. Since "there is no man who does not have his moment,"[61] it doesn't make sense to expend so much energy when failure is likely. With a little patience, we can wait for the right moment and work with it to progress more easily.

> Michael, who had trouble keeping friends, had been told a number of times that his sharp tongue was to blame. He decided to try to go to the other extreme and go out of his way to speak gently and encouragingly to others.
>
> For a day and a half his project was a success. Then he began to feel uneasy inside. To make matters worse, someone made a sarcastic remark to him about his sudden reformation. Since

Michael was determined to change himself, he decided to try to be even nicer. That just didn't seem to work, and he felt ready to throw in the towel.

Michael's teacher noticed that something was going on and called him aside to ask him about it. Michael decided to speak up frankly and found that his teacher had encouraging words to offer. "There are times when the going will be rough. When that happens, don't try to be extra nice. Just acknowledge your negative feelings and allow them to pass on, and try not to be outright nasty. Then, when your mood improves, push a little further ahead with your project."

Michael followed his teacher's advice. After about six months, both he and his friends could hardly believe the change.

Needless to say, we have to be honest with ourselves and not use a bad mood or some external obstacle as a pretext for giving up — even temporarily. We could spend our whole lives excusing ourselves for the same, or similar reasons!

Malka had a closed, timid personality. She even felt too shy to greet anyone except the two friends that she had somehow managed to make. So she decided that every day when she came to school, she would try to greet one other girl. The day after she formulated her plan, Malka got to school late and had to hurry silently into her classroom. Over the following two days she was in a bad mood, and told herself that it wasn't a time to be greeting people.

Malka was disappointed that her project wasn't getting off the ground, though. After a little reflection, she realized that she had been setting up obstacles for herself. On the way to school she had been looking for a reason to be in a bad mood, so that she could avoid taking the difficult step of greeting people. Malka really did want to overcome her timidity, so she decided that on the way to school she would think positively. That way, she would be in a good mood and it would be easier to start her greeting project.

Malka was very pleased with her determination and her progress. She was even more pleased to notice that many of her schoolmates were beginning to relate to her in a friendly, natural way.

A tense person will find it hard to wait patiently until the "days of aversion," or the external obstacles, pass by. His tension itself also compounds his aversion. When a person is relaxed, however, he is capable of making a logical evaluation of his situation to clarify whether it is a time to act, or a time to wait — as Shlomo HaMelech points out, "How good is something in its proper time!"[62] The Meiri comments on this verse:

> Sometimes, a person fails because he is convinced that if he succeeded once in a certain situation, that he'll always succeed. Since every moment is unique, what worked once won't necessarily work again; because time and the variables are always in flux, an approach always needs some readjustment. This is why a person should always consult with the aged — those who have experienced life's challenges — "For wisdom is with the elders."[63]

When a person is ready to wait for the right moment before acting, he will surely enjoy the fruits of success.

THINK ABOUT IT

HOW DOES THIS EXPLAIN WHY WE MAY:

◆ overexert ourselves to succeed?

◆ be overly concerned about the decisions we make?

How might what's written above modify our expectations?

How might it contribute to a more wholesome sense of responsibility?

It Doesn't Pay to Push

The person who is tensely preoccupied with some project may push himself to achieve a goal that is not even appropriate for him. Even if he temporarily achieves that goal, his accomplishment will not endure. Our Sages taught:

> *The Holy One, Blessed be He, created three gifts in this world: wisdom, strength, and wealth. When a person merits one of these, he holds the key to the world's most precious treasures.... When? Only as long as they are gifts of Heaven, coming from the power of Hashem's Glory. But a person's own strength and wealth are worth nothing. This is what Shlomo said: "Once more I saw under the sun that the race is not won by the swift, nor the battle by the strong, nor does bread come to the wise...."[64] These gifts, when they do not come from Hashem, are destined to leave the person....*
>
> *Our Sages taught: Two wise men came into the world, one from the Jewish people and one from the gentiles — Achitofel from the Jewish people and Bila'am from the gentiles — and both of them were lost from this world and from the World to Come.*
>
> *Two mighty people came into the world, one from the Jewish people and one from the gentiles — Shimshon from the Jewish people and Goliath from the gentiles — and both were lost from this world.*
>
> *Two wealthy people came into the world, one from the Jewish people and one from the gentiles — Korach from the Jewish people and Haman from the gentiles — and both were lost from this world. Why? Because their gift did not come from the Holy One, Blessed be He, but they snatched the gift for themselves.*
>
> *So we see, as well, with the tribes of Gad and Reuven, who were very wealthy, had huge herds, and cherished their riches, and therefore settled outside of the Land. For this reason, they were the first of the tribes to go into exile....[65]*

Wisdom is clearly desirable, and a person should certainly strive to acquire it. So, in many cases, are strength and wealth. But if a person tries *too* hard to attain those blessings, and attempts to reach the level beyond what Hashem wants for him at that time, it is as if that person is trying to snatch those blessings without permission. In some cases, he will be allowed to take hold of the thing he is reaching for — but only temporarily. In the end, it slips through his fingers, or — worse still — what should have been a blessing, instead, causes his downfall. Our Sages explain:

> "Whoever presses the moment, the moment presses upon him [and causes him to fail]..." — *this is the one who labors hard at making his*

> *fortune and achieving fame and, though he sees that he is not succeeding, still continues to travel great distances and force himself into higher circles —* "But whoever allows himself to be pushed aside by the moment, the moment awaits him." *— In due time, he will have his successful hour.*[66]

Yet there is another good reason to avoid being sucked into a state of pressure and tension: the anxious striver may fail to evaluate his situation accurately, and may aim for a level beyond what is suitable for him to achieve. Since he has saddled himself with an oversized goal, the pressure he feels only escalates. Deep within, he also may sense that his efforts are fruitless and misdirected. In the end, this unfortunate person will either fail or manage to accomplish the opposite of what he had hoped for.

Although achievement and self-improvement are such important parts of our lives, we should not, for these reasons, push *too* hard to attain our objectives. Instead, we should save ourselves a great deal of tension and heartache, and advance toward our destination step by step. In a state of lightness and tranquility we can move forward without "pressing the moment."

Don't Try To Jump Up the Ladder!

Pushing for oversized goals can be dangerous even when the goal is spiritual. If a person is overly tense and anxious to progress, he is likely to try to circumvent vital steps. Perhaps he will succeed in reaching his goal for the time being, and come to an exalted level in one particular area. He may become a master of abstinence, strictness, even diligence, before the other aspects of his personality have had a chance to keep pace. The outcome is an unbalanced personality, and like any lopsided structure, it is in danger of toppling over.

A famous example of such a person was Ben Zoma.[67] The Talmud describes him as trying to access deeper insights into the Divine than he was worthy of grasping. Because of this, the insights that he did attain were distorted, and he lost his mind. The verse "If you find honey, eat only enough for you, lest you be over-satiated and vomit it out,"[68] is applied to him.[69] Even a food as pure as honey can cause harm if a person eats too much of it. The same is true of the spiritual: a person should not push himself toward higher levels when he is not ready for them.

Similarly, the Vilna Gaon comments on Mishlei:

> "Without knowledge, the spirit is not good..." — *when a person does mitzvos without knowledge, it is not good for the soul because the soul gets no pleasure from them — without knowing the root of an act, it is done without desire* — "and one who is hurried with his feet sins." — *"Feet" signify character traits. When a person accustoms himself to good character traits, they become second nature to him. But one has to advance from one character level to the next, like someone climbing a ladder, and not jump to a rung for which he is not suited. This is the meaning of "hurried with his feet": if someone jumps to an elevated character trait that he does not deserve, he sins and loses everything, since he will fall from there.*[70]

The Torah speaks of a place called *Kivros HaTa'avah*, the "graves of longing."[71] The *Reishis Chochmah* offers an astounding explanation of this name:

> *Every angel who longs to rise beyond its appointed level will cease to exist. This is what is meant by the burial that comes about because of longing.*[72]

We can well imagine that an angel, to whom the brilliance of eternal truth is clear, would desire and yearn to draw as close as possible to its Creator. Even it, however, is obligated to recognize its abilities and its limitations, and if it attempts to effect a closeness that is beyond its level, it will be destroyed.[73]

We must also take note of the words of the Vilna Gaon in his commentary on Mishlei:

> "Wisdom is before the understanding person..." — *the understanding person does not look to jump ahead, but looks to understand what is before him* — "...But the fool's eyes are on the ends of the earth." — *As soon as he starts learning, he sets his eyes on the time when he will finish the whole Talmud or [at least] the tractate.*[74]

The understanding person enjoys the process of learning even more than the prospect of finishing his studies. The fool does not enjoy the learning itself, but only derives pleasure when he has completed what he set out to accomplish — regardless of the quality of his accomplishment.

Again, in spiritual matters, as in material ones, a person should not try to snatch a level that is beyond him. His steps toward his goal should be steady and tranquil. His purpose should be to do Hashem's Will, keeping in mind that "the one who accomplishes much and the one who accomplishes little are equal, as long as their intentions are pure."[75] With this awareness, free from tension, a person can invest all of his energy to do the Will of Hashem.

The Results of Tension

To sum up, we have seen that tension and pressure can have a range of harmful effects, and so, the tense person is likely to:

- *Decrease the Quality of the Results:* He may fail or get less than optimal results in the very area in which he is so anxious to succeed, because he is working under pressure.
- *Make Mistakes in Judgment:* Tension can often cause mistakes in judgment because he is incapable of evaluating his situation calmly and clearly.
- *Leave a Path of Misery Behind Him:* The tense person will surely make life unpleasant — sometimes even miserable — for the people around him.

- 👎 *Lose Cooperation:* A tense person can't work in harmony with others, and his atmosphere of tension will discourage other people from cooperating with him.
- 👎 *Develop into a Habit:* A constantly tense person will develop a general tendency toward nervousness and irritability.
- 👎 *Jump Ahead Prematurely:* When a person is anxious, he often will try to progress at an inappropriate time or place because of his impatience to wait for the right opportunity.
- 👎 *Move Too Fast:* There's nothing like stress to make people feel driven to advance at an unrealistic speed.
- 👎 *Reach Too Far:* He might set his sight on goals that are beyond his level.
- 👎 *Make Unrealistic Assessments:* He may even see his goal or the process of achieving it as harder than it really is — which puts him under even more pressure.
- 👎 *Stop in the Middle:* A person in the throes of anxiety may just throw up his hands in defeat and give up entirely if he does not realize his goal as quickly or as perfectly as he expected to.
- 👎 *Get Depressed:* All these attitudes can snowball until the tense person can come to the conclusion that he is a failure at everything.

Our Goal — The Harmonious Balance

Our aim is to be *both* bold as a leopard *and* light as an eagle to work toward our goals with determination and enthusiasm, but without tension and anxiety.

The harmonious synchronization of these two factors is necessary when we deal with life's challenges, too. While we actively work to improve our situation, we free ourselves of anxiety by accepting matters as they are. This allows us to take the right direction and decide on the right measure of effort needed to achieve our goal.

We may feel, at first, that this is a contradiction in terms. How can we intensely feel the need to accomplish something, be unsure of the outcome, and, simultaneously radiate calmness and serenity? How can we act to improve a difficult situation, doing everything possible to bring about change, and at the same time be emotionally prepared to accept the situation as it is?

The secret of achieving this balance lies in understanding the concept of "lightness" and in developing it as a habit.

We sometimes relate to things too seriously, being overly conscious of our responsibility. This seriousness acts like dead weight, causing heaviness and sluggishness. Trying to move ahead with this dead weight, or even trying to become happier while maintaining the original seriousness, becomes an ordeal of fighting against resistance. This pushing against our inner resistance causes tension and stress. In contrast, we apply the term "lightness" to a state of mind characterized by mental distance from worry or feelings of exaggerated responsibility. Lightness, here, connotes a casual, even carefree attitude — the ability to take things easily, and remain undemanding. In proper measure, this feeling is positive and counterbalances the tendency to be weighed down by tension-inducing feelings of accountability.

Emotional lightness makes us feel physically light and buoyant, and emotionally delighted and spirited. These states help us feel how easy it is to move ahead and act — so with them, we pursue our goals energetically and enthusiastically.

In the first step of Rabbi Yehuda ben Teima's program, we work on our will, strengthening it and consolidating it, until we achieve rock-solid determination. In the second step, we encourage ourselves to be somewhat lightheaded in order to counterbalance excessive seriousness. We bring ourselves to buoyancy and vivacity and replace leaded determination with facility and enthusiasm.

As we adopt this approach, we may find ourselves leaning toward either tense determination or flightiness. We need to counterbalance each with the opposite until we become skilled at striking a harmonious balance and creating a blend: buoyant determination.

With Lightness and Joy

Using anxiety as a motivating force is certainly unhealthy — but how *can* a person motivate himself to do things that he doesn't enjoy? In volume 2, chapter 5 and throughout volume 4 we will learn how to derive genuine pleasure from our worthwhile activities for their intrinsic value. For now, we will simply try to maintain a mental image of our aim: to function out of pleasure and willingness, without feeling forced or obligated.

When you practice functioning in this way, you will feel a weight being lifted off your heart; you will feel lighter, no longer so somber and anxious.

The Beis Yosef goes even further. He teaches us that being "light as an eagle" implies having a mindset of near lightheadedness to enhance his service of Hashem. We should do *mitzvos* with a sense of joviality, of good cheer![76]

Our Sages taught:

> "Be bold as a leopard, light as an eagle, swift as a deer, and strong as a lion to do the Will of your Father in Heaven." *This teaches you that there is no [place for] haughtiness before Hashem.*
>
> *We see this of Dovid, the king of Israel, who did not conduct himself with haughtiness before Hashem, but humbled himself like a commoner in His Honor.*[77] *Dovid and all the people of Israel made merry before Hashem.... He gathered the elders of Israel and the officials, and the officers of the* Kohanim *and the* Levi'im *to bring up the Holy Ark with great joy....*
>
> "And Dovid danced about with all his might before Hashem..."[78] *When they reached Yerushalayim, all the women peered at Dovid*

> *from the rooftops and the windows and saw how he danced and made merry, and he did not care.... When she [Dovid's wife Michal, the daughter of King Shaul] saw him acting like a commoner, he was degraded in her eyes.*
>
> *What did he do? Our Sages say: he was dressed in gold-ornamented garments... and he clapped his hands, and the gold ornaments jingled. Was that all Dovid did? No! He turned cartwheels and jumped up and down....*
>
> *After all the people of Israel took their leave of him, he turned homeward to his wife, to share with her the great joy of the Holy Ark. Michal came out to meet him and vilified him for debasing himself before the Holy Ark and in front of all the women... she said, "How honored today is the king of Israel, who uncovered himself before the eyes of the mothers of his servants!" ...She said to him... "Look at the difference between you and my father's family. All of my father's family was modest and holy. It was said of the House of Shaul that their heels and their toes were never seen all of their days... and you stand and uncover your clothing like some boor."*
>
> *He replied to her, "But did I make merry before a flesh and blood king? I rejoiced before the King of all kings, Who chose me above your father and all of his house... and I would be [willing to be] disgraced even more than this."*
>
> *And because Michal spoke this way, she was punished.... No man in Israel degraded himself for the sake of mitzvos more than Dovid....*[79]

We see how, for the Honor of his Creator, Dovid could make merry and be light as an eagle by making light of his own dignity.[80]

Priming Your Environment

Generally speaking, tense people tend to develop unhealthy daily habits. To avoid falling prey to these habits, it's worthwhile to spot-check for the following points:

♦ *A Balanced Schedule:* Diversify your activities, and be sure to include physical exercise. Staying glued to a project all day long is not a healthy option.

- *Being Prepared:* When planning a new activity, prepare yourself sufficiently by knowing what to do, and how to do it; set up preliminary details, and when applicable, arrange for review time.
- *An Improved Atmosphere:* Initiate congeniality among family members and acquaintances, and maintain an atmosphere of humor, joy, hope, mutual interest, and appreciation.
- *A Healthy Diet:* Choose healthy food, eat slowly in a relaxed way, and chew well.
- *Down-Time:* Take several breaks a day from work. During that time, a walk may be in order. Or, spend the time strengthening inner joy and patience, being mindful of the pleasure of the work itself; or just take a short rest so that you can return to work with a feeling of freshness.
- *Sufficient, Sound Sleep:* Go to sleep relaxed — a drink of warm milk or a soothing bath may help. Focus on the pleasures of the day, without getting caught up in what didn't get accomplished or what didn't work out. Try to connect to your Creator mentally for a few moments, and get up in the morning feeling refreshed!

It was for the very best of reasons that the Rambam elaborated on the "middle path" in behavior, health, deeds, and daily schedule at the very beginning of his magnum opus, the *Yad Chazakah* (see *Hilchos De'os*). With a good balance in the basic elements of life, the energy that a person invests in his *avodas Hashem* and work in the world has the best chance of bearing real fruit.

Light As an Eagle

The eagle is a large, heavy bird, but Hashem has endowed it with especially wide, long wings that enable it to take advantage of rising or moving air currents. Despite its size, it can sail through the skies at great speeds and travel long distances, hardly flapping its wings. The eagle glides on air currents at high altitudes and cruises the skies, seemingly effortlessly. It just lets the wind carry it to its destination.

We should learn from the eagle and allow currents of joy and energetic enthusiasm, good will, and ease carry us toward our goals.

This process has two distinct stages:

1. *Freedom from All Thoughts and Feelings of Heaviness:* a person should review the damaging thought patterns that were listed throughout this chapter and identify those that are relevant to his situation. He should analyze the subject until he feels emotionally disassociated from the problems.

2. *Repeating Positive Affirmations:* At the same time, he should ask himself, "What elements of my tasks do I really enjoy?" He should try to occasionally repeat mental affirmations of encouragement and enjoyment while he shunts aside worries and expectations — in this way he will get used to positive thinking until it becomes natural.

For example, the intelligent housewife cleans her home not out of a sense of compulsion, but because she desires to care for herself and those who are dear to her. As she works, she looks back on what she has done, and focuses on the benefits of her work. She frees herself from concern about just how long the room will remain spotless and orderly, and so she feels a tremendous sense of relief. She no longer snaps at the one who forgets to hang up his coat or the child who slips and spills something. She still keeps the house clean and neat, and trains her children to do their part, too. She doesn't take the condition of the house too much to heart, though. Her old tensions slowly dissipate. Eventually she may even develop a sort of lightheadedness, like that of Dovid HaMelech:

tending to her home with a light, high-spirited step, as if she were skipping to a tune. In such a tranquil state of mind, she is even more open to enjoying her achievements: the fact that the room really is neat and clean, and that the children are learning, little by little, to do what is expected of them. She has learned to walk the golden middle road between tension and apathy, and can achieve a wonderful state of lightness when doing her work.

The working man feels content with the fact that he is doing an honest day's work. He recognizes its value, foresees its contribution to others, and chooses to focus on that. In addition, he takes pride and pleasure in providing for his loved ones. Feelings of contentment and appreciation provide him with a constant, cheerful motivation to continue in his day's tasks.

A light attitude is important in intellectual activities, as well. Rabbi Shlomo Wolbe teaches:

> *All the masters of thought advised that one should not contemplate in a state of pressure and exertion, but rather in a state of calmness, even pleasure. Thinking is not like chopping wood, but like playing a violin. This is a major principle in the art of thought.*[81]

Anyone can understand that the violinist who is having trouble getting the right sound from his instrument will not improve matters with stiffened fingers and a vise-like grip. This is just not the way to bring out sweet tones from a violin. Instead, the violinist who wants to perfect his art has to relax his muscles, to bring himself to a calm, trance-like state that allows his fingers to express his soul's feelings through his instrument. Any tension in his heart or muscles will gum up the delicate tones that only a violin can produce.

In the same way, thought is most fluid when a person reaches the greatest level of tranquility. A calm state enables his mind to examine any matter with the greatest possible clarity, just like the still, clear waters of a pond allow a person to peer into its depths.

The way to learn Torah, then, is by not forcing ourselves.[82] Instead, we should relieve ourselves of all anxiety about how well we will concentrate, whether we will understand the material properly, and whether we will cover enough ground in the time available to us. We should focus on the times that we've taken genuine pleasure from our learning and value the opportunity to be involved in studying Hashem's Torah. We are wise enough to know how to learn without pushing ourselves. We can let the flow of pleasure, appreciation, and love of learning carry us on to the next point in our studies, and then to the next. We can simply *allow* ourselves to learn, encouraging ourselves to progress without stress. We can count the various opinions in the Talmud in the same happy, light way that we would count a hundred dollar bills that we earned unexpectedly. We can let the Torah thoughts well up from within like a fountain bubbling with the purest of waters.

In *tefillah*, too, a person should not force himself to concentrate and to become emotional. As it says in *Avos:* "Do not make your prayer a set one, but entreaties and [pleas for] mercy before Hashem."[83] With the material in this section in mind, we may understand from this mishnah that a person shouldn't force himself to pray, but that the prayer should flow from his heart as though by itself.

We must learn the art of opening our hearts until our lips express the words of the *tefillah* naturally and spontaneously.

This ease should be our attitude when we do other *mitzvos*, as well. We can and should do all *mitzvos* joyfully — even those few that call for sobriety or sadness! Fasting on Tisha B'Av is profoundly sad, but, at the same time, we should feel an undercurrent of joy at doing Hashem's Will. This prevents our mourning from turning into depression.

Remember: even Dovid, King of Israel, behaved with light-headedness in front of the entire nation when that was the appropriate way to serve Hashem.

Once you accustom yourself to this approach, you will feel a tremendous sense of relief, as if you were dancing through your everyday routine, and you will soar like the eagle toward your highest goals.

FINDING YOURSELF IN WHAT YOU'VE LEARNED

A. Self-Awareness

1. Arrange a list of personal or interpersonal projects that didn't work out. Determine if tension is playing a role in these situations, and determine how the tension created obstacles which prevented your success. Try to remind yourself of these tension-caused obstacles from time to time.
2. Organize a list of objectives that you managed to handle with a more relaxed approach. Enjoy it.
3. Do you feel that the explanations of deeper causes of tension are relevant to you? If you have other insights into the roots of your tension, think about them for a while and then write them down, too. (The author welcomes any of your insights that you feel might be helpful to others; please mail your ideas to: Rabbi Eisenblatt, PO Box 23399, Jerusalem, Israel.)

B. For Further Study

When dealing with the following roots of tension, learning pertinent and appropriate text can help reshape our perceptions so that we become more motivated to change our behavior.

1. Insufficient faith and trust in Hashem: *Chovos HaLevavos, "Sha'ar HaBitachon"; Sefer HaBitachon* of Rav Shmuel Hominer, *ztz"l*.
2. Insufficient understanding and awareness: *Chovos HaLevavos; Mesillas Yesharim; and Derech Hashem*.

3. Insufficient appreciation of good deeds: in this series, volume 2, chapters 5-7; also in the following book: Rabbi Shmuel D Eisenblatt, *Fulfillment in Marriage*, 2 volumes (Jerusalem: Feldheim, 5748), volume 1, chapters 2, 4, and 5; volume 2, part 1, chapter 5 and part 2, chapter 1.

APPLYING WHAT YOU'VE LEARNED

A. Playing "The Opposite Extreme" Game

Try this game to turn down the tension level and help empty yourself of harmful emotions:

Instead of trying to free yourself of some feeling, do the opposite. Decide on a period of time — say, half an hour, although sometimes a quarter of an hour or even ten minutes will do the trick — during which you will not think about anything else but the unwanted feeling. Focus only on experiencing that negative emotion. If you want to escape from sadness, be sad for half an hour. If you are a worrier, go ahead and worry for half an hour. If you are angry, nurse your anger for half an hour.

Most likely, by the time the half-hour is up — and perhaps long before — you'll be sick and tired of wallowing in that feeling. You'll have an acute sense of how foolish and what a waste of time and energy that emotion is. In the course of this game, you'll also be releasing yourself from the pressure to change. Instead of fighting the unwanted feeling, you are joining it, encouraging it to excess. This will allow you to feel satiated and ready to let go without tension or a fight. You'll come out of it feeling free to really jettison that negative emotion.

B. Charting Habits

1. Refer back to page 246; do any of the "Results of Tension" listed there apply to you? Try to list which three elements affect

you most acutely and copy them onto a separate sheet of paper. Place it, or hang it up, in the place you find yourself most often, or even better, in your "tension spot," that is the area in your home or workplace where you get tense most often, e.g., the kitchen table, your desk, near the stove, etc. Glance at it periodically to remind yourself of the negative repercussions of tension.

2. Review the section on "Priming Your Environment" found on page 250. Mentally rate your present standing in each area. Using the chart on the following page, plot out the concrete changes you intend to introduce (when, what, and how much), and any other ideas that you may have to improve your lifestyle. Hang the list next to the "Results" list in your "tension spot."

Habit / Progress	A Balanced Schedule	An Improved Atmosphere	A Healthy Diet	Down-time	Sufficient Sleep
Week no. 1					
Week no. 2					
Week no. 3					
Week no. 4					
Week no. 5					

C. Crisis Intervention

If you find yourself feeling tense, here are some on-the-spot neutralizers:

1. Take a deep breath, in through your nose and out through your mouth. Do this as many times as you need until you feel more under control.
2. Step away from the situation for a few minutes and try this visualization to help you relax: If you feel your tension mainly as a knot in your chest, close your eyes and picture that tightness as a blown-up balloon inside you. As you breathe deeply, and with every exhalation, envision the balloon losing its air and slowly deflating. By the time you have emptied the balloon, you should be feeling much more calm. You can transfer this visualization to any place where you feel tension.
3. Step away from the situation for a few minutes and try venting your frustrations using the technique described in chapter 7, in the section called "Neutralizing Resistance." Depending on the circumstances, one of two options will be more practicable:
    a) Vent your feelings onto paper. Write down exactly what's bothering you; be specific and don't hold back. After writing down your feelings, take a few moments and practice the breathing or visualization techniques. When you feel more settled, return to what you've written — most likely, the issue will not seem as earth-shattering as it had a few minutes earlier.
    b) Vent your feelings out loud. Give voice to your frustrations (privately, where no one can hear you) and keep on doing it until you lose your steam.
4. Step away from the situation for a few minutes and use this as an opportunity to deepen your relationship with Hashem. Rather than just vent, speak out what's bothering you in the

form of a spontaneous prayer. Instead of "I'm fuming!" it can be, "Hashem, I'm so frustrated and angry! I hate this feeling — help me get out of it!"

5. Walk off your tension. Fresh air, improved circulation, a change of scene, and space to think can do wonders.

NOTES TO CHAPTER EIGHT

1. *Bava Basra* 16a.
2. Heard from my father, Rav Shlomo Eisenblatt, *ztz"l*.
3. *Shabbos* 82a.
4. *Avos D'Rabbi Nosson* 1:4.
5. *Ruach Chayim* on *Avos* 6:6.
6. *Chayei HaMussar*, part II, p. 211.
7. *Mishneh Torah*, end of *Hilchos Issurei Biyah*.
8. Bamidbar 15:39. See also *Avodah Zarah* 20b on the verse "*V'nismachta*" (Devarim 23:10).
9. Since we are discussing task-related tension in this chapter, most of what will be covered is relevant to unhealthy expectations of ourselves and "life." In volume 2 of this series, chapter 2, situation-oriented tension is the focus of the discussion; unbalanced expectations of others and "life" will be covered then.
10. See the beginning of *Mesillas Yesharim*. See also *Derech Hashem*, part I, chapter 4:5. The Talmud (*Nazir* 23a) states that every sin has two elements: rebellion against Hashem's Will and the spiritual defect caused by the sin. Likewise, a *mitzvah* has two parts: its value includes both compliance with Hashem's Will and the spiritual improvement it causes.
11. *Midrash Tehillim* 16.
12. *Bava Metzia* 38a, and Rashi there.
13. *Ma'amar Toras HaBayis*, chapter 1.
14. "I toil and receive reward" (*Berachos* 28b); "'If you toil in Torah, He has much reward to give you.' The reward is according to the degree of toil and effort, not according to the amount studied" (*Midrash Shmuel* on *Avos* 4:12).

   "Hashem does not withhold reward from any person in any instance; when a person exerts himself and puts his soul into something, Hashem does not withhold his reward" (*Bamidbar Rabbah* 12:11).

"'The soul, too, shall not be filled.' Because the soul knows that all the effort it exerts, it exerts for itself, it is never satisfied with the *mitzvos* and good deeds it has already done [but always wants to do more]" (*Yalkut Shimoni*, Koheles 972 [on Koheles 6:7]).

15. See also the *Maggid Meisharim, Parashas* Bereishis, Shabbos, Teves 14 on *nehama d'kisufa* (bread of shame); and *Derech Hashem*, part I, chapter 2 on the subject: Why a person should try to be a "master of his good."
16. *Avos* 5:24.
17. "One thing accomplished with pain is better for a person than a hundred things accomplished easily" (*Avos D'Rabbi Nosson* 3:6). This lesson in effort goes hand in hand with the phrase we say in morning *berachos*, asking Hashem "not to bring us to challenges." We do not seek difficulties. But if Hashem should send them to us, we greet them with the willingness to invest whatever energy it would take to prevail.
18. See the Rambam on *Avos* 3:15, "Everything is according to the abundance of good deeds."
19. "If a person tells you, 'I toiled, but I didn't achieve,' don't believe him. 'I didn't toil, but I achieved,' don't believe him. 'I toiled and I achieved,' believe him!" (*Megillah* 6b).
20. *Bava Metzia* 85b.
21. See "The *Beraisa* of Thirty-Two *Middos*," *Mishnas Rabbi Eliezer* 20; and *Mechilta D'Rashbi*, Yisro 9, quoted in Rav Shumel D. Eisenblatt, *Chayim Shel Osher*, 2 volumes (Jerusalem: The Foundation for the Advancement of Torah Study, 5749), volume 2, pp. 195-196.
22. *Chovos HaLevavos*, "*Sha'ar Avodas HaElokim*," chapter 4.
23. See volume 2 of this series, appendix B, called *"Chavivim Yesurim."*
24. See volume 2 of this series, chapter 2 on the "Tension Family."
25. Bereishis 3:16-19.
26. See volume 2 of this series, chapter 6, and all of volume 4.
27. See volume 2 of this series, chapter 1.
28. See Rambam, *Mishneh Torah, Hilchos Gerushin*, chapter 2, halachah 2.
29. *Kiddushin* 40a-b.
30. *Avos* 2:13.
31. *Avos* 2:4.
32. See *Pesachim* 68b, and Rashi there.

33. See *Sotah* 5b where it discusses the person who weighs his steps. Also see the Rambam's *Eight Chapters*, end of chapter 8.
34. *Bava Basra* 21a.
35. Mishnah, *Yoma* 22a.
36. *Yoma* 23a.
37. *Ohr Yechezkel, Middos* 290.
38. See Targum, Rashi, and Metzudos on Koheles 4:4.
39. Ibn Ezra on Koheles 4:4.
40. Koheles 4:4.
41. *Chovos HaLevavos*, "Sha'ar HaBitachon," chapter 4.
42. See volume 2 of this series, chapter 4. The poor self-image engendered by failure may actually stem from exaggerated expectations of ourselves, or perhaps from a fear of rejection.
43. Such a person would do well to work on developing joy with what he possesses, and would find it worth his while to look into volume 2 of this series, chapter 4 and onward.
44. *Menachos* 110a.
45. *Zohar*, Bereishis 11. See *Sha'arei Ora* end of *sha'ar* 7, recommended by the Arizal on the subject of kindness and fear.
46. Devarim 6:5.
47. Devarim 6:13.
48. Yerushalmi, *Sotah* 5:5 (25a).
49. See *Sifri*, end of *Parashas* Kedoshim.
50. Devarim 28:47. See also, in this series, volume 2 chapter 5; and all of volume 4.
51. See volume 2 of this series, chapters 5 and 6.
52. Meiri on Mishlei 29:20.
53. Mishlei 9:17.
54. *Gittin* 6b-7a. See also *Orchos Tzaddikim*, section 13.
55. See also the discussion of communication in the section entitled "Choosing the Right Mode of Action" in chapter 1 of this volume.
56. *Sefer HaYashar*, chapter 6.
57. Ibid.
58. Rav Chayim of Volozhin on *Avos*, chapter 2.
59. "When praying during a spiritual slump, one should just read the letters and words clearly. A period of inspiration is the time to invest a lot of

effort into the deeper intentions of the prayers." *Toldos Aharon* on the Torah portions of Ki Sisa and Shlach.
60. Koheles 7:14.
61. *Avos* 4:3.
62. Mishlei 15:23.
63. Meiri on Mishlei 15:23.
64. Koheles 9:11.
65. *Midrash Tanchuma* on Matos 5.
66. *Eruvin* 13b, and Rashi there.
67. *Chagigah* 14b.
68. Mishlei 25:16.
69. *Chagigah* 14b; see Rashi and Maharsha there.
70. Vilna Gaon on Mishlei 19:2.
71. Bamidbar 11:34. This idea may be hinted to in *Sefer HaYetzirah*, chapter 1: "If your heart hurries on, return to the place!"
72. *Sha'ar HaYirah*, chapters 2 and 10 in the name of *Bris Menuchah*.
73. See *Reishis Chochmah*, beginning of chapter 40.
74. Vilna Gaon on Mishlei 17:24.
75. Mishnah, end of *Menachos*. We will, with Hashem's help, discuss this subject at length in volume 2 of this series, chapter 4.
76. Beginning of *Tur, Orach Chayim*.
77. II Shmuel, chapter 6.
78. II Shmuel 6:14.
79. *Bamidbar Rabbah* 4:20.
80. See also Yerushalmi, *Sukkah* 85:4, and *Sanhedrin* 83:4.
81. Rav Shlomo Wolbe, *Alei Shur*, 2 volumes (Jerusalem: Tzor Os, 5748), volume 2, p. 260.
82. Perhaps this was Rabbi Yishmael's intention when he said, "The words of Torah should not be an obligation upon you, but you are not permitted to exempt yourself from them" (*Menachos* 99b).
83. *Avos* 2:13 (2:18 in *siddur*); order changed slightly.

9

Swift As a Deer

Shaking Off Laziness

Until now we have focused on balancing our approach: we've learned how to pursue our goals with a consolidated will, and eliminate the conflicting motives and desires which interfere with our success, while at the same time approaching our projects with a relaxed disposition, free of tension. Now it is time for us to talk *tachlis*, action, and learn how to get down to work with alacrity.

Alacrity — *zerizus* — is fired by inner enthusiasm, and denotes readiness to act swiftly and briskly.[1] It is the very opposite of laziness, and infuses us with energy to get right down to our tasks instead of putting them off. But is alacrity all that important? Couldn't we manage our responsibilities well enough without overflowing enthusiasm?

Ambivalence isn't the only factor that inhibits wholehearted devotion to a project. There is another form of internal resistance that is more general, and also very common. This type of inner opposition is unconnected to the specific nature of the goal, and manifests as an overall feeling of lethargy. This feeling makes us balk at the prospect of exertion for the sake of any goal at all.

In chapter 7, we explained that the resistance created by a divided will comes from a deep-seated concern that attaining a specific goal will result in a significant loss. Accordingly, we discussed ways to identify the secondary concerns, and then neutralize or sidestep them. The kind of resistance under discussion now is different. Here, although there is no real reason why the person should not truly want to achieve his goal, he still feels weighted down. In this case, the obstacle is probably a product of laziness or a general resistance to change.

How can we overcome this resistance? How can we cast off our lethargy and advance swiftly toward our goals with energetic enthusiasm?

Justifying Sluggishness

The lazy person doesn't just sit idle — his mind may be amazingly active devising justifications for his inactivity. As soon as a situation arises that might obligate him, he responds like a creative, well-organized business manager. On a moment's notice, he whips up a dozen tailor-made rationalizations that explain why he cannot possibly take action. That is why "The lazy person is wiser in his own eyes than seven royal advisors."[2] For the sake of his laziness, he is shrewd enough to find any excuse to avoid work.[3] He is, however, seldom aware of this process. Rather, convinced of his sincerity, he offers excuses of two types: "It's so hard!" and "It's not necessary."

"IT'S SO HARD!"

This is the most common excuse, easily adapted to all sorts of situations that require active involvement. It is usually generated by simple indolence.[4] When a person lacks the drive to invest effort, he paints a mental picture of the situation that is overwhelmingly daunting. He may then respond with a variety of arguments:

♦ "It's too hard! I just can't!" (But is he really trying his best?)

- "Do I need more headaches? I have enough responsibilities to think about without starting another project!" (But this goal might just save him from some of his other "headaches.")
- "I'm too old to change; you can't teach an old dog new tricks, can you?" (Even though he relishes trying out new food or diversions — as long as they promise to be enjoyable.)
- "I'd like to, but there are so many obstacles preventing me from doing it." (The wise person realizes that there are obstacles in the way of accomplishing *anything* of value. The person who really wants to achieve manages to overcome most of them. He who finds obstacles overwhelmingly intimidating, however, is usually looking for a way out.)
- "I won't succeed anyway; it doesn't pay to try." (Does he relate that way to things he really wants for himself, too?)
- "I just don't have time for this. I have a lot of other things to take care of. I can't fit this in, too." (But are the other things more important than this one? Are his priorities in order?)

"IT'S NOT NECESSARY"

This response is also common, especially when the issue is a change in character. For example:

- "My life will still be just fine, even if I don't do..." (But is he really so compliant and uncomplaining about the situation as it is now?)
- "What's so terrible if I don't...?" (But is he really paying attention to the disadvantages?)
- "Why, all of a sudden, do I need to..." (Does he always resist change, or only when it's a challenge?)
- "I'm still young; give me a chance to enjoy life." (Actually, the change would help him to enjoy life even more.)

- "As I see it, for me to change would amount to putting on a show, and I'm no hypocrite!" (Of course, he is perfectly willing to put on a show when it comes to being interviewed for a new job, meeting a potential *shidduch*, or dealing with a client.)
- "Everyone has his share of faults. What's so terrible about this one?" (But does he tolerate other people's faults so easily?)
- And, of course: "That's the way I am — period!"

The "It's not necessary" mentality isn't only attributable to laziness; a tendency toward arrogance, a lack of flexibility, or a general sense of insecurity might also be responsible. The person loves himself — as he is right now. Or, the insecure person fears that, by making improvements, he or the world around him will suddenly become so different that he will lose his (already weak) grip on the old and familiar. Either possibility can feel threatening.

The truth, though, is that moderate character improvement doesn't transform us into new people. On the contrary, every one of us comes equipped with an innate ability to adapt to different situations; this flexibility is a natural part of our potential. True, we should not try to institute extreme or fundamental changes in our core personality — it isn't readily altered. But as long as we aim for reasonable improvements, we are actually enhancing the better elements within, and allowing our original good nature to express itself freely. Being flexible and using our potential for self-change to strengthen the good in our natural personality — makes us feel fulfilled, not alienated from our real selves. Similarly, we can work to change outside factors (job, friends, schedule, etc.), yet take care to retain what we know and love in our world. Whether the changes we make are internal or external, the positive effects are far reaching; we feel open to appreciate ourselves for the work we've done, and feel reassuringly secure since we've proven to ourselves that we aren't as helpless as we might have thought.

Conversely, if a person allows himself to fall victim to laziness, he paints a picture for himself that is all in shadow, and uses that dismal picture to convince himself that change would be either too difficult, or unnecessary. Lethargy leads him to throw up his hands in defeat or to develop more sophisticated rationalizations for his lack of constructive action. Beyond that, he lacks the feeling of fulfillment that can inspire him to progress further in his life. Those excuses, then, form a vicious cycle that effectively blocks him from advancing on his path in life.

Why Do Today What You Can Put Off Till Tomorrow?

Some people prefer to play a more subtle game. Instead of saying flat out, "It's too hard for me," they say, "It's too hard for me *right now*." The procrastinator can convince himself, "It's hard for me to concentrate now," "I'm not in the right frame of mind," or "I'm in a hurry now; another time would be better."

Of course, we can only hope and pray that when that "other" time finally comes along, he won't concoct some new excuse for why he can't do it then, either. The Ramchal writes:

> There is nothing as dangerous as this, because with each new moment, a new obstacle can arise to prevent him from doing the good deed.[5]

Contrast this with Boaz, of whom Naomi was certain that "the man will not rest unless he concludes the matter today."[6] How did she know this? Our Sages answer, "Because, for righteous people — their 'yes' is 'yes' and their 'no' is 'no'."[7]

Naomi knew that an intention that isn't acted upon immediately cannot be considered a true resolution; that is simply not the meaning of a real "yes." When a righteous person says something, however, he acts on it at once.

> **THINK ABOUT IT**
>
> **HOW DOES THIS EXPLAIN:**
>
> ♦ how the lazy person makes life more difficult for himself?
> ♦ how investing energy in change can actually make life easier?
>
> How can a feeling of lethargy create a Spiral Effect?

Emotional Arteriosclerosis

The Torah describes both the "It's too hard" and the "It's not necessary" brands of rationalization. "It's too hard" means that a person knows what he should do, but feels sluggish; it is described as "heaviness" or "hardness" of the heart.

> *Paroh's heart is heavy; he refuses to send out the nation.... Paroh hardened his heart this time, as well, and did not send out the nation.*[8]

Paroh was an eyewitness to all the plagues and miracles and had already made up his mind to free the Jewish people. When it came down to it, though, he didn't carry his decision through.[9] Like a dead weight, his heart felt that movement and change was too strenuous, despite his knowledge of what was right. When a person starts out inflexible, his heart hardens even more, and it becomes all the more difficult for him to surrender and compromise.

"It's not necessary" is a refusal to recognize the value of the proposed action, and that attitude is referred to as an "uncircumcised heart" in the Torah. The heart can become somewhat impervious and obtuse when it comes to the importance of the issue in question.[10] In contrast to the "stony heart," which recognizes the truth but hardly responds, a "covered" or "clogged" heart finds it difficult to hear the argument in the first place. The uncircumcised heart is *uninterested* in hearing the argument and, at the same time, finds it hard to comprehend finer concepts and understand the truth.[11] Therefore the Torah commands: "Circumcise the foreskin of your heart"[12] — don't behave as if your emotional heart was covered or clogged.[13]

Sometimes a person who refuses to see is described as having a "fat-covered heart." These words are used in the Torah to describe *B'nei Yisrael*:

> *And Israel became fat, and kicked... you became fat, thick, and covered over... and [Israel] rejected the G-d Who created him....*[14]

When a person refuses to exercise his heart by deeply attending to words of wisdom, it becomes (figuratively) fat, clogged, and out of shape. This makes it even more difficult for him to absorb and understand such words. He can change all this, though, by attuning his heart to matters of truth and introspection, and actualizing what he has heard. Through this, he heals his heart and opens the doors of his perception.[15] But how, if we just said that it is so difficult for him to absorb wise words, can he even begin to comprehend matters of faith and repentance?

Working Off the Excess Fat

Most people understand how important it is to maintain a healthy, well-functioning heart. Innumerable books and articles are printed and sold, full of advice on how to feel alert and energetic with the best diet and exercise program. Most of us also recognize how important it is for the emotional heart to be healthy, and this, too, requires a unique diet and exercise regimen. The ideal program would be geared to reduce the "excess fat" that weighs on our understanding, blurs our emotional vision, and inhibits our comprehension of spiritual truth. Such clarity would open our eyes to the greatness of taking appropriate action, and inspire us to act. At the same time, we would do "emotional calisthenics" to develop our flexibility, so that we feel free to act in any way that we know is right.

So how do we get into this emotional fitness regimen? Every time we drop an excuse for inaction from our repertoire, we work off some of the accumulated fat that was weighing us down and making us lazy. This makes us feel lighter and more energetic, so that we can advance more quickly and smoothly in life. It is important to see right through our excuses, so that they don't inhibit us from meeting the challenges that will help us grow. We need to be alert to the strategies of our own *yetzer hara* and disarm these excuses the moment they enter our minds — before we are convinced by any glib rationalizations, like: "I can't... I don't want to... It's not so terrible..." and "I so badly want to..."

An important part of our exercise program for developing energetic enthusiasm is to make a habit of acting on our decisions as soon as we make them. Regular, vigorous physical activity and flexible muscles are needed to keep the body in tone; active functioning and emotional flexibility are no less essential when we want to keep our emotional selves trim and fit.

This habit of acting immediately on our decisions helps us in another way, too: the longer we hesitate, the more time we have to waver and get into internal debates. Such philosophizing buys the time needed for excuses and obstacles to materialize, but when we get to work immediately and energetically, we put all those pitfalls behind us.

> **Note**: Acting immediately doesn't mean that our decision should be made impetuously. Most complex issues do require careful deliberation. There is a middle road, however. Once an issue has been thought out and feels resolved, we should act on it without delay. When we are accustomed to taking prompt and energetic action, it becomes easier to distinguish

between an issue that really calls for deep consideration and the *yetzer hara's* stalling tactics.

Inflated Concerns

In addition to "It's too hard" and "It's not necessary," there is another brand of rationalization: *"It's not worth it."* Variations on this theme may sound something like this:

- "What?! Do you know what might happen if I try to do that?!" This refrain mirrors the lame excuse of the lazy person that appears in Mishlei: "There is a lion on the way; I'll get killed if I go into the streets."[16]
- "I'm afraid I will do more harm than good." (See chapter 4 of this volume, the section called "Subtle Handicaps," for a discussion of when this is and is not a legitimate cause for concern.)
- "I won't succeed anyway." (Is that what he says about goals that he *really does* want for himself?)
- "Everyone will just laugh at me and say, 'What a *tzaddik!* Since when is he such a big shot?'" (But are we permitted to be swayed by the opinion of others when *avodas Hashem* is at stake?)[17]

To support the "It's not worth it" attitude, the *yetzer* manipulates our mental image of a task. This is accomplished in two main ways: by questioning the significance of the outcome or by incorrectly estimating what the results will be.

QUESTIONING THE SIGNIFICANCE OF THE OUTCOME
Our leaning toward laziness can determine the level of importance we ascribe to a goal and miscalculate the factors involved in

success. When faced with a new project, our lazy side does a quick accounting: it looks at the path to success and compares the degree of difficulties to the goal. It then may decide that the difficulties involved don't justify that goal. Thus, the value of our tasks fluctuates according to our lazy side's vested interests. This type of rationalization has a few forms:

- *Downplaying the Significance of Inaction:* A person can wriggle out of feeling the need to act immediately by adopting a casual attitude about the importance of success or inaction. By convincing himself that inaction would only result in a trivial loss, all motivation to act disappears. It is as if our lazy side is saying: "If success won't bring me any great benefit, it's not worth it to even try."
- *Inflating the Severity of Potential Obstacles:* A person may focus on the likelihood of problems arising as he works toward his goal, convincing himself that the negative consequences of trying outweigh the value of success. For example, if failure were to mean minor discomfort; and success (which is likely) would involve much more significant gains — the fear of losing that negligible amount will prevent him from trying at all.
- *Exaggerating the Investment:* A person inflates his estimate of the time, money, or effort that he will need to put into a project, or his feelings about that investment. He then convinces himself that what he stands to gain is minor compared to what he'll lose as an investment.

EXAGGERATING OUR CHANCES OF FAILURE
Our leaning toward laziness can also affect the way we see the viability of the outcome — making success seem less (or more) likely, according to our lazy side's whims. This type of rationalization has a few forms:

- *Minimizing the Chance of Success:* A person may magnify his chances of failure and see himself as bound to fail even when there is a good chance of success. A person who has suffered a crushing defeat in the past may be especially prone to fear taking another risk. He may feel that way even if the task at hand is completely different and even if his past failure was related to circumstances that no longer exist. He tells himself: "If success is so unlikely, it's not worth it to even make the attempt."
- *Minimizing the Possibility of Danger:* Even if he sees success as a good statistical bet, a person can still wriggle out of constructive action by convincing himself that the chances that passivity will cause trouble are negligible.
- *Inflating the Probability of Problems:* A person may exaggerate the likelihood that obstacles will crop up in the course of his project. He will find himself using these problems to scare himself away from undertaking any project that he doesn't like.

The inclination to laziness fosters inaccuracies and distortions so that a person will reach the conclusion that he should not take action. If, however, we are attuned to the *yetzer's* tactics, we can learn to recognize when these lines are valid arguments, and when they are simply overblown excuses.

THINK ABOUT IT

HOW DOES THIS EXPLAIN...

- how laziness affects the way we assess situations?
- the way laziness interferes with our life's direction?

How would a person find the "middle road" between laziness and careful deliberation?

Honest Judgment

When it comes to inventing tailor-made excuses for his inaction, the lazy person can be remarkably creative. Yet the question presents itself: some objectives really *are* unnecessary; some goals *are* beyond a person's capability. Sometimes a mode of action isn't worthwhile because the chances of success are so remote, or because that action really would cause more harm than good. How, then, are we to know when to attend to these concerns, and when to ignore them? How do we free ourselves from the distorting influence that laziness has over our mental image? How can we know when to trust our own assessments?

The bottom line of "It's too hard" and "It's not necessary" is usually "It's not worth it" — the goal just doesn't justify putting in the required effort. This is the conclusion that the *yetzer hara* wants us to come to, and it tries to lead us there by making us think of the goal as not very valuable, after all. Here are some guidelines to help you make an honest judgment. Consider your goal and ask yourself:

1. "If I could get there effortlessly, would I want to?" If your answer is "yes," it shows that you do attribute a certain amount of importance to the goal. So try to understand *why* you would like the benefits of achieving that goal and try to build on that feeling of importance bit by bit.

2. Then ask yourself, "Now that I attribute more importance to this goal, is my estimate of its benefit more accurate, or not?"

3. Better still, ask yourself, "If I were already working toward this goal, would I *stop* because of one of these reasons — the reasons that the *yetzer hara* is using to prevent me from even *starting*, like: fear that harm will result, it isn't worth my while, etc.; or would I stick with it?" If you answer that you would keep on going, then ask yourself, "Why would I continue? Doesn't that prove that my goal *is* important to me?"

Some people are generally apathetic or lazy. They need to change that habit, and bit by bit, begin taking on more initiative. Others may basically accept responsibility, or demonstrate initiative, while other times they evade it. With them, the "It isn't necessary" excuse takes on an interesting shape. Although they may be ordinary people, they suddenly become paragons of tolerance. If their goal is not too interesting or demands a bit of effort, they assure themselves that they can manage without it. The risks of failing to achieve those goals or rid themselves of those particular problems don't register. If you find yourself selecting your goals in a way that is not constructive, ask yourself: "Am I just as satisfied with my lot when it comes to other things, like my salary or how much people respect me? If not, then why am I willing to invest effort to further those goals, while I feel perfectly satisfied to maintain the status quo of others?" This will help you put your finger on the specific type of projects which are problematic for you.

Even people who don't consider themselves lazy, people who are prompt and responsible in practical matters, may slacken when it comes to their responsibility to make internal changes. Intellectually speaking, this is not very logical. Consider the following: If someone were ill, G-d forbid, and he spotted his doctor whispering something to one of the members of his family, he would definitely try to find out what the doctor had said, trying to clarify the details of his diagnosis and what could be done to cure his illness. He would certainly not say to himself, "It's surely nothing" or, "So what if my body's not in great shape", but would try to consult with experts in the field.

Why don't we do the same in emotional matters? Why are we ashamed to clarify precisely what it is that we lack and how we can overcome our deficiencies?

Have you ever met a sick person who said, "Since other people are sick, I'm entitled to be sick, too. So why should I bother trying to get better?" Why is it, then, that when it comes to character flaws, so many of us say to ourselves, "Other people have this same fault, so why should I bother to change myself?" Many people even turn their attention to other people's faults to remove the spotlight from their own deficiencies.

Again, we need to always sharpen our awareness of the *yetzer hara's* contrived arguments — the way it dismisses emotional and spiritual progress and downplays the benefits that it brings us. That way, we can more effectively rebut its reasoning and free ourselves of its influence. Whenever you notice that it has become difficult to take the initiative in some area, you can try some of these suggestions to help ferret out the "It's not necessary" excuse which may be lurking in your thoughts.

1. Imagine what you would advise someone else in the same situation. How might you look at the issue a few years down the line? Or, imagine how a respected figure in your life would advise you.

2. You may, even with these suggestions, still find it hard to get an objective picture of your situation, free of exaggerations, since you only have your own, subjective self with whom to work. To get an accurate understanding, it may be best to actually ask another person — someone whose honesty you can count on — whether or not he thinks your excuse is adequate. Of course, this approach does have its drawbacks. The idler in you may hold back crucial information or present it in a way that minimizes it, so make sure you present all sides of the issue. It is also important to choose as your sounding board someone who doesn't suffer from a similar problem; if he does, he may give a subjective answer to cover himself.

3. Here's another possible solution: scan the arena. Is there anyone who has a vested interest in your completion of the project? Would *he* think your version of the issue is valid?

If you can't motivate yourself enough to bother examining the validity of your reasons, reconsider that sick person we mentioned. Also ask yourself whether you have some particular reason for not using the methods described above. For example, if you're ashamed to let a third party hear your reasoning, it may indicate that you already don't believe that it's valid.

Overblown Excuses

For some people, the arguments that their goal is too difficult, unnecessary, or not important enough don't quiet their stirrings of conscience. To justify inaction, they develop intense concerns about all the possible negative results of jumping in. They prophesize doom, and their pessimistic predictions develop into actual fears that breed anxiety.

This disquiet can have limiting, as well as ludicrous results. A person may, for example, pass up excellent opportunities to solve his problems or advance in life because he is he is unwilling to invest the energy needed to tackle a new situation. It can feel much easier to deal with a familiar situation; a person may resist expending the energy that a new situation requires, such as the need for alertness, meeting new people, and the effort to make decisions. That unwillingness can snowball into a fear of trying anything new. This fear becomes more real to him than the opportunity itself, and encourages a preference of what is already familiar, shortcomings and all. Some single people, therefore, won't even take a chance at a very good *shidduch* because the world of married life is just too much uncharted territory for them to be interested in crossing.

Fear of failure can be another offshoot of lethargy. The devitalized person can work himself into being so intimidated by risks that he won't do anything to help himself unless success is assured. The results can be equally ridiculous. Even if the temporary discomfort of having to admit to failure is about the worst that can happen, suffering with his problems may still appear to him to be his best option. With such an escalated fear of having to acknowledge any degree of failure, is it any wonder that he is convinced that it is a waste to invest any effort without a guarantee of success?

Another aspect of the fear of failure is the fear of disappointment. The sluggish person can become concerned that making an effort means getting his hopes up — which allows for the possibility of disappointment, This is unbearable for him. Therefore, he conveniently concludes that he would rather not try at all.

Others develop anxiety about what people will think of them. They reshape an inhibition born of laziness into a social concern. They believe that chances are that someone is going to have some comment about the job that they would like to do. When they have problems with a neighbor or coworker, they avoid discussing the issue directly because they are wary of the other person's possible reaction. Their laziness impels them to create unjustified concerns over raising a few eyebrows, which in turn may inhibit them from accepting important challenges or trying new things.

If only they could internalize the awareness that feelings of embarrassment and disappointment are so fleeting, but the rewards of being enriched and improved by a new challenge last a lifetime.

Furthermore, the person who approaches a challenge with energetic enthusiasm is more likely to excel than the one who hesitates and is anxious. Bear in mind, too, that — contrary to what we might expect — the person who is preoccupied with other people's opinions is often the one who has the hardest time getting people to like and respect him. His anxiety keeps him from feeling comfortable and behaving naturally around them. But the person who does what is right without dwelling on what anyone else may think usually wins the approval and respect of others.

Obviously, when we have to make a decision, we must work out a clear picture of the subject at hand that includes both sides of any questions. Our next move can only be planned on the basis of this information. It is usually prudent to compile a list of all the advantages and disadvantages of the project before we start. When we see the data in black and white, it is easier to get an accurate understanding. Unwillingness to make such a list may indicate that we are not prepared to see the problem honestly and without exaggeration because we are concerned that such an understanding would obligate us in a way that we would have to act against our original bias.

> **Note**: All this doesn't mean that a fear of failure or a disappointment in what others say always finds its roots in laziness. Such fears can be a result of pathology, negative experiences, etc. The point we are discussing here is how laziness can nurture subtle concerns and turn them into substantial inhibiting factors. Leanings toward laziness encourage a person to capitalize on any technical or emotional suspicion it can set its hands on.

The wise person doesn't fear failure; he considers it to be a valuable, custom-fit lesson for life — one that may not be available in any other way.[18]

Proceed with (Not Too Much!) Caution

The idle person allows himself to be possessed by foolish fears about factors that are beyond his control. He piles safeguard upon safeguard, and fritters away time or energy that would be better spent on constructive activities.

The Ramchal provides guidelines for evaluating our fears and weeding out illogical excuses:

> Another obstacle to alacrity is an inordinate fear and a great terror of what time may bring about. One time a person may be afraid of the cold or the heat; another time, of accidents; and a different time, of

> disease, or the wind, and so on.... Instead, his heart should be firm in the trust of Hashem and he should not fear the consequences of time or the dangers it may bring.
>
> You may object that we find many places where our Sages say that a person is obligated to guard himself well and not put himself into danger, even if he is righteous and has good deeds to his credit....
>
> But know that there is appropriate fear, and there is foolish fear. There is trust, and there is folly. For the Blessed Master created man with common sense and sound logic so that he can conduct himself properly and guard himself from the harmful things that were created to punish evildoers. If someone does not wish to conduct himself wisely, but exposes himself to dangers — this is not trust, but folly. Such a person is a sinner, for he transgresses the Will of the Blessed Creator, Who wants him to guard himself. Consequently, in addition to the inherent danger of the situation in which he places himself because of his recklessness, he also becomes liable to punishment because of having done a sinful act. Therefore, the sin itself [of recklessness] leads him to be punished.
>
> This safeguarding of himself and this fear, which is based on reason and logic, is appropriate. Of fear it is said: "The shrewd one sees evil and takes cover, but fools pass through and are punished."[19]
>
> But foolish fear is when a person wishes to add protection upon protection and fear upon fear. He makes safeguards for his safeguards in such a way that it results in the obstruction of his Torah learning and his service of Hashem.
>
> The principle by which we can differentiate between the two kinds of fear is the rule stated by the Sages, "In a case where the danger of harm is common, we relate differently to the situation." For when harm is probable and well known, one should take precautions. But in a case where there is no known risk of harm, there is no reason to be afraid. About such cases it is said, "If we do not see a problem, we do not presume one to exist."[20] And "The wise person judges only by what he sees[21] [actual facts, not imagined possibilities.]"[22]

The principle by which the Ramchal differentiates between the two kinds of fear is established by our Sages: "In a case where the danger of harm is common, we relate differently to the situation."[23] When harm is probable, precautions are in order. In a case when there is no known risk, however, there is no reason to be afraid. Consequently, "If we do not see a problem, we do not presume one to exist." In addition, "The wise person judges only by what he sees [actual facts, not imagined possibilities]."

Laziness leads to destructive fear; together they generate a distorted picture of our situation. We can only hope to reach an accurate picture after we free ourselves of the influence of these harmful inclinations. Once we are willing to act, we must collect all the relevant information and check if we have an accurate picture. We must use our common sense to judge whether anything really important is at stake, and whether the risk is significant, or only a distant possibility.

"If I Am Not for Myself..."

Laziness and the feeling that "It's so hard" are sometimes related to what we expect from others — the assumption that somebody else should be doing the job. A person can suddenly seem to have a marvelous appreciation for the abilities of his friend, spouse, or coworker. He tells himself:

- ◆ "I'd better leave this to him. He would do the job much better than I ever could."
- ◆ "I think he really loves this kind of work."
- ◆ "It would take me so long to do this, but he can get it done in no time at all."
- ◆ "This would be a wonderful challenge for him. It would really boost his self-confidence!"

Laziness can make a person give up on himself easily and exaggerate everyone else's abilities. "I can't do it; only he can." Or, "I can only do it with his help." It pays for the lazy person to humble himself — as long as someone else will be honored with the task that he wants to escape from doing!

> It was noon on a hot day. Six people were sitting in a seven-seater inter-city taxi, anxiously waiting for a seventh passenger to turn up so that the taxi could depart.
>
> As time dragged on and no additional passenger appeared, they began to demand that the driver set out with just the six of them. "How long do you expect us to wait? Nobody's going to come. Hardly anyone is even out on the street in this heat!"
>
> But the driver insisted that going with less than a full taxi would mean that he would make no profit on the trip.
>
> Finally, the passengers' patience ran out and they decided to teach the driver a lesson. They all got out off the taxi and went their separate ways, leaving the driver high and dry.

Of course, the passengers could have opted for the simple solution: each of them just had to pay an additional sixth of their fare to compensate for the missing passenger. The difference would have been negligible, and it certainly would have been worth their while to pay it rather than wait in the heat of the day and perhaps even cancel their plans.

Yet none of the passengers spoke up to suggest this solution. In fact, because they were all handicapped by the same mindset, they probably didn't even consider it. They were so sure that the solution had to come from a seventh passenger, or from the driver — it never occurred to them that they, themselves, could solve the problem. Or, perhaps they were blinded by the attitude that it wasn't fair to pay a higher-than-usual price.

Isn't it a shame, though, to sit and wait for other people to take action? Isn't it a pity to rely on others when we have the power to help ourselves?

When everyone relies on someone else to do the job, not much gets accomplished. In the words of our Sages, "The dish prepared by two chefs is neither hot nor cold" — because each of them expects the other to take care of it![24]

This tendency to leave responsibility to others applies not only to jobs and problems. In the world of character improvement, as well, a person often waits... for *others* to change! He expects *them* to learn to avoid doing things that annoy him. He expects the other guy to smile at him first, the new classmate sitting next to him to strike up the conversation, and the neighbor who passes by to be the one to greet *him*.

The same can be said of a group of people who are about to do something wrong. Consider a group of boys planning some kind of mischief. If they stop to think about it, a good number of them would actually prefer not to join in — but each one is cowed by his unwillingness to play the role of *tzaddik* in front of the others. Each of them waits for someone to speak up, back out, and encourage everyone else to drop the idea, too. If only *someone* would step forward and take that responsibility!

People usually have especially high expectations of their spouses. Each one waits for the other to lend a hand not only in practical matters, but also in emotional and spiritual ones. Each feels that the other should be the one to apologize for yesterday's argument without making any demands of his own. If these "reasonable" expectations are not fully met, he feels that his own development is being stifled.

Interestingly, in the business world, people do not have any trouble at all about taking the initiative with a smile and a friendly greeting. When people are eager to close a deal or to advance in their careers, everyone can be mature enough to project affability. They see opportunity in front of them, which arouses their good side in a very natural way — so they find no need to wait for the other guy to start being nice. When it comes to other areas, unfortunately, many of us seem to lose this easy geniality.

Many people who would like to improve themselves and overcome their negative traits keep putting off the project — they are waiting for someone else to make the first move. Sadly, they are still waiting…

We need to drop the assumption that we are incapable of helping ourselves. We must pick up, instead, the motto of Hillel: "If I am not for myself, who will be for me?"[25] We all encounter situations when we have no choice but to strike out on our own. At such times, we find new powers and new horizons unfolding before us because we are finally free of our expectations of others.

Even when we *can* get other people to do something for us or help us, it's often worth our while to tackle it on our own. As our Sages say, "If someone is dependent on the mercies of others, the world is darkened for him, and his life is not worth living."[26] The less we depend on others, the more accomplished we feel. Our constructive abilities become stronger and more deeply ingrained as we exercise them; we get ourselves in shape so that we can accept future challenges without relying on others.

> **Note**: This is not to say that we should swing to the opposite extreme and never ask for anyone's help as a matter of principle, or believe that asking for it is always a sign of weakness. The golden mean is to accept responsibility and enjoy doing a job ourselves as long as we aren't ashamed to ask for help after we've done our best.

Sometimes we're so out of practice in helping ourselves that we don't believe that we have the internal resources to meet life's challenges, grow, or change. The Talmud provides an example of a person who thought that he was too far gone to help himself. That man was Elazar ben Durdaya. After coming to an abrupt and shattering awareness of the depth of his sin, Elazar ben Durdaya sought his path to *teshuvah*.

> *He went and sat between two mountains and said, "Mountains and hills, ask mercy for me!" They told him, "Before we ask for you, we must ask for ourselves, for it says, 'For the mountains shall be moved*

> and the hills shall collapse.'"[27] [He asked similarly of the heaven and earth, the sun and moon, and the stars and constellations, and all gave him similar answers]. Finally, he said, "It depends on me alone."
>
> He put his head between his knees and sobbed hysterically until his soul left him. A Divine voice proclaimed, "Rabbi Elazar ben Durdaya is destined for the World to Come." ...Not only was his repentance accepted; he was even designated "Rabbi."[28]

Ultimately, Elazar ben Durdaya realized that nothing in the universe could compensate for his own role, and that the responsibility for himself was his alone.

To end on a happier note, here is the story of Elkana, who didn't wait 'till the last minute to take advantage of his potential.

> "That man [Elkana] *went up from his town.*" — *He became elevated in his household; he became elevated in his courtyard; he became elevated in his town; he became elevated in all of Israel. And all this elevation was caused by no one but himself.*[29]

So, when one of life's challenges comes your way, don't procrastinate or be quick to pass the buck to someone else. Take a second motto from Hillel, "And if not now, when?"[30]

"Haste Makes Waste"

You might have a question: throughout chapter 8, we discussed the consequences of pushing too hard or too fast toward our goals. How does this new, positive mode of swiftness fit into the picture? We learn from the *Orchos Tzaddikim*:

> *Although alacrity is beneficial, a person should take care not to be too rushed in the efforts he makes — the speeding driver courts disaster, and the one that races on foot is bound to stumble. In any event, it's impossible to make constructive changes in hurried confusion. Corrections are effected only with patient deliberation. What, then, is positive alacrity? A person's heart and mind should be alert, and his limbs ready to work — but in no way should he rush in*

> *a panic. This requires great wisdom, knowing when to be quick and when to stall.*[31]

It has been said that alacrity is a virtue — as long as it is an expression of an internal quality rather than active rushing.[32] It should reflect a simple readiness to act, as well as promptness. Haste, on the other hand, is usually nonconstructive and should be avoided when:

◆ handling sudden inspiration;

◆ planning a project;

◆ reaching conclusions;

◆ dealing with household responsibilities;

◆ managing at work;

◆ trying to succeed in one's studies.

Let's take a closer look at some scenarios in which these extremes of haste and procrastination complicate a situation, while the golden mean of alacrity — or promptness — provides a healthy solution which gets results. Notice the differences between the responses people chose.

HANDLING SUDDEN INSPIRATION

👎 *Haste*

> Immediately following an inspiring Yom Kippur with his yeshivah, Aharon felt as if he had been totally renewed. He wanted to make the most of his sense of elevation and decided to inaugurate a fresh rededication to Torah by learning all night. Since the fast had been especially difficult — the weather was stifling and the air-conditioning in the *beis medrash* had conked out during *Mussaf* — Aharon wasn't really in shape for an all-nighter. Although the first few hours flew by with Aharon feeling on top of the world, by 2 A.M. he was ready to collapse, and had to force himself to abandon his

Talmud and crawl to bed. The next morning, Aharon was so exhausted that he failed to hear his alarm ring. He missed the first *zman krias Shema*, and by the time he finished *Shacharis* and some sluggish learning, he felt like a failure...

👎 Procrastination

Yankel finished all six *sedarim* of *mishnayos* in a year's time. His friend Chatzkel encouraged him to start again immediately so as not to lose his momentum. He urged him to get into the habit of finishing every year, just as he had that first year. Yankel agreed in principle, but insisted that he felt "burnt-out" and needed to take a few weeks vacation.... He never got back into it again.

👍 Promptness

After a most exhilarating Simchas Torah, during the fervent dancing of *hakafos shnios*, Daniel felt as though a new world was opening up for him in his *avodas Hashem*. With the singing of *"Tov li Toras picha"* reverberating in his ears, Daniel tried to figure out how he could make this feeling of love and commitment to the Torah last. "What use is feeling this way, if tomorrow I'm back to business as usual?" He decided, then and there, to get up twenty minutes earlier than usual every day. That way, he could learn the *sifrei machshavah* he usually couldn't find the time for — before the yeshivah *minyan* began.

PLANNING A PROJECT

👎 Haste

Mrs. Zimmerman was struck with a brilliant idea: why not organize a *shiur* for the women of her community every Rosh Chodesh? It would provide some much-needed cohesion among the women, and perhaps she could even serve light refreshments so that they ladies would enjoy a little monthly celebration of their own? Since Rosh Chodesh Kislev was only four days away, Mrs. Zimmerman (always efficient) set to work immediately: getting the speaker, arranging for the use of the shul, designing and putting up flyers, and ordering cakes. She got so carried away that, until *erev Rosh Chodesh,* she failed to realize that the Mendelson wedding (planned three months earlier) was scheduled for the same night, effectively cutting her intended crowd down to a fifth.

👎 *Procrastination*

Two days before Purim, Chaya Adler decided that it would be a good idea to organize a *shiur* (with refreshments, of course) for Rosh Chodesh Nisan. By then, most women were already up to their ears making Pesach and could appreciate the opportunity to get out from under the bleach for an evening. Since Purim was just around the corner, she thought that it would be better to leave the details for afterward. She left a note for herself on the refrigerator as a reminder and got busy with baking and *shalach manos.* Each day that went by after Purim found Chaya more deeply entrenched in her own Pesach cleaning; every time she passed her refrigerator she thought, "Let me just finish… and then I'll get right down to making some phone calls." On *erev Rosh Chodesh*, she finally managed to sit down with her phone book to make the calls — but by then, not one of the women she called was willing to commit to coming, since they hadn't made room in their tight schedules.

👍 *Promptness*

Mrs. Harari felt inspired — she wanted to begin a Shabbos afternoon *shiur* in her home on the laws of *Shemiras HaLashon.* Since it was already Wednesday, she realized that if she started making phone calls now, she might not get a very good response. Mrs. Harari smiled, shrugged, and said, "I can start making phone calls now — for the Shabbos *after* this one!"

REACHING CONCLUSIONS/TAKING ACTION

👎 *Haste*

As Mrs. Green checked the mailbox on her way into the building, she found an envelope without a stamp. She opened it and found a scribbled note: "Yossi doesn't put the garbage bag into the can neatly. He should be punished. He shouldn't have sweets for two days' time." There was no signature. She thought to herself — "Who could have written this note if not for Mr. Brown, my downstairs neighbor? Two weeks ago, he mentioned a problem about the garbage, and half a year ago he sent a note to a different neighbor." But Mrs. Green thought that this time he had gone way overboard, telling her just how to train her children!

She went upstairs and wrote a response, thanking Mr. Brown for his concern but admonishing him for his lack of tact and consideration of boundaries. She went downstairs and quietly slipped the note under her neighbor's door.

When Mr. Green called later in the morning, Mrs. Green told him about the note and what she had done. Mr. Green was silent for a moment and said, "But dear, when I noticed the garbage this morning as I left with Yossi for *cheder*, I was in a rush and scribbled the note off to you so I wouldn't forget..."

👎 *Procrastination*

Mrs. Shalomi looked down from her front porch at the children playing in the yard. To her shock and dismay, she caught a glimpse of her neighbor's son, Eliyahu Zeller, as he boxed her son Ya'akov's ear! Ya'akov looked up at the house and saw his mother standing on the porch. His ear was smarting; he saw her wave him upstairs, but he decided that he didn't want to go in just yet. Ya'akov stayed in the courtyard for another fifteen minutes before coming upstairs, and by the time he did he had forgotten about his ear entirely.

As he walked into the house, Mrs. Shalomi asked him what had happened. Ya'akov shrugged and said, "We were playing and Eli got mad at me. It's no big deal." This wasn't the first time that Eliyahu Zeller, who outweighed Ya'akov by about twenty pounds, had gone overboard and gotten too rough, and lately it had been getting worse. But since Ya'akov didn't seem too concerned, Mrs. Shalomi didn't feel that it was necessary to intervene.

The following week, Mrs. Shalomi was preparing supper when she heard screams coming from the courtyard. She ran out to the porch and saw Ya'akov sitting on the ground with his hands on his head, shrieking. Mrs. Shalomi ran downstairs. On the way she passed one of the Zeller boys who blurted, "Eliyahu pushed Ya'akov and he fell and hurt his head." Mrs. Shalomi bolted past a gang of small children huddled around her son and scooped him into her arms. Eliyahu Zeller stood to the side with his hands in his pockets, looking guilty. Some twelve stitches later (thank G-d the cut wasn't too deep), Mrs. Shalomi sorely regretted ignoring the situation with the neighbor's boy for as long as she had. She resolved to speak to Mrs. Zeller as soon as she got home from the emergency room.

Promptness

Dov Cohen put on his most pitiful expression. He knocked on his mother's bedroom door. "Imma? Imma?"

"What is it?" He heard her wash her hands and get up from her bed. "Imma, I don't feel well."

"Dov, what's bothering you this morning? Don't you feel better since yesterday? You said you had a headache," she emerged from her room, "and I let you stay home from *cheder*. What's the problem now?"

"Imma," he looked up and pretended to blink back a tear, "my stomach hurts me. It really does! I feel too sick to go back to *cheder* today."

It was difficult for Mrs. Cohen to suppress a giggle, his playacting was so transparent. At the same time, she felt a little knot in her own stomach. Why didn't her sweet, little boy want to go to *cheder*? He always loved going! True, he just started with a new Rebbe, but she had met him and he seemed so dedicated and patient. What was going on?

"Let me give you some breakfast, sweetie, and we'll see what we'll do..."

As Mrs. Cohen bustled around her kitchen, she tried to come up with a game plan for getting to the bottom of this. Should she wait until tonight and call the Rebbe? Or should she bring him in late and speak to the Rebbe during recess? Mrs. Cohen was not the type to put things off, so she decided to bring Dov in herself and try to elicit information from him on the way in to *cheder*.

An hour and a half later, Mrs. Cohen, Dov, and little Shimmy in the stroller made their way toward school.

"Is there something bothering you about *cheder*, Dovy?" Mrs. Cohen probed gently.

Dov thought a minute. "Not really. I like going to *cheder*."

"How do you feel about your new Rebbe?" She let the question fall softly.

"He's really great. It's not him, just..." He didn't seem to want to continue.

"Just what, sweetie?" Mrs. Cohen held her breath.

"Well, one of the other boys told the class not to let me play with the rest of them during recess. Rebbe Yosef never let things like that happen! But this boy knows that the new Rebbe won't stop him, so he keeps telling people not to play with me." They walked through the building quietly and met Dov's class just as they were heading outside for recess. Mrs. Cohen had a quick word with the new Rebbe, pointed out the situation, and headed for home. Most of all, she felt satisfied with herself for having tackled the issue head-on instead of waiting for the problem to solve itself.

DEALING WITH HOUSEHOLD RESPONSIBILITIES
👎 Haste

One Sunday afternoon, Mr. Berger finally got around to hanging those bookshelves his wife had bought weeks before. He carefully laid out his drill, bits, and screws on the telephone table so they would be handy. Mr. Berger glanced at his watch and remembered, "I have to pick Dvori up from *gan* in ten minutes! I'd better get this done quickly now, otherwise it will never get done." He marked the holes at lightning speed, checking his watch all the while. True, he had the holes drilled ten minutes later as he shot out the door, but, unfortunately, most of them were not placed properly at all. When he returned, he had to remeasure all over again, refill, and redrill five of the holes.

👎 *Procrastination*

It's a good thing that Mrs. Landsman has a home with more than adequate closet space. That way, she has room to store all her undone mending, unironed shirts, and unfolded laundry as it piles up. Unfortunately, once the piles get too big, the thought of all that work waiting to be done puts Mrs. Landsman into a state of high anxiety. To calm her nerves, she usually sits down with a cup of coffee and a good book.

The day of reckoning eventually arrives (no more clean underwear, no unwrinkled shirts, no socks without holes...) and Mrs. Landsman is forced to open one of her many closets and get to work. When that time comes, she spends hours on the backlog, barely making a dent. Invariably, she closes the closets up with a sigh and says to herself, "I wonder why I even bother. After hours of work, it doesn't seem as though I've gotten anywhere!" This feeling makes it all the more difficult for her to approach the piles until the next day of reckoning rolls around.

👍 *Promptness*

Mrs. Furst smiled as she taped her neatly written sign to her refrigerator door. She had just finished reading a popular household management guidebook, and she wanted to put what she had learned into practice right away. Her small, angular script read:

"As you move around the house, pick things up as you go along."

"If you're waiting for the water to boil, don't watch the pot; fold laundry instead!"

"If you're talking on the phone, do the dishes or peel vegetables."

"If you're doing dishes, clean the sink and the counter while you're there."

"And don't forget: the time you waste is your own!"

Just then, the phone rang. It was Mrs. Furst's sister. She grabbed a bowl, her peeler, and a bag of potatoes and got to work as they chatted. By the time Mrs. Furst got off the phone, she had prepared all the vegetables for the *cholent* and kugel, without even realizing it!

STAYING ON TOP OF SCHOOL/WORK/LEARNING

👎 *Haste (in school)*

At her teacher's signal, Ariella turned her exam face up on her desk. Her pen was poised over her paper and her watch stared at her from its station on the table in front of her, to the left of her test. Although two hours were allotted for the exam, her anxiety about the presence of a time limit made her feel as if she were (sorry to say) a horse at the racetrack and they had just let up the gate. And they're off! She ran through the first two sections with ease, but around midway through the exam, she began to feel tired. Since Ariella was afraid that a moment's rest wouldn't leave her time to finish, she didn't pause at all and pushed herself to finish the third section. She began the essay questions feeling none too confident about that hastily completed third section and raced through the final two questions, supplying sloppy long-winded answers when the test demanded well-organized, concise, and well thought-out responses. She turned in her paper with half an hour to spare, relieved to have it out of her hands, and left the room to get some air.

👎 Procrastination (at work)

Mr. Ashkenazi, a freelance wedding photographer, handed out his card at the Simon wedding along with his warmest smile. "Do you think you might be free on July the 12th?" asked Mr. Levi. "We're making a *bar mitzvah* and we still haven't settled on a photographer. My wife is very particular," he shrugged noncommittally.

"I'll have to check my reservation list," said Mr. Ashkenazi, "but I'm fairly certain it's fine. Why don't you have your wife give me a call and I'll make an appointment for her to come by and see my work?"

Mr. Levi said that he would do just that — he "much preferred to have a *heimishe Yid* shoot the *simchah* than some anonymous photographer out of the yellow pages." And that was that.

Two weeks later, Mrs. Levi came in for her appointment. She said she liked what she saw and that she was pretty much settled on taking Mr. Ashkenazi. She asked him to call her in a few days to remind her to come in to sign the contract.

Mr. Ashkenzi was confident that the Levi's wouldn't find anyone who does better work at a better price and left a note for himself to call her in three days.

Over the next few days, every time he saw the note he said, "Let me just finish what I'm doing and I'll make that call." On the fourth day, he was called by a repeat customer who wanted to book him for a wedding on the same night. Mr. Ashkenazi turned him down. "I'm sorry, Mr. BenTov, but I have a prior engagement."

On July 7th, a full week later, Mr. Ashkenazi finally called Mrs. Levi to remind her to come in and sign the contract. "Oh, but Mr. Ashkenazi!" she gasped, "I found someone else *ages* ago! Since you didn't get back to me, I just went with my second choice. You know how it is, making a *simchah* and everything..." He was flabbergasted and quickly ended the conversation.

Naturally, Mr. BenTov had also hired his second-choice photographer and Mr. Ashkenazi spent the evening of July 12th wondering where he had gone wrong.

✏️ Promptness (while studying)

As Eliezer sat to review the halachos in the *Mishnah Berurah* that he needed to know for Sukkos, he remembered the resolution that he had made while going over *Hilchos Yom HaKippurim*: to always follow up on the sources in the *Be'er HaGolah* and the *Sha'ar HaTziun*. The fact that the *Orchos Tzaddikim* lists the promptness to research thoroughly as a manifestation of the attribute of *zerizus* made him feel all the more motivated. Even though, to be honest, it took him much longer than he had anticipated, by the time he finished the laws of the festival he felt he knew them more deeply than he had ever known them before. The time he had invested had been repaid to him many times over in the feeling of satisfaction that he carried with him all *Yom Tov* long.

These stories demonstrate the risks of haste and procrastination, and highlight the way the golden mean of promptness operates in day-to-day life. We have seen haste leading the characters in the stories to unrealistic and foolhardy expectations and rash decisions. Some of the characters in the stories skipped crucial steps, felt pressured, and sometimes even acted with a bit of hysteria, which caused mistakes.

Those who procrastinated fared no better; they let their inspiration fade, leaving them with insufficient motivation to proceed. They let their responsibilities lay by the wayside, ignoring them to the point that even when they did try to do something, by that time the situation had become uncorrectable. This procrastination led the person, at times, to feel unfulfilled out of a lack of satisfactory functioning or achievement. At other times it led to dangerous realms of irresponsibility.

Those characters who acted with promptness activated their inspiration. They made practical, realistic decisions which they were able to — and did — carry out successfully. They were able to avoid problems, and felt satisfied and fulfilled.

Life really can be smooth sailing — as long as we make promptness a priority, keep an eye out for haste, and don't procrastinate!

> **THINK ABOUT IT**
>
> **HOW DOES THIS EXPLAIN:**
> ◆ why people confuse haste and promptness?
> ◆ the dangers of procrastination?
>
> How do each of the scenarios above illustrate finding the golden mean between haste and procrastination?

Worth It or Not?

Let's review. When you face some challenge and have to decide whether or not to accept it, you can keep laziness from influencing your decision by using the following techniques:

1. Imagine that you are ready and willing to do whatever may turn out to be necessary,
2. Honestly examine all sides of the question. Screen out all rationalizations and flawed reasoning that prevent you from getting an accurate picture of the situation. Be on the lookout for the classic excuses:
   ◆ "It's too hard."
   ◆ "It's not necessary."
   ◆ "It's not worth the effort."
   ◆ "Someone else can do it better."

3. If you're inclined to believe one of these statements, and think that it isn't simply an excuse, ask yourself:
   - *"It's too hard":* Is my attitude unreasonably negative about this job? Might it not be so difficult, after all? If the whole job *is* too hard, is there some part of it that I can do? Am I ready to do that much?
   - *"It's not necessary":* Do I really appreciate how much I can benefit from doing this? And if I really *don't* need to do this, what other constructive course of action do I need to take instead?
   - *"It's not worth the effort":* How valuable is this goal really? If I could accomplish it without much effort, would I want it? If I were already working toward it, would I consider it worth my while to keep going so as not to waste the effort I'd already put in? Would I, instead, feel that I shouldn't waste any more time than I already had?

If you're still in doubt, talk it over with an unbiased person whose opinion you trust.

Weeding out these excuses will free you to make correct decisions and break the bonds of laziness. Once you have learned to do whatever is within your capabilities, you will feel less dependent on others, and experience a new sense of power and accomplishment. Move ahead with alacrity — with energetic enthusiasm — and you will be swift as the deer to reach your goals and fulfill the Will of your Father in Heaven!

FINDING YOURSELF IN WHAT YOU'VE LEARNED

1. Organize a list of the times when you managed to reject any lame excuses that you wanted to make. Add to it the times that

you succeeded in doing things that you had considered difficult. Feel good about it.

2. On what occasions have you managed to take the initiative or accept responsibility when you could have pushed it on to someone else instead?

3. Make a list of the rationalizations that you use to generally avoid taking constructive action. Are these reasons really justified?

APPLYING WHAT YOU'VE LEARNED

1. Create a chart of your daily activities and obligations. Over the course of a few days, experiment with the way you manage your routines. On one day, time how long it takes to do the job sluggishly; the following day, do it with alacrity and time it again. Keep track of the difference in time saved and your general mood, and post it up as a model and motivator.

2. Now refer back to your list of rationalizations in question 3 above. If what keeps you from undertaking a new project is a lack of time, tell yourself that saving time with *zerizus* can help open up new slots in your schedule.[33]

3. Refer back to your list of rationalizations in question 3 above. Compare them with the lists beginning on pages 265-272 of this chapter. What counter-arguments could you supply to *your* list of excuses? Write them down, and try reading them aloud.

NOTES TO CHAPTER NINE

1. Based on *Mesillas Yesharim*, chapters 6 and 7.
2. Mishlei 26:16.
3. *Metzudos* on Mishlei 26:16.

4. According to *Kabbalah*, a human being is composed of different elements. Two of them are fire/energy and earth/passivity. It is this element of passivity that causes laziness, or the tendency toward inertia. In other words, human beings possess a life force that encourages action and spiritual rising, and an inanimate force that pulls us toward inaction, spiritual stagnation, and death. See *Sha'ar HaKedushah*, part I, *sha'ar 2*.
5. *Mesillas Yesharim*, chapter 7.
6. Rus 3:18.
7. *Rus Rabbah* 7:6.
8. Shemos 7:14, 8:28.
9. Similarly in Shemos 4:21, 9:34, 10:20, 11:10, 14:8. See also Yechezkel 11:19-20: "And I shall remove the stone heart from their body and give them a heart of flesh so that they shall follow My laws and observe My statutes." These sources all attribute a failure to make accomplishments to a hard or "stony" heart.
10. "Only for this the proud one may praise himself: for understanding and knowing Me... but the House of Israel all have uncircumcised hearts" (Yirmeyahu 9:23-25).
11. Rabbeinu Bachaya on Devarim 10:16; see Malbim there.
12. Devarim 10:16.
13. *Moreh Nevuchim*, section 3, chapter 33. There is a difference of opinions among the translators/ interpreters of the Rambam. According to the Narvonne, "foreskin of the heart" is a euphemism for lack of inspiration and failure to hear, as if a barrier exists so that other people's words don't register. According to Rav Shmuel ibn Tibbon, "circumcise the foreskin of your heart" is an exhortation to pay attention to what other people are saying — not only to hear, but to listen and respond to the will of others. According to Rav Yosef Kapach, the term means that a person should not be stubborn or arrogant, but responsive, attentive, deliberate, and flexible.
14. Devarim 32:15.
15. See Yeshaya 6:10 and 44:18.
16. Mishlei 22:13.
17. See *Tur* and *Beis Yosef* on *Orach Chayim*, chapter 1.
18. See volume 2 of this series, chapter 3.
19. Mishlei 22:3.
20. *Chullin* 56b.

21. *Bava Basra* 131a.
22. *Mesillas Yesharim*, chapter 9.
23. *Pesachim* 8b.
24. *Eruvin* 3a, see Maharsha there.
25. *Avos* 1:14.
26. *Beitzah* 32b.
27. Yeshaya 54:10.
28. *Avodah Zarah* 17a.
29. *Midrash Shmuel* on I Shmuel 1:3.
30. *Avos* 1:14.
31. *Orchos Tzaddikim*, end of *sha'ar* 15.
32. *Ma'alas HaMiddos, ma'alah* 20, see edition published by Eshkol with vowels, p. 259.
33. For a further discussion of time management (particularly for the homemaker), you might want to refer to Nechama Berg and Chaya Levine, *It's About Time* (Brooklyn: Mesorah Publications, 1992).

🕮 10 🕮
Strong As a Lion

Marching Forward with Fortitude

Now that we have learned to be bold as leopards, light as eagles, and swift as deer, we come to the fourth dimension of Rabbi Yehuda ben Teima's formula: being strong as lions by approaching our goals with inner strength and confidence.

We have already reviewed several tactics that our *yetzer hara* uses to try to hinder our progress. Yet another tactic is its attempt to make us underestimate our own potential. Our *yetzer hara* makes us doubt our ability to rise to the challenges that we face. If it successfully convinces us that we lack the energy, skill, or merit to succeed, we may be left feeling that expending effort for the sake of our goal is a waste of time. Furthermore, even if we do attempt to complete a project, we approach it apprehensively. With this half-discouraging mindset, we can actually talk ourselves into failure.

Other times, we do undertake the project, but we are accompanied more by a fear of failure or encountering difficulty than by the hope for success. Here a person might fall prey to a disposition which we will call Partial Despair. This applies to situations where a person's concern that he might fail can keep him from fully committing to the project, and can dampen the enthusiasm and optimism that would contribute to the quality of what he is doing. The result of partial despair is work well below our potential.

Feeling less than adequate can harm us in many ways. It keeps us from trying new things which may be unfamiliar to us or developing our potential in realms where we lack experience or proven success. When we decide at the outset that we don't have what it takes to succeed, we close ourselves off to many opportunities for developing our potential.[1]

Emotional strength is not acquired immediately. As we rid ourselves of our inner resistance and conflicts of will, and try to reach our goals with enthusiasm, we prepare the groundwork from which inner strength unfolds. Such staunchness makes us feel like emotional powerhouses, and the obstacles in our way fade, appearing insignificant.[2] Intellectually, we recognize that those obstacles are real, and determine the best way to deal with them — but emotionally, they lose their provocative edge. We pursue our objectives with the natural self-possession of a lion pursuing its prey, a kind of confidence that infuses us with even more strength to reach our goals.[3]

The *mitzvah* of "you shall walk in His ways"[4] obliges us to emulate Hashem by imitating the Divine attributes. According to the Rambam, these characteristics are to be found among the praises that the prophets offered to Hashem by calling Him "'Righteous...', 'Perfect...', '*Courageous* and *Strong*', and so on."[5] This means that every time we make an effort to fortify ourselves, we've fulfilled a positive commandment. When we face an emotional or spiritual challenge, we should remember that Hashem never gives us impossible tests.[6] We should not feel like a bird trying to escape from a trap, or a lone soldier on the battlefield. We should, instead, see ourselves as accomplished warriors that have been assigned to merely chase away a few scrawny cats.

For example, when a person finds himself surrounded by people who are speaking *lashon hara* (derogatory words about others), he should calmly plan his response, without feeling ashamed or intimidated. Is it worthwhile to try to rebuke the others, or might this lead them to speak even more *lashon hara* as they try to justify themselves? Would changing the subject work? Should he simply walk away? He can only evaluate these options freely if he is strong and confident and not cowed by what anyone may think or say.

Inner strength and courage are the polar opposite of despair. Despair smothers a person's energies and dulls his will to act. With it, he imagines pitfalls at every turn and feels unable to cope with them or his own dismal emotions. A robust heart, however, provides us with the courage to easily clear away the many obstacles before us so that we can accomplish great things. This courage makes us feel in control of our spirit and able to maneuver our emotions in any direction that we choose.

This fourth stage of development — a sense of inner strength and confidence — reinforces what we achieve in the first three stages: determination, lightness and ease, and alacrity. Being "strong as a lion" not only allows us to march bravely forward, making our obstacles fade before us. Armed with a sense of fortitude, our challenges appear simpler — we feel in control of our emotions. We therefore find it easier to resolve our will. Tension isn't a problem because we do not feel the need to exert great emotional effort to carry out our decisions. Our inner strength makes it easy for us to shake off lethargy and maintain energetic enthusiasm. Armed with might and courage, secure in the knowledge that Hashem is at our side, we allow our resolve and the complete spectrum of our emotional strengths to shine and work harmoniously toward the realization of our goals.

> **THINK ABOUT IT**
>
> **HOW DOES THIS EXPLAIN:**
> ◆ how inner strength reinforces the other stages of development?
> ◆ how a lack of emotional stamina can stymie even intense efforts toward personal growth?
>
> How does inner strength operate within us?

Impinging on the Quality of Our Functioning

If failure to accomplish difficult tasks, overcome obstacles, or develop opportunities were the only disadvantages of insufficient emotional strength — we would have sufficient cause to approach the subject seriously, and make every effort to acquire it. The damage, however, is much more fundamental and extensive — a weak approach has a profound effect on the entire quality of our functioning. In contrast, inner strength will not only keep you from setting yourself up for Partial Failure, or from giving up completely, but with a confident approach, you will have more vitality and enthusiasm, feeling motivated through the various stages of the project. You will find yourself appreciating the goal and its rewards — you'll even enjoy the challenges involved and find that the process offers a deep sense of fulfillment.

It is in the *yetzer hara's* interest that any positive action we take — no matter how noble — will be devoid of enthusiasm. To throttle our desire, he pulls out his trump card and tries to make us feel weak and apathetic. As those feelings take hold, we might find ourselves thinking: "I'm just *barely* able to... [accomplish the good deed, or avoid the negative act]." "It's so hard for me to focus right now." "Why do I always have to try so hard?" "Either way, I'm going to fail — so why bother putting in so much effort?" The person who has a reasonable chance to accomplish more, might find himself saying, "I'll never finish it; besides, whatever I accomplished already is enough." Even if we manage to implement positive steps, our lack of enthusiasm restricts our progress and debilitates our inner drive.

In a similar vein, a person may complain to himself — while undertaking a reasonable project or chore — "Why do I have to do this myself? Why am I not getting help, encouragement, and appreciation from others?" A person may even justify himself by saying "the reason that I am not doing this *mitzvah* happily is because my [parent, teacher, spouse, friend] is not giving me adequate emotional support." Or even worse, "how can I do the right thing if... is always getting in the way?" In this sense, lack of emotional fortitude causes the person to feel the need to lean on others and develop a habit of feeling inadequate unless he gets their support.

The person who chooses to focus on the (sometimes too real) difficulties of the task before him, can never complete it in the best possible manner. When he does a good deed (or avoids evil), he acts as if he half regrets what he's doing. Since he doesn't focus on and enjoy the good that he accomplishes, he does it all by rote — or worse, with a bad attitude. Being caught up in an unproductive mindset makes it a challenge to act graciously and lovingly even when offering assistance to someone in need.

Many Torah sources discuss the necessary attitude for performance of a *mitzvah*: the need for great joy; that one should race to perform a *mitzvah*; that one should long for the opportunity to perform a *mitzvah*; that one should do *mitzvos* imbued with love of Hashem... not out of a feeling of obligation and wanting to be done with it, as if it were a burden, but out of love; that even without being commanded, he would have longed to do it and bring *nachas* to Hashem. Rabbi Shimon bar Yochai even goes so far as to say that any *mitzvah* performed without love and awe of Hashem isn't a *mitzvah!*[7]

We do many good deeds, each of which is essentially the fulfillment of a *mitzvah*, or even several *mitzvos*. However, when our activities are accompanied by background feelings of weakness, (either emotional or physical), it becomes hard for us to approach *mitzvos* joyfully. When we are preoccupied with our exhaustion, we seldom long for the opportunities to do *mitzvos* (and we certainly don't race to perform them). It becomes a real challenge to overcome the feeling that we'd like to be over and done with them.

The Tur explains that the term "strong as a lion" refers to the heart, since "Strength in *avodas Hashem* is in the heart." This means "That he should fortify his heart and eliminate any division in it... to do the *mitzvos* with all [his] heart. There is a world of difference between one who performs a *mitzvah* with deep mindfulness, and one who does it by rote."[8] We already do so much good, it would be a shame if our accomplishments would be devoid of mental and emotional content — just for lack of inner fortitude.

When a person is staunchly bringing some task to completion, it's natural that he feel happy with his deeds, that he see their good points, and feel completely devoted to his mission. As he activates that feeling of inner power, he clears more mental space to be filled with good intentions, and he feels suffused with love and joy, enthusiasm, and alacrity.

The Danger of Feeling Unfortunate

One feeling that corrodes the sense of inner strength is feeling unfortunate. Alongside a lack of emotional preparedness for the positive (discussed in chapter 6 of this volume), self-pity undermines our inner fortitude. The person who is overwhelmed with such feelings parallels the *"misonen"* of the *Tanach*. Rashi says that "*onen*" means lowly and weak,[9] and the Ramban, in his commentary on the sin of the *misonenim* in the desert, explains:

> *They got themselves upset by saying, "What will we do, how will we survive in this desert? What will we eat and drink, and how will we tolerate the toil and the affliction — and when will we get out of it?" The [word* misonen*] connotes pain and travail over himself.... For they spoke from embittered spirits.... And it was evil in the Eyes of Hashem. They should have followed Him joyfully, willingly, enjoying all the good He gave them — but, they acted as though they were coerced, full of sorrow and complaints over their situation. That is why the second verse says, "And Bnei Yisrael also [again] sat and cried..."; since they sinned at first by complaining about their discomfort in the desert, [then] they sat and cried again....*[10]

With a "poor me" mentality, a person can get caught up in his irritation when things don't work out in a way that suits him, when progress doesn't conform to the rate he would prefer, or when his considerable investments of energy don't produce satisfying results.

When a person's thoughts turn to how much he's suffered, or that he is still suffering — he starts to feel as though he doesn't have the emotional strength to sacrifice much more. And if a person is beset by the feeling that he has already invested too much time and energy — he loses the willpower to pull himself together and continue to invest effort. It is even possible for him to justify his slackening by thinking that Hashem knows his troubles and certainly understands; that He will have mercy on him and be lenient.

This is how "poor me" thoughts cause a weakening of the heart. The good that he actually does is lackluster because he feels that, since he already worked so hard or sacrificed so much, he deserves a break. He will feel a lack of enthusiasm, apathy, and even pain when approaching his tasks — and perhaps even after completing them. This, in turn, will sap him of his inner strength and deprive him of all its advantages.

On the other hand, when a person feels that his life is full of goodness, he approaches his tasks willingly and joyfully, and with the feeling that he has the energy and motivation to get things done. He also feels as though he could, relatively easily, handle any obstacles which may arise.

Most of us wouldn't like to define ourselves as unfortunate, nor consider ourselves to be complainers. Even so, if we were to examine ourselves, we would recognize that we may tend to mull over subtle feelings of discontentment or anger because we haven't gotten our way. The fact that we aren't as satisfied as we could be affects the quality of our lives and our deeds. It also saps us of much emotional and spiritual strength.

Conversely, when a person activates his feelings of strength, it becomes easy for him to work on his emotions until he attains the perspective that he has so much, and that he is ready to enjoy what is his. Rather than think about how much he's already worked, he focuses on how much energy he really has. That way, his interest and will are aroused in order to avoid doing that which he shouldn't, and to accomplish that which he must. Regarding such a person, the verse proclaims, "And [Hashem's] loved ones are like the sun rising in its strength."[11]

Therefore, when we take steps to fortify our hearts, we need to relate to two points:

1. We should focus on feelings of power, security, and ability (as opposed to weakness and despair). We will deal with this point presently.

2. We should emphasize feelings of happiness, calmness, and enthusiasm (as opposed to self-pity and withdrawal). The upcoming volumes will, with Hashem's help, be devoted to this important subject.

Beware of Bravado!

While we are concerned with all the redeeming qualities of emotional strength, we need to take care not to abuse it. Bravado, or an overdone sense of inner courage, can lead a person to convince himself that he can draw on physical reserves that he doesn't really possess, like attempting to stay awake several extra hours or assuming other responsibilities that are beyond his ability. He may try to refine himself on a very elevated plane, even though he has skipped over the basics.

A person may also demand a constant output of energy from himself. It is possible that he has just put in great effort, and it is, therefore, entirely natural that he feels tired. The person who insists upon always being powerful, and fails to recognize the genuine qualities and limits of emotional strength, is prone to deny real exhaustion and continue to push himself.

A person that forces himself to reach levels for which he isn't physically or emotionally ready, or to accomplish tasks that really are beyond his abilities, is courting a twofold danger. He will either stumble into tension by overextending himself as he struggles to succeed, or descend into despair if he should fail. When that happens, he has actually distanced himself from attaining the attribute of "strong like a lion"; he surely hasn't brought himself closer at all. In such a case, overenthusiasm has ironically backfired into despair — not only neutralizing tactics for growth, but creating new problems as well.

It should be clear, then, that even a strong person has his weak moments. During those times, how does such a person express his attribute of strength? To answer that, we need to become familiar with the "emotional strongman" from all angles.

Only a very small portion of the strongman's life is dedicated to very challenging or unusual tasks. His strength is expressed and observable in his conduct, in his regular activity, and even when he is tired or weak.

Normally, our strongman is happy and energized, yet calm whether approaching a task or bringing it to completion. His emotions are occupied with the reward or the purpose of the action, not with its potential pitfalls, or the time and effort involved. He relates to obstacles only as far as is necessary to decide, in a deliberate and balanced way, the correct course of action. When he has the necessary capabilities, and he sees that the action is profitable, thoughts about effort and exhaustion merely bore him. On the contrary, he derives a special satisfaction from overcoming challenges and succeeding at his endeavor.

In a condition of weakness or exhaustion, the strongman doesn't avoid doing what he can, and he doesn't look to gain from his weakness. He feels free to allow himself the rest he genuinely needs, but he doesn't permit his exhaustion to be the master of his emotions. He is able to evaluate, rather accurately, what he is capable of doing without being manipulated by a bothersome tiredness that can skew his judgment and the quality of his functioning. With careful consideration and a wholehearted commitment to succeed, he estimates whether the program before him suits his current abilities or not. He determines, with an eye to the demands of the moment, just how much rest he needs, and when he can allow himself that time. If he is forced to take care of certain things while tired — he manages as well as he can.

Let's take a look at the approach of Dovid HaMelech: on the one hand, he was a strongman.[12] On the other, he was pursued for part of his life by people plotting to destroy him or humiliate him in the worst way. When he had the strength, he prayed to the Holy One out loud saying,

> "Hear my words, Hashem..." — *when I have the strength to pray. When I lack that strength, and the worry remains locked inside me,* "...know my musings" — *understand my heart's contemplation.*[13]

There were times that Dovid HaMelech was so weak that he wasn't even able to *daven*. Even then he didn't allow himself to fall into passivity; he focused instead on the musings of his heart, and begged Hashem to read his unexpressed thoughts.

The Talmud speaks of Rabbi Zeira who, when he was too weak to learn, would go to sit by the entrance of the *beis medrash* so that when the students passed, he could rise before them in respect and accrue Heavenly reward.[14] He wasn't paralyzed by his situation, but found within himself the strength to rise before scholars, and took full advantage of that strength.

This doesn't negate the fact that sometimes we *do* need absolute rest. There are ample accounts of Torah giants that needed to take a break from learning for a set time since they had overextended themselves; they checked their enthusiasm when they saw that they were overdoing it.

The strongman knows his strengths and recognizes his limitations. He acknowledges that if he were to override his limits, he would, most likely, pay dearly — with tension and exhaustion, which could lead to despair. Therefore, his general disposition is composed and confident. As he focuses on the positive, and on the abilities that he does have, he assesses his goals and decides how much he can undertake while still proceeding powerfully and resolutely.

The strongman's attitude is not limited to professional weight lifters or muscle-bound athletes. It applies just as well to an ill person trying to lift his fallen pillow. Anybody can be a strongman — to the extent that he recognizes his strengths and limitations, and tackles his goals powerfully and resolutely, with the force of a lion.

THINK ABOUT IT

HOW DOES THIS EXPLAIN:

◆ the definition of inner strength?
◆ the problems caused by an exaggerated sense of bravado?

What can a person gain from a healthy sense of his capabilities?

Building Our Inner Strength

The first three stages of Yehuda ben Teima's approach, a resolved will, equanimity, and alacrity, have a reciprocal relationship with inner strength: each contributes to and is reinforced by the other. With the fourth step, inner strength, it becomes easy to develop resolve, composure, and an ability to approach goals swiftly. At the same time, resolve increases stamina, and freedom from tension and fear allows our inner strength the space to develop. When we face the challenges before us with energy and enthusiasm, we also feel flooded with power.

There are still more ways we can build our inner strength and courage:

- *Recognize Your Strengths:* Develop an awareness and inner conviction that you do have the emotional capacity to cope with a wide variety of challenges.
- *Recall Past Successes:* Pull up from your memory those times when you succeeded in controlling your emotions.
- *Set Reasonable Goals:* Make it a habit to modify your goals so that they are within your grasp.
- *Identify Your Talents:* Recognize the many skills and abilities with which you are gifted.
- *Avoid False Humility:* Understand that the true definition of humility includes an honest awareness of your strengths.
- *Recognize Your Worth:* Appreciate your noble stature as a Jew.
- *Trust in Hashem:* Strengthen your conviction that Hashem is always there, near you, to support you through your constructive endeavors.
- *Learn the Rewards of Inner Strength:* Uncover the benefits of emotional fortitude.

Let's examine these points individually and absorb the strength that they can give us.

RECOGNIZE YOUR STRENGTHS: SURPRISE! YOU CAN!

> Eliyahu HaNavi told Rav Anan:
> Once when I was walking, a certain person met me and mocked and scorned my words. I asked him, "What will you answer your Creator on the day of judgment?"
> He told me, "Understanding and knowledge were not given to me that I should read and study."
> I asked him, "My son, what is your occupation?"
> He told me, "Fishing."
> And I asked him, "Who taught you to take linen and weave it into nets and throw them into the sea and catch fish from the sea?"
> He answered me, "Understanding was given to me from Heaven."
> I said to him, "What?! To take linen and weave nets to throw into the sea to catch fish — for that you were given knowledge and understanding from Heaven? But words of Torah, of which it is written, 'For this thing is very close to you'[15] — for that you were not given understanding and knowledge from Heaven?!"
> Immediately [the fisherman] raised his voice and wept, until I said to him, "Do not feel bad. Everyone who passes through this world gives the same answer, but their deeds testify against them."[16]

"*Everyone who passes through this world gives the same answer.*" Implying that *none* of us properly appreciates what treasures our abilities are. Eliyahu, however, warns us that our deeds testify against us because, when we really want something, we somehow come up with the means to procure it and exhibit our dormant talents. This proves that we have reservoirs of potential which extend far beyond what we currently use for our goals, even those we find important.

We have to do some digging to unearth the treasure trove of abilities that lies hidden within us. As we discover it, we can begin to determine which areas demand a more firm and effective approach than we are now providing. Simply knowing that we possess greater gifts than we had realized will, itself, help renew our courage and confidence.

RECALL PAST SUCCESSES: WE ALREADY CONTROL OUR EMOTIONS

Many people accept it as an article of faith that changing their emotional state is pretty much impossible. "This is how I feel, period. What can I do about it?" The angry person doesn't believe that he could *not* explode, the depressed person sees no way of escaping from his melancholy. The nervous, anxious person doesn't understand how he could ever feel calm and confident. Even those people who concede that they could (theoretically) change their emotions are convinced that it's the hardest thing in the world to do.

Many *mitzvos* in the Torah, however, demand certain emotions of us. Love, eliminating hatred, abandoning a grudge, and freedom from jealousy are all part and parcel of our obligations to Hashem and our fellow Jews.[17] Clearly, the Torah assumes that we *are* capable of controlling our emotions.[18]

The Rambam describes the Torah's command to the heart of the Jewish soldier that stands in the thick of battle, as well as a technique to achieve what seems almost impossible. The bracketed terms have been added in order to identify and highlight the various suggestions which the Rambam offers.

> Once he has entered the thick of battle, he must rely on the Help of Israel, its Savior in times of trouble [trust in Hashem], and know that he is fighting for the unity of G-d's Name [focus on the objective]. He must risk his life and not be fearful or frightened. He must not think about his wife and children, but must block out all memory of them, turn away from all other matters [block out distracting thoughts], and concentrate on the battle [focus on the technicalities of the objective]. Whoever begins to have second thoughts and worry about the battle and who terrifies himself, violates... "Do not

> *let your hearts be faint; do not fear or be alarmed, and do not be intimidated by them."*[19] *If he does not conquer [his fears] and does not do battle with all his heart and soul, it is as if he spilled [Jewish] blood, as it says, "So that he not make his brethren's hearts faint like his...."*[20] *Whoever fights with all his heart, fearlessly, and whose sole intention is to sanctify Hashem's Name — he is assured that no harm will befall him and that he will live to build an established home in Israel. He will create merit for himself and his children to eternity and will merit the World to Come.*[21]

When a soldier faces the enemy on the battlefield knowing that his life is in jeopardy, fear and anxiety would seem to be entirely natural and justified. Yet, the Rambam makes it quite clear that this soldier is capable of controlling his emotions, is expected to do so, and will be amply rewarded for fulfilling this obligation.

If a person has the power to reign in his thoughts and direct his will in such an extreme situation, clearly we can manage it while under more mundane pressures.[22] Knowing that we can transcend our emotional state empowers us as we approach our goals. In many cases, we can fortify ourselves until unalterable realities cease to be obstacles — since they no longer overwhelm us.

And here's some more good news: we also have the power to change our bad habits, even those that are deeply entrenched.

Although we may not have thought of it this way, everyone who *davens* does change a habit twice a year. At Pesach and Sukkos, when we rearrange the wording of our prayers to suit the season by referring to wind and rain or to dew, we uproot a six-month-old habit from our minds and transplant a new one. The well-known halachah proves this point: if a person is unsure whether he said the correct phrase, we judge his situation according to the amount of time that has passed since the change began. If at least thirty days have gone by, we assume that the person said the right words because, by the end of thirty days, the *new habit has surely taken root.*[23] Just as a habit of six months can be overturned in thirty days, so too, our individual habits that may have taken root long ago can be weeded out and supplanted with healthier ones in comparatively less time than they took to sprout.

Many people don't realize how much they actually *do* control their will, thoughts, and emotions.

> Once, when the Alter of Slobodka was in the central marketplace of Vilna, he saw a merchant standing behind a stall of knickknacks, venting his rage on a shopper. From the vendor's ranting, the Alter understood that the fellow had badgered him with a litany of questions and had, in the end, bought nothing.
>
> In the midst of this tantrum, another passer-by stopped and expressed an interest in some item on the stand. Instantly the merchant's rage fizzled. He turned to his new customer with a smile, graciously assisting him with the purchase he was considering.
>
> The Alter considered what he had witnessed. Even if the second customer would end up buying something, the merchant's profit on the sale would be negligible. And, of course, the vendor couldn't be certain that he would buy anything. But even the possibility of making a sale was enough to motivate the merchant to take control of himself, remove every trace of his previous anger, and make himself calm and affable for his new customer.
>
> If so, concluded the Alter, all a person has to do to control himself is to envision the profit (even if it is only a potential profit) that awaits him for behaving properly. As it says,[24] "And he saw that tranquility was good and that the land was pleasant, so he inclined his shoulder to accept the burden."[25]

Each of us has surely had similar experiences — times when we were jolted out of a bad mood by suddenly meeting up with a friend or an unexpected, but welcome, guest. Instantly, we snapped out of our gloom to smile warmly and offer a friendly greeting. Such incidents prove that, when we consider it worthwhile, we can control our behavior and state of mind rather easily. We could even draw on such experiences to pull ourselves out of a negative state of mind by *imagining* that such a friend or guest came our way! That way, the memory of those incidents can fortify us to succeed in controlling our emotions again in the future.

Visualizing the vast reward that is reserved for those who overcome their negative impulses should certainly provide ample motivation and inner strength to take control of our emotions and adopt a positive, constructive frame of mind.

Anxiousness is another emotion that we often control without realizing it.

> Baruch had a four o'clock doctor's appointment. Since buses to the office came infrequently, Baruch was forced to take an early bus, and arrived at the doctor's office twenty minutes early. During those twenty minutes, he waited patiently. He had come equipped with a book, and he settled back, relaxed, and read it.
>
> As soon as the hands of the clock reached four o'clock, and then crept toward ten minutes after four, and Baruch's turn still hadn't come, he began to lose his patience. He started thinking about all the errands that he still had to take care of after the appointment, and he began to get tense and anxious. From that point on, he found it too difficult to concentrate on reading. He sat on the edge of his chair, glanced repeatedly at his watch, and couldn't get his mind off of all the other things he had to do. Over and over again he wondered, "*Nu?* When will it be my turn already?"

Why was it that during the first twenty minutes, Baruch was calm, but for the last few minutes, he started to feel anxious?

The answer is that Baruch had known in advance that he would have to wait until four o'clock. He had accepted the situation and prepared himself for it both practically and emotionally. In a sense, he had "agreed" to control himself. But he hadn't agreed to any further delays. His resistance to the situation made it difficult for him to control his annoyance. And once he had become annoyed, he didn't *feel like* controlling himself any longer.[26] Even if Baruch had a tight schedule, feeling anxious about the wait was not constructive.

Again we see how a person can change his mood from one extreme to the other in mere moments. Of course, in this case, Baruch did not change his mood deliberately. We do see, though, that he was able to relate to a potentially nerve-wracking situation calmly for as long as he had agreed to be in control of his state of mind. After that, he let his state of mind take control of him!

> Five-year-old Moshe was running along not far from his house when he tripped and fell, scraping his knee and the palms of his hands. His parents were at home and he didn't see any other adults around to help him, so after a minute, Moshe picked himself up and headed for home. It was a little hard to bend his knee, and he moaned with pain, but as he walked along, his moans became fainter and fainter. As he limped along, he noticed an interesting truck on the street and stopped for a few minutes to investigate.
>
> When he finally reached his house, Moshe suddenly remembered the fall that had made him come home. He burst out crying, his mind occupied again only with his pain.

Moshe wasn't fooling himself; his scrapes really did hurt. But while he was outside, he had no reason to cry; there was no one to hear him. There was also something interesting to look at: the truck, which distracted him. It was more worth his while to examine the truck, which he enjoyed doing, than to cry and not be heard, so he temporarily blocked out his pain. In other words, something inside little Moshe made a calculation: when to pay attention to his bruises and when not to.

Of course, all children are different. Some cry immediately because they are particularly sensitive to pain. Some cry outdoors as a warm-up for crying at home. The point stands, however: a person has the power to ignore his pain if he has a good enough reason to do so. Don't we, too, as adults, occasionally ignore pain or minor troubles when there is no one around to commiserate, and magnify them when we hope to receive a little sympathy?

We see from these three examples of anger, tension, and pain, that controlling our emotions when it is advantageous can come very naturally. This is equally true of other emotions and qualities.

Each of us can find our own examples of times when we succeeded in controlling ourselves. Keep those examples at the forefront of your mind so that you can pull them out when you need a boost. They'll remind you of how much power you *do* have over your emotions, and thus make it easier to face your future goals with a strong will, courage, and trust in Hashem.

SET REASONABLE GOALS: DON'T BITE OFF MORE THAN YOU CAN CHEW!

There is a point that has been made before that takes on new meaning as we learn to become strong as lions. We have already discussed many advantages of setting manageable goals, including: preventing the despair that can be caused by over-ambitious goals (especially ones we don't achieve), unifying the will, and reducing tension. Another advantage of setting reasonable goals: it becomes easier to feel strong and confident about tackling them.

The Midrash illustrates the benefit of advancing slowly and steadily:

> *Regarding a mound of dirt: What does the fool say? "Who can [manage to] clear this away?" What does the wise man say? "I'll haul away two baskets-full today and two baskets-full tomorrow, until I clear away the whole thing."*
>
> *In the same way, the fool says, "Who can learn the Torah? Nezikin has thirty chapters; Keilim has thirty chapters." What does the wise man say? "I will learn two laws today and two laws tomorrow, until I have learned the whole Torah."*
>
> *Rav Ami said: "Wisdom is like* ra'amos *[a rare gem] to the fool."*[27]
>
> *Rabbi Yochanan said: "It is like a loaf of bread hanging from the ceiling of a house. The fool says, 'Who can ever get it down?' The wise man says, 'Did not someone hang it there?' He brings two poles, claps them together, and takes it down. In the same way, the fool says, 'Who can learn the Torah that is in a Sage's heart?' But the wise man says, 'Did he not learn it from someone else? I, too, will learn two laws today and two tomorrow, until I learn the whole Torah.'"*[28]

We have already spoken[29] of the yetzer hara's favorite strategies: when it comes to sin, the *yetzer* works its way in slowly, so that a person, gradually and almost imperceptibly, falls into bad habits.[30] When it comes to virtue, however, the *yetzer hara* urges rapid progress that invites failure and discouragement. What is the best way to fight the *yetzer hara*? By adopting its own strategy. The method that the *yetzer* uses to lead us to sin can be used, instead, to bring ourselves to virtue. We can thus avoid its push for rapid advancement, that really distances us from our ultimate goals, and instead lead ourselves toward our goals gradually.

Advancing gradually will help us to become confident and strong as a lion; we will set before ourselves moderate intermediate goals so that we will know that we can accomplish them. The greater success we achieve will serve as proof that we have what it takes to keep on climbing toward our future goals.

IDENTIFY YOUR TALENTS: WHAT'S SPECIAL ABOUT YOU?

Reb Yerucham Leibovitz, the Mirrer *mashgiach*, used to say that while the person who fails to recognize his own defects is at a loss when it comes to self-improvement, the one that can't see his own *strengths* is in *deeper* trouble — for even if he knows his shortcomings, he isn't familiar or even aware of the tools he has with which he can refine himself.[31] Truly, there is nothing as beneficial as an intimate knowledge of one's own assets, intellectual ability, and wisdom.[32]

> Yosef had a close friend and confidante, Motti, who was an extremely successful businessman. One day when Yosef was visiting him, Motti leaned across the table and said, "I've just been offered an opportunity like none I've ever heard of before in all my years in business. A person can make hundreds of thousands on this deal. I've checked it out, and it's solid and reliable. The only problem is that it takes an investment of a hundred thousand dollars, and right now I can't put in more than fifty thousand. Do you want to go in with me on it? If you can put up the other fifty thousand, we'll be equal partners and split the profits evenly. Can you do it?"
>
> Yosef was taken aback. "Come on, Motti, old friend, are you teasing me or something? Of course I'd love to do it, but you know

that all my life's savings don't amount to more than fifteen thousand dollars."

But the next day Yosef stopped in at his bank and discovered that he had a balance of fifty-five thousand dollars! He was sure that a mistake must have been made, but when he checked, the manager told him that a week earlier, a rich, old uncle of Yosef's had come into the bank and deposited forty thousand dollars in his account without telling him. "I've been redoing my will," the uncle had explained to the manager, "and I decided to give this to my favorite, hardworking nephew now, while we can both enjoy his having it. No, I haven't told him yet." He added with a chuckle, "I want it to be a surprise."

Astounded, Yosef dashed to the nearest phone to call Motti and ask if it wasn't too late to take him up on his offer.

From time to time we read or hear about some suggestion or inspiration for improving ourselves. We would love to achieve that goal, but are stymied by a conviction that we don't have the qualities that success demands. Once in a while, though, we discover unexpectedly that we do, indeed, have the emotional mettle, and that our abilities far exceed our estimation. Or, we may suddenly feel that Hashem has just granted us new abilities, ones that we never really possessed. Once we make this discovery, wouldn't it be wise to promptly make the most of our newly found potential by investing it in a profitable emotional or spiritual endeavor? This promptness is nothing like the overreaching hastiness about which we've been forewarned, in which perceived pressure led people to try to accomplish goals too quickly or without enough deliberation (perhaps skipping crucial steps). Rather, it is a calculated move to "strike while the iron is hot" and capitalize on inspiration when it comes.

You can benefit from compiling a mental "picture album" of your abilities and strengths. Take spiritual and emotional faculties as well as practical skills into account. Include in your album images of all the spheres of your competence, all the times you mastered something difficult or accomplished that which you had previously considered impossible. The benefit of such a list is twofold: you will see that you really are strong and capable in many areas, and examining your practical successes will provide hints as to which emotional strengths made them possible.

Next, list your three strongest assets. Then work out how each can be used to improve your life. Here's how Yanky used his mental photo album to his best advantage:

> Yanky came up with this list:
>
> I am precise and pay attention to detail.
>
> I am neat and organized in my work.
>
> I tend to be very logical.
>
> He also hit upon those weaknesses that caused the most problems:
>
> I tend to be critical.
>
> I am not as understanding of others as I should be.
>
> Yanky had tried to work on these shortcomings before, without success. He now decided, instead, to work *with* his strong points. Precision and attention to detail could help him get an accurate picture of other people and notice all of their good points. Thinking logically could help him assess how excessive criticism had gotten him poor results. He could then determine a course of action that might elicit more positive responses from people.

Emphasizing his assets gave Yanky the strength to overcome his tendency to criticize, and provided a means to become more understanding of others.

AVOID FALSE MODESTY: WHAT IS REAL HUMILITY?

"But wait a minute," you may object, "what's all this talk about appreciating ourselves? Aren't we supposed to be humble and not think that anything about us is so great? And what's this business of "self-confidence"? How could anyone always feel confident of success? People fail, that's life... and anyway, don't we have to trust in Hashem, not in ourselves?"

Chovos HaLevavos explains the relationship between humility and appreciation of our unique strengths. As the author describes it, failure to take responsible action to improve a situation is a form of foolishness, and is not symptomatic of true humility or submission to Divine Will. A person may feel that he has achieved noble levels of tolerance of difficulties. But if any harm he was experiencing was preventable, his tolerance may be no more than feelings of inferiority and exaggerated helplessness that come through ignorance. The author of *Chovos HaLevavos* explains that this type of false humility is actually a form of helplessness; like the ostrich who buries his head in the sand instead of running from danger, a person ignores his own capabilities instead of using them to improve the situation. In this way, he experiences a type of myopia that prevents him from seeing his worth and ability and how he can be assertive to correct situations. The *yetzer hara* encourages this emotional and practical passivity, since its function is to block constructive action and the development of spiritual self-esteem.

True humility, on the other hand, is the product of the soul's elevation and transcendence of crass materialism and mundane behavior. The truly humble person strives to reach higher levels out of appreciation of wisdom and the value of good *middos*. The humility that follows is truly praiseworthy.[33]

Scripture indicates that Yehoshafat HaMelech lived with this type of appropriate self-esteem: "His heart was proud in the ways of Hashem" — he prided himself for walking only in Hashem's ways.[34] Yehoshafat was truly humble; he was faithful and devoted to Hashem, and submissive to His Will in all that he did. At the same time, he was profoundly aware of the value of this virtue, and his achievement of it. This did not make him vain, rather it gave him the energy to continue in his exalted path.

We, too, need the self-esteem derived from having a clear and accurate awareness of our strengths and virtues. That way, we can recognize what lies within the realm of our capabilities as well as determine how, exactly, we should "walk with Hashem."[35]

Similarly, self-confidence does not mean that we trust in ourselves instead of in Hashem. And it does not mean that we are absolutely certain and confident that we will succeed in accomplishing that which we set out to do. Healthy self-confidence is a complete and wholesome appreciation of all of our potential. It is supported by several convictions: that all our abilities are Hashem's gifts to us; that He has put us into the world for certain purposes; and that He grants us the choice and ability to utilize our potential in accordance with His rules of nature and Divine Providence. This kind of self-confidence is really an appreciation of the myriad powers that Hashem has instilled in us.[36]

RECOGNIZE YOUR WORTH: "A KINGDOM OF PRIESTS AND A HOLY NATION"

Strength and confidence come not only from recognizing our own value as individuals. Each one of us can also derive strength from an appreciation of our exalted status as human beings created in the Divine Image, and of the spiritual inheritance that is ours, as members of the people of Israel.

When we disregard our noble heritage and ancestry, we become easy prey for the *yetzer hara*. Once our royal lineage is forgotten and confused with the superstition of crude and earthy people, we can easily be intimidated by spiritual challenge. If, however, we stop to consider that Divine Providence accompanies us every step of our way, then we realize how privileged and close to Hashem we really are. When that happens, we are able to see that the *yetzer's* offers are beneath our dignity — and we are able to rise above any disturbance. It is as though the thought of sin itself loses its allure and becomes almost distasteful. [37]

If you're still tempted, follow the advice of Rabbeinu Yonah: a person, by appreciating his noble origins, can still remain unaffected. When he is tempted to do something improper, he can reflect on those who came before him. He will then be ashamed of himself and ashamed before his forefathers. "He will say to himself, 'Someone as important as myself — someone who possesses such great, sublime virtues, and who is of such honorable lineage, the descendant of ancient kings — how can I possibly do such a terrible act and sin for all time against Hashem and my ancestors?'"[38]

The Chovos HaLevavos and Rabbeinu Yonah speak about refraining from negative behavior. Rav Shlomo Wolbe, shlit"a, offers us similar advice, reapplied to the pursuit of positive goals:

> A person cannot acquire Torah without an awareness of his own importance. In preparation for receiving the Torah, the people of Israel were told, "You shall be to Me a kingdom of priests."[39] Rashi explains "priests" here to mean "noblemen." Every single Jew is a nobleman, a man of esteem, and a personage of responsibility....
>
> The first step of every program for self-improvement must include an experience of the exaltedness of being human. If someone has never fully understood that a human being is glorious from his very inception, and his sole self-involvement is devoted to broadening his awareness of the evil within him and agonizing about it, he will just sink deeper and deeper into despair. He will end up accepting himself as evil, having lost all hope of correcting his flaws....
>
> Every person must know that he is important. That is, not a pretentious sort of conceit... but an awareness that he has a profound, even shocking, significance. Every single person is required to say of himself, "The world was created for my sake." Rashi explains:[40] "I am as important as the entire world, and I will not banish myself from it over one transgression."[41]

We all have the capacity for spiritual greatness — but to draw on this source of strength, we must stay aware of its existence. One way would be to pay attention to the reminders sprinkled throughout our daily prayers: the morning blessings of "Who girds Israel with strength" and "Who crowns Israel with splendor"; the words "He gives strength and power to the nation"[42] in the *Pesukei D'Zimrah*; and the verse "Hashem gives strength to His nation,"[43] found in a number of places in our *tefillah*. Being conscious of the implications of these words and working on *living* them every day will empower us. Their strength will enable us to succeed in our daily obligations and our individual goals.

"TRUST IN HASHEM AND DO WHAT IS GOOD"[44]

One of the prime reasons for us to be strong and courageous is the knowledge that the Rock of Israel is there to help us. Since the dawn of mankind, Hashem has promised that we can win our fight against the *yetzer hara*: "[The temptation to] sin lies at the doorway, and it longs for you, but you can rule over it."[45] Provided, that is, that *we* supply the requisite determination.

With every effort that we make and every step that we take, Hashem lights our way and fortifies us so that we can advance still further.[46] "Whoever comes to purify himself is helped,"[47] and "The Pure of Hands shall increase the strength [of the righteous ones who do His Will]."[48]

Actually, the help that Hashem promises us is disproportionate to the quantity, and quality, of our efforts. When we open our hearts to repentance by as much as the width of a needle's eye, Hashem assures us, "I will open for you entranceways so wide that even wagons and carriages can enter through them."[49]

When we work toward our goals calmly and confidently, with resolve, energetic enthusiasm, and trust in Hashem's help, we will find that "The joy in Hashem — *that* is [our] fortress."[50]

The very joy that we feel in doing Hashem's Will and knowing that He is with us strengthens us to transcend our handicaps and actualize additional dimensions of our potential. We are to be living examples of the prophetess Devora's song: "Those who love Him are like the sun emerging in its glory."[51]

LEARN THE REWARDS OF INNER STRENGTH: IT PAYS TO BE BRAVE

Strength and bravery bring great rewards, and bearing that in mind can help us charge forward dauntlessly. Aside from the obvious, that they make you far more likely to succeed in meeting the challenge before you, there are also fringe benefits. Courage and inner strength sometimes open the door to pleasant surprises.

> In Hamburg, many years ago, a young scholar was chosen to serve as the city's Rabbi. The very day he arrived in town to take up his position, a simple market woman came to him and said that she had a dispute with Mr. P., one of Hamburg's notables, and she needed the Rabbi to judge between them. The Rabbi asked her if the matter could wait until the following day, since he was still exhausted from his journey. The woman gave the Rabbi a number of reasons why her suit needed to be heard immediately.
>
> The Rabbi called in his shamash and told him, "Go to Mr. P. and tell him that I summon him to court because a certain woman has a complaint against him."
>
> The shamash was terrified at the thought of serving a summons to the wealthy man — and especially, of having to tell him that a pauper woman had made the complaint. The Rabbi understood his hesitation, but he urged the shamash repeatedly until he reluctantly set out on his mission, his teeth chattering with fear.
>
> When the shamash reached the entrance of the rich man's mansion, his fear once again overcame him, and he could not bring himself to ring the bell. He paced back and forth in front of the gate, hoping that Mr. P. would happen to come outside. Finally, he did come out, and the shamash approached him meekly.
>
> "What do you want?" Mr. P. barked.
>
> The frightened shamash managed to stutter out a few incoherent half-sentences about the Rabbi's summons — and couldn't continue.
>
> The wealthy man shouted at him, "Nu? Speak up!" and the shamash finally managed to get out the message that the Rabbi was summoning him to court.
>
> Mr. P. snapped back, "Tell the Rabbi that it will have to wait. I don't have time for it right now."

The shamash *returned to the Rabbi and delivered the response. On hearing it, the Rabbi asked the woman if she was willing to wait until a later date. She replied, "Rabbi, I beg of you, don't put it off. It is very hard for me to wait."*

The Rabbi ordered the shamash *to go back again, instructing him, "Tell Mr. P. that the woman does not agree to wait, and he must come today."*

When the shamash *heard that he had to undertake this errand a second time, he was scared half to death. How could he say such harsh words to one of the richest, most powerful men in Hamburg? But the Rabbi explained to the* shamash *that he had nothing to fear since he, the sender, was responsible for the demand being made of the rich man.*

When he came before the rich man again, the shamash *could not bring himself to repeat the message. Finally the rich man demanded, "Well, what did the Rabbi say?" and the* shamash *managed to answer that the woman did not agree to the delay, and he must come that very day.*

At that, Mr. P. turned purple with rage and screamed, "Go tell the Rabbi that I am the wealthiest man in Hamburg and he is still just a guest in this town and is not yet familiar with the way things work here. If I say that I'll come when I have time, then I will keep my word, but I cannot, and will not, give a definite time, and that's that."

The shamash *went to the Rabbi and delivered the reply. On hearing it, the Rabbi immediately rose to his feet and told the* shamash, *"Go straight back to Mr. P. and tell him that he may be the richest man in Hamburg, but if I say that he should come today, then he had better come today and no later. And though I may not have an army at my disposal to bring him here against his will, I do have the power to put him in* cherem *(excommunicate him) — and I will not hesitate to do so if I must."*

When the shamash *heard that, he began to tremble in terror and begged the Rabbi to find a different messenger. But the Rabbi insisted that he go, and without delay.*

When the shamash *came back to Mr. P., he begged his forgiveness and said that he could not bring himself to say what he must tell him. The wealthy man drew him out, forcing him to repeat everything the Rabbi had told him, word for word. When it had all been said, the* shamash *made a beeline for the door and ran back to the Rabbi's house as fast as his feet could carry him.*

> *An hour later, Mr. P. himself was shown into the Rabbi's house, a broad smile on his face. He greeted the Rabbi with "Mazal tov! Mazal tov! Your Honor is well suited to be our Rabbi!" He went on to explain, "I am not a defendant, and that woman has no real claim against me. You see, since Your Honor is so young and the established, wealthy people of the city are so powerful, we were concerned whether Your Honor would be able to stand up to them to fulfill the obligation of a judge, 'Do not be intimidated.'[52] And so we staged this episode so that we could test the Rabbi's fortitude. And since Your Honor fulfilled the commandment without conceding even in the slightest, you have proven yourself more than worthy to be the Rabbi of Hamburg."*

It is clear that, had the Rabbi been afraid to carry out the halachah, he would have lost both his integrity and his prestigious position. By being strong and remaining firm, he gained a double profit, because, as a result of this incident, he lived the rest of his days in Hamburg in honor and tranquility. This incident gave him the uncontested authority to enforce halachah in the city. Everyone obeyed his instructions, and no one ever suspected him of wrongdoing.[53]

The young Rabbi's courage and fortitude not only enabled him to carry out his responsibility properly, but they were precisely what won him esteem and success in his community.

Each of us can recall experiences of our own in which our inner strength, properly used, brought us unanticipated reward. Keep those incidents in mind; they will encourage you and strengthen your resolve when you again need to be stalwart and brave when facing a challenge. You will begin to really feel "How fortunate is the person who finds strength in [Hashem]!"[54]

Strong As a Lion

The goal in becoming "strong as a lion" is not to conquer uncharted land, nor is it to work miracles. The goal, in essence, is to improve the way in which we approach the things we do in life. Instead of avoiding responsibility and regarding it as somewhat of a burden, one can relate to responsibility as a challenge, as an intriguing riddle which needs solving, as a simple, yet profitable task, as a longed-for objective, which draws the person to stride ever forward on the path of life.

A person who adopts the approach of "strong as a lion" generally goes through life with a sense of energy. He is aware of his strength and talents, he takes the responsibility to utilize these strengths and talents, and he indeed utilizes them with joy. The strong person does not retreat when he is confronted by the *yetzer hara*. And as Rashi explained, one who overcomes his *yetzer hara* is defined as one who "Rouses his *yetzer hatov* (good inclination) against the *yetzer hara*. If the *yetzer hara* tells him, 'Commit this sin,' not only does he refrain from the sin, but he goes a step further and does a *mitzvah*...."[55]

When a person grasps on to the quality of strength in the proper way, he may merit the status of being identified with the verse "For the nation shall rise like a lion cub and raise itself up like a lion: it shall not rest until it has consumed its prey."[56]

Ready, Set, Go!

In these last four chapters we have examined the four dimensions of Rabbi Yehuda ben Teima's formula for achieving our goals in life. Mulling over these concepts and working to apply them can spark the realization that this formula is not a combination of disparate elements. It is, rather, an overall attitude that is an organic whole, and greater than the sum of its parts. It is an uplifted, composed feeling of total readiness to tackle the challenges that come our way. With Hashem's help, the coming volumes will fill in more details by providing examples of how to put this system to use in many areas of life.

The best way to start developing the overall balanced attitude suggested by Rabbi Yehuda ben Teima's formula is by examining yourself: "In which of the four characteristics am I weak? Do I lack a clearly defined and determined will? Am I inclined to become tense and anxious? Do I have a tendency toward laziness and apathy? Do I face my goals with feelings of timidity and inadequacy?"

Once you have identified your weak spots, you will know where to concentrate your efforts. Keep in mind that you are aiming for balance. If you become tense easily, don't try to strengthen your determination — try to lighten up your attitude, instead. On the other hand, if you are low on resolve, don't work on developing a more easygoing manner — strengthen your will. If you tend to drag your feet and get bogged down in laziness and apathy, work on developing energetic enthusiasm. But if you tend to be rash and don't emphasize the need for alacrity — learn to address your goals in a more relaxed, deliberate way, with slow, patient steps.

FINDING YOURSELF IN WHAT YOU'VE LEARNED

1. Make a list of all the things you accomplished when you adopted a strong, confident attitude.
2. List those times when you discovered that you were actually able to do things that you previously assumed you were unable to handle.
3. What negative feelings and tendencies have you managed to overcome? Keep this and the last two lists handy and refer to them from time to time to remind yourself of your hidden strengths.
4. Have you ever felt Hashem's help in the path that you chose to take?

APPLYING WHAT YOU'VE LEARNED

1. What are your assets and strong points? How could you use them to your best advantage?
2. Picture yourself as the leader of a community or some other distinguished person. How might this mental image have a positive effect on your conduct?
3. Reread Shemos 19:5-6, which describes our special relationship with Hashem. How does reading the verses make you feel? Uplifted, overwhelmed, uncomfortable?
4. Refer to the list in the section called "What's Special About You," page 323. Create such a list for yourself, being careful to list both weaknesses and strengths. Try to capitalize on your strong points; perhaps you can even use them to work through your weak points.

NOTES TO CHAPTER TEN

1. Refer back to chapter 3 of this volume, which discusses defeatism and despair, and chapter 9 which discusses sluggishness and rationalization.
2. See the Ya'avetz on *Avos* 5:22.
3. See Rashi and Midrash Shmuel on *Avos* 5:22.
4. Devarim 28:9.
5. "In explaining this *mitzvah*, [our Sages] said: 'Just as He is called Kind, so you be kind. Just as He is called Merciful, so you be merciful. Just as He is called holy, so you be Holy.' In the same way, the prophets called G-d by all those terms: 'Slow to anger', 'Great in Kindness', 'Righteous and Upright', 'Perfect', *'Courageous* and *Strong',* and so on. [This was] to make it known that they are good, proper ways, and that a person must conduct himself according to them and to imitate Him as much as he can." (*Hilchos De'os* 1:6) (emphasis mine)
6. Devarim 32:11, Ohr HaChayim there, "As the Sages said, Hashem does not test a person to a degree that he cannot tolerate."
7. See *Sefer Chareidim,* Introduction to *Mitzvos,* preconditions 2, 4, 7, 13; *Chayei Adam,* section 68, halachos 13-15, 17.

8. *Orach Chayim* 1, according to the Bach and Prisha.
9. I *Divrei HaYamim* 2:26.
10. See *Ramban* on *Bamidbar* 11:1.
11. *Shoftim* 5:31.
12. See *Moed Katan* 16, where Dovid HaMelech's strengths are enumerated.
13. *Tehillim* 5:2, and *Rashi*; see *Medrash Shochar Tov* 5.
14. *Berachos* 28a; *Eruvin* 28b.
15. *Devarim* 30:14.
16. *Tanna D'Bei Eliyahu Zuta*, chapter 14.
17. "Love Hashem, your G-d" (*Devarim* 6:5); "Do not hate your brother in your heart" (*Vayikra* 19:17); "Do not bear a grudge... Love your fellow man as yourself" (Ibid., verse 18); "Do not covet" (*Shemos* 20:14).
18. "For this thing [the Torah] is very close to you... to do it." Regarding this, our Sages said, "Hashem does not make unreasonable demands on His creations" (*Shemos Rabbah* 34:1; *Tanchuma, Ki Sisa* 10).
19. *Devarim* 20:3.
20. *Devarim* 20:8.
21. *Hilchos Melachim* 7:15.
22. See *Rabbeinu Bachaya* on *Devarim* 29:18; *Likutei Amarim: Tanya*, chapter 27; and *Ibn Ezra* on *Shemos* 20:14.
23. *Orach Chayim* 114:8.
24. *Bereishis* 49:15.
25. A different version of the same story appears in Rabbi Chayim Efrayim Zaitchik, *Sparks of Mussar* (Jerusalem: Feldheim, 1985), p. 187.
26. See chapter 5 of this volume for an exploration of this "vicious cycle."
27. *Mishlei* 24:7.
28. *Vayikra Rabbah* 19:2.
29. See chapters 7 and 8 of this volume.
30. See *Shabbos* 105b.
31. Rav Shlomo Wolbe, *Alei Shur*, 2 volumes (Jerusalem: Tzor Os, 5748), part I, p. 169.
32. Rabbi Yehuda ibn Tibbon, in his Introduction to *sha'ar* II of *Chovos HaLevavos*, quoting the *Mivchar HaPeninim*.

33. *Chovos HaLevavos, sha'ar HaKni'a*, chapter 2; also see Rav Shlomo Wolbe, *Alei Shur*, 2 volumes (Jerusalem: Tzor Os, 5748), part I, *sha'ar 3*, chapter 3.
34. II Divrei HaYamim 17:6, and Rashi there.
35. See *Sotah* 49b, "Rav Yosef said to a *Tanna*, 'Do not say that humility [has ceased from the world] for there is me.'" Similarly, it is clear that Moshe Rabbeinu recognized his own humility, since the Torah says (Bamidbar 12:3), "The man Moshe was very humble, more than any person on the face of the earth." Moshe Rabbeinu surely taught that verse publicly, as he did the entirety of the Torah.

    The Talmud in *Nedarim* 62a asks how Ovadyahu could have said (I Melachim 18:12), "Your servant [i.e., the speaker himself] has feared Hashem since his youth," when the verse in Mishlei cautions, "Let a stranger praise you, and not your own mouth" (Mishlei 27:2). The Talmud answers that the advice of Mishlei applies in a place where other people know the person, but in a place where they do not know him, it is permissible for him to make his own virtues known. The Talmud adds that a scholar is permitted to say, "I am a scholar."
36. "Remember Hashem, your G-d — that it is He Who gives you the power to do great things" (Devarim 8:18).
37. Introduction to the *Siddur Beis Ya'akov*.
38. *Sha'arei HaAvodah*, essay 1.
39. Shemos 19:6.
40. *Sanhedrin* 37a; For a further treatment of this subject, see Rebbe Kalonymos Kalman Shapira's *Chovas HaTalmidim*, particularly the "Talk with Teachers and Parents" at the beginning of the book.
41. Rav Shlomo Wolbe, *Alei Shur*, 2 volumes (Jerusalem: Tzor Os, 5748), part I, p. 168.
42. Tehillim 68:36.
43. Ibid., 29:11.
44. Ibid., 37:3.
45. Bereishis 4:7 (emphasis mine).
46. "A person is led in the path in which he wants to go" (*Makos* 10b).
47. *Shabbos* 104a; *Yoma* 38b.
48. Iyov 17:9 and *Yalkut Shimoni* 907.
49. *Shir HaShirim Rabbah* 5:2(3).
50. Nechemia 8:10.

51. Shoftim 5:31.
52. Devarim 1:17.
53. The Alter of Novardok, *Madreigas HaAdam*, ed. Rabbi Moshe Yemini (New York: Congregation Beith Yosef, 5736), p. 268.
54. Tehillim 84:6.
55. *Sanhedrin* 111b, starting at the words "And he overcomes his *yetzer*..."
56. Bamidbar 23:24.

Epilogue: The Power To Choose

To make it easier for you to keep in mind what you've read, let's quickly review the main points of this first volume.

Chapter 1: Expanding the Power of Free Choice

In the course of our lives, we often find ourselves having to make decisions about how to relate to a situation, whether or not to take on a particular challenge, or what course of action to choose. Unfortunately, we often resort to approaches that are either ineffective or cause harmful side effects. We may do this because we assume that there are no better alternatives, because we have not taken the time to consider other options, or simply out of habit.

In almost every situation, though, if we take the trouble to look, we will find that we are capable of choosing to respond in a variety of ways. These may include disregard, escape, submission, emotionalization/internalization, or initiating change. When deciding on a course of action, then, we should stop to consider what the real range of options is and which would be best, considering our particular circumstances. This is especially true after trying a particular route a number of times without reasonable success. Outside factors aren't always to blame — there may be a more appropriate way to deal with the problems and issues involved. Try increasing the range of your options and allow yourself to choose the best route.

Chapters 2-6: The Obstacles

Even after we have considered our options and chosen among them, certain obstacles may interfere with our ability to actualize our decisions.

The obstacles discussed in **Chapters 2-4** included embarrassment, the fear that we lack the ability to achieve our goals (despair), and other negative character traits. We must learn to recognize these handicaps so that we can overcome them.

In **Chapter 5** we saw why it is sometimes difficult to escape from a particular state of mind and discussed the advantages of temporary escape.

In **Chapter 6** we learned to recognize various deep, unconscious motivations that can splinter our determination. We saw that the first step toward personal growth is to determine if things are progressing smoothly. If not, it's important to try to identify what may be getting in the way.

Chapters 7-10: On to the Solutions!

These chapters each describe one stage of Rabbi Yehudah ben Teima's four-point formula for achieving goals.

Chapter 7: *Bold As a Leopard* — When we face a challenge or set ourselves a goal, we must resolve our will in order to succeed.

Chapter 8: *Light As an Eagle* — At the same time, we must not develop an intense determination that engenders tension. Instead, we should take a relaxed, buoyant approach to our challenges.

Chapter 9: *Swift As a Deer* — We must rise above feelings of laziness and apathy and develop alacrity — energetic enthusiasm.

Chapter 10: *Strong As a Lion* — We must overcome timidity and feelings of inadequacy to develop confidence, courage, and inner strength.

This program for success in life is not a complicated method comprising many details. It is an overall healthy attitude that is determined yet relaxed, enthusiastic and not easily discouraged. As we develop this attitude, we discover that we can handle more types of situations, and are able to achieve so many more of life's goals. When we finally make this approach our own, we experience a wonderful, exalted feeling as we march, calmly and courageously, to do the Will of our Father in Heaven.

Appendix A
Comparative Success*

Excerpt #1

Sha'arei HaAvodah of Rabbeinu Yona, ztz"l

[49] ... A person should take to heart all that I've explained until this point and completely focus on serving Hashem "with all his heart, with all his soul, and with all his might." With this attitude, he can aspire to attain the spiritual levels of the giants of the spirit — Avraham, Yitzchak, Ya'akov, Moshe, Aharon, Dovid, and Shlomo — *since they, too, only served their Creator as far as their abilities allowed.* The intelligent person will certainly realize that someone who seeks wealth or honor will maximize his motivation and not slacken, even though these qualities are transient and meaningless and draw him away from his *avodas Hashem*. It is the case that in service of Hashem a person can attain the most sublime levels — the levels of Avraham, Yitzchak, Ya'akov, Moshe, Aharon, Dovid, and Shlomo. And these levels are greater than any kingdom on earth; and if he makes the effort, he will succeed! How much more so, then, should he be willing to strive constantly, with all his heart, soul, and might, and not slacken for an hour or lose sight of his goal for a moment?! Every day he should increase his stamina and

---

* In chapter 8, we discussed being ready to invest what is necessary in order to succeed, without being anxious about the results or the need for achievement. The following excerpts reinforce this idea; some of the relevant sections have been emphasized.

rise from one quality to the next, from one level to the next, in the service of his Creator. A person must desire and yearn to attain that which he is still unable to achieve in *avodas Hashem*, and pay attention to those who have accomplished it, connect to them, and choose to follow in their ways and learn from their deeds and wisdom. As it says, "The one who goes with the wise becomes wise."[1] This is what a person must do with every attribute that he has not yet attained — he should long for it and connect to it in any way he can to acquire it; more than he would to attain all the silver and gold in the world. As it says, "They are more desirable than gold or great amounts of the finest gold."[2] For making the choice [to desire what is good], a person receives reward as if he had acquired the attribute, since he has already pushed himself to his limit. Making the choice itself is the fulfillment of a positive commandment, as it says, "Therefore choose life."[3]

Excerpt #2
Letter of Encouragement from the author of the *Pachad Yitzchak, ztz"l*[★]

The second day of Rosh Chodesh Iyar, 5723

My dear one,

Shalom u'vracha!

I received your letter and your words touched me. You should know, my dear one, that the very essence of your letter contradicts

---

[★] A reprint of letter #128 to be found in the Letters section of the work *Pachad Yitzchak* of Rav Yitzchak Hutner, *ztz"l; emphasis mine.* Reprinted with permission of Rav Yonasan Dovid, *shlit"a*, the Rosh Yeshivah of Pachad Yitzchak.

everything that you describe in it. And I'll explain what that sentence means shortly.

There is an epidemic among us — when we are involved in learning about the aspects of greatness of our *Gedolim*, we only focus on the end product. We speak of their perfected ways, their stature, their character, and skip over the inner struggles that they went through. Everyone discusses, wonders at, [and] places the Chofetz Chayim's purity of speech on a pedestal. But who knows how many battles, struggles, stumblings, failures, and regressions occurred in the course of his war with his *yetzer hara*? This is just one example among many. I'm sure that someone as intelligent as you are can extrapolate a general principle from a specific case. The result of this is, though, that when a spirited, inspired, excitable youth finds himself stumbling and falling, he assumes that he isn't "flourishing in the house of Hashem." This youth imagines that to blossom in Hashem's house means to sit with equanimity on the smoothest of grassy plains; to sit back and enjoy his *yetzer tov* just like the *Tzaddikim* in *Gan Eden* sit back with their crowns on their heads basking in Hashem's Presence. The youth does not believe he should be involved in the turmoil of the *yetzer hara* — as we find in the verse "The dead are free [of responsibility]."[4]

But know, my dear one, that the root to your soul is to be found in the *yetzer tov*'s struggles, not its equanimity. Your precious, heartfelt letter is like a hundred witnesses to the fact that you are to be counted among the faithful fighters of its army. People say, "Lose a battle and win the war." You've failed before and you're certain to fail again (articulating this fact of life is not called "opening the mouth of the *Satan*"). But I promise you that, when all is said and done, you'll emerge with the victor's laurel on your head, and with that elusive prey quivering in your grasp. *"Lose a battle, but win wars."* The wisest man of all said, "The *tzaddik* falls seven times and gets up."[5] Fools think that Shlomo HaMelech intended this to be something remarkable — despite the fact that the *tzaddik* falls seven times, he still gets up. Wise people understand well, though, that the intention of the verse is that the essence of the "getting up" of the *tzaddik* is *through* his "seven fallings." "'And He saw everything that He had made, and behold it was very good.' 'Good' implies the *yetzer tov;* 'Very' implies the *yetzer hara.*"[6]

My dear, I'm holding you close to my heart and whispering in your ear. If your letter had related all the *mitzvos* and good deeds that you're doing, I would have said that I received a good letter. Now that your letter tells me about stumblings and failings, I can say that I received a very good letter. Your spirit is in turmoil as a reaction to your aspiration to be great. But please don't envision *Gedolim* who were in total harmony with their *yetzer tov*. In contrast, picture the greatness of the *Gedolim* in the signs of the incredible battle they fought with all types of low and base inclinations. And when you feel your *yetzer* raging within you, know that at *that moment* you resemble the *Gedolim* much more than when you find yourself in that state of complete tranquility that you yearn for. It is precisely in those places that you find yourself failing the most that you have the greatest potential of becoming an exemplary vessel for revealing the glory of Heaven.

You don't want to fool me, that I should think that you are doing well when you're really such and such, and seven times that, no less. And why should you concern me with the "seven times"? For me, the main thing is that, this past winter, you gained a good understanding of the laws of monetary damages. You reviewed the tractate you learned several times; you don't deny it. This is the deciding factor. Buried within that fact is the key to victory in your struggle with your *yetzer*.

You write, "I'll never forget the desire I had to succeed and climb ever higher; unfortunately, I've lost all hope." I don't understand how you have the audacity to deny a living reality — haven't you climbed ever higher since you entered the *beis medrash?!* I know you, you don't have that kind of chutzpah. It's only that it's like this: when you find that your *yetzer hara* has won a round, your foolishness and naivete tell you that there's no more hope. Your words are almost funny. I empathize with your suffering, but this suffering is the womb of greatness. I've seen your face as you delve into the halachah. I've watched you listen attentively to the *shiurim*. I've seen your expression on the seventh night of Pesach. The words that are etched on your face at those times are "Glory will come at the end." The road to glory doesn't meander across a plain; it winds like a serpent on its way. So the venom of the serpent is in you? "He will strike at your heel, and you will crush its head."[7]

I found it appropriate to present these words to you in writing. That way, you will be able to look them over whenever you need them. It should be self-evident that I only refer here to the general gist of your letter. As regards the particular points, it would be better to speak face-to-face. *You* are the one who is "flourishing in the house of Hashem"!

> Sharing in your troubles,
> Confident of your ultimate victory,
> Praying for your success,
> Yitzchak Hutner

P.S. Now you understand the opening sentence of this letter — that the essence of your letter contradicts everything that you describe there.

NOTES TO APPENDIX A

1. Mishlei 13:20.
2. Tehillim 19:11.
3. Devarim 30:19.
4. Tehillim 88:6.
5. Mishlei 24:16.
6. *Bereishis Rabbah* 9.
7. A rearrangement of the verse in Bereishis 3:15.

Appendix B
Tension in Real Life Scenes

In chapter 8, we explained the concept "light as an eagle" and broadly discussed the causes and deeper origins of stress. Since tension plays such a significant role in preventing people from attaining their goals and in damaging the quality of their lives, in this appendix we will explore its role on a more practical plane, using illustrations from everyday life. Here is a list of common situations and conditions in which we usually find ourselves. To make it more practical, these predicaments are divided into a few groups, representing incidents which happen to a diverse group of people. There will be stories that are typical to the life of the yeshivah student, the *kollel avreich*, the working man, the high school girl, the married woman, couples, and parents, as follows:

Yeshivah Student: 1. Tension due to impatience and lack of self-encouragement

2. Stress due to lack of clarity about the future

Kollel Avreich: 3. Pressure due to feeling a lack of self-worth

4. Stress brought on when attempting to prepare for the future

Working Man: 5. Tension due to accumulated stress

Adolescent Girl: 6. Pressure brought on when preparing for exams

7. Stress that comes with developing potential

8. Tension brought about by attempting to achieve social status

Married Woman: 9. Pressure felt by a hard-working mother

Spouses: 10. Stress that comes from attempting to improve the atmosphere at home
11. Stress that is part of dealing with adolescent children

It will be possible to find, within the stories, the deeper origins of tension discussed in chapter 8. Some points will be more clearly spelled out, and others will be part and parcel of the narrative. The attentive reader will discover, while following the story line, just how the protagonists are affected by the different sources of stress. He will be able to see from "up close" how the characters discover their problems and relate to their feelings as they begin to try to improve their situations. As in real life, the stories don't always end once one set of difficulties is surmounted; new difficulties always arise. The characters featured here will sometimes grapple with a few different life situations in succession.

Some of the stories may seem far out of the reader's own life context — that's fine. They can still help clarify the points covered in chapter 8 and allow them to penetrate more deeply. They can also enhance the reader's skills for dealing with stress in his own life. To make it easier, here is a review of the main points of chapter 8; this list should help you to be conscious of those points and discover them within the stories:

I. Causes of Tension

A. *Exaggerated Expectations*

- The need to invest energy
- The quality of the results
- The time it takes to see results

B. *Exaggerated Responsibility*

- Hyper-exertion for success
- Hyper-responsibility about decisions
- The need to prove "I care"
- Stress, the motivator

II. Deeper Causes of Tension

- Insufficient understanding of the function of difficulties
- Insufficient awareness of the fact that difficulties are commonplace
- egocentricity
- Preoccupation with self-image
- Insufficient faith and trust in Hashem
- Insufficient appreciation of good deeds
- Preoccupation with the opinions of others

Scenario #1 — Stress in the life of a yeshivah student
Stress Due to Impatience and Lack of Self-Encouragement

"When will my deeds measure up to the deeds of Avraham, Yitzchak, and Ya'akov?"[1] "If you strive to be like the Vilna Gaon — you might become a Rabbi Akiva Eiger; but if you aim to be 'only' a Rabbi Akiva Eiger — you'll barely get as far as being a Rav Chayim Ozer..."

Ze'evi, a serious student with an agile mind, was occupied with such thoughts just moments before the start of *Minchah* on Yom Kippur in his yeshivah. He had high ambitions and a strong will, fired by a near-certain conviction that he would be victorious in achieving his intended goal. While immersed in thought, Ze'evi noticed Yanky take the seat at his side. Ze'evi's opinion of Yanky was none too generous. "Yanky is such a hotshot," he remarked to himself. "His *pilpulim* are totally not meant seriously... he's only out to impress." At that moment, Ze'evi caught himself. "This is definitely the worst time to be critical; we all need to be worthy of Divine Mercy now. Yanky is probably doing as well as he can..."

Ze'evi had already organized his resolutions for the coming year during the Ten Days of Repentance. He planned to say the *Amidah* with an awareness of standing before the King of kings, naturally with undivided attention to the meaning of the words, and to intensify his *mussar* learning with enthusiasm, in order to strengthen his *yiras Shamayim*. He committed himself to doing one act of *chessed* graciously every single day. Last but not least, he was determined to develop clarity in penetrating to the depths of his Torah studies without interrupting with any unnecessary conversation. He recalled having made similar resolutions the previous year, but this year he felt that he was approaching the task with absolute resolve — and that he would accomplish his goals, come what may.

More than two months have flown by and Ze'evi finds himself reviewing the recent past and looking into his future. Chanukah, the Festival of Lights, with all that it symbolizes, inspires some introspection. Ze'evi realizes that he isn't as prepared for the holiday as he would like to be, and his analysis of his recent track record leads him to conclusions that aren't too encouraging. Following Yom Kippur he put in a lot of effort to concentrate on his *davening*, without much success. True, there were times that parts of the *Amidah* had been "quality," but part is certainly a far cry from all, and even that had been infrequent. When the Sukkos break arrived, he decided that it wasn't an ideal time to start implementing any changes, and that it would be better to wait until the beginning of the winter *zman*. When it arrived, he again pushed himself to succeed, and again waited, full of longing, for the week during which he would manage to pray the *Amidah* "properly." None of this bore fruit and as a result he suffered from disappointment and terrible frustration. Even his other priorities — enthusiastic study of *mussar* and performing acts of *chessed* graciously — didn't amount to much, and his learning schedule failed to measure up, too.

But Ze'evi didn't give up completely. His jealousy of his friend Yanky that had been quietly fermenting deep in his heart rose to the surface. "Yanky always has some sort of a brilliant brain-twister on the tip of his tongue — his own, or some *Acharon's*." Ze'evi decided, then, that if the "duties of the heart" weren't his strong point, at the very least he should attempt to excel in his studies and be a warrior on the battlefield of the Torah.

―・◇◯◇◉◇◯◇・―

For the time being, let us shift our focus to Yanky. He is a bubbly teenager who is well accepted socially — however, he is somewhat short of brilliant. Although Yanky is not to blame, he is unable to compete with the sharper minds in his class. Even so, he has found a niche for himself — he has an uncanny ability to conjure up some difficult question he has once heard or learned and toss it into a group of boys learning. At times this has had an explosive effect that has earned Yanky a level of respect from his classmates that, to put it bluntly, extends way beyond what a boy of his intellect and diligence seems to deserve. Oftentimes, the arguments that whirl around him are incomprehensible to him; he tries his best to laugh off being intellectually overwhelmed. Occasionally, though, this theatricality and the honor extended to him have felt uncomfortable. At such times, he feels empty and resents the constant pressure to always discover the brilliant question — and to struggle for superficial recognition. Which is why Yanky approaches the Festival of Lights feeling a genuine, inner stirring to gradually take leave of the "theater" and recreate himself as a person whose actions have meaning.

The winter term progressed at its usual pace, and during the week after Purim, the boys got busy setting up *chavrusos* for the coming *zman*. You may not believe this, but every student managed to find a partner — except for our two friends, Ze'evi and Yanky. It seemed an unlikely match to everyone, but it was Yanky that broke the ice. He approached Ze'evi and blurted, "It looks like we're partners for the coming *zman*." Ze'evi responded with a smile and settled back into his usual thoughtful stance. "What's the problem?" asked Yanky. He said it with such simple concern that it touched a nerve in Ze'evi. Somehow, a deep and open conversation emerged from the question, what people call a "heart to heart talk." Each was surprised by the common ground between them, their parallel roller coaster rides of working on *middos*, throwing themselves into their studies, and periods of dejection and despair. True, their general tendencies were so different — but each one found the ups and downs of the other so familiar!

The summer *zman* arrived, and Ze'evi and Yanky were still learning together. The partnership had not only been a successful study venture — they had come out of it the best of friends. In Ze'evi, Yanky found the sincerity, calm, and intellectual depth he had been seeking. And in Yanky, Ze'evi found the lightheartedness and effervescence he had been lacking. During one of their late-night conversations, they both decided to discover the solution to the riddle: why all the ups and downs, the struggles, and the failures?

After some discussion, they arrived at the following conclusion: While each of them was in the process of working toward their goals, they had expected to see immediate results. The fact that they had, at some point, managed to concentrate on several of the *berachos* of the *Amidah* somehow hadn't given them a feeling of satisfaction or accomplishment. The fact that Ze'evi did manage, occasionally, to graciously perform an act of *chessed*, or learn *mussar* enthusiastically, wasn't enough to ignite a warm satisfied glow inside him. This drive for immediate results without wanting to invest the necessary time led to overexertion and, consequently, to a feeling of failure.

Furthermore, all that they accomplished in their Torah studies didn't satisfy them, since their aspirations had been so much higher than that which came to be. They wound up feeling dejected and miserable.

"Who says that my learning has really developed, anyway?" Ze'evi asked Yanky, straight out.

"You've definitely been moving ahead nicely... what's the question?" Yanky waved his hand in the air as if to brush the issue aside.

"*Nu*, so prove it!" demanded Ze'evi.

Yanky was silent for a moment. He gave it some thought, and suddenly came up with an idea. "Hey, just a minute! Where were you two years ago?" he asked.

"I don't understand the question," Ze'evi said. He had been in the second *shiur* of his *yeshivah ketanah*.

"Aha!" said Yanky, as if he was about to discover America, jabbing his index finger right at Ze'evi. "You were just average, right?"

"Right. I was a pretty serious student, maybe more than average," answered Ze'evi, not quite following just where Yanky was heading.

"And now," Yanky started to glow as if he was moving in for the kill, "if you were to learn together with a boy from that same second *shiur*, would you feel a bit better than average? Or would you feel that you were way beyond him?"

Ze'evi suddenly caught Yanky's drift. He had really worked hard on his learning, but when checking his progress, he had only compared himself to other boys his own age. Since he hadn't noticed any great difference between his level and that of his peers, he had felt as though all his work had been for nothing. As he compared his present level with his own two years earlier, he was suddenly able to see an unbelievable change.

Then it was Ze'evi's turn to offer Yanky some support. "Once, when I was in a lousy mood, I approached my *Rosh Mesivta* and poured my heart out to him. I have to admit that he was really great and identified with me. He did say, though, that he couldn't help me much since his business is the preparation of the *shiur* and not guidance. He told me that if I needed advice, I should go see the *mashgiach*.

"Even so," continued Ze'evi, "he said that he wanted to tell me two things. The first, that I shouldn't think that I'm the only one in the world with ups and downs. He opened the *Ruach Chayim* (of Rav Chayim Volozhin) on *Avos* to the first *mishnah* of the second chapter. 'A person always has ups and downs, and during the time that he is down he feels that all his Torah and *avodah* are halfhearted, and don't manage to inspire him. And this is familiar to anyone who walks in the Torah's ways....' He pointed out to me that Rav Chayim Volozhin claimed generations ago that the phenomenon of ups and downs is well known. He told me that it's obvious that my situation isn't novel at all.

"My Rebbe went on, 'The second thing isn't pleasant to admit. But when I prepare a new subject in an unfamiliar *mesechta*, I sometimes have ups and downs, too. Even worse, I say to myself... "How will you put on a show when you give over the *shiur* as if you are so well versed in the material that you learn for the sheer pleasure of it?" Because, between me, myself, and I... when learning a difficult *mesechta*, I feel just like a plodding beginner. Even so, I get myself going again with those words of Rav Chayim.'"

Yanky listened, with his mouth agape. "What?" he asked. "The *maggid shiur* said that? But he's an incredible *Talmid Chacham*, and finds the deepest subjects totally transparent! I guess it's just the human condition — having to work hard, and finding sometimes that the work is rough or confusing."

"That feeling definitely has its benefits," offered Ze'evi. "At least the rough spots make it easy to see that we aren't so great, and that we have nothing to be conceited about..."

"But I thought we were supposed to be encouraging ourselves," asked Ya'akov wonderingly.

"Yes," answered Ze'evi elaborating with new clarity. "If a person isn't conceited, he can reach the golden mean. He may strive for greatness, but that doesn't mean that it should happen at once. The road to greatness is long; I don't think that you can just parachute into Torah as if it were an open field. Maybe we should just enjoy the small victories. Instead of pressure, we'll feel like we did it, like we accomplished something — which might just make it easier to go on."

So the two talked on and made an agreement. "If I see you pushing too hard, Ze'evi, I'm going to remind you to be more patient," warned Yanky.

"Fine — but don't let me catch you slacking off, or you'll hear it from me!" responded Ze'evi. The boys laughed at each other's mock seriousness and made their way out of the near-empty *beis medrash*. Let's hope they kept to their words.

> **THINK ABOUT IT**
>
> **WAS THE BEGINNING OF THE SOLUTION:**
> ◆ their emotional openness?
> ◆ or their intellectual awareness?
>
> What was the relationship between their expectations and their disappointments?

Scenario #2 — Stress in the life of a yeshivah student
Stress Due to Lack of Clarity About the Future

The dog days of summer. The tension in the air of the graduating *shiur* of the *yeshivah ketanah* was palpable. The students were all preoccupied with thoughts (and concerns) about the coming term, and where they would be learning. The public phones were constantly tied up, and the overall hubbub was too distinct to ignore. The great question mark hanging over everyone's heads was: to which *yeshivah gedolah* would each boy now go? Would each be accepted to his first choice?

Those that had already received negative responses seemed more subdued and serious. They tried to handle the rejection and work on registering at a different school. The ones that had still not heard waited in suspense to find out where they stood, and whether or not they needed to look into other options for the coming year. Even Those that had already been accepted were proud of it, and they radiated an aura of delight — as if they were all set to greet the brightest of futures. Beneath the cool exteriors, though, these boys had stomachs full of knots. What would it be like? How would they manage in a new place? How would they fit in scholastically and socially?

Like his good friends, Yechiel (a capable and successful boy) also applied to a reputable and rather demanding yeshivah. Yechiel tried his best to hide his tension in yeshivah and at home. From time to time, however, his suppressed feelings exploded and manifested themselves in a distorted way: he would suddenly act either silly or moody. These behaviors didn't escape the eagle eyes of his father, who grasped just what was eating at his Yechiel. Every so often he would comment, "You know, Yechiel, human beings are really myopic. We don't really know what's good for us, and we usually can't see where Hashem is leading us." Or, "It's good when a person makes a *hishtadlus* like you did... but after he's done all he can, he has to stop worrying about it."

That said, Yechiel still found it difficult to relax. He couldn't come to terms with the possibility of his rejection from the *yeshivah gedolah*, the effect that it would have on him socially, and the embarrassment of having to settle for a second-rate school. He also suspected that perhaps he could have done more, somehow, to assure himself a place in the yeshivah of his choice. Maybe if he could pull some strings, his name would magically appear on the list of accepted students? Yechiel felt torn; even though he knew his father was in the right, and that everything would turn out in line with Hashem's plan, he couldn't shake his nagging doubts.

Deep inside, very different concerns tugged at him. Yechiel felt pressured by a possible positive response. Even if he were to be accepted, would the high academic standard prove too much for him? "Maybe it would be better to just hear a 'no.' That way I wouldn't have a choice; I would have to settle for a less impressive and less pressured yeshivah. At least there I would be more likely to be at the top of my class!" Yechiel tossed these arguments back and forth in his mind.

"If I only had the letter in front of me right now," grumbled Yechiel, "I would at least know where I stand!" Yechiel continued, "And anyway, why have so many of my friends already gotten acceptance letters? I'm definitely second-rate, otherwise why would they have to deliberate about whether or not to accept me?" He felt so worthless.

Yechiel assumed that his misery was unique. "All of my friends are happy and relaxed; you can see it on their faces. I'm the only one who's falling apart!" This thought ate at him until, one evening, Yechiel found himself opening up to his older, married brother Yonasan, and letting out a stream of emotion that had been pent up for too long. Yonasan felt obliged to enlighten his younger brother about some of the harsh realities of life he had learned of through his own experiences. He judged Yechiel mature enough and began, much to Yechiel's amazement, to tell him about the period of his life when he was looking for a *shidduch*.

"Every prospect that came up then made me so stressed out," Yonasan recalled. "I felt like I was under so much under pressure, especially until an answer would come from the girl's side. Maybe they'd refuse, maybe they'd say no... Usually, there *wasn't* a clear 'no'; instead it would be like they were trying to wriggle out of it, 'For now, it's not clear. Maybe call back in a few weeks.' That kind of an answer was the worst, it used to make me so nervous — what did they really mean? Do they really need a few weeks to consider, or is this just a nice way to say 'no'? And if it's 'no', then *why* is it 'no'? Maybe somebody suggested someone else, and they're leaving me on hold if *that* doesn't work out, and then we'll meet again?! You do see that sometimes people pick up a *shidduch* again after a time... Or, maybe they spoke to the wrong person and heard something terrible about me? Who is this guy, and should I be angry with him? Or, maybe I need to just decide that this *shiddduch* isn't really for me, or maybe even... that I'm just fooling myself and think too much of myself. Maybe I'm not even ready for *shidduchim* at all.

"There were some 'spectacular' prospects, and less impressive ones too." Yonasan was carried away by his memories. "I wanted to make an impact on everyone with a really impressive *shidduch*. I was proud that I had been getting such great offers, and it's hard to describe my longing that just one of them would work out all right."

Yonasan took a deep breath, sat back in his chair, and went on with his story.

"When I look back now at my mindset then," Yonasan concluded with a smile, "I get a good laugh. How immature I was, that I thought I was running the world and knew what was best for my future!"

"You probably don't remember, Yechiel, since you were very young then." Yechiel shot his older brother a penetrating look. "I had just about gotten engaged to a girl from a very special family when they broke it off. I fell apart — I got so depressed, it took me weeks to get back to myself. A few months later, we discovered that the girl in question was extremely domineering."

Yechiel's older brother wrapped up his story by adding, "I learned an important lesson from those experiences, and it accompanies me everywhere I go — when choosing a *kollel*, a job... anything, really. Life rarely presents you with what you need on a silver platter. This world is a world of action, full of pitfalls and tests. It could be that in one week, one person has it easy while his friend is being run through the mill; the next week, it's the reverse. The main point is that a person can really grow from the rough times; *especially* from those rough times.

"And I learned something else... There is Someone watching out for us. He knows what's really for our benefit in the long run. Our job is only to try to choose wisely after considering what is good for us in the long run; not to be overly concerned with the results. You did your part by applying to the yeshivah that seems to be the most suitable for you. All your worries about what will happen — dump them, and trust that Hashem will lead you the way you need to go."

Feeling deeply grateful, Yechiel took leave of his brother and went on his way. A kind of calm security was making its way into his heart, and, for the first time in a while, Yechiel started to relax. Yechiel understood that his tension wasn't unique, and that everyone goes through the same, or similar, trials at different times of their lives. He recalled something he had read, that the *hashgachah pratis* that a person sees in his life corresponds exactly to the degree of his trust in Hashem.

Not long afterward, Yechiel received notice of his acceptance into his first-choice yeshivah. He might have thought that from now on life would be smooth sailing. But, naturally, just when everything seems to be shipshape, tests are arranged from Upstairs. And so Yechiel soon entered into a whole new merry-go-round of stress.

As always, the topic in the spotlight at the beginning of the term was *chavrusos*. Perhaps Yechiel relied too much on his standing in his old yeshivah, and half-expected his *chavrusah* to be deposited before him with a sign taped to his lapel, "Here I am. Learn with me!" He started to feel dejected that landing a good partner was proving to be so difficult.

It also wasn't clear to Yechiel exactly what he was seeking. On the one hand, he wanted the right *shidduch*, where they would succeed together. On the other hand, he longed for a "star," an impressive boy who could, by association, make Yechiel a star, too. And everyone knows that, once you've learned well with a well-respected *chavrusah*, it becomes all the more likely to land a similar one the next time around.

So Yechiel paced in the study hall among the students, sending out searching looks to all sides, waiting for "something" to happen.

Yechiel's mood went into a downslide when he realized that a majority of the boys were already set up and learning well while he was still making the rounds without any prospects.

During one of his tours of the study hall, he remembered something his older brother Yonasan had said. "A person can really grow... especially from the rough times. I would recommend to you, dear brother, that you choose wisely based on what you think will be best for you in the long term."

Yechiel grasped that his unwillingness to put in effort to make a friend, and his insistence that it had to be someone "special" were what had been keeping him from accomplishing this fairly routine task. Yechiel reviewed the list of "free" *bochurim* yet again, and within minutes was sitting at a table with a pleasant boy. The story is far from over, for new challenges arose as soon as the old were behind him. And as his challenges grew, so did Yechiel.

THINK ABOUT IT

HOW DID YECHIEL'S NEED FOR APPROVAL:

◆ interfere with his natural motivation?

◆ cause him to put too much pressure on himself?

How did renewed trust in Hashem help him to achieve more?

Scenario #3 — Stress in the life of a yeshivah / kollel student

Stress Due to Feeling a Lack of Self-Worth

The word "happiness" hardly does justice to the emotions that flooded Elimelech's heart during his first weeks at the yeshivah. He had come from a small town where he had learned in the local, and unknown, *yeshivah ketanah*. Elimelech had excelled at his studies and had been accepted with ease to a well-known Chassidic *yeshivah gedolah*. The *kol Torah* that filled the study hall and radiated to the street outside made Elimelech feel so happy and alive! The serious attitude with which the other *bochurim* approached *davening* inspired him and made him feel as if warm waves of *kedushah* were passing through him. He admired those boys that stood still a moment to recite a *berachah* with the proper awe. The opportunity to be in a big city and to visit the various Chassidic courts Friday night after the meal and be swept away with such fervor, was a new and holy experience for him — and it penetrated deeply.

Furthermore, he felt a unique kind of freedom. In the *yeshivah ketanah* where he had spent the last three years, there were a few sharp-tounged lads who felt as if they had to prove their cleverness, twenty-four hours a day. One boy would ask his friend a simple question, and the other would feel the need to respond with a wisecrack, to spice things up a little... Unfortunately, most often, these witticisms were expressed sarcastically — whether at the expense of other people, or serious issues. For example, the boys often played a nasty guessing game: who had the *mashgiach* been alluding to in his last *mussar shmuess*? Elimelech would sit to the side, serious and disappointed, pained by the jokers and distressed for the victims.

Unfortunately, Elimelech's sense of liberation didn't last too long in his new yeshivah. This time, the problems centered around the dining room. At the table, the conversations generally revolved around the Chassidic world. Sometimes, a boy would reveal some news that hadn't yet been heard; other times, they would share old stories that were inspiring, or thrilling. Occasionally, a boy would offer a spontaneous speech to those assembled, and at times a discussion would evolve into a debate over the origins of a particular custom, or a question about the details of a certain story.

The common denominator was always Elimelech's passivity. He always listened attentively, and quickly became an expert nodder. Since he came from a simple background, his treasury of stories and information was especially poor. What would he say, what *could* he say to interest everyone?

Even worse, the boys of the yeshivah were mainly connected to various famous Chassidic groups. Although Elimelech enjoyed his visits to the various Chassidic courts, and benefited from them spiritually, he was still completely devoted to his Rebbe from his little town. When his father, a broken orphan, had arrived in Israel after the *churban*, it was this Rebbe that had breathed new life into him, and arranged for the wedding to Elimelech's mother; he was like a surrogate *zeide* to Elimelech and his siblings. He was always there with his kind face and infinite patience — it was so easy to approach him and pour out your heart. You always came away from him feeling encouraged and well-advised. Elimelech, an *eidel* and somewhat closed boy, didn't feel he had much to "sell" from his Rebbe, and felt so detached from the other boys.

Elimelech considered approaching the *mashgiach*, Rav Tzvi — a friendly, wise middle-aged man — to discuss his problem. Elimelech, however, crossed off the possibility of approaching him. "The *mashgiach* is for a *bochur* with a real problem," he thought. "Take Chatzkel, for example. He's a boy without the sharpest mind, he probably hasn't found his place socially. That's why he's always fooling around — he must need attention. Those secret meetings in the kitchen, his chumminess with the cook, the extra portions on the side — for sure he's convinced the cook he's dying of hunger. But why, then, did he put the lights out in the *beis medrash* two days before Purim? Evidently, it was only a ploy to get some attention. *Nu*, it would be good for someone like him to consult the *mashgiach*, who, I'm sure, would be only too happy to help him out. But me? I'm just a regular guy, learning well, coming on time to *minyan*, and even trying to develop my *yiras Shamayim*.

The only problem is the dining room, so why bother with the *mashgiach*?"

Elimelech continued to think. "One minute — Chatzkel also, apparently, hasn't approached the *mashgiach*. So maybe it's just a trick of the *yetzer hara*? Doesn't Chatzkel also have his reasons for not going to the *mashgiach*? Perhaps we're both just copping out? No, no, it's impossible..." Elimelech continued his internal debate, "Chatzkel is the one who's copping out! He's the boy with problems, not me! I'm not trying to get out of anything; I just don't know who to talk to about something like this." In short, to his detriment, Elimelech wasn't able to approach his *mashgiach* (or anyone, for that matter), to open up and ask for advice.

The distress accumulated within him and caused him increasing pain. Because of it, he decided that it would be best for him to get married as soon as possible — that it would be the ideal solution to his problems. On the one hand, he wouldn't need to be present at the group meals. On the other, as a *balebos*, he would feel more established and immune to the differences between himself and the others.

And so, not much time passed before the offers began to pour in. Elimelech made a good *shidduch*, with a refined and modest girl.

It took Elimelech some time to adjust to married life — to learn how to express himself clearly and work together, side by side, with another person. As the months passed, though, it became clearer to Elimelech that his old problem had never really disappeared; it had only taken on a new form. His learning and *davening* did, indeed, fill him with light and joy. When it came to his life at home, however, he would get all balled up. He wanted to permeate his home with certain values, but it didn't always go smoothly. Elimelech was torn between wanting to get back to his learning and wanting to help his wife — particularly after the birth of their second child — and to be more mature and patient when educating the children. In addition, they were in a constant financial crisis. Elimelech was troubled with a question: should he stay in learning, with the financial pressures that it entailed, or seek work?

Somewhere in his heart, Elimelech was jealous of Yitzchak Eliezer. Now there was an impressive personality; his whole being pulsed self-confidence and strength, his face radiated equanimity, his wit was pleasantly sharp. It seemed as if nothing in the world could possibly bother and get under the skin of Yitzchak Eliezer. Deep inside, Elimelech longed for the chance to have a talk with him, to learn his tricks and apply them to his own life.

One day, Elimelech's hopes materialized, albeit in a somewhat surprising way. It was one of those days when he was in a lousy mood, every word, every gesture was a picture of unease and stress. It happened in the evening, after *Ma'ariv*, some ninety seconds before Elimelech was to leave for his home. Without any prior warning, Reb Yitzchak Eliezer slapped a massive hand on Elimelech's rounded upper back and said determinedly, "If you don't broaden your shoulders a bit, you'll be crushed under that tiny load you're carrying." With that, he vanished out the front door of the *shul*.

Elimelech was bewildered, it felt as if he had been hit with a ton of bricks. What nerve? Who was Yitzchak Eliezer to decide how heavy his load was! And then, before he had even been able to grasp what had happened and respond, Yitzchak Eliezer had disappeared.

As Elimelech approached his house, he realized more and more clearly how right Yitzchak Eliezer had been with his "love pat." He was conscious of how, with every step he took going home, his tension mounted and his doubts crystallized. He also saw how senseless this tension was; he had a wonderful wife, sweet children. He couldn't expect that everything would run like clockwork from sunrise to sunset. He shouldn't take everything so much to heart. It occurred to Elimelech that if he had those "broad shoulders" when he was younger, he would have had much more success in dealing with his difficulties.

After a few weeks, Elimelech took a look at himself; he was beginning to like what he saw. He wanted to say something to Yitzchak Eliezer, but he also wanted to wait for just the right moment. That was why, one evening, after *Ma'ariv*, Elimelech approached him and slapped a hand on his broad back with a mischievous smile playing on his lips. "Thanks for the longest and shortest *shiur* I ever heard in my life..."

THINK ABOUT IT

HOW DID ELIMELECH'S NEED TO FIT IN:

♦ interfere with his ability to make clear-headed decisions?

♦ cause him to be jealous of Yitzchak Eliezer?

How does "broadening your shoulders" enable a person to better cope with the stresses of life?

Scenario #4 — Stress in the life of a *kollel avreich*

Stress Brought on When Attempting to Prepare for the Future

Chayim felt like he had come to a dead end. He did not have the vaguest idea of how to resolve a serious problem: his rapidly dwindling ability to concentrate on his Torah learning.

Chayim remembered that when he was newly married, he had made several iron-clad decisions. At that point, the hectic period of the engagement and the wedding were behind him. He had a wonderful wife, Esther, who very much wanted him to grow in his learning. In short, his future lay paved before him. He took on himself a solidly packed learning schedule, with a number of different objectives, and he relied on his diligence and determination to carry him to success in meeting his various goals.

At first, everything was wonderful. He progressed quickly both in his *iyun seder* (in-depth focus on one section at a time), and in *bekius seder* (learning in order to cover ground and get the big picture), as well as a number of smaller learning sessions at night in halachah (Jewish law) and *chazarah* (general review). He invariably came on time, always put his whole self into it, and consistently accomplished a great deal. True, he did not always manage to cover as much ground as he had planned — but he understood that you cannot always know in advance how complex a subject in Talmud will be. Granted, Esther complained from time to time that his schedule was too demanding for her, but in general, she accepted the situation with understanding, bless her. She was more bothered when, about two years ago, after they had been married for some three years, he started to be irritable occasionally. But nobody is an angel, he thought to himself, and she has to learn that it's not possible to always remain perfectly calm.

In the last several months, however, he began to feel a sense of fatigue, and a corresponding difficulty in concentration. Interestingly, after a few weeks, he also began to have trouble sleeping. At first, it happened only about once a week, but gradually, the phenomenon began to occur more frequently — at times he had difficulty falling asleep, while at other times, he would wake up in the middle of the night with a sense of tension and have trouble falling back asleep. Chayim did not understand how his sleep could be disturbed, when he felt so exhausted. He decided that his sleeping problem probably emanated from concern over the drop in his learning — and therefore, he would have to devote every bit of energy he had to strengthen his learning.

Then something unexpected occurred. Little Motti got an ear infection, and I'm sure you can imagine what it's like when a child has an ear infection: there's a screaming baby, a worried and wiped-out mother, a tense atmosphere at home, and sleepless nights. Chayim got all tangled up in it. On the one hand, he really wanted to help his wife; on the other, he felt that now wasn't the time. He felt as if he stood at a crossroads, and that if he wouldn't succeed at his new venture — learning with all his might — he would just fall apart altogether.

Unfortunately, the situation deteriorated so much that Chayim's marriage began to show the strain. It was too much for his wife to continue working for the family with a sick child and an unresponsive and unhelpful husband. Despite this, Chayim tried to explain to her how important it was for him to focus on his learning just then. His unarticulated complaint always resounded in his ears, "Why doesn't she appreciate all the times that I helped her before?"

Chayim left his house bitterly disappointed. He recalled that, as an older *bochur*, he also hadn't amounted to much in his learning. At the time he had decided that it was so hard for him because he lacked support; his parents didn't encourage him enough, nor did his friends. It seemed to him then that what he needed was a supportive wife who would help him focus on his Torah learning. To Chayim, it seemed that in the first period after marriage (when his wife had less responsibilities, and therefore needed less help), Esther was more supportive and his studies blossomed. Whereas lately, for whatever reason (like a child, a new job, or the current ear infection), his wife had become less appreciative of both his learning and whatever help he did manage to offer her, and as a result, his learning was suffering immensely.

Chayim felt like he had no choice but to share his feelings with his wife. He figured that the easiest way would be to call her immediately on the phone and tell her right away. Said and done. Esther was shocked. After all the encouragement she gave him throughout the years, after all the times she was willing to forgo her comfort so that he could learn, after she went out to work to support him, and after she had to stand by and watch her husband's situation deteriorating — now he has the audacity to claim that everything is *her* fault?! She did not say a word, for fear that it would irritate him even more. But she felt that she could not allow the situation to continue, both because of the pain of her husband's accusations, and because of her very real concern for her husband's distress. She did not know how to relate to the situation. With no alternative in sight, she turned to her brother-in-law, a successful *Rosh Kollel*. He said that he too had noticed recently that something was not right with Chayim, and that in his opinion, she should seek professional help as soon as possible.

When her husband returned, Esther told him about the conversation she had had with her brother-in-law and his recommendation. At that, Chayim exploded. "Don't you know that the worst possible thing is to reveal personal problems to a family member?!" he thundered. This time, Esther did not remain silent. "All right, so I made a terrible mistake. You'll never understand why I did it. But what do we do now to improve the situation here?" Esther gave a clear message that she would not be silent until Chayim took the necessary measures to extricate himself from his situation.

Chayim saw that he did not have much of a choice, but he still refused to go for professional help. "Your brother-in-law is not going to be the one to decide exactly what we have to do. Look, we have a neighbor, Rabbi Kugel, whom I'm very friendly with. He's also a *Rosh Kollel* and he has experience with many *avreichim* (married men who learn full time). Maybe he can help."

Esther listened, and then replied, "I'm not completely comfortable with the situation. But meanwhile, I'm willing to compromise, and then we'll see how things develop. If he can really help you — that's wonderful. What difference does it make to me who will be the good angel who can help us?"

That night, Chayim mustered up the courage to go to see Rabbi Kugel. As soon as Chayim spoke with him, Chayim saw serious worry register on his neighbor's face.

"Are you aware," Rabbi Yudel asked Chayim slowly, deliberately, "that life isn't child's play? It's a little dangerous to put yourself under so much pressure. I don't want to scare you, Chayim, but there have been grown men that needed to take a few *months* off of learning because they pushed themselves too hard. Sometimes, the pressure makes these boys start to act a little strange — they call it 'nerves.' Psychologists call it 'compulsive behaviors.' For example, a person may wash his hands for *netilas yadayim* many times, because he doubts whether or not he's fulfilled the *mitzvah* properly."

"I don't follow you," Yechiel argued with Rav Kugel, "I've read the biographies of a number of *Gedolim;* all of them were super-diligent in their learning and worked on their *avodas Hashem* with all they had. Why can't I try to do the same?"

"Think a minute, Chayim," the Rav tried to explain calmly and patiently. "If you were writing the biography of some *Gadol*, would you include stories about his marital difficulties, his trouble learning? Would you portray all his struggles, and even his failures? I think I even saw this point in *Cheshbon HaNefesh* once. Listen, don't get me wrong, it's definitely important to read these biographies, to get a picture of what it is to be an elevated person. But you have to do it wisely, and use common sense. You have to understand that our *Gedolim* are very much human beings, with their own strong and weak points, and that their path to greatness was full of peaks and valleys."

"But how does the *Gadol* become so great?" asked Chayim.

"With perseverance and determination, together with calmness and enthusiasm."

"But how do you do *that?*"

"You slowly build up your perseverance, and at the same time you develop a pleasure from learning — you learn with determination *and* enjoyment. Instead of focusing on how to squeeze more time out of yourself for learning, you work on the quality of the time that you already spend."

Until now, Chayim had perceived his outstanding learning schedule as a remarkable, heroic effort in the area of total devotion to Torah study. Suddenly, Chayim began to see the other side of the coin — the price that was being paid, not only by himself, but by those around him. Still...

Chayim had his doubts and wasn't too clear about how to strike the delicate balance between lightheartedness, motivation, and vivaciousness. He did commit to trying, though. He would work on valuing his own efforts, not expecting immediate results, and he would pray that Hashem should lead him in the right direction and care for him.

The openness of Chayim's discussion with his neighbor helped him touch base with his own delusions. He realized that his number one priority was going to have to be developing a more relaxed and fulfilled attitude — one that would help him to truly grow — in his studies and in the life and family he was building with his wife. Let us hope that Chayim is brave enough to loosen his grasp on the exaggerated picture of success, and move ahead to a life filled with appreciation for his work and enjoyment of his progress — along with a pleasant atmosphere in his home.

> **THINK ABOUT IT**
>
> **HOW WERE CHAYIM'S EXPECTATIONS OF HIMSELF:**
>
> ♦ a sign of healthy ambition, but with a mistaken perspective?
>
> ♦ keeping Chayim from actualizing his potential?
>
> How could Chayim redirect his desire for excellence to encompass a larger, more complete (and enduring) picture of success?

Scenario #5 — Stress in the life of a working man

Accumulated Stress

Mr. Edelman, a successful attorney, sat at his desk with his well-groomed head in his hands. Had he been looking out the broad picture window behind him, he might have been calmed by the view of the city laid out before him like a toy town. Mr. Edelman, though, had no time to look out windows. He usually didn't even make time to eat at the office. From 8:30 A.M. until he finally made it home (sometimes as late as 1 A.M.), he would drink huge quantities of coffee (milk, no sugar), seltzer with ice, and the occasional bagel or danish. By the time he walked into his locked and silent house on those late, late nights, he would feel as if he were about to burst.

Generally speaking, Mr. Edelman walked in the door at a reasonable 8 or 9 P.M.., hungry, tired, and barely in control of himself. The slightest problem could set him off. Was supper not made? Was it too hot, too cold, the wrong food, not enough food?

Don't misunderstand — Mr. Edelman was a wonderful guy. Everybody loved him, as long as they weren't getting "on his nerves." Dedicated to *mitzvos*, dedicated to his family, loving to his wife, committed to building up the *shul* and helping people in the neighborhood. But... he could be edgy sometimes.

"Mr. Edelman?" his secretary poked her head into his office. "You didn't hear the intercom, I guess. Mrs. Lazerson is on the phone. Again." She smirked, and retired to her corner. Harry Edelman picked his head up out of his palms and gulped down some cold coffee. "I can't believe that woman! She owes me eight thousand dollars in overdue fees and she thinks that I'm going to jump when she calls! She probably wants me to fight it out with the co-op board again over the maintenance agreement. Why is it that people with money are always the most obnoxious?" He took a deep breath and picked up the receiver.

"Harry? Harry? Are you there?" That nasal whine.

"Yes, Mrs. Lazerson. What can I do for you today?"

"Harry, as my attorney, I really think you ought to be protecting my interests a little bit better. I got another nasty letter in the mail from that guy in Florida over that little golf course incident. Isn't it your job to make sure that people like that don't annoy me? Am I rrrright?" Oh, that awful grating noise in her voice again. Silence. "Harry," he could almost hear her clicking her nails on her desk, "I'm beginning to think that maybe I should go shopping for a new lawyer."

Mr. Edelman, normally a paragon of self-restraint and tact, felt the caffeine surge through his veins. His head was pounding as he said to himself, "Is this what my life is for, to get harangued by crazy ladies from Connecticut?" He groped for a response. "Why is she bothering me, today of all days? The *shul* is in the middle of a lawsuit, my wife told me that if I don't come home by 7:30 P.M., she's not making supper or waiting around, my cardiologist wants me in for a stress test soon... I just don't have the energy to take care of everything right now." He cleared his throat.

"Mrs. Lazerson. If that's what you'd like to do, by all means. Please be advised, though, that you have an outstanding bill with me for my retainer. All the documentation for all your legal work is my property until that bill is cleared. And, no, I have no control over what people send you in the mail. Good afternoon, Mrs. Lazerson." He set the receiver down softly.

Harry Edelman needed a breath of fresh air. "You would think that, after paying fifty thousand dollars a year in rent on these offices, I'd be able to open a window around here." Anyway, it was almost time for *Minchah*. He put on his hat and coat, called out, "Katie, I'm going out!" and headed for the elevators. It was a long trip down and it seemed as if the entire building was going out to lunch simultaneously. He nodded to the doorman and burst out into the sunshine, feeling as if the balloon that had been expanding in his chest all morning had suddenly taken flight. He felt almost giddy. Harry Edelman glanced at his watch; he had twenty minutes to walk until *Minchah* time at Sanders and Fleckman on 34th Street. "Park Avenue is broad enough, and it has those flowers down the middle. Maybe I'll be able to breathe there." The gaudy parade of tulips relaxed him and he felt his shoulders beginning to unwind.

"I'm fifty-two years old. I've been working as a lawyer all my adult life. I realize that I haven't exactly been Mr. Calm all these years (what lawyer is?), but lately, I feel as if I'm drowning. What's happening to me?" Harry Edelman was strolling now. The day was crisp and clear — he was actually beginning to enjoy it. "I need to sit down and prioritize. Who do I think I am, Superman? I guess I have always thought that I'm the man of steel. I always worked every Sunday, never took a vacation; if my kids wanted to spend time with me, they had to come into the office. I always worked late hours, and then took my work home with me. So, why does it feel like everything's falling apart now? Maybe it's my age. Who knows?" He sat down on a bench, drinking in the sunshine, not thinking much. He had four minutes to get over to 34th Street. He liked *davening Minchah* there because they had an interesting *daf yomi shiur* afterward. Even so, Harry Edelman sighed and got up regretfully.

—·⋄⟨⋄⟩⟨⋄⟩⋄·—

When he returned to the pile of papers awaiting his attention, it was already 5:30 P.M. "I have an hour to work if I'm going to get home by 7:30, so I'd better get moving." The office was clearing out already. Harry Edelman heard a knock at his half-opened door and looked up. His partner, Bernie Sherer, was leaning on the doorframe, looking pensive.

"Harry, we need to talk. Can I come in?"

"Sure. Sit down. I thought you were in court today, counselor."

"I went down there and spent the whole day running around. I just came uptown on my way home to pick up some papers for tomorrow. I also wanted to touch base with you. We've got a problem, Harry."

"What kind of a problem?" Harry Edelman felt the ever-present knot tightening in his chest.

"A cash flow problem."

"Us, Bernie? We're so busy we don't have time to think. We're overloaded with work..."

"But, Harry, too many of your clients haven't been paying their fees. You have to be firmer with them." Bernie Sherer looked pained. "Harry, I spoke to our bookkeeper today. We're behind on the rent. Really behind. We haven't paid for the new computer system yet, and it cost us thirty thousand dollars. We're down a lot of money all of a sudden."

The phone rang and Katie had already left for the day. Harry Edelman picked it up. "Mr. Edelman, please."

"Speaking. How can I help you?"

"Mr. Edelman, this is Mindy Goldblum from the *shul*. I was asked to call all of the new members of the board to remind them that there will be a compulsory meeting tonight at 7 P.M."

"Thank you for calling — I had forgotten about it entirely... You too... Be well. Goodbye." He hung up and turned back to his partner. "Bernie, I know it's all my fault. I'm sure that if I were more up front about unpaid fees, the clients would come up with the money. I'll try to have everything ironed out by next week. Okay?"

Bernie Sherer looked skeptical. "Next week? You think a problem that's taken months to develop will be solved by next week?"

Harry began to get agitated, "Look, Bernie, it's my fault and I'll take care of it! If I say I'll do something, then I'll do it!"

"Relax, Harry. I didn't mean to get you upset; we just need to start addressing the problem. You've also been seeming a little edgy lately... But look what time it is! We'd both better pack up — I know my wife hates it when I'm late!" He headed for his office. "I'll walk you down when you're ready."

Harry Edelman looked at his watch and realized that if he was going to make the meeting, he'd have to get on the 6:15 p.m. express bus. "The *shul* business shouldn't take longer than half an hour," he thought. "I should be able to make it home by about quarter to eight. What's fifteen minutes? I'm sure Linda will understand." He snapped his attaché case closed and grabbed his coat and hat. "Bernie, I'm ready to go!" They both were preoccupied in the elevator and didn't speak until they were out on the street. "Take care! Bye!" They went their separate ways.

Harry Edelman stood at his front door and checked his watch. 10:34 p.m.! Linda would be furious. He dreaded going in the house, but decided to bite the bullet. Where would he sleep? In the car?

Linda was reading in her favorite chair when he walked into the living room. She didn't look up as he hung up his coat. "What was it this time? Any reason why you didn't call?"

"We had a meeting, I mean a brawl, at the *shul* at 7:00. It dragged on until just now..."

"More about the lawsuit, Harry? What a waste of time and energy! You're getting much more involved in the *shul* than is really necessary. Let the president and the *gabbai* work out their differences on their own. Quit the board and just do the legal work for them."

"Linda, let me sit down and eat something before I collapse, okay?"

Over cold meatloaf and potatoes, Harry went over the night's proceedings. "I just can't leave the *shul*. It's just assumed that I'll be an active member of the board. If I don't take care of the case, the whole place will just fall apart! How can I abandon it?"

"Harry, doesn't it say in the Talmud that your life comes first?" Was that pity he saw in her eyes?

It was 11:28 P.M. It was beginning to dawn on Harry Edelman that the time had come to let Linda know about what had been going on at the office. She wasn't trying to hand him ultimatums — she was just concerned. "I had some unpleasant news from Bernie today. Money problems. We're really behind paying bills and it's hard to imagine how I'm going to make good on a lot of uncollected fees."

"Sounds like things are piling up. Maybe you need to prioritize."

"Right. So I'm trying to do that, but I don't even have a minute to think, much less get to work on figuring out how to maximize my time."

"I meant, it sounds like maybe you're trying to do too much."

"Sweetheart, you can't understand — Bernie is relying on me, there are bills to pay, the *shul* is in the middle of a crisis, and I'm struggling to get *daf yomi* done every day... What am I supposed to do?" Harry Edelman was at a total loss.

"Harry, I don't mean to offend you, but it just seems like you're driving yourself too hard. I'm sure there's a way to be involved with the *shul* in a less taxing and much more efficient way. And, as for *daf yomi* — we're so proud of you! But you haven't let anything off. I've been so worried about you. And Doctor Ingram called today; he wants you to go in for a stress test. I made an appointment for you for the day after tomorrow."

Mr. Edelman composed himself. "I know you mean well, Linda, but I just don't know if I can let go so easily. You know, I'm used to being the hero. I hate giving up."

"Harry, is it giving up to admit that you're human? Scale down your involvement in the *shul*. Maybe you should break up with Bernie and work from the house. You mentioned bills before — I'll bet you'd be a lot less tense if you didn't have such a high overhead! What's your rent in midtown, anyway? And you can't even open a window in your office!" Mr. Edelman smiled.

"What you're saying makes sense. I just don't see how I could manage it."

"Rabbi Greenberg said something in his Tehillim class last week: '*Hashem yigmor ba'adi*' — 'Hashem will complete it for me.'[2] The *Shiurei Da'as* says that that means that I have to do my part, but to push myself past reasonable limits is like a lack of trust in Hashem."[3]

"I feel like I need to sleep on this. Maybe tomorrow I'll take the morning off to talk with you about this some more."

"It's about time, Harry. It's been many weeks that I've been waiting for you to realize the condition that you're in. Maybe that will give you the push you need to finally make real changes."

> **THINK ABOUT IT**
>
> **WHY DOES HARRY EDELMAN:**
> ♦ take on more responsibility than he can handle?
> ♦ not realize how much pressure he's under?
>
> How was his wife able to maintain an open channel of constructive communication despite her personal disappointment?

Scenario #6 — Stress in the life of an adolescent girl

Stress Brought on When Preparing for Exams

Tzipporah was a year and a half older than her sister, Shoshana. The two sisters tried to get along and in years past they were like partners in everything they did. Gradually though, over the last few months, an atmosphere of competitiveness had sprung up between the girls, along with tension that followed them wherever they went.

Tzipporah was a sweet and simple girl that loved to pitch in and help, whether in her home or someone else's. In contrast, Shoshana was the brilliant one. She loved to learn, and was at the top (or close to it) of her class. Consequently, she was quite popular.

Several years earlier, jealousy of her younger sister began to sneak into Tzipporah's heart. For her part, she always tried to hold her own in her schoolwork and occasionally exerted herself quite a bit. Even so, her grades were never too impressive. Tzipporah's parents did their best to encourage her, and explained to her over and over that, for them, the important thing was that she had done her best. When Tzipporah heard this, she would relax for some time but, sooner or later, when confronted by the image of her sister and the spectacular grades she seemed to pull out of a hat, jealousy would again rear its ugly head. "Why do I always have to work so hard," she wondered. "I spend hours studying for every test!"

At the end of the year, the school held final exams on a huge amount of material. Since the exam in question was to cover a great amount of difficult material, she suspected that she wouldn't even be able to get average. This worry cut into Tzipporah's ability to concentrate; even when she managed to focus, she tired easily.

In the middle of this, as Tzipporah struggled to focus on preparing for the exam, she noticed how her younger sister sat at the table, opened her books with great energy, and began to review her own schoolwork with the greatest of ease and pleasure. After a while she finished, and radiating self-satisfaction, stood up from her place and turned to other things.

Tzipporah's mood deteriorated even further. She only wanted the whole business to be over and done with — that she should be finished reviewing, that all the charts should be imprinted in her memory, that the test (successfully completed) should already be behind her. These stressful thoughts plagued her. With these emotions, she pushed herself to review the material.

Tzipporah heard a knock at the front door. Dragging her feet, she made her way over to open it.

"Oh, Tzipporah, just who I came looking for!" A neighbor's face greeted her with a warm smile. "Could you baby-sit tonight?" She didn't give Tzipporah much time to consider, and went on enthusiastically, "I can't forget how, when I was out for a few hours last week, you managed so well with the children. I wouldn't have dreamed that a girl as young as you are would have known how to accommodate the feelings of the little ones, and keep track of everything so smoothly."

Tzipporah stood, bewildered, a confused smile tugging at her mouth.

The neighbor didn't let up. "I'll tell you the truth. Even much older girls rarely succeed with my kids the way that you did. I think that it would be in my children's best interest to be exposed to your approach more often. So, we're on for tonight?"

Tzipporah nodded her head in the affirmative, and the conversation ended with heartfelt thanks from the neighbor.

Tzipporah returned to her table and went back to stooping over her books. An unexpected ray of light had burst in from somewhere off to the side to dispel her gloom. She finally had caught on that everyone has their strong points and their way of being — and their own job to do, too. She realized that she ought to focus on and enjoy her specialty, without giving up entirely on those areas that tend to be difficult. It was only after Tzipporah had freed herself from her recent malaise that she proved able to focus constructively. She understood that the more she appreciated her achievements in other fields, the more satisfied she would feel with her academic accomplishments, whatever they might be.

That evening, Tzipporah approached her neighbor's house with a sprightly step. The woman welcomed her warmly and gratefully and, once again, showered her with praise. Tzipporah decided that she would try her best to prepare for the exam and enjoy what interested her without getting her hopes up for a super grade. That was how Tzipporah managed to continue her review feeling at ease, and learned the material to the maximum of her capabilities.

—·◇◯◇◉◇◯◇·—

Two days after the test, in the afternoon...

Shoshana stormed in with a face that registered anger and disappointment. Barely minutes passed before she broke out in hysterics, wailing, "My teacher hates me!" Her behavior was completely out of character.

By way of explanation she complained that they had just received the test results, and she had only gotten a 95. As Shoshana saw it, she had been unjustly cheated of extra points. With her face streaked with tears she went on, "I worked so hard for this exam! I stayed awake two whole nights! And Ruthie (the queen of the class) got a 97, even though I'm smarter! Where's the justice?"

Tzipporah, standing to the side, observed the goings-on. With her new outlook, she felt even more encouraged. She saw even more clearly now how anyone could get tense when their aspirations were too high. Everything clicked all at once: She could feel for her sister and keep her jealousy at bay by remembering that Shoshana wasn't just enjoying success; she clearly had problems of her own. Tzipporah was starting to internalize, "That's her work, and developing my own potential is mine. How could I confuse the two?"

> **THINK ABOUT IT**
>
> **HOW DID OVER-CONCERN FOR SUCCESS:**
>
> ◆ affect Tzipporah and Shoshana similarly?
> ◆ affect them differently?
>
> What helped Tzipporah to gain a healthy recognition of the value of her accomplishments?

Appendix B: Tension in Real Life Scenes 381

Scenario #7 — Stress in the life of an adolescent girl

Stress That Is Part of Developing Potential

Beruriah, a creative and sociable seventeen-year-old-girl, sat and pored over her seminary's course catalog for the coming year. She wanted to expand her horizons, had decided to take part in some course as an elective, and sat there vacillating over which one to choose.

As she reviewed the listings for what seemed the tenth time, a computer course caught her eye. She had no particular love for the devices, but the field had an important and impressive sound to it that appealed to her. "Now *that's* a profession," said Beruriah to herself. "I'm sure it's fascinating and would help me land a good job in the long run." She daydreamed about telling her cousins how she's decided to "...specialize in computers, and I'm considering working in the field in the future." Beruriah was also a bit nervous — maybe the course would be too difficult for her? Even so, she was determined to do it and pushed aside her quiet doubts as she signed up for the class.

On the first day of classes, her normally steady and confident tread had an air of hesitancy about it as she made her way to a seat. She was a bit intimidated by the size of the room and the large number of computers it held. The atmosphere was quite formal; soon enough, the first lecture began.

The majority of concepts covered that first day were entirely new to Beruriah. At the start of the class, she tried her best to follow the train of ideas. As the hour went on, though, she got tired. And disappointed. She had hoped for a stimulating hour and had discovered, instead, that she really needed to exert herself to catch the concepts and hold on to them as they went whizzing over her head.

During the lessons, an occasional question or comment would be thrown in by one of the other girls. Whenever Beruriah heard a particularly astute question from one of the students, she felt pressured. Beruriah got tense because she believed that the others were absorbing the material or progressing faster than she was.

While doing one of the classroom exercises, Beruriah felt as if every minor error tightened a chokehold on her heart. "That's how you learn," the instructor consoled all the girls that made mistakes. Beruriah, however, couldn't relax — she wanted to be perfect right off the bat.

Beruriah had a passion for devouring new information. She always wanted to know everything "on one foot" since the world and all its wonder stretched out before her, and there was so much to find out. Beruriah paid dearly for this lofty goal. She found it difficult to invest the time necessary to get a solid foundation in any subject. Naturally, it was difficult to fully comprehend the more difficult material without knowing the basics, and so she was often frustrated with her progress. In this course as well, this tendency ran wild and blocked her advancement. It explained why, during the lectures, Beruriah was busy flipping through the guidebook to get to the really interesting stuff and didn't bother with mastering the material that was being painstakingly reviewed by everyone else.

Beruriah had opted for the computer course because she reasoned that the subject was important and respectable. As the classes continued, though, Beruriah felt more dissatisfied with her performance, and blamed herself more and more. She began to suspect that there was something not right about her, that perhaps she had been mistaken for thinking she was bright and capable.

—·◇◆◇—

Several more lessons flew by and Beruriah continued to participate, tired and uninterested. To motivate herself a little to focus better, she resorted to pushing herself by getting tense about the work.

Beruriah impatiently waited for the semester's end, and when it did, she walked out of the last class feeling disappointed in herself.

The following fall, when registration time came around again, Beruriah remembered the previous year's failure. She decided to choose her courses more intelligently and deliberately than she had the year before. She recognized that she already had a well-developed creative flair, and that she loved to sew and even dream up new styles that were tasteful, refined, and artistic. She therefore chose to participate in a sewing course.

Since Beruriah was determined not to repeat the previous year's mistakes, she decided to make some advanced preparation. She did some introspecting and asked herself, what problems does she always run into when learning a new subject? Beruriah came to a basic conclusion that she always wanted to reap the rewards before the time was ripe. She resolved to enjoy each stage at its time, and approach the project patiently.

Beruriah went to each sewing class patiently, filled with pleasure and appreciation of her gradual progress. She succeeded in acquiring knowledge and skill at a reasonable pace and with a lot of enjoyment. In addition, above and beyond her technical know-how, she had a great deal of satisfaction from the number of beautiful outfits that hung in her closet, and her wise decision of that fall.

THINK ABOUT IT

HOW WAS BERURIAH FINALLY ABLE TO:

◆ understand that learning a new skill takes investment?

◆ motivate herself in a healthy way?

How did Beruriah finally learn to enjoy healthy goals?

Scenario #8 — Stress in the life of an adolescent girl

Stress Brought on by Attempting to Achieve Social Status

Wednesday, Iyar 21, 5757

Hi there, Dear Diary!

To be a "chevraman" or not to be; now that is a confusing question.

I don't know if you understand me, Diary. But that's the way I feel. I saw Rivky and Brachi organizing the class for the social; everyone was talking to them, everyone admired them. I so much want to be like them!

I longed for the rest of the girls to see that I can also do something. That I'm not just some dumb sheep tagging along, afraid to say a word of her own, with nothing to contribute... You know me, Diary, and you know how much I hate terms like those being applied to me.

That was why I decided to demonstrate my abilities too; to prove to everyone (including myself) that I can be just as much of a "chevraman" as anyone else. I decided to take advantage of whatever opportunity presents itself to show them all that I can also be a leader.

On that very day, during recess, I thought my opportunity had arrived. The girls had gathered together to strategize. They wanted to present a definite recommendation for the yearly trip. "If we all go together to ask, there's a good chance that they'll listen to our suggestion," said Rivky. Everyone agreed enthusiastically.

I tried my luck. "Maybe it's worthwhile to visit the electric power station in Ashdod. My cousin was there last month with her family and they had a great time. You can even see the sea from there..."

Some heads turned my way for a few seconds and immediately snapped back. The discussion went on, and no one even bothered to respond to my suggestion. I was so disappointed, but I wasn't going to give up. If they won't listen to me willingly, I'll find some way to make them listen.

The first class after recess was history. The teacher pointed out that King Chizkiyahu had lived in the middle of the time of the first Beis HaMikdash. I remembered all the times that I was afraid to ask a question — or was too embarrassed to offer an answer — and found instead that some other girl would say exactly what I had thought a few seconds later. I was determined not to let that happen any more, no matter what. Wanting to sound like I knew what I was talking about, I raised my hand and asked, "But didn't the Chashmona'im live during the middle of that period?" Again, heads turned my way inquisitively, and they were smiling (as if to say, "Why are you, all of a sudden, putting your two cents in when you don't even understand the subject?") I was shown my mistake, that the Chashmona'im had lived during the second Beis HaMikdash and the teacher was discussing the first... I wished the ground could have swallowed me up, I was so embarrassed!

I'm so confused, I don't even know what to think; do you know what I mean? On the one hand, I don't want to be so quiet anymore; I want to feel like I have some status in the class. On the other hand, I'm afraid I'm going too lose my own, natural personality with these deliberate attempts.

I'm all out of ideas, Diary. Maybe you have some?

Miri

Thursday, Iyar 22, 5757

Hi. It's me again. I couldn't sleep at all last night, I was so tense and anxious. I guess yesterday's question really is a hard one.

Toward dawn, I came to a conclusion. I can't be a chevraman; it's just not me, it doesn't work. The title doesn't suit me. Maybe it fits

Rivky, Brachi, Chaggiti, or Lea'le. They know just how to run the class through hoops and make everyone happy. They do everything perfectly.

It seems to me, though, that I'm just not made for this; it's not me. It's got to be something you have at birth, and I just never got it.

After thinking this, I started to calm down, "There's no happiness like the resolution of doubt," even if the reality isn't so complimentary.

It's possible that what bothered me the most was that, out of wanting to score points in class, I had actually lost some. I can deal with that, but I want to be straight with myself. I can tell that something is still bothering me, irritating me... How can I get the other girls to appreciate me? Simply know that I'm alive...

Sunday, Iyar 25, 5757

Dear Diary,

I'm totally confused today. No, not confused. Shocked! Basically, I don't know how to express my feelings. All I know is that this definitely couldn't have happened to Devora; not Devora!

But I heard it with my own ears...

Shabbos afternoon, Imma whispered to Abba that my cousin Devora was getting a divorce! That whisper knocked me over like a gale-force wind.

How could it be that our Devora, who always organized the family get-togethers, who danced in that way of hers at weddings, so joyfully, that she... *she* is getting a divorce?! I just don't understand it. Doesn't popularity mean that you are succeeding in life? How could it happen to her? And aside from that, what will happen to little Chayim'ke and Yanky? How will they feel? How will they grow up? What's it like to live in a house with only one parent?

It really worries me! How can you take little children and separate them from one of their parents? How???

I hope that a good night's sleep will help settle at least some of the questions that are racing around my brain.

Sunday, Elul 5, 5757

Good morning, Diary,

I'm going to tell you something totally new this time. This time it's not anxieties and questions. I sort of got tired of all those fantasies about nonsense. All that analyzing and trying doesn't seem to help anyway. So today I decided to get a bit more serious, so I made a resolution.

I told you about my new teacher, the one who just drops those pearls of wisdom? Today, after a class on *teshuvah*, I decided that I need to make some changes.

And... I decided!

Bli neder, I'm going to work on my *tznius*. That's why I'm going to list those areas that I need to improve: I will no longer go around in those semi-transparent tights. Thicker ones won't hurt my legs at all; my neckline should be better put together, not lying open carelessly; there probably is some way to make my hair more orderly, you know what I mean, Diary, so I don't need to spell it out; it should just be pretty and modest.

All in all, it doesn't seem like too much, but I'm really worried about the other girls' reaction.

Miri

Tuesday, Elul 7, 5757

I was right, Dear Diary, I knew what I felt. That was why it didn't take me altogether by surprise; even so, it wasn't too pleasant.

As soon as I walked into class, I saw how they were all examining me in surprise. It was as if I were some space alien that had suddenly landed smack in the middle of the classroom. They raked me over from top to toe until they were satisfied that, yes, it was just their friend Miri. I heard all these whispers, "What a *tzadekes!*" "*Yachne,*" "*Rebbetzin!*" or just "*Bubbie* Miri." I still don't understand just what all those names have to do with the matter at hand, but anyway, that's not my business right now.

My problem is that I'm afraid that I'm going to have to call it quits; I'm worried that I won't be strong enough to hold to my resolutions. Maybe this challenge is just too much for me? Perhaps I didn't really need to take this on? Maybe I'm too weak to really change the way I dress? I distinctly remember how, when Brachi became *bas mitzvah*, she started to be more careful about her sleeve length and didn't pay any attention to any wisecracks from anyone. And Rivky once got everyone to follow the school's dress code more closely. So how come it doesn't work for me?

So the problem really has two parts. On the one hand, I'm not strong enough. I just don't have it in me to stroll casually into class as if nothing's happened and totally ignore those girls that feel obliged to make some comment.

On the other hand, the reaction of some of the girls is definitely a problem. Why do they tease the girls who are trying to be a little more careful about halachah? Why do they have to call names? What does it matter to them?

Just a second. Maybe those names aren't really so bad — doesn't every Jewish girl aspire to become a *tzadekes*? Maybe making fun of *tznius*, or any other *mitzvah* that they aren't so strict about, stems from jealousy! They're jealous! They know what's right, but they just aren't strong enough to fight their *yetzer*, they're too weak.

Maybe they also feel guilty and, to hide it, they create this image as if the other girl is the weirdo so that they won't feel too small and their guilty conscience won't bother them. Somewhere in their hearts, though, they really want to be the same way.

Dear Diary, I have a question for you: why does such a simple step to do *teshuvah* have to be so full of tension? I just don't have the strength to stand up to the girls teasing me, to feel like such an oddball. I'm not strong enough to hold to my path, even though I'm sure it's the right way to go.

Do you have any advice for me?

Miri

Monday, Elul 13, 5757

Hello,

If I hadn't noticed that something was wrong with Esti, I never would have figured it out. She's such a quiet girl. Socially, she's not really ever in the middle of things, so it wasn't so obvious that, during the last week, she was more serious. No one noticed that she also came an hour late twice. In my heart, though, I knew something was going on. I wanted to approach her and ask if there was anything the matter, but I already knew what the answer would be, "Nothing." Esti is smart and a hard worker with a heart of gold, she willingly helps everyone with homework, but she's very quiet and shy and doesn't usually talk about herself.

I got an idea. At the end of last year, I needed to make up some work and went to her house for help. I should pass by and go in on the pretext that I'm missing some grammar notes. That way, maybe I could talk with her a little bit more freely. And that's what I did...

I knocked on her door yesterday afternoon and when it opened, I was dumbstruck. Instead of the orderly house I saw a few months earlier, the place looked as if an earthquake had hit it. Toys and dirty laundry were piled up in the corners, the little children were going wild, and every so often you could hear some baby screaming. In the middle of this mess I saw Esti trying to put things in order and feed two-and-a-half-year-old Yitzchak.

Esti didn't know how to react when she saw me; she looked as if I had caught her "red-handed" and, after a minute, she came to the door and got right to the point. A few weeks earlier, her mother had a baby girl, but the doctors told them that she had a heart problem. Her mother was at the hospital all day, and her father went there directly from work to relieve her. Because her parents are such quiet people, they didn't ask for much help from relatives and neighbors, just that the small children should be taken care of in the mornings while Esti, the eldest, is in school.

"But Esti, how are you managing?! Isn't it too much for you to take care of six children?"

"Of course I can't do it all," answered Esti. "I do as much as I can."

"I actually have some time right now," I said. "I came to copy some notes, but it's not really important. In the meanwhile, I can stay a bit; I love to watch little children. I'll play with Nechami while you feed Yitzchak." Naturally, I didn't only play with Nechami, but also helped here and there for two or three hours until the children were in bed.

Last night, I could hardly sleep. I was so shaken up by the news about the baby and also (maybe even more so) by the huge burden weighing on Esti. I decided that I wouldn't leave matters alone. Esti was falling apart. I told my parents what was happening and they agreed that something needs to be done.

In the morning, I jumped out of bed like a tiger. I went to the phone and dialed Rivky's number. I asked her rather urgently to come to school early, because I had something important to discuss with her.

Rivky showed up and listened, barely breathing, to what I had to say. Without speaking much, we put together a list of help that had to be provided: baby-sitting, straightening up, cooking, etc. During recess, quietly, we organized the girls of the class into a rotation. When the girls heard about what happened to their beloved Esti, some of them jumped as if a snake had bitten them. By then, I was calmer since steps had already been taken to help Esti and her family.

I'm signing off now because I have to get over to Esti's for my turn...

Miri

Sunday, Elul 19, 5757

Hello Diary,

The truth is that our class is out of the ordinary. Each girl took on the task that suited her and went about doing it in the most quiet and refined way imaginable (to minimize Esti's family's discomfort). On Wednesday, the baby went through successful surgery, *baruch Hashem*. Even Esti's parents felt as if we had really eased their burden and thanked us from the bottom of their hearts for the help that we had offered without their having to ask for it.

This is hard to put down in writing, but I feel like I have to point out that, even though I feel awful about Esti's family, I do feel a certain satisfaction about what we're doing for them. More than once I heard the girls complimenting me on my sharpness — that I had noticed that something was wrong with Esti — and the smart way I had opened the issue.

Apparently, everyone has their place. Instead of pushing myself into some ill-fitting niche, I should make my way through the gate that suits me. It's not for nothing that Shlomo HaMelech said that there's a time and a place for everything.

But do you know what I did today, dear Diary? At the beginning of last week I started connecting to Rivky, right? During the week we got closer, and so I decided to open up to her about what's been bothering me. I actually was brave enough to do it! After I told her everything, do you know what happened? She looked at me and blurted out, "What? I don't believe it!"

She then discussed the issue with me from her perspective. "You know well enough," she began, "what kinds of expectations everyone has of me. If they decide to organize a social, everything falls on me. If the teacher decided that there should be a presentation, I get the honor of arranging everything. If she decides that some letter needs to be written, I get to compose it and make sure that it gets to where it needs to go. It is sort of fun to be in the middle of what's happening but it's still very stressful. My presentation has to be 'triple A'; if not, everyone would be disappointed. I always have to come up with new ideas for our activities, because that's what everyone expects from me. Naturally, every idea has to be approved by Brachi — the class queen — if not, my reputation in the class would be ruined. I also always have to be in a good mood and you can imagine how, as it gets closer to Adar, the pressure builds to be so happy that the whole class just vibrates with joy.

"You might not believe me but there were times that I was actually jealous of you! You're so *eidel*, you don't bother anyone, you don't make any disturbances. You can be yourself without worrying about being in the spotlight. So what's your problem...?"

Miri

Tuesday, Elul 21, 5757

My dear, dear Diary,

Maybe you can help me???

I have to admit that I'm completely perplexed. I suddenly remembered the feelings that have been with me these last two years, how deprived I am because I'm not a chevraman; instead of having the approval of the class, I'm shunted off to the side. But then there's Esti, she's no chevraman and look at how much everyone loves her! Then again, she's so smart and diligent and always helps everyone out with their work. I'm no genius like her, so what about me? True, I succeeded with Esti's problem, but that only happened because of a flash of inspiration. But what will be in a few months? Certainly I won't have any special status because of some worn-out story.

I also think about Devora's divorce. I guess none of her "chevraman" tendencies helped her much. I'm confused, I don't see any way out of all the questions swimming around nonstop in my head.

What does it mean to be a chevraman? Does it mean being involved? Happy? Lighthearted? Or maybe more than that? It seems to mean something more, but what?

And anyway, I already decided not to be a chevraman. But is it, essentially good or not to be one? Maybe it's only good in school, but not in real life. But why? And what's real life, then? Aren't we alive even though we're in school? If family life is the only real one, then what life are we living now? Isn't *it* real?

Miri

Wednesday, Elul 22, 5757

Wow! What a class today! Instead of teaching about *Selichos*, the teacher spoke about the Chofetz Chayim since his *yahrtzeit* comes out on Friday. What did she point out? The contrast. Here he was, the simplest Jew. But he also was a *Gadol* in the fullest sense of the word. On the one hand, he fled from honor. On the other, he was a unique personality to be counted among the greats of all the generations in *golus*, who united all segments of Jewry under his direction. A person who didn't believe he had so much to offer the next person, but his gifts and influence on *Klal Yisrael* were legendary.

I can tell there's some lesson here for me, personally, but I can't seem to draw it out...

Miri

Motza'ei Shabbos Kodesh, Parashas Netzavim/Vayelech

Dear Diary,

A flash of clarity came to me on Shabbos; probably because of it. I suddenly felt an amazing lightness, as if a burden weighing several tons had slid off of me.

I discovered, simply, that there are two kinds of honor: superficial and real. A person can make a presentation and afterward receive thunderous applause — but what does it say about him? About his character? Nothing. Sometimes you see a person who withstood a challenge, or saved a life — what then? Deep admiration.

I guess the chevraman has a good chance of succeeding with superficial life, just like she has a good chance of organizing a good performance. But the more we move into "real life," the more we begin to appreciate the value of things more real. I even heard about some real chevramen who, after getting married, became very simple. I never understood why they went through such a drastic change. It sounded as if they had undergone some kind of weird personality degeneration; as if getting married were something to worry about. After thinking about it, though, it seems that they must have just realized that, in the long run, it doesn't really amount to much (to be a chevraman).

Suddenly, my whole desire to become a chevraman has dwindled. I feel a kind of liberation, as though I'm almost ready to just be myself (even Rivky appreciates me the way I am!). Even the simple side of myself! I just shouldn't be embarrassed of my personality, because, really, there's nothing to be ashamed of.

Miri

Wednesday, Elul 29, 5757

Dear Diary!

This last year has been very tricky. I tried to find my place, and still haven't exactly managed it. I'm still unclear about a lot of ideas and my understanding of why people act the way they do. So I wish for everyone, including myself, to be inscribed and sealed for a good year; a good *shidduch* for my brother; all should turn out well for Devora and her little ones; good news for everyone; and that Hashem should guide us in the best possible path...

Have a good and sweet new year!

Miri

> **THINK ABOUT IT**
>
> **TO WHAT EXTENT WAS MIRI'S SELF-IMAGE:**
>
> ◆ determined by other girls' opinions?
> ◆ affecting the way some of the girls in Miri's class thought of her?
>
> Why was she unable to see that her apprehension was making it even more difficult to be popular?

Scenario #9 — Stress in the life of a married woman

Stress Felt by a Hard-Working Mother

Mrs. M. considers herself a thinking mother. She certainly does invest a great deal of her thought into the area of child raising. She is forever vigilant to attend to the needs of her children, keep track of their behavior, and even mark down any area that requires some correction.

Despite her vigilant and energetic efforts, Mrs. M. does understand that it isn't desirable to expect too much of the children, all at once. Which is why she always focuses on one goal that seems important and reasonable, and resolves to dedicate several weeks to tackling it. During that time, she makes consistent progress in her scaled-down objective. In that way she wants, slowly and steadily, to instill healthy habits and exemplary behavior in her children.

For instance, recently, Mrs. M. chose the topic of speaking calmly. She recognized a need to ensure that a calm and pleasant atmosphere should prevail in the house — and that the way to do it would be by working on everyone's speech.

Mrs. M. understood that if she wanted her children to change, she would have to motivate them with love and wisdom. She sat, then, in the evening, surrounded by her children, and told them a

Appendix B: Tension in Real Life Scenes 397

captivating tale about the subject. After telling the story, she asked the children if they would like to try a similar project. The children enthusiastically accepted the moral and agreed to the project. Mrs. M., feeling satisfied and happy about their response, put them to bed, expecting excellent results.

In the morning, Mrs. M. gently reminded the children of the previous night's interesting story. She was almost certain that her job was pretty much done. She was even more certain of her coming success because, several weeks earlier, she had worked on a different project in which she invested much less preparation, and had seen great improvement. She had wanted each child to be responsible for hanging up his own coat and knapsack as soon as he came home from school; *baruch Hashem*, she had seen terrific results almost immediately. Following this smashing success, she was certain that things would progress even more smoothly this time around.

That afternoon, her two little ones returned from *gan* tired and thirsty and asked for what they wanted a bit stridently.

Mrs. M.'s first reaction was, "But didn't we hear that wonderful story just yesterday that taught us how to speak nicely? Have you forgotten already?" She said to herself, "Little children are allowed to forget once." In that way, she pushed off her feelings of disappointment that were beginning to erupt.

In the course of the afternoon, Mrs. M. felt that she needed a rest. She lay down with her eyes closed, trying to catch a nap, but fully aware of what was going on outside her bedroom door. She heard voices in the background that sounded like the girls doing their homework.

"Give me your eraser for a minute," Brachi said to her sister.

"You're always losing your things, and afterward you ask to borrow from everyone," Racheli raised her voice. "This one time, I'm not giving you anything. That way, you'll learn to be more orderly and take care of your stuff."

"What does it matter to you," complained Brachi, "it's only for a second."

"Every day it's 'only for a second,'" Racheli's voice went up a few decibels. "From now on you'll learn to be responsible for yourself."

"Fine. Today I'll buy a new eraser, and I'll take good care of it from tomorrow on," Brachi tried for the third time.

"I've said what I had to say, and don't bother me while I'm doing my homework anymore." Racheli was practically yelling.

"Imma!" A shout could be heard reverberating around the house, "Racheli won't loan me her eraser. Imma, tell her..."

Mrs. M. shrank in her bed. She couldn't rest with an argument going on and quickly jumped up and hurried out of the room. Without thinking, she burst out, "Again there's screaming in this house. Only yesterday we decided that things were going to be quiet around here — is this what's come of it? There must be something wrong with me. Otherwise, how could it be that I've put in so much effort and haven't seen results?"

That evening, at the close of a stressful day, Mrs. M. was immersed in her thoughts. She wanted so much to see her home transformed into an oasis of harmony; but the reality was far from her dream.

On one clear, run-of-the-mill day, Mrs. M. caught on to what had been at the root of her tension and resulting failure. It happened when she surprised the children with a trip to their cousins who live on a *moshav*, whom they hadn't seen for almost two years. Not long ago, Mrs. M.'s brother had made a tactless comment about her approach to the children that had kept her from going for a visit. Now, the coming trip made her feel as though she were under terrible pressure; it lasted as they were preparing for the outing and even during the entire visit. She had a hidden expectation in her heart that her children's behavior would be exemplary and impress everyone that laid eyes on them. Naturally, on the outside, Mrs. M. was trying to create a light and

Appendix B: Tension in Real Life Scenes   399

pleasant atmosphere as she attempted to hide any hint of family conflict from the eyes of her children. The family, then, proceeded joyfully on to the home of their relatives.

After a warm reception and introductions, the children found common ground quickly and raced off to play together.

Mrs. M. kept up a laughing and sociable front, but one eye was constantly focused on her children's behavior.

After a while, the children got a little bored and went in search of more interesting diversions. Curious about everything in this new place, one of them discovered a large and breathtakingly colorful ball. In absolute innocence he made his way toward it, and in one daring move leaped on it in an effort to perch on top of the thing. To everyone's shock, the ball exploded.

Mrs. M. was so confused and embarrassed, she didn't know what to do with herself. She was unresponsive when her sister-in-law joked with the children about what happened to the poor ball.

Somehow the visit dragged to a close and Mrs. M. and the children politely took their leave.

On the way back home, Mrs. M. sat withdrawn into her own thoughts. She did a real internal inventory about what had happened at her brother's house. She was ready to be straight with herself and came, after examining her emotions, to a deep and honest conclusion.

First and foremost she asked herself what had made her "lose it" when the ball burst? Hadn't her children just been acting like any others would have upon finding an interesting new toy?

Upon further introspection, Mrs. M. noticed that she had felt a sort of tension working on her during the entire ride to the cousins. She had tried to implant a sense of calmness in her children while she was, herself, completely tense. "How could I work on toning down their behavior in general when I was tense the whole time?"

The return trip ended. The children got themselves ready for bed happily enough — they were exhausted from the trip. They fell asleep soon after their heads hit their pillows and quiet reigned in the house.

That evening, Mrs. M. let her husband in on her thoughts and conclusions. He expressed an appreciation of her dedication to child raising, but pointed out an aspect of her approach that he felt needed some improvement. "Sometimes, your 'campaigns' come along in a cloud of tension, since you obviously expect positive and quick results. Especially when other people are around."

After thinking about her own feelings and her conversation with her husband, Mrs. M. realized that her sensitivity to the opinion of others was intertwined with her desire to improve her children's behavior. Meaning: a good part of her motivation for her child-raising projects was her hope to receive applause from the world around her for her children's wonderful conduct. It was that anticipation that was causing so much anxiety. "If I were concerned only with their behavior and not with everyone's opinion," she admitted to herself, "I would definitely be more understanding and patient. I wouldn't ask so much of myself or the children — I would be more relaxed. If I were, we could all progress joyfully and succeed slowly but surely."

Convinced by her own arguments, Mrs. M. resolved to begin by undertaking her own self-improvement project. She was satisfied with what she had gained from the trip. One would hope that she really will continue on her chosen path and experience much *nachas* from her children, and her own efforts.

THINK ABOUT IT

HOW WERE MRS. M.'S IMPROVEMENT PROJECTS:

♦ overly ambitious?

♦ focused more on ulterior motives than she realized?

How did Mrs. M's criteria for progress change once she understood what was going on?

Scenario #10 — Stress in the lives of spouses
Stress That Comes from Trying To Improve the Atmosphere at Home

In the Levenstein home, the Shabbos meals are not running as they should. The atmosphere was tense: and rather often, one of the parents would be in a bad mood, the children would fight, sometimes they would be disobedient or they lacked the patience to stay seated during the meal. Because of this, the couple has decided to take steps to improve the situation. Each of them has taken stock of themselves to determine what can be done to make the overall feeling in the house more *Shabbosdik*.

Efrayim, the husband, decided that he needs to do more spiritual preparation. He realized how much better it would be if he would prepare *divrei Torah* or perhaps some story ahead of time to interest the children and involve them.

Shifra, the wife, thought that if she managed to rest Friday afternoon she might be more relaxed in the evening and would be able to function that much better.

Efrayim and Shifra resolved that, starting the very next Thursday, they would work on their assigned areas. Efrayim delved into various *seforim* and marked the pieces that seemed appropriate. Shifra tried to get a jump start on the Shabbos preparations so that she would find the time to rest.

That week, the Shabbos Queen made her way into the Levenstein home with quiet, calm majesty and the couple looked forward to a change for the better. For some reason, though, it failed to materialize.

Although both parents had looked for causes and had even come to some reasonable conclusions, they still went through the motions of making their changes with some reservation. A quiet thought had stolen into both of their hearts, "If my husband/wife had really done his/her part, I wouldn't have to put in so much effort on my end." On the heels of that, a whisper, "If my husband/wife were acting the way he/she should, we wouldn't be having this problem at all."

So even though both Efrayim and Shifra had actually done their parts, neither had really made peace with the fact that they had to invest some of their precious time and energy to make the thing work; they both believed that the other person was the main source of the problem. Their complaints stemmed from an unwillingness to acknowledge that they had a personal responsibility to invest energy into building the home. They thought that if the other would only correct *his* (or her) problem, everything would be fixed. Those complaints were left unsaid and hung heavily in the air. They caused the couple to forget about their original goal: to foster a positive atmosphere.

Aside from his general dissatisfaction, Efrayim was burdened with additional anxieties. After working to prepare something for the Shabbos table for nearly two hours, would the family participate? Would they enjoy what he had to say? Would Shifra appreciate his investment and cleverness?

Shifra was similarly preoccupied. Did Efrayim appreciate how hard she had pushed herself to finish the cooking early so that she could rest and enter Shabbos like a mensch? Would they appreciate what she's doing and be grateful for having such a warm, calm wife and mother? Or would they just look at any improvement as par for the course, not noticing the fundamental changes that had taken place, both in her personally and in the general atmosphere in the house?

Unfortunately, Efrayim and Shifra's anxieties affected, against their own wills, the outcome. He began to speak in a cold and stiff manner, his eyes probing his family seated around him to judge whether they were radiating sufficient joy. She was wound up like a spring waiting to see the fruits of her efforts; she, naturally, bore no resemblance to the pleasant wife and mother she had imagined herself becoming.

In short, at the beginning of the meal there were definite signs of improvement in the general ambience. Each spouse's latent anxieties and tension, however, made the atmosphere ripe for an explosion. Which, of course, occurred when one of the children lost his patience and began to rock in his chair. Efrayim let out his pent-up anxieties on the child, and Shifra let out hers on Efrayim, supposedly for the way he mishandled the situation.

"How is it possible," Efrayim later thought to himself, "that precisely when I am trying my best to interest the children in something meaningful that all of this had to happen?"

The parents expected that, on the very first Shabbos, the children would be models of perfect conduct and everything would run like clockwork. Since they were focused only on total success, their partial progress held no allure for them, and they lost out on the bit of pleasure they might have had from their efforts.

Furthermore, both of them were concerned about the outcome — maybe they wouldn't be as good as they had hoped, maybe they wouldn't see a change right away. Their high expectations blocked them from noticing the small improvements that *were* made.

Even though each spouse blamed the other, in their hearts they both began to suspect that maybe something about them was not quite right.

"If I was more capable and had a stronger personality," thought Efrayim, "I would certainly be able to run my Shabbos table properly." Shifra said bitterly to herself, "Why aren't I privileged to *siyata di'Shemaya* after putting in all this effort?"

—·⋄⋄⋄⋄·—

Following that depressing Shabbos, Efrayim and Shifra decided to try again. To their good fortune, however, an interesting surprise unfolded.

Because the previous Shabbos had been such a flop, they didn't expect success the second time around and didn't really consider themselves capable of achieving their goal. Precisely because of their lack of expectations, they were open to see a degree of improvement and they were able to enjoy it — and express appreciation to one another.

Another week flew by. This time, they approached Shabbos feeling encouraged — by the partial success of the previous week, and the appreciative words they had exchanged then, too, that still echoed in both their ears. They were able to proceed in a more lighthearted spirit, were motivated, and could appreciate achievements made one step at a time. It was natural, then, that they radiated a placid joy during the Shabbos meals. Every so often one or the other of them would let out some encouraging word, even to the children, and pleasant smiles graced the table. Efrayim and Shifra managed to maintain a warm atmosphere, even though the children did lapse into misbehavior at times.

After Shabbos, Efrayim and Shifra reviewed what had transpired that day and noticed that the most important point seemed to be approaching their task happily and patiently. They both agreed that it was fairly certain that, in the future, they wouldn't always live up to that. They understood, though, that even that failure shouldn't turn into an excuse for becoming tense; they should just remember to be happy with their overall progress.

In this way, happiness reigned in the Levenstein home until the next challenge presented itself. It wasn't purposeful — Efrayim was supposed to travel to Bnei Brak at 7 P.M. and stay there for an hour at the wedding of a distant cousin. He was then scheduled to hop over to his brother-in-law's (Shifra's brother) for a few seconds to take care of a minor matter. They had worked out that he should be arriving home no later than 11 P.M. By 10 P.M., all the children were sleeping and Shifra, too, was exhausted, and retired for the evening.

Shifra woke with a start at 1 A.M. to the baby's cries. She looked around — no sign of Efrayim. Her heart began to pound and her imagination went into overdrive. Where is Efrayim? What happened to him? Is everything all right? Shifra took care of the baby as if her head and her body were two separate entities. The baby went on sleeping sweetly but Shifra couldn't sleep. She called her brother in Bnei Brak but the phone was busy; apparently they had taken it off the hook. They often did that past 11:30 P.M. Shifra didn't know what to do with herself.

To her misfortune, she heard suddenly the wail of an ambulance. Her mind told her that there probably was no connection, but the sound of the siren did nothing to ease her anxieties and wild imaginings. The clock ran so slowly, the hands seemed to be moving backward. 1:20 A.M. 1:25 A.M. 1:30 A.M.... Shifra nearly fainted from terror. At 2:15 A.M., Shifra heard the familiar scrape of Efrayim's key in the door followed by him tiptoeing in, hoping not to wake anyone.

The storm was quick in coming. "Where were you?!" Shifra shrieked. "I was half-dead from fear. Why didn't you call?!"

"I'm sorry," Efrayim whispered, so as not to wake the children. "I arrived at your brother's house; I thought it would only take a few minutes. It turned out that we had a bit of a problem, and we sat down to discuss it. I didn't imagine it would take as long as it did. When I saw how late it was, I wanted to call but I was sure that you were sleeping and I didn't want to wake you. It's no big deal."

"Is it no big deal when I go out of my mind with worry?!"

Efrayim was also tired and began to lose his patience. "Excuse me, Madame. It was your brother that I was trying to help. I wasn't doing anything for myself."

"I don't care who it was for. You need to learn how to be more considerate of your wife's feelings..." Unfortunately, the fight continued for no less than twenty minutes and was only called off on account of mutual exhaustion. They both went to bed angry and hurt.

The next day, Efrayim and Shifra discussed what had happened. Efrayim began, "I understand that I caused you a lot of aggravation, and I'm sorry. But why did you have to yell at me? I didn't do anything wrong."

"What?!" Shifra was amazed. "It shouldn't bother me that my husband is nowhere to be found? I screamed because I care about you."

"I'll tell you the truth," responded Efrayim. "At the time, the last thing I felt was that you cared about me."

"So what should I have done instead?" asked Shifra.

"Well, what were you feeling when I walked in?" Efrayim analyzed the issue. "I'll bet you breathed a big sigh of relief, you felt much more calm. So why didn't you express your real feelings? You should have told me how much better you felt now that I was home safe. Afterward, you could have asked me what happened, and then shared the panic you had felt."

"You're right. I was so wound up that it was hard for me to express my happiness that you'd come home. And I am so happy that you came back safe and sound, and grateful that you helped my brother. For future reference, I give you advance permission to wake me up — just make sure not to put me through something like this again, all right?"

They both sat thinking a moment. Shifra broke the silence. "One minute. I've seen you get tense about other things, like *mitzvos*, many times. Preparing for Shabbos, putting up the *sukkah* or getting your *esrog*... even if one of the children disturbs you while you're learning. What are you trying to express with that? That you love the Torah and care about the *mitzvos*? None of us get such a great impression when you're tense like that."

Efrayim gave some thought to what Shifra said and confessed, "You're right. I guess I make the same mistake. I have this feeling that if I don't get all wound up and nervous about learning and *mitzvos*, it proves that I don't really care about them. You're right. It's possible to express those feelings more appropriately. I need to emphasize the joy instead of such nit-picky seriousness.

So, together, the Levensteins began to focus on the positive. Joy returned to their home where, hopefully, by now, it has taken up permanent residence.

THINK ABOUT IT

HOW DID EFRAYIM AND SHIFRA:

♦ mistakenly use tension to show they cared?
♦ use positive emotions to relax the tension?

How did lower expectations actually help Efrayim and Shifra's table to improve?

Scenario #11 — Stress in the lives of spouses

Stress That Is Part of Dealing with Adolescent Children

One of the hardest things in the world to guess at is Nachman's mood. You get the feeling that it would be easier to predict the weather in London ten days in advance than foresee what Nachman's reaction to anything will be.

When Dina, Nachman's older sister, had been his age, their parents had assumed that her bizarre behavior could be attributed to something going on at school. There wasn't any other way for them to interpret her sudden fits of crying, her strident demands which were completely out of character. Suddenly, she would get sick of a certain dress or abruptly resolve to help her mother. Being witnesses to Nachman's conduct, they have begun to understand a few things retroactively.

Mr. and Mrs. Levy were so caught up in the whirlwind of their lives, their work and responsibilities, that they didn't make the effort to walk in their children's shoes. They did, however, find themselves having to deal with more and more issues in their home. For example, sometimes on Friday Dina suddenly disappeared from the kitchen, only to be found (oblivious to the need to finish the preparations before Shabbos) in some corner absorbed in a book. Tension had long been developing between Mrs. Levy and the children, but now they see that Nachman is acting the same way, and they are starting to ask themselves, what was it like for them when they were teenagers? They couldn't remember much, so they worked on analyzing the present situation instead.

The child is in the middle of the process of transforming into an adult — or is it — the adolescent is in the process of emerging from his childhood. Sometimes it seems like Nachman wants to try his hand at being responsible, even though he may not yet be ready for it. Because he doesn't quite know where or what he is, he wants to prove himself. One can only wonder whether you call this a lack of self-confidence, or too much self-confidence. Maybe it's a little of both, or something in the middle. The fact remains, though, that it seems like Nachman wants to prove himself — either his ability, or his social standing, or his very independence. And he doesn't always know whether he wants support from his parents, or whether they should let him try on his own, or maybe a little bit of both. (Sorry for the confusion, but it is a similar type of confusion that teenagers experience.)

Although Mr. and Mrs. Levy did try to understand their children's moods, they didn't make any significant changes in their overall parenting style — that is, until the day that Nachman sailed in and told them how one of the neighborhood boys had decided to run away from home. A red light went on in both of his parents' heads, for more than one reason. They got a frightening glimpse of what can happen when the parent-child relationship deteriorates. And the very fact that Nachman had deigned to tell them made them terrified. Who knew what was going through the mind of the boy?

Unfortunately, this new development that should have forced Mr. and Mrs. Levy to stop, reassess, and correct, had the exact opposite effect. The father blamed the mother for causing Nachman's problems with her too-soft and inconsistent approach. "The boy needs discipline and firm guidance," Mr. Levy argued pointedly. "Everyone knows the effect that anarchy has on a child."

"Quite the contrary," countered Mrs. Levy, "it's your rigidity and coldness that kills Nachman. Everyone has seen children that rejected their parents for being too unyielding." Sorry to say that it got so bad that the Levys practically stopped speaking to one another (aside from when their pent-up feelings would explode). The Levys were both so bothered by the fact that their spouse's approach was so wrong, and the only way they knew how to show that they cared was by demonstrating anger. And Nachman's behavior continued to get worse...

If that weren't enough, out of nowhere, a new chapter opened up with Dina. Dina came home from school wiped out. She sighed as she dropped her book-bag at the door. This wasn't one of her better days. First, the teacher called on her for an answer that she didn't know. After that, she got back a test and the grade wasn't exactly what you would call thrilling. On top of it all, she got into that stupid fight with Yocheved.

She plodded into her room and slammed the door behind her. Dina wanted some peace and quiet, a little time to herself. She sat on her bed, trying to mentally review her day. Just then, Rutie, Dina's little sister, quietly entered the bedroom. She asked Dina if she would read her the story of the little lost sheep. Dina, strung out to begin with, felt her nerves stretch to the breaking point.

Dina muttered under her breath, "That Rutie, she doesn't give me a moment's peace. I just got home from school and already she comes around bothering me. Again that dumb story! How many times does she think I can repeat the same one? What does she think, that when I was her age, that they read me stories all the time, whenever I wanted?" She lashed out at her younger sister, "I haven't got the energy to read you a story; go find someone else to do it!"

Rutie, however, wouldn't give up. She insisted that she only wanted Dina to read to her. Dina felt as though she were about to explode. She shouted at Rutie, "I'm not reading you that story! Go and play before I give you a *potch!*" Rutie burst out crying. By the time Dina had calmed her little sister down, she felt completely drained.

After that ordeal, Dina went out to the porch to get a breath of fresh air. She ran into her mother, who was happy to see her. "Hi, Dina! I'm glad to see you. Do you think you can go down to the grocery store and pick up some bread?" Dina didn't have the patience to go out and didn't mince her words. "I'm too tired to go; I still haven't taken a break since I got home from school. Anyway, I don't need the bread — whoever wants it should go and get it himself! I'm not anyone's maid!" Mrs. Levy got upset. "If you want to explain yourself, that isn't the way to do it, Dina. Say what's on your mind with a little more tact. And go down to the grocery store right this minute."

Infuriated and holding back her tears, Dina left the house and slammed the door behind her. "Why don't they understand me? Why can't Imma see that I'm wiped out — how could she force me to go out now? And Rutie thinks she's an only child. You have to give her everything she wants on a silver platter the second she asks for it. Why couldn't Yocheved figure out that I didn't mean

Appendix B: Tension in Real Life Scenes

anything bad by what I said? Couldn't that teacher have been more considerate? Everyone slips every once in a while — for that she had to flunk me?"

Dina trudged to the grocery store, bought the bread, and headed home. "At least now they'll appreciate me. Despite the way I feel, I went out and got the bread that they need so badly for lunch. Maybe now they'll even try to understand what I'm going through." When she got home, however, she realized her error. Her mother and father were talking in loud tones, apparently something to do with Dina's disrespect. She heard her mother say to her father: "Why is Dina acting this way? Why can't she help out more? I would have expected a little more maturity from a girl her age. She's old enough to understand how hard it is for me; she knows that Shloim'ke is sick today. Doesn't she understand that I had a terrible morning with him? And what did I ask of her, anyway? Just to go down and buy a loaf of bread. Is that too much for her? You should have heard how she talked back to me! What will be with her? Will she stay like this?"

Dina waited to hear her father's response to see if he would take her side. Would he explain that she's really not so bad? Instead, she heard her father blame her mother for Dina's indifference and chutzpah, and a fight developed over whose fault it was.

Dina slunk into her room, threw her pillow on her bed angrily without really understanding why, and sprawled dramatically across her bed. "I couldn't care less about anyone in this house. They definitely don't care about me. And if... if I would disappear suddenly from this house, who would even notice, who would care?

Dina and Mrs. Levy's argument really stemmed from two misunderstandings. Had Mrs. Levy known how hard Dina's day had been, she certainly would have given her some time to relax and offered her some encouragement. Had Dina been a little more considerate of her mother and how hard her morning had been, she wouldn't have been so opposed to going out to the store. The whole incident would have been (and should have been) insignificant and everything would have returned to its normal, peaceful state.

Since each of them was preoccupied with her own concerns, however, what could have been a minor incident blew up into a major conflict that created emotional distance between mother and daughter, and left a negative impression that lasted weeks.

Help finally arrived, but from an unanticipated source. Uncle Zevulun and Aunt Malki decided to come from America during the summer, and everyone knows that when they visit, they come with presents. And not just any presents, either! They brought a sewing machine for Chava, a laptop computer for Nachman, for nine-year-old Yitzchak a two-wheeler, and so on.

A few days later, Yitzchak asked his parents to help him learn to ride his new bike. Both parents went out to the courtyard, and their efforts were crowned with success. Mr. Levy held on the bicycle as Yitzchak got on and started moving, trying his best to keep his balance. At first, Yitzchak could only manage riding a foot or two. Mrs. Levy stood at the sidelines, applauding every bit of progress and encouraging Yitzchak to keep on trying. All in all, it took no more than an hour for the boy to get the hang of riding alone.

Both parents watched Yitzchak make his way around the courtyard with pride in their eyes. They looked at each other. This little collective victory had broken the ice between them. "How on earth did it go so smoothly?" asked Mr. Levy. His wife thought a minute. "We each did our part — you're stronger, so you took care of the technicalities. You held onto the bike, you helped him physically, and I helped him along emotionally. The harmony between us definitely contributed, too." Mrs. Levy looked up to find her husband immersed in his thoughts. "What happened" she asked. "What's on your mind?"

"Tell me, isn't adolescence like learning to ride a two-wheeler? Isn't it also about teaching a child to be independent?" Mr. Levy went on deliberately, "Why can't we learn from this how to deal with Nachman?"

"You know, you're so right!" Mrs. Levy was amazed. "That's a great idea. Each of us has a different function, but they're meant to synchronize. Perhaps your job is to give the practical assistance, and mine is to provide the encouragement. We probably shouldn't have overly grand expectations of him; we should just try to understand what he's going through in his search for independence. If we could let Nachman know that we're trying to understand, it might help him feel better."

"When a child knows that his parents are there for him," added Mr. Levy, "it helps a lot. We can give him space without being indifferent. We can guide him slowly, and let go as he is more capable of handling himself, just like we did with the bicycle."

They both took a minute to mentally digest the image until Mr. Levy realized something. "Now I remember something I learned recently in *Maseches Kiddushin*. The Talmud explains that children naturally honor their mothers more than their fathers because mothers always offer encouraging words. That's why the Torah mentions the father first in the command to honor parents — because the child needs an extra reminder to honor his father like his mother. The inverse is also true: children naturally fear their fathers more than their mothers; that's why the mother precedes the father in the command to fear parents — as if to say, 'don't forget, you need to fear your mother, too.' Mr. Levy took a deep breath. "That means that, in a healthy family, both parents fulfill different functions. Apparently, the father is usually better suited to the role of disciplinarian, whereas the mother radiates warmth and softness. It's clear that each parent need not be a copy of the other; their approach doesn't have to be the same. It is actually healthy that a child is given two parents; from one he receives love mixed mostly with softness, from the other love mixed mostly with firmness. Isn't it harder for a single parent to raise two children than for two parents to raise ten? And the children will probably grow up healthier, too. So the Talmud suggests a similar framework to the one that you described before."

"If we have to show that we're in harmony," Mrs. Levy smiled, "then my job is to support your disciplining, and yours it to support my gentle encouragement, isn't that right?" Mrs. Levy caught herself. "Just a minute. What are we going to do about Dina? Haven't you noticed that sour face she's had on recently?"

Mr. Levy answered, "In my opinion, Dina is pretty mature. I think that if you would be a little bit more open with her, you'd be able to work things out like two adults."

"Maybe I should have explained to her that I'm human, too, and that I also have my bad days. If she would understand that, she wouldn't take it so much to heart when I get anxious and upset."

"It's true," Mr. Levy nodded. "But while it's very important for you to be open about your feelings, it's just as important to listen to what Dina has to say for herself."

It would be difficult to describe how much tension dissipated from Mr. and Mrs. Levy's hearts after these "revelations." I'm sure you can imagine how much better Dina and Nachman began to feel, too.

THINK ABOUT IT

HOW WERE MR. AND MRS. LEVY ABLE TO CORRECT:

- ◆ their expectations of each other?
- ◆ their expectations of their children?

How were the Levys' difficulties diminished when Mr. and Mrs. Levy realized they could demonstrate their care in other ways, aside from tension?

In Conclusion

Libraries are filled with thrilling stories which leave us breathless as dizzying surprises unfold. Some people look for these stories for entertainment, or to temporarily escape the pressures of life. This, however, was not our intention when writing the stories for this section. Instead, these stories deal with everyday life, and tell us about normal human beings with their common, stressful struggles. The goal when creating these stories was to help the reader look at routine situations in his own life from the point of view of an observer, and to discover, when possible, ways to improve them.

We hope the reader can benefit from the stories in the following ways:

- *Recognize that these events are commonplace:* We have already pointed out that one cause of tension is a lack of awareness that difficulties are part of life in this world. Some people assume that when their progress gets bogged down by difficulties, it means that they are worthless. This assumption makes them feel uncomfortable, and fighting this feeling of discomfort causes tension. Therefore, one goal of these stories was to demonstrate that the very existence of these types of stumbling blocks in our lives should not make us overly excited or concerned.

- *Recognize that the reactions are also common:* In these stories, it becomes clear that not only are the events common, but the way people respond can be (and often is) far from ideal. These types of events, and the way a person chooses to respond to them, are part of his process of growth. A person with a leaning toward tension is not alone. Occasional entanglement in everyday events is normal. So you need not get tense because you feel tense! Success will be yours if you apply yourself to learning from these and your own life's events.

- *See the events from a different angle:* On one hand, since the stories are realistic, it's very easy to identify with the characters. On the other hand, since the reader isn't personally involved, he can assess the events as an outsider, and more easily discover twisted logic or distortions within them. Many times the tension will appear almost ridiculous, such as expecting too much in too little time. This will enable him to clearly see how such distortions often cause tension, and how unnecessary that tension is.
- *Be impressed by the suffering caused by tension:* In story form, it is easy to identify with the suffering of the characters that is caused by their tension. This can motivate him to overcome his own anxiousness in order to avoid going through these types of ordeals.
- *Detect other side effects of tension:* As is clear from the stories, tension itself can be a source for more harm. Ze'evi and Yanky weren't aware of their need to develop patience and self-motivation — because of their tension. Consequently, their progress was stunted. Yonasan was anxious about finding his life's partner, and tension may have caused him to accept an unsuitable match. Yechiel's search for a learning partner was complicated by his anxiety; it was only after he calmed down that he was able to find a suitable *chavrusah*, and so on. Their stories should inspire us to avoid tension, since it only complicates our ability to improve situations.
- *Discover how easy it is to release oneself from tension:* Most importantly, almost every character managed to find a solution to his problem — without a sudden change in his circumstances or weird experience like a startling dream. Instead, their success came through their efforts to select an appropriate approach, along with the patience and the stamina to let the process run its natural course.

This bears a vital message: Regardless of where life may lead us, there will always be different doors open before us. These opportunities to help ourselves are much more common than we might think. Once we take advantage of them, we will develop a more constructive attitude toward difficulties sooner or later; we might even discover the benefit gained through struggle (see volume 2, chapter 3). We should be on the alert for these opportunities and take full advantage of them.

For a deeper understanding of tension and how to deal with it, refer to chapter 8 of this volume. Other techniques will be forthcoming in future volumes. Armed with these ideas, and reinforced by the stories here, a person can begin to take steps toward change. He can begin to refocus and redirect his thoughts and actions in small ways each day, until his tension melts away, and he remains alert, poised, and ready to take full advantage of all the gifts and talents that Hashem implanted within him.

NOTES TO APPENDIX B

1. *Tanna D'Bei Eliyahu*, chapter 25.
2. Tehillim 138:8.
3. Rabbi Yehuda Leib Bloch, "*Dor HaFlaga*" in *Shiurei Da'as* (Jerusalem: Feldheim, 5749), volume 1, pp. 262-263.

Glossary

abba - Hebrew for "father"

Acharon, *pl.* **Achronim** - lit. later; name for Torah commentators from the 15th century until today

Adam HaRishon - Adam, the First Man

agunah - a married woman who, although separated from her husband, has not been given a bill of divorce and therefore cannot remarry

Aharon HaKohen - Aharon, the High Priest; the brother of Moses and first high priest of the Tabernacle

Amalek - a nation which is an ancient enemy of Israel

Amidah - see *Shemoneh Esrei*

Amoraim - Rabbis who lived and taught after the closing of the Mishnah until the sealing of the Talmud, in approximately 400 C.E.

amos - see *daled amos*

avodah - see *avodas Hashem*

avodas Hashem - service of G-d

Avraham Avinu - Abraham, Our Father

avreich - a married man who learns in *kollel*

B'nei Yisrael - lit. "Children of Israel"; the Jewish people

balebos - a married man with a household

baruch Hashem - praise G-d

bas mitzvah - a girl who has reached the age of twelve, considered an adult in the eyes of the Torah, with the accompanying responsibilities

Beis HaMikdash - the Holy Temple

Beis Hillel and Beis Shammai - two schools of thought during the era of the Second Temple, each led by the Rabbi for which they are named

beis medrash - house of study

bekius - a style of Talmudic learning that focuses on covering ground as opposed to in-depth analysis

berachah, *pl.* **berachos** - blessing

bimah - the central table in a synagogue used for reading the Torah

bli neder - lit. "without making any promises"; said because breaking an oath or a promise is a serious sin

bochur, *pl.* **bochurim** - a young man who learns in yeshivah

bubbie - Yiddish for "grandmother"

chaburah - a presentation which brings together the material that a group of Torah scholars has been learning

chavrusah, *pl.* chavrusos - study partner

cheder - primary school for boys

cherem - excommunication

chessed - kindness

chevraman - a popular, capable, efficient person

chinuch - education

cholent - a meat and grain dish that is cooked all night, usually to be served on Shabbos morning

chosson - groom

chuppah - wedding canopy

churban - lit. "catastrophe"; also used to refer to the most recent *Churban Europa* (Holocaust)

daf yomi - lit. "daily page"; the name given to the worldwide lear-ning program in which participants all learn the same page of Talmud each day, in sequence

daled amos - lit. four cubits; commonly used to refer to a person's inner sphere, his private life

daven, davening - to pray, praying

dayan - a judge

din Torah - a legal ruling in a case before a court of Jewish law

divrei Torah - lit. "words of Torah"; a brief speech which presents an idea from the Torah and its commentators

Dovid HaMelech - King David

Edomites - a nation which is an ancient enemy of Israel

eidel - sweet, delicate, refined

emunah - faith

Eretz Yisrael - the Land of Israel

erev - lit. "evening"; when used in conjunction with a holiday, means the day before that holiday, as in *erev Shabbos*

Eisav - the evil brother of Jacob

esrog - a citron, one of the four species which are used for a *mitzvah* on Sukkos

evil inclination - see yetzer hara

gabbai - the beadle of the *shul*, the person who takes care of the technicalities of the prayer services

Gadol, *pl.* Gedolim - lit. the "great ones"; used to refer to Torah leaders

Gan Eden - the Garden of Eden

gan - kindergarten or nursery school

Gehennom - purgatory

golus - the Diaspora

Hadrian - the Roman emperor who conquered much of Europe and the Middle East in the first century of the common era; he passed harsh decrees restricting the Jews from learning Torah

hakafos shnios - lit. "second encircling"; the name of the second round of dancing around the *bimah*, done on Simchas Torah

halachah, *pl*. halachos - Jewish law

halachic - legal

hashgachah pratis - Divine Providence bestowed to each Jew on an individual level

heimishe Yid - someone permeated by Jewish culture and values

hilchos Yom HaKippurim - the laws pertaining to the Day of Atonement

hisbonenus - inward reflection

hishtadlus - personal effort

Holy Ark - in a synagogue, the place where Torah scrolls are stored; historically in the Tabernacle and First and Second Temples, the Holy Ark, or *Aron HaKodesh*, also held other holy articles

imma - Hebrew for "mother"

iyun - a style of Talmudic learning that focuses on in-depth analysis as opposed to covering ground

kallah - bride

kaparah - a Divinely sent means of atonement

kashrus - the quality of being kosher

kavanah - intention, concentration

kedushah - holiness

kiddush, *pl*. kiddushim - the blessing over wine said on Shabbos, festivals, and weddings; also refers to a spread of food which is often offered to people on Shabbos morning after *davening* to celebrate a *simchah*

Klal Yisrael - the Nation of Israel; refers to all Jews as one group

Kohen, *pl*. Kohanim - priests in the Tabernacle and Holy Temple, and their descendants

kol Torah - lit. the "voice of Torah"; refers to the uplifting sound of a large group of people learning Torah

kollel - a yeshivah for married men

Korach - a biblical insurrectionist who led a group of people to try to unseat Aharon, the High Priest

kvetchy - complaining, whining

lashon hara - derogatory words about others, which in most cases are legally forbidden to speak

Lavan - the father-in-law of Jacob, and father of Leah and Rachel

Levy, *pl*. Levi'im - ministers in the Tabernacle and Holy Temple, and their descendants

Ma'ariv - the evening prayer service

ma'asim tovim - good deeds

Maccabees - group of Hasmonean fighters who led the rebellion against Greek rule in the Second

Temple period

maggid shiur - a teacher who gives a *shiur*

mashgiach - lit. "overseer"; term used for guidance counselor in yeshivos, also used in terms of overseeing *kashrus* in commercial kitchens

mensch - a decent and mature person

mesechta - a tractate of the Talmud

Michal - one of King David's wives

middah, *pl.* **middos** - character traits

middas chassidus - piety, going beyond the letter of the law

Midrash, *pl.* **midrashim** - various works compiled by Talmudic Sages, usually as commentary on the Torah

Minchah - the afternoon prayer service

minyan - a quorum of ten men

Mishnah Berurah - a seminal commentary on Jewish law, arranged by the Chofetz Chayim

Mishnah - the teachings of the *Tannaim*, compiled by Rabbi Yehuda HaNasi; also used as a name of a passage within the Mishnah

misonen, *pl.* **misonenim** - complainer

mitzvah, *pl.* **mitzvos** - Torah commandment

moshav - a variation of the kibbutz; families live on and sometimes work privately-owned land, but share communal equipment

Moshe Rabbeinu - Moses, Our Teacher

Motza'ei Shabbos Kodesh - the night that Shabbos ends

Mussaf - an extra prayer service on the Sabbath and Holidays

mussar - lit. "self-discipline"; relates to schools or works written on the topic of self-discipline and character refinement

mussar shmuess - a lecture or lesson in *mussar*

nachas - lit. "relief"; enjoying your own success or that of a child, student, or others who are close to you, especially when it is preceded by concern

navi - prophet

nazir - a legal category for a person who adopts a temporary set of prescribed stringencies as an aid in spiritual growth, most common in the First and Second Temple eras

nebuch - a pitiful person; pitiful

neshamah - soul

netilas yadayim - lit. the "raising of the hands"; refers to the ritual washing of the hands

nisayon - a Heaven-sent test

Nu? - lit. "So?" "Well?" Often used to urge another person to respond

Glossary

osek b'mitzvah - involved in doing a *mitzvah* (other than the one currently being presented to you)

Paroh - Pharaoh

parashah - section of the Torah

Pesach - Passover

Pesukei D'Zimrah - psalms of praise read toward the beginning of the morning prayer service

pilpul, *pl.* **pilpulim** - a Talmudic discourse which covers many sides of one issue

potch - a smack

Potiphar's wife - the wife of Joseph's master when Joseph was in Egypt; her efforts to seduce Joseph, though unsuccessful, eventually landed him in prison

Purim - holiday four weeks before Pesach commemorating the rescue of Jews from the wicked Haman, who intended to destroy them. One of the *mitzvos* of this holiday is to prepare and distribute *shalach manos*

Rabbeinu - our Rabbi or teacher

Rav - Rabbi, teacher, and/or mentor

Rebbe - teacher or mentor; amongst Chassidim, the title given to the main spiritual leader of the sect

Rivka Imeinu - Rebecca, Our Mother

Rosh Chodesh - the holiday celebrating the first day(s) of the new month

Rosh Mesivta - the dean of a *mesivta* (yeshivah high school)

Rosh Yeshivah - the dean of a yeshivah

Rov - see *Rav*

Sages - special term which applies to the Rabbis of the Talmud

Satan, the - the angel of bad counsel

savta - Hebrew for "grandmother"

seder of mishnayos, *pl.* **sedarim of mishnayos** - any of the six volumes of Mishnah

seforim - books, especially books on Torah topics

segulah - a paraphysical remedy; also used to describe the nation of Israel - an *am segulah*, a special nation

semichah - Rabbinical ordination

seudas mitzvah - a meal that is a *mitzvah* itself

Shabbos - the Sabbath

Shabbosdik - having the atmosphere of Shabbos

shadchan - matchmaker

shalach manos - gifts of foodstuffs sent on Purim

shalom bayis - lit. "peace in the home"; refers to the harmony between husband and wife

shamash - beadle, assistant to the Rabbi

Shaul HaMelech - King Saul

Shemiras HaLashon - lit. "guarding the tongue"; used to refer to the teachings against libel and slander

Shemoneh Esrei - lit. "eighteen"; the name of the central part of every Jewish prayer service; also called the *tefillas Amidah* and silent benediction, it is said in a whisper while standing

sheva berachos - the seven blessings made under the wedding canopy and after a festive meal for a bride and groom; also the name for the festive meals given for the bride and groom during the week following their wedding

shidduch - a match; the term can describe, but is not limited to, a bride and groom

shidduchim - dating

shiur, *pl.* **shiurim** - a lecture

shlit"a - an acronym, lit. "he should live for many long, good years, Amen"; said in praise of a Torah scholar

Shlomo HaMelech - King Solomon

shochet - a slaughterer of meat in accordance with Jewish law

shtender - a small, high table or stand designed specifically to hold a book

shul - synagogue

Shulchan Aruch - code of Jewish law, codified from the Talmud by Rabbi Yosef Caro

sifrei machshavah - books of Jewish philosophy

simchah - lit. "happiness"; also used as a name for a celebration or celebratory meal

Simchas Torah - the holiday that celebrates the completion of the cycle of the Torah

siyata di'Shemaya - lit. "help from Heaven"; Divine assistance

sukkah - a small booth built on Sukkos according to prescribed guidelines; one of the *mitzvos* of Sukkos is to sit in this booth

Sukkos - the Festival of Tabernacles

tachlis - lit "aim, point, goal"; often used when the speaker wants to encourage immediate, constructive action

Talmid Chacham, *pl.* **Talmidei Chachomim** - lit. "students of the wise"; refers to Torah scholars

Tanach - acronym for *Torah, Nevi'im,* and *Kesuvim* (the Five Books of Moses, the Prophets, and the Writings), the three parts of the Written Torah

Tanna, *pl.* **Tannaim** - Rabbis who lived and taught during the Second Temple period until Rebbe Yehuda HaNasi encoded the Mishnah, approximately in the year 150 of the common era

tefillah, *pl.* **tefillos** - a prayer

tefillas Amidah - see *Shemoneh Esrei*

Tehillim - Psalms

teshuvah - lit. "return"; used in terms of repentance

Tisha B'Av - the day on which we commemorate the destruction of the Holy Temple and other tragedies

tithe - before using the produce of *Eretz Yisrael,* one tenth of it must be set aside to give to the poor, the *Levi'im,* and the *Kohanim*

Toras Chayim - Torah as the source of spiritual life; also the application of Torah to daily life

Tov li Toras picha - lit. "the teachings of your mouth are sweet to me"

treife - non-kosher

tzaddekes, *pl.* **tzidkaniyos** - a righteous lady

tzaddik, *pl.* **tzaddikim** - a righteous man (the plural can also include women)

tznius - modest dress and/or actions

Ya'akov Avinu - Jacob, Our Father

yachne - a chatterbox; usually refers to the stereotype of a gossiping old lady

yahrtzeit - the anniversary of someone's passing

Yehoshafat HaMelech - King Jehosofat

yeshivah gedolah - yeshivah for post-high school-aged boys

yeshivah ketanah - yeshivah high school

yeshivah - school for Jewish learning

yetzer - inner drive; often used as the short form for *yetzer hara*

yetzer hara - the inner drive which is inclined toward negativity

yetzer hatov - the inner drive which is inclined toward goodness

yiras Shamayim - fear of Heaven

yirei Shamayim - a person who fears Heaven

Yom Tov - a holiday

Yosef - Joseph, a son of Jacob

z"l - an acronym, lit. "may his memory be blessed"

zeide - Yiddish for "grandfather"

zerizus - alacrity

zman - lit. "time"; used to refer to a semester in yeshivah or *kollel,* or the specified time to do a *mitzvah*

zman krias Shema - the time proscribed for reciting the biblical verses of the *Shema*

ztz"l - an acronym, lit. "the memory of a *tzaddik* should serve as a blessing"; said in praise of a righteous person who has passed away

Index

A

Adolescent
   description, 408
   resolving conflict, 411
Agression
   caused by shyness, 62
Alacrity
   examples, 288
   healthy balance, 287
Anger
   as a way to initiate change, 25
   caused by shyness, 62
   defusing, 177
   difficulties in overcoming, 170
   effects, 101, 121
   overcoming, 89
Anxiousness
   controlling, 318
   effects, 202, 378, 402
Apathy
   Torah's view of, 85
Approval-seeking
   causing anxiousness, 216
   expectations and, 215
   in parenting, 71, 399
   overcoming, 219
   shyness and, 279
   tension and, 361

Arguments
   origins, 69, 134
   resolving, 18, 19, 118, 128
Arrogance. *See* Pride
Assertiveness
   lack of, 19
Attention
   for children, 151
   need for, 68

B

Bashfulness. *See* Shyness
Biographies of Torah Giants, 9, 342, 368
Bitachon
   applying, 229
   decisions and, 358
   effects of a lack of, 207
Boldness
   dangers of, 193
   vs. shyness, 59, 66

C

Calmness
   advantages, 254
Change
   fear of, 149
   initiating change, 24
   lack of interest in, 148

Children. See Parenting
Clarity, 187
Communication
   effective, 46, 67, 118
   improving to avoid anger, 174
Competition
   achievement and, 221
   compulsive winner, 102
   risks of, 222
Complaining
   and self-pity, 151, 159
   types of, 149
Contentment
   inner balance, 21, 193
   personal fulfillment, 6
Control
   and laziness, 280
Criticism
   and self-pity, 159

D

Dating
   tension and, 203, 356
Decisions
   acting on, 271
   ambivalence, 264
   bitachon, 358
   making, 52, 279
Defeatism. See chapter 3
   recognizing, 76
Depression, 98, 102
Despair
   effects, 78
   origin, 84

Determination
   accomplishment and, 41
   power of, 78
   self-esteem and, 80
Disappointment
   expectations and, 214
   fear of, 279
Downward spiral. See Spiral Effect

E

Effort
   channeling, 88
   importance of, 210, 211, 223
   limitations and, 99
   progress and, 93
   unreasonable, 16, 17
Egocentricity. See Self-pity
   effects, 226
Embarrassment. See Shyness
Emotions
   affecting actions, 305
   channeling, 18, 21
   controlling, 315, 319
   emotional response, 21, 23
   improper channeling, 105
Encouragement
   effects, 404
   need for, 69
Enthusiasm
   importance of, 264
   studying Torah and, 234
Equanimity
   maintaining, 134

Escape. *See* chapter 1
  when appropriate, 62
Exams
  fear and, 103
  tension and, 225
Excuses
  deflating, 277
  evaluating, 275
  hindering effect, 278
  types, 265, 272
Exhaustion
  effects, 132
  respecting, 312
Expectations
  causing tension, 199, 366
  dangers of, 351
  exaggerated, 198
  flexibility within, 200
  in marriage, 284
  objects of, 199
  of others, 282
  patience and, 226

F

Failure
  benefits, 280
  exaggerating likelihood of, 274
  fear of, 100
  origins, 145, 146
Faults
  dealing with, 277
  ignoring them, 16
  looking for, 157

Fear
  channeling, 280
  limiting effects, 99, 107
  of disappointment, 279
  of failure, 278
  of new things, 278
Friendship
  developing, 63, 67
  improving communication, 174
  making amends, 110
  overcoming shyness, 66
Frustration
  overcoming, 93
Fulfillment
  when lacking, 216
Functioning
  improving, 305

G

Goals
  achieving, 77, 93, 369
  ambition and, 88
  choosing properly, 84, 90
  healthy, 88
  hesitations, 86, 87
  inappropriate, 243, 382
  investing energy, 208
  managing, 320
  modifying, 92, 182
  patience and, 244
  practical steps, 88
  self-doubt, 85
  spiritual, 227, 244

Guilt
  expectations and, 214

H

Habits
  changing, 41, 316
Honor
  types of, 394
Housekeeping
  approval seeking and, 71
  attitudes, 252
  limitations, 83
  planning a *simcha*, 216
  priorities, 217
  when overwhelmed, 80
Humility
  definition, 313, 323
Hypersensitivity, 101

I

Ignoring
  and forgiveness, 23
  when it is productive, 16
  when it is counterproductive, 17
Imagination
  brainstorming, 38
  unhealthy use of, 132
Impatience. See chapter 8
  causing tension, 201
  dangers, 237, 310
  overcoming, 383
  risks, 286, 295, 322
Inner conflicts
  effects, 148
  resolving, 169
  short-term solutions, 176
Inner strength. See also Self-confidence
  benefits, 309
  building, 309, 313
  correct usage, 310
  definition, 310
Inspiration
  harnessing, 287

J

Jealousy
  constructive, 363
  reciprocal, 392
  tension and, 382
Judgment
  distorted, 148

L

Laziness. See chapter 9
  as a form of activity, 265
  as an obstacle to growth, 265
  benefits of overcoming, 270
  causing fear, 282
  combating, 172
  effects, 267
Limitations. See chapters 2, 3, and 4
  defeatism, 76
  healthy awareness, 83
  identifying, 98
  ignoring, 83
  making problems worse, 59
  respecting, 312
  shyness and, 70
  tension, 194

M

Marriage
  communication, 46, 129, 362, 406
  conflict in, 19, 30
  considered escape, 362
  developing closeness, 63
  disappointment in, 128
  expectations in, 401
  problem solving, 235
  self-pity and, 158
  shyness in, 68
  solving conflicts, 174
Mindset. *See also* Moods, Thoughts
  benefits of positive, 138
Moods
  dealing with, 135, 352
Motivation
  love of Hashem, 231
  stress and, 232, 383
  using stress, 232
  wholesome, 369

N

Negativity
  complaining, 149
  internalizing, 23
Neighbors
  developing relationship, 63

O

Obstacles
  benefits of identifying, 98
  exaggerated, 76
  overcoming, 14, 15
  self-image and, 223
  strengthening a person, 77
  ultimate reward for, 211

P

Parenting
  adolescents, 407
  anxiousness, 407
  children crying, 153
  conflict in styles, 409
  cooperation (between parents), 412
  dealing with conflict, 118, 235
  developing the relationship, 144
  expectations, 227
  fear of failure and, 108
  giving attention, 16, 151
  guilt in, 144
  impatience, 397
  limitations, 83
  methods, 40, 396
  misbehavior, 24
  needing approval, 399
  offering guidance, 129
  patience, 228
  priorities, 217
  problems in school, 109
  protectiveness, 235
  resolving conflict, 411
  teaching order, 252
  teaching problem solving, 37
  weaning a child from self-pity, 153
  when overwhelmed, 80

Perfection
  working for, 210
Perfectionism
  discouraging, 349
  neutralizing, 363
  self-image and, 224
Pessimism
  anxiety and, 278
  limiting effect, 99
Physical needs
  spirituality and, 214
Potential
  appreciating, 75
  developing, 85
  overestimation, 83
  underestimation, 79
  vivid awareness of, 76
Praying
  concentrating, 88, 197
  properly, 170, 254
Pressure. See chapter 8
  dangers of, 368
  sensitivity to, 102
Pride
  arrogance, 267
  healthy balance, 23
Priorities
  determining, 219
Problems
  accepting instead of solving, 19
  accepting while solving, 20
  avoiding, 17, 19
  benefits of having, 344
  benefits of solving, 2
  failure to overcome, 76
  learning to solve, 41
Procrastination
  examples, 268, 288
Projects
  completing, 239
  implementing, 290
  planning, 217, 288
Promptness. See Alacrity
Punishment
  of self, 149

R

Relationships. See also Friends, Marriage, Parenting, Student/teacher, Neighbor
  attitudes and, 103
  communication, 241
  difficulties, 123
  effects of tension on, 106
  encouragement, 106
  expectations, 199, 366
  friends, 31
  neighbors, 28
  parent and child, 16, 118, 151
  self-pity and, 157
  shyness, 241
Responsibility
  accepting, 282
  at home, 293
  aversion to, 149
  inappropriate, 198
  tension and, 201
Rewarding
  for difficulties, 211

self, 179

S

Sadness, 102
Self-confidence. *See also* Inner strength
  benefits, 285, 304
  building, 303
  healthy, 325
  lack of, 267, 303
Self-discipline
  responsibility and, 231
Self-esteem
  appreciation of self, 207
  building, 22
  defeatism and, 76
  respect of others, 79
  shyness and, 71
Self-evaluation
  advantages, 148
Self-image
  as a tool for growth, 321
  challenges to, 206
  distorted, 84
  evaluating, 86, 323
  failure and, 223
  healthy, 379
  humility and, 324
  identifying strengths, 321
  influence on relationships, 68
  needing approval, 361, 384
  needing success, 355
  obstacles and, 223
  over-estimating, dangers of, 199
  perfectionism and, 224
  preoccupation with, 206, 219
  problems and, 206
  seeking approval, 216
Self-improvement
  and *avodas Hashem*, 210
  assumptions, 3
  conditions for, 238
  explained, 267
  pitfalls, 237
  planning for, 332
  stable results, 212
Self-pity
  and success, 155
  benefits, 159
  effect on inner strength, 307
  effects, 308
  in adolescents, 154
  in marriage, 155
  origins, 151
  overcoming, 156, 160
  weaning from, 153
Self-sympathy. *See* Self-pity
Shame. *See* Shyness
Shidduchim. See Dating
Shyness. *See* chapter 2
  as cause of anger, 62
  causing loss, 70
  in marriage, 68
  influenced by self-image, 62
  narrowing options, 58
  overcoming, 66, 241
  rewards of overcoming, 72
  stunting relationships, 63
  test for proper measure, 61

when appropriate, 59, 60
Spiral Effect. *See* chapter 5
   defined, 121
   escaping, 125
   reversing, 126, 135
Student
   adjusting to school, 109
   fear and, 99
Student/teacher
   developing relationship, 63, 64
Studying
   being relaxed, 196
   competition, 221
   extremes, 83
   finding partners, 358
   focusing, 170, 197
   how to, 254
   patience, 353
   pitfalls, 239
   promptness, 296
   self-inhibitions, 80
   self-motivation, 351
   tension and, 225, 234, 348
Subconscious. *See* chapters 6 and 7
   obstacles and, 108
   power of, 143
Submission
   improper use, 21
Success. *See also* Self-confidence
   anxiety about, 203, 355, 400
   judging value of, 91, 273

T

Tension. *See* chapter 8
   acceptance and, 200
   definition, 198
   effects, 25, 194, 195, 246
   focus of, 200
   limiting effects, 98, 102
   neutralizing, 195, 363
   origins, 205
   purposefully creating, 204
Thoughts. *See also* Moods
   effects, 121
   eliminating improper, 196

W

Will
   conflicts within, 142, 145, 169
   resolving conflicts within, 170
Work
   fear and, 99
   fulfillment, 253
   tension in, 370
   value of, 213
Worrying
   proper perspective, 280

Y

Yehudah ben Teima's plan. *See* chapter 7
   review of, 337

An Expression of Gratitude

I would like to express my appreciation to a man with unique potential who is a dynamic pioneer of Torah,

Rabbi Chaim Coffman *shlit"a*

and his wife **Melanie** *tichye*

who generously gave of their practical resources and emotional support during the rougher spots of this work. My dear friend, may Hashem help you see the realization of your noble visions, and have many happy, healthy years together and much *nachas* from your children.